A Powerhouse of a Man
Tom Farrell

Published by Brolga Publishing Pty Ltd
ABN 46 063 962 443
PO Box 12544
A'Beckett St
Melbourne,VIC, 8006
Australia

email: markzocchi@brolgapublishing.com.au

National Library of Australia Cataloguing-in-Publication entry
    Mooney, Christopher, author
    A powerhouse of a man : Tom Farrell
    ISBN: 9781922175793 (paperback)
    Subjects: Farrell, Tom, 1917-2012.
    War correspondents--Australia--Biography.
    Journalists--Australia--Biography.
    Dewey Number: 070.4333092

Cover design & typesetting by Wanissa Somsuphangsri
Photographs & Illustrations: Unless otherwise indicated, all photographs and illustrations were provided by the Farrell families.

BE PUBLISHED

Publish through a successful publisher. National distribution, Macmillan & International distribution to the United Kingdom, North America. Sales Representation to South East Asia
Email: markzocchi@brolgapublishing.com.au

A POWERHOUSE OF A MAN
Tom Farrell

A BIOGRAPHY OF ROLF EVERIST FARRELL

CHRISTOPHER MOONEY

TOM FARRELL INSTITUTE FOR THE ENVIRONMENT
UNIVERSITY OF NEWCASTLE

For my parents, Ida and Frank Mooney
who, like Kath and Tom Farrell,
lived exemplary lives.

Sic itur ad astra (Virgil).

Acknowledgements

I wish to thank John Farrell, Beverley Hincks, Joan Manson, Claire Nelmes and Kay Talty for sharing with me the memories of their parents. Such memories are precious and not normally shared with a stranger. I thank them for their trust. Without their support this project would not have been possible.

I wish also to thank the relatives and friends of Kath and Tom Farrell for sharing their memories with me. I am indebted to Mr Doug Lithgow, President of the Parks and Playgrounds Movement and Freeman of the City of Newcastle, New South Wales, for his input regarding Tom's involvement in the Northern Parks and Playgrounds Movement.

I wish to thank Professor Tim Roberts and the Tom Farrell Institute for the Environment, University of Newcastle, for supporting and funding this project. Without Tim's leadership this project would not have been brought to fruition. I would also like to acknowledge the contribution of Dr Bernie Curran, University of Newcastle Foundation Executive Officer, International Division, and Mr Peter Kofler.

I wish to thank Emeritus Professor John Ramsland, Faculty of Education and Arts, University of Newcastle, for his continuing support and assistance. His mentoring of my work over many years has been much appreciated.

I wish to thank Mr Gionni Di Gravio, University Archivist, and the staff of the Cultural Collections, University of Newcastle, for their assistance. I wish to acknowledge also the assistance of the staff of the NSW State Records Authority, Kingswood, the Mitchell Library, Sydney, the Newcastle Region Library, Local Studies & Archives, and the University of Sydney Archives.

I wish to thank Ms Gillean Shaw, Art Curator, University Gallery, University of Newcastle, for her assistance with the layout and graphic design of the book and Mr Olivier Rey-Lescure, Technical Officer, School of Environmental & Life Sciences, University of Newcastle, for designing the maps included in the text. I also wish to thank Mr Grahame Marjoribanks, Chief Librarian, Newcastle Morning Herald, for his assistance with the illustrations and photographs.

Finally, I wish to thank my family for their ongoing support and encouragement.

Christopher Mooney
September 2014

INTRODUCTION

In this e-world we now live in, with its instant and easy communication modes and instant access to information from anywhere at any time, it seems hard to comprehend that communication by typewriter, carbon copies and letters enabled some to accomplish more in those days than ten of us can today. One such monumental achiever was Tom Farrell and I am sure you will marvel with me, the enormity of his legacy achieved without the computer, without email and without the web.

Our University is testament to his foresight, his ability to garner local supporters, his dogged determination to take on and to win, against the centralists of Sydney, who then as now saw Newcastle as a second tier settlement unworthy of expenditure from the public purse.

Our environmental treasures of Blackbutt, Mount Sugarloaf, Glenrock Lagoon, Barrington Tops and Myall Lakes all owe their existence in not a small way to Tom Farrell. He was a visionary for environmental sustainability. He succeeded in the dream of a viable economy nested within an equitable society nurtured by a nurturing and natural ecosystem.

We at the TFI are proud to bear Tom Farrell's name as it serves as a constant reminder that finding regional solutions for a sustainable future is possible if we draw inspirations from such giants of the past.

Professor Tim Roberts
Director, Tom Farrell Institute For The Environment,
University of Newcastle
September 2014

Foreword

I believe my father's inspiration and foresight, came from his parents' influence and example, and my mother and her family. At mum's death, Dad lamented that he had lost his 'only real friend'. He highly regarded mum and her family (the Mahers) as an exemplary family unit.

Growing up in the Farrell family seemed to be frequent gatherings at home, initially at 19 Collaroy Road and then from 1941 at 137 Russell Road, New Lambton and at Rally Round, the family weekender at Fishing Point on the foreshore of Lake Macquarie. These gatherings with family, relatives, and friends, from all walks of life, were memorable occasions.

At home, mum would be whistling or singing ('Whistle While You Work', 'The Ferry Boat Serenade', 'Always Let Your Conscious Be Your Guide'), as she tended to the care of her family (cooking, cleaning, washing, ironing, reading to/with her children). When we had visitors, the women and children often congregated round mum playing the piano, as she led us in sing songs. The men would be in the sunroom or the lounge-room engrossed in discussions of many issues, planning strategies and action plans to achieve the best level of community involvement and other positive outcomes.

In contrast to home, Rally Round was a real change. Prior to 1948 there was no electricity, it lacked town water until about 1960 and the sewer was not connected until September 1995. Our times at Rally Round included the numerous card games on wet days and most evenings in the glow from kerosene lamps, swimming, fishing, cricket on the front lawn (Rally Round rules?!) the ongoing maintenance and renovations to 'the shack' and rowboat, then the construction of 'Topside' from 1948.

Both home and Rally Round provided the 'free space', a private retreat, for dad to contemplate and reflect on the various problems and issues, which resulted from his busy life of work and community service. Weekends and holidays at Rally Round are some of my most enjoyable experiences of my life. That's what made and makes for so many unique memories.

My mother and father were dedicated to family life and could not have done more for my sisters and I. They worked tirelessly throughout their lives to achieve the best for us. They also gave this support and encouragement to relatives and friends and many others to whom they offered the hand of friendship. They were supportive, inclusive and generous to all who came into their lives.

I reflect on the many evenings of dad attending a variety of meetings connected with community issues, including the Friday after work 'think tank' group, who met at 'The Duke' (Duke of Wellington Hotel, New Lambton). Dad still found time for the 7 pm ABC news and news review (mandatory), teaching my sisters and I to swim, excursions to Nobbys and Merewether Beach, the many weekends, Easter and Christmas holidays at Rally Round, the games of 'footie', local club games (Western Suburbs) and Test matches at the Sydney Cricket Ground, and collecting 'waste', recycled to construct paths and garden terraces at home and Rally Round; the working bees at Blackbutt, and home building inspections associated with Starr Bowkett loans for members.

In this biography you will meet people from all walks of life who came into our lives through the projects dad was involved. There was no great divide between his public life and family life. Privately, he helped many in need and much of this will never be known. He put others before himself and the accomplishment of his work for the community was of great satisfaction to him, more so than his own personal gain.

Born in 1904, my father, like so many of his generation left school at an early age. Life and the challenges thrown at him meant that 'survival' was his great educator. He listened to others, quickly developing a keen understanding of the broader issues, and the need to develop practical solutions. This biography exposes his dedication to environmental activism (i.e. the broad sense of the environment in which we live and work), social justice, financial security and independence, sport and recreation, and education.

Through his own experience, he could see the value of formal education and hence the value of university education. But he despaired at the practical irrelevance some academics brought to the table. What he wanted was a traditional university, which would be innovative and relevant to the needs and challenges of the time. As with most parents, he wanted his family to have the opportunity of a university education. The difference with Tom Farrell was that by the time he had joined the campaign for an autonomous university for Newcastle, he had a much bigger family – the community of the Hunter.

I hope that this biography provides a greater insight into my father's life, and inspires the reader to understand what any individual—working collaboratively with others—can achieve, in the interest of their community.

John Sayce Farrell
September 2014

FOREWORD

This book reveals how one man Tom Farrell shaped the destiny of the Newcastle and Hunter region in NSW throughout the 20th century. It takes you on Tom's lifetime journey of outstanding community achievements. He was truly a remarkable man: a role model for present day leaders.

Over a period of some fifty years Tom helped develop much needed home ownership lending facilities especially for families on low incomes, assisted in creating the University of Newcastle as an important centre for regional higher learning, fought to preserve unique natural bush land habitat " Blackbutt" located in the centre of Newcastle, as a reserve for everyone to enjoy, established the Northern Parks and Playground Movement to handle the whole region's environmental development and enhanced a range of community sporting activities.

Tom's achievements were really remarkable when you realize that throughout the 20th century, no internet or social media network existed. Yet Tom was a master networker. He travelled for hours to meet up with people, attend meetings, fulfil appointments, and rally support. Within a digital world, one can hardly imagine the speed with which he would have gained public support and the immediate impact of his efforts.

What motivated Tom was his overwhelming 'community spirit'. He wanted as many families as possible to have access to much needed services. In his quiet unassuming way he made it his priority to find innovative practical solutions.

This book presents Tom's lifetime work, taking the reader through each pursuit, involving challenges, heartbreaks, determination and triumphs. It represents a tapestry, rich in context, laid out in a chronological pattern. You will marvel at his people skills, the ability to catch the mood of the moment, his resiliency and his realistic assessment of himself. He was a remarkable leader who led from behind.

Each major project Tom tackled was different requiring contrasting approaches. For example, in developing new financial funding mechanisms for low income earners, Tom identified the unfulfilled community need and helped establish a range of practical, funding mechanisms. These were innovative processes. No vested interests existed, fighting to preserve the status quo because there was nothing available. No-one would want to deny poorer folk the opportunity to buy their home without incurring unsustainable financial hardship. Once Tom had helped organize affordable home funding options the benefits soon emerged.

In contrast, identifying and establishing a need for a university in Newcastle met with stiff opposition even though there was a regional need to establish a higher educational facility in the region. Such a local university would make it both affordable and accessible for many potential students living in the Newcastle and Hunter areas. But resistance came from outside the region. State Government funding apathy, opposition from other existing NSW universities frightened of losing their share of public funding and even differences about the type of university to create. Once these obstacles were overcome, and a start made to operate the new regional university, positive benefits soon emerged.

One of the most difficult projects Tom tackled was in establishing a parkland reserve at Blackbutt in the face of commercial interests who wanted the land for development. The battle extended for a period of some forty years or more, indicating how determined the opposing forces were to drag out the fight for as long as possible. Yet Tom, who inspired so many of his community with his vision for Blackbutt, saw the matter through. These are just three examples of the many interesting challenges and activities which Tom undertook, all represented in this book's coverage of Tom's life work.

Throughout the book you will find numerous recurring instances where Tom encountered the problem of the regional demands of the Hunter and Newcastle communities being decided upon by a remote State Government located far-away in Sydney. This is a problem which still exists today.

Of modest disposition, Tom was the first to admit that he could not have achieved so much without the support of his beloved partner and wife, Kath, rearing five children and extending their warmth and hospitality to many extended families and friends. Kath provided Tom with the love, care and stability which enabled him to effectively focus on his work. As Tom was involved in so many major community projects, he often encountered many problems. This placed him under great mental stress. Kath's encouragement and support were essential for him to overcome those times.

Whilst he was doing all this community work, Tom had to provide for his family's well-being. As was his way, Tom started from the ground floor in his working life career at the Newcastle Abattoirs, rising to General Manager. On his journey he qualified as an accountant, earned a Meat Inspector's License, and worked in all areas of the Abattoir before entering senior management.

The book contains frequent reference to Tom acknowledging that any positive achievements resulted from the combined efforts of his many community supporters who willingly gave their knowhow, energy, time and comradeship to fight on and win. There were many partners and associates who actively worked with Tom. However, just like the conductor of an orchestra, Tom was the catalyst and 'lifeline' of those projects. It should be recognized that all this community work was done voluntarily, free of any financial cost to the community.

This book takes you on Tom's outstanding lifelong pursuit to enhance the quality of life for his beloved Newcastle and Hunter communities. His legacy and passions live on. There is no doubt he would want his biography to inspire others to go on with that work. This book is a wonderful endorsement of that wish.

Peter Kofler
Dr Bernard Curran
September 2014

Abbreviations

BAC	Blackbutt Reserve Action Committee
CHLSSC	Cook's Hill Life Saving & Surf Club
DMR	Department of Main Roads
LMSC	Lake Macquarie Shire Council
ML	Mitchell Library, Sydney
NBNENSM	Newcastle Branch of the New England New State Movement
NCC	Newcastle City Council
NHRSBS	Newcastle Hunter River Public Service Starr Bowkett Society
NUC	Newcastle University College
NUEG	Newcastle University Establishment Group
NRLLSA	Newcastle Regional Library, Local Studies & Archives
TFP	Tom Farrell Papers, University of Newcastle Archives
TFPJF	Tom Farrell Papers, in the possession of John Farrell
TFPTFI	Tom Farrell Papers, in possession of Professor Tim Roberts, Tom Farrell Institute for the Environment, University of Newcastle
UNA	University of Newcastle Archives
USA	University of Sydney Archives

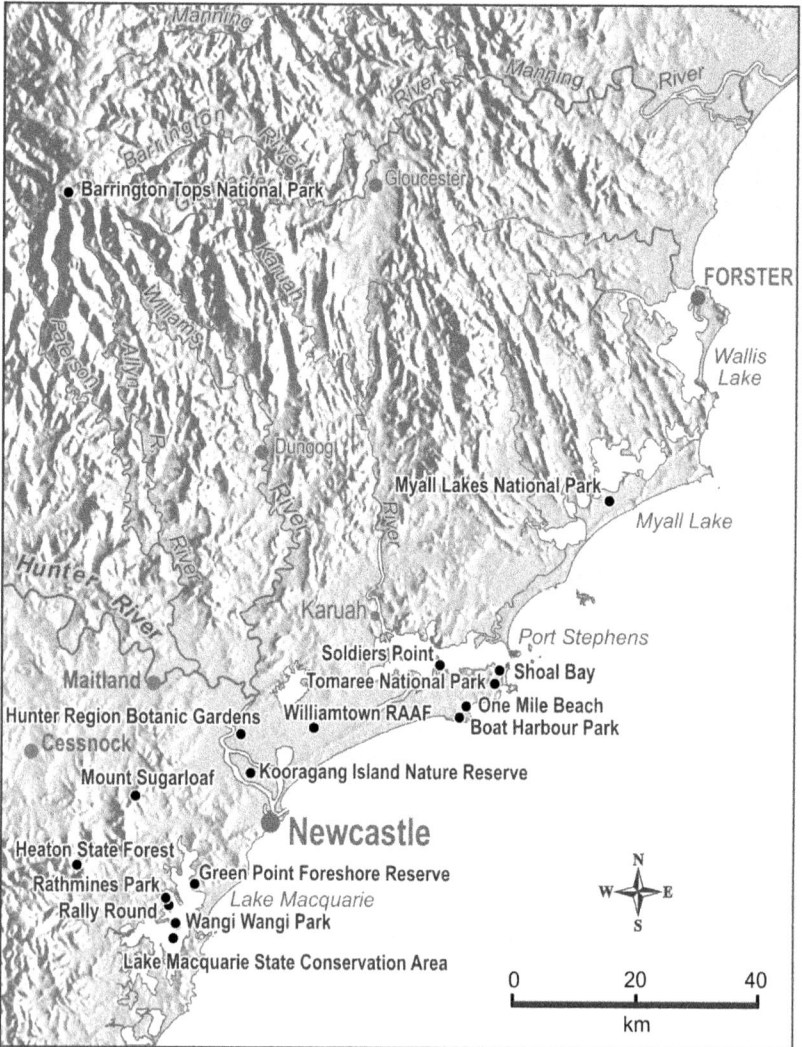

The Greater Newcastle region, Lake Macquarie, Port Stephens, Myall Lakes and Barrington Tops. Map designed by Mr Olivier Rey-Lescure.

CONTENTS

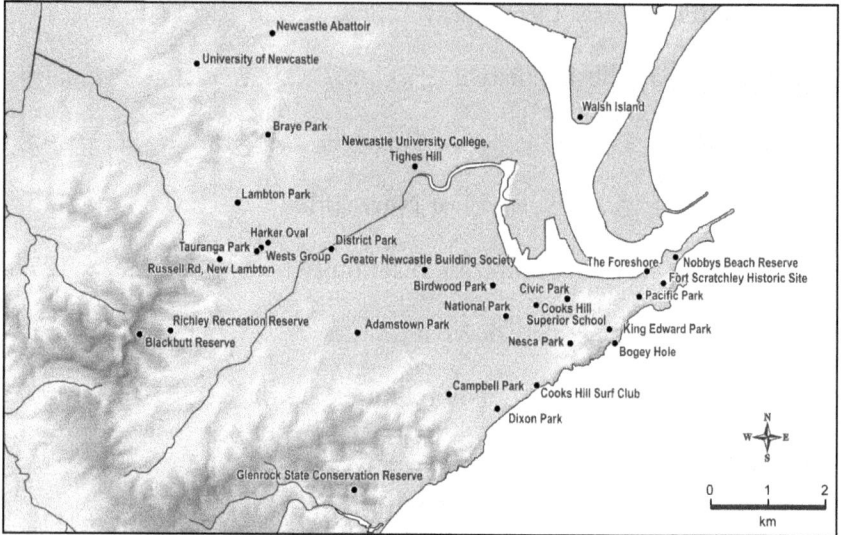

Places of interest in and around Newcastle.
Map designed by Mr Olivier Rey-Lescure.

1: Early Life

Rolf Everist (Tom) Farrell was born on 21 May 1904 in Brisbane, the third son of William and Deborah Farrell. Tom's father was an eminent professional photographer who had business interests throughout Queensland, country New South Wales and New Zealand before establishing a photographic studio in Queen Street, Brisbane. His purchase of the first cinematographic cameras in Australia allowed him to photograph leading socialites and prominent politicians in his studios. Among the famous who posed at the Farrell studio in Brisbane for photographic portraits were Dame Nellie Melba, the famed Australian soprano, and George, Prince of Wales, the son of King Edward VII. William was commissioned in 1901 to take a number of portraits of Sir Edmund Barton, the first Commonwealth Prime Minister, and Alfred Deakin, the second Prime Minister, on the occasion of the opening of the Commonwealth Parliament on 1 January 1901. He was among the first photographers to capture the moment when Australian troops departed for the Boer War. These images were later displayed to an eager public in a make-shift open air cinema set up in Queen Street, Brisbane. Such was the popularity of these cinematographic events that the traffic in downtown Brisbane was brought to a stand-still. As a result the Brisbane Council felt bound to prohibit any future displays of the same nature.

By the time the Farrell family moved from Brisbane to Newcastle, New South Wales, in 1908 William and Deborah had three sons (Charles, Edward and Tom) and one daughter (Mabel). It was Deborah's poor health that had provided the impetus for the move – unfortunately, Tom's mother had contracted tuberculosis. It was hoped that Newcastle's proximity to the Blue Mountains would provide some relief from the condition. William ensured that his children visited their mother as regularly as possible. Tom later recalled how impressed he was by the scenery he observed from the train on his way to Katoomba. Unfortunately, Deborah succumbed to her illness on the 6 April 1926. She was laid to rest in the Church of England section of Katoomba cemetery. In Newcastle William continued to work as a photographer establishing a studio ('Tosca Studio') in a building in Hunter Street between Auckland and Union Streets. The family home was established in rooms above the studio. The business did well with William acquiring enough income to indulge his interest in horse racing. The family purchased a number of race horses which had moderate success at local, Sydney and northern racetracks. For example, the imported Irish mare, 'Fair Desmond', won the Maitland Cup (1919) and Grafton Cup (1921). The 'Farrell Stables' were located at the rear of the Black Diamond Hotel near what is now Wheeler Place. The Farrell brothers exercised their horses at the eastern end of what is now Civic Park.[1]

William was keen to ensure that his children received the best education possible. In June 1909, his sons were enrolled at Cooks Hill Superior Public School, considered one of the best schools in Newcastle, situated at the corner of Lamen and Union Streets. In 1908 the District Inspector of Schools referred to the school as 'the 'chief centre' to which people in Newcastle have been drawn for higher primary instruction'. Such was the school's popularity that the District Inspector had taken the decision to restrict the enrolment exclusively to students who resided in the area of inner Newcastle. Fortunately for Tom, his brothers and sister, the Farrell residence was located within the designated area. The status of the school only grew in the years following the arrival of the Farrell children. In July 1913, Peter Board, the first Director-General of Education in New South Wales, referred to the school, in terms of its numbers and its work, as 'the most important school outside Sydney'. [2]

In the early years of their primary schooling, Tom and his brothers were exposed to a curriculum which gave great emphasis to reading, writing and arithmetic. In the final two years, the boys (aged between twelve and fourteen) undertook 'superior classes' which were more vocational in character. At Cooks Hill Superior Public School the emphasis was on commercial training which provided the boys with 'two years start in the ABC of business'. On completion of the superior classes, students were expected to find employment in industry or commerce. The work of the pupils attending the superior classes was regularly exhibited. For example, in 1915 the work of the Commercial Class was regarded by one commentator as 'one of the most conspicuous and interesting exhibits at the recent Newcastle show'. [3]

Deborah & William Farrell

Given their interests later in life, it is clear that Tom and his brothers would have enjoyed the extra-curricula activities offered by the school. The records show that the school hosted a number of social and sporting clubs where pupils could engage in activities like swimming, football, band practice and rifle shooting. Tom was encouraged by the sports-master, Mr Cecil Walker, to play rugby league for the school. This was the start of his association with the sport that was to last a lifetime. The swimming club was particularly popular with an average weekly attendance of 127 boys at the Bogey Hole Baths. Having completed their training, the boys were awarded certificates and medallions by the Royal Life Saving Club, Newcastle. It appears that on occasions Tom preferred to spend his time on these activities rather than his academic studies. He later confessed to his son that he found it difficult to resist a trip to the beach during school hours particularly in the summer. Tom's misdeed did not go unpunished – a letter was sent by the school to his parents asking for an explanation. Tom later recalled the gentle reprimand he received from his mother. But such so-called misbehaviour was not typical – in fact, Tom was a hard-working student who did well at school.

Cooks Hill Superior Public School

It is clear that 'a good education' was important to Tom Farrell. He (with the support of his wife) successfully communicated this to his own children. As his son later explained:

> My father always insisted we maximise our individual education opportunities, and both Tom and Kath did everything possible to ensure we all received a good education, hopefully attaining tertiary levels. He believed this would give his children the capability to be independently employed...our education could not have been achieved if it had not been for the sacrifices both mum and dad made to support and encourage us throughout their life.

Tom (on left) with his siblings, Edward, Charles and Mabel in the yard at Lindsay Street, Hamilton (early 1920s). Edward (Mick) is standing next to Tom, then Charles (Chas) and Mabel seated.

Bev Hincks, one of Tom's daughters, argues that her father was a man 'ahead of his times' in regards to 'girls' education'. He encouraged all of his children (including his daughters) to undertake university studies at the end of their secondary schooling. Their subsequent careers are a testament to their parents' commitment to education. Such was his commitment in this area that Tom and his two brothers later assisted and financed the education of their sister at the University of Sydney and Sydney Teachers College. As Joan Manson points out her mother also played a significant role: 'mum believed in education – she was a marvellous wife and fully supportive of all dad did'. Such sentiments were shared by all the Farrell children. Both parents took an active interest in their children's education – taking time to check their homework, participate in school

Tom's wife, Kath Farrell (aged in her early 20s).

working-bees, attend sporting carnivals, help raise funds and attend parent-teacher evenings. It is clear that Tom and Kath worked as a team in this regard. Like her husband, Kath placed a high value on a good education – she had been trained at the Sydney Business College as a comptometer operator before being employed at Walsh Island.[4]

The Farrell children remember their home as a happy and busy place where Tom (supported by his wife) devoted his time to his family. Although much of Tom's week was taken up with work and his involvement in various community activities, he always found time for his wife and children. His children recall fondly the discussions they had around the dinner table, their sing-alongs with their mother at the piano and various weekend excursions with their parents. Blackbutt was a favourite destination at the weekend but so was Nobbys Beach, Newcastle Ocean Baths for swimming and trips to Rally Round where they swam, fished and enjoyed the beach. Although discipline was valued in the Farrell household, the children were encouraged to think for themselves. They were encouraged to read the newspaper, listen to the radio to be informed of current affairs. Each evening Tom in the company of his wife and children listened to the ABC news and News Review. The children were free to enjoy their leisure time with their parents – reading a good book (one of Tom's favourite past-times), learning to swim, watching a football match at Harker Oval or driving to a spot near Fort Scratchley on a hot summer's night to await the arrival of the 'southerly'. In their later life, Kath and Tom Farrell displayed the same level of love and commitment to their grandchildren as they had with their own children. Tom and Kath Farrell were much loved by their twenty-three grandchildren whom they adored.[5]

Tom passed on to his children his love for the great 'outdoors'. He later recalled the fun he had enjoyed growing up in Newcastle. He especially remembered the games he played as a child:

> many boys in the area had fun jumping on the back step of the (horse-drawn) bus for a free ride. This was called 'whip behind' because the bus driver had a long handle with a whip attached and he used this to remove the urchins on the back step. This was great sport for the children in those days. The area bounded by Hunter, Union, Auckland and King Streets, was in those days a labyrinth of lanes, where many families lived. The children of these families congregated in some of the smaller areas to pursue their childhood games.

But not all outside activities were pleasant. Tom remembered the anxiety he felt as a young boy following his brothers along the

Rally Round, Fishing Point, Lake Macquarie (1990) where
Tom spent much time with his family and friends from 1922 to 1996.

cliff edge between Bar Beach and the Bogey Hole, a favourite swimming spot. As he later admitted, his brothers in getting as close to the edge as possible, were more adventurous than he. He enjoyed wandering around Newcastle Harbour, a busy port, watching the cargo boats tie up at Lee Wharf or the iron ore ships making their way up to the newly founded Steel Works to unload their cargo. Later he was happy to share these childhood memories with his children.[6]

Tom completed his schooling at the age of thirteen, having achieved the Qualifying Certificate. On leaving school Tom was keen to put into practise the commercial skills he had learnt at school. He first found employment in the office of Breckenridge & Co Timber Merchants, a leading Novocastrian company, situated on the site of what was to become Civic Park. Here he gained some clerical experience, before moving to the Walsh Island Dockyard in 1920. He changed employment a year later gaining a position as a junior clerk in the office at the Newcastle Abattoir, Waratah West. Here he was to remain for the next forty-seven years, applying his commercial knowledge and business acumen. Given his ability, it is not surprising that he rose through the ranks, finally achieving the position of General Manager.[7]

Having achieved permanent employment and financial security, Tom decided to propose to Kathleen Mary Maher whom he had met while working at the Dockyard. Kath Maher came from a family of eight being the eldest of seven daughters. Tom met his future wife on the Dockyard ferry where both travelled to work in the front office. After a six year courtship, the couple married in 1926. They began their new life together in Lawson Street, Hamilton, living with Tom's father, now a widower. The Farrell family next moved to 'Desmond' in Collaroy Road, New Lambton, then built a new home on land purchased in Russell Road, New Lambton. This was to remain the family home for the next fifty-four years. Here the Farrells settled down to suburban life with their five children - Beverley, Claire, Joan, John and Kay.

Throughout their sixty-two years of married life, Kath and Tom were devoted to each other. Both shared a similar value system which drove them to assist the local community in any way they could. Both at home and in the community, the couple worked as a team. Kath worked alongside her husband on various campaigns when time allowed. When domestic matters needed her attention, she allowed her husband the freedom to continue his work for the community regardless of the number of hours that this involved. Despite the need for him to be away from home on many evenings and on weekends, Tom always knew he had the full support of his wife. There is no doubt that without Kath by his side, Tom would not have been able to achieve what he did. In 1984 one of Tom's friends remarked how lucky he was to have had a wife of the calibre and character of Kath Farrell. Tom would have needed no prompting in completely agreeing with this sentiment. In later life Tom simply expressed to one of his daughters his debt to his wife: 'I have had a wonderful life and a wonderful wife'. In the years after her death, Tom would frequently refer to Kath as 'the only friend I ever had'.[8]

Newcastle Abattoir also provided employment for Tom's father and brother. William Farrell had sold his photographic business in 1920 to pursue other business interests. When his wife died in 1926 he opened a butcher shop in Vincent Street, Cessnock, later acting as a buyer for the abattoir. Charles Farrell, Tom's brother, took up employment at the abattoir in 1924, eventually becoming a qualified meat inspector and head of the Bacon Department. Tom's other brother, Edward, also followed a business career, first travelling for Maxam Bacon which took him to Brisbane. There he joined Brown & Dureau and eventually becoming the Department Manager (Scrap Metal) at Hunter's Hill. After graduating with a Science Degree from the University of Sydney, Mabel rose through the ranks of the New South Wales Department of Education, first serving in the country at Junee and Hay Girls High, before joining the Science Staff at Newcastle High School in 1942. From here she gained the position of Principal of Wickham Girls Junior High, then Acting Principal at Maitland Girls High and finally Head Mistress of Hunter Girls High.

Tom and his brothers built themselves a weekend retreat at Fishing Point, Lake Macquarie in the 1920s. This was to become a 'rallying point' for all the family and friends. Initially the property had no road access resulting in all materials having to be transported by boat from Toronto. Prior to the war the property had no running water, electricity or sewerage. The Farrell boys had to rely on a large circle of friends (drawn especially from the football and surf clubs with which they were associated) to help the family complete the building. In recognition of this fact they named the weekender 'Rally Round'. Here for decades both family and friends could meet to relax and enjoy each-others company — a practice that continues today. In the company of his family and friends Tom was able to fully relax — using the time to think through various projects and problems. He always enjoyed his time on the lake. It gave him an opportunity to indulge his passion for boats, swimming and fishing. He was especially fond of a Townes clinker rowing boat with which he took both family and friends out fishing. His children and grandchildren all played their part in the maintenance and repair of the vessel. A niece later recalled: 'their hospitality was remarkable; everyone was given a warm welcome. I can still picture Uncle Tom beside the lake cooking a freshly caught fish for me determined to change my idea that I didn't like fish'. A nephew remembered that 'Uncle Tom took us to dig worms on the lakeside then out in his row boat for a few hours of fishing. He would then show us how to scale and gut the fish we caught; that evening Aunty Kath would cook them on the old wood burning stove for our tea'. It is no surprise that the small boat shed at Fishing Point known as 'Rally Round' became (in the words of his daughter, Bev) 'a retreat with a welcome mat for all friends and extended family'. Such was the hospitality of the Farrell family. Tom's support for his extended family also involved the provision of financial assistance when difficult circumstances arose. 'Rally Round' remains in the possession of the Farrell family today – it continues to be a place where 'the door is always open' for family and friends.[9]

A typical summer sunrise looking east from Rally Round.

2: *The Formative Years*

In the 1930s Tom settled down to married life with his wife and five children in New Lambton. A permanent position at the Newcastle Abattoir allowed him to build a well sustained career - his clerical and administrative duties led to more responsibility, further study by correspondence and a position as a qualified accountant. With the help of a local Starr-Bowkett Society, he purchased his first home in Russell Road, New Lambton. Although much of his time was taken up with work and family, he managed to maintain his association with a number of local sporting clubs. Football and swimming were to remain passions for the rest of his life. Tom's permanent position provided the family with financial security during the depression years when unemployment rates doubled. No doubt Tom had concerns that the relative prosperity of the second half of the 1930s was interrupted by the advent of the Second World War. His daughter, Bev, vividly recalls the day when her family gathered around a radio at 'Rally Round' in September 1939 to hear the news that Australia was now at war. Tom no doubt grew increasingly alarmed by the growing Japanese threat to Australia. The year 1942 brought the war ever closer to home with Japanese airborne attacks on Darwin and midget submarine activity against Sydney and Newcastle. The rapid advance of Japanese Imperial Forces throughout South-East Asia, seemed to suggest that an invasion of Australia was imminent. Although Tom's occupation was designated as 'restricted', he decided to enlist after the Fall of Singapore in February 1942. He was thirty-eight years of age. It has been noted that sportsmen and servicemen share many qualities in common – courage, teamwork, leadership, physical prowess, mateship and loyalty. Tom would draw on such qualities as he faced the challenges of these formative years.[1]

In April 1942 Tom Farrell was given a Commission in the Administrative Branch of the Royal Australian Air Force (RAAF). While his application outlined his educational qualifications, administrative experience and sporting ability, it also provided details of his seven year's military service in the Militia (Commonwealth Military Forces - CMF) where he had served the prescribed time as a senior cadet and driver for the army service corps. Tom's application to the RAAF was successful – he enlisted in the Citizen Air Force in October 1942. The exact reason for his enlistment in the RAAF is not known. He was one of 189,000 men and 27,000 women who enlisted in the RAAF in World War II. There is no doubt that

Insignia 76 Squadron

Flying Officer Rolf (Tom) Farrell

Tom wanted to do his part to prevent a Japanese invasion of Australia. The Fall of Singapore had confirmed his resolve. Although the enemy had faced recent setbacks at Midway and Kakoda, the Japanese Imperial Forces were still a force to be reckoned with. The Japanese attacks on mainland Australia (Darwin, Sydney and Newcastle) in February and June 1942 had clearly shown this. His choice to enlist in the RAAF may have been influenced by the fact that the Australian airborne division had played a key role in the defence of Darwin and Port Morseby. He may also have been influenced by a recent recruitment drive for the Volunteer Air Force, 'Make Them Mightier Yet'.

During 1942 it was clear that the war was having an impact on the local area. Properties in the vicinity of Russell Road, including the New Lambton Public School, were commandeered by the military. The closure of the school meant that the Farrell children had to travel to Hamilton to attend school. The Farrell house was inspected for its suitability to accommodate the office of the army commander. After the residents of rental properties were evicted, Tom led a delegation of home-owners to argue against the further acquisition of houses in the area. His efforts were successful. On enlistment he assured his wife that he was confident that 'the army would not turn a woman and five children out of their home when her husband is off fighting'. Although the house was not commandeered, Tom made all the necessary arrangements to look after his family while on military service. He constructed an air-raid shelter in the backyard and rented a property in Gresford (near his brother-in-law) to provide a safe haven for his wife and children in the eventuality of an invasion. Kath did her bit as well ensuring that the children went to school each day with an emergency kit containing food, essential utensils and spare underwear just in case an emergency evacuation was ordered from school.

Tom's enlistment in the RAAF was voluntarily. At the outbreak of the war, the Menzies United Australia Party (UAP) Government had reintroduced compulsory military training for unmarried men who were over the age of twenty-one. Tom had already completed this requirement after leaving school. In January 1943, two months after he enlisted, the Curtin Labor Government enacted The Defence (Citizen Military Forces) Act which obliged soldiers in the Militia to serve outside of Australia in New Guinea and areas of the south-west Pacific. These conscripts were to reinforce the volunteer forces (which included Tom Farrell) in various theatres of war overseas. Tom's decision to enlist did not come without risk – death and serious injury were real possibilities. There was also the financial strain that enlistment placed on a serviceman's family – it is clear that Tom's decision to leave behind a secure position at the abattoir exposed his wife and family to financial difficulty. John Farrell recalls that his father was so concerned about the family's budget during his absence that he made arrangements to pay a number of bills on his return.[2]

The medical examination which Tom was required to complete before enlistment, reveals that he was a very fit thirty-eight year old male. Clearly his regular participation in sporting activities like football and swimming had maintained his physical fitness. The medical notes record that the candidate was 5 feet and 7½ inches tall, weighed 149 pounds and was of perfect vision (except for the need to use reading glasses at work). The only matters of note in the medical records were the appearance of two scars on the left thigh and evidence of Harrison's Sulcus. Having indicated a preparedness 'to serve anywhere', the candidate was passed 'fit for service'. After a three month personal course at the Officer Training School,

Scenes of Tom on active service in
West Papua (Island of Numfoor) and Borneo (Labuan)

University of Melbourne, Tom was commissioned into the RAAF at the end of 1942.[3]

On enlistment Tom was sent to Bradfield Park, Lindfield, New South Wales, for Officer Training. It is no surprise, given his background, that he was attached to the 'Accounting and Pay' division as a Pilot Officer. He was to remain in this division throughout his enlistment. In May 1943 he was promoted to the rank of 'Flying Officer' and attached to the '76 Squadron', a division that had given distinguished service since its formation in March 1942. In August 1944 he was deployed to the headquarters of 'No 73 Wing' and then to 'No 81 Wing'. In January 1945 Tom was promoted to the rank of Flight Lieutenant. From 1944 onwards Tom served outside Australia in New Guinea, the Dutch East Indies, the Philippines and Borneo. He later explained to a friend that:

> From Bradfield Park I was posted to New Guinea to 76 Squadron (Kittyhawks). Later, 76 Squadron moved to a small island off the coast of New Guinea (Numfoor) and after a short period there, 82 Squadron joined the same Wing as 76 Squadron…We then joined together again in New Guinea and then later moved to what we called the Dutch East Indies, an Island Moratoi where the Australian divisions were gathering for the eventual invasion of Borneo. Later 76 Squadron moved to Zulu Archipelago of the Philippines and then later joined 81 Squadron at Lubuan where the invasion had taken place by Australian forces.

On discharge he was eligible for the 'Return from Active Service Badge' and the 'Pacific Star'.[4]

It is clear that the war could not end quickly enough for the Farrell family. A number of letters contained in the Farrell Papers show how much Tom was missed by his wife and children. The children communicated with their father while he was away – writing letters and sending him small gifts. In turn Tom sent his children gifts from overseas including bracelets made with pearl shell set in silver which the soldiers had illegally made by melting down twenty florin coins, money boxes made of coconut shell and American chocolate and sweets (the children's favourite) obtained from the American forces.

Tom was so keen to get home from Borneo in 1945 that he hitched a ride on a Catalina bound for Darwin. He eventually made his way to Williamtown, near Newcastle, where he served out the final months of his war service. His daughter remembers being alarmed by the sight of her father – like many servicemen, he was emaciated, thin and jaundiced caused by the prescribed drugs he had taken to prevent malaria. He was based at Williamtown as an Accountant Officer at the Headquarters of the 'No 81 Wing'. A routine report prepared in November 1945 for Captain I.D.McLachlan, Commanding Officer

Tom with Kath and Kay (1946) while stationed at Williamtown, near Newcastle

No 81 (Fighter) Wing, gives some insight into Tom's time in the RAAF. Flight Lieutenant R. E. Farrell was found to be completely dependable for all ordinary duties. He had the necessary mental alertness, self-expression and self-confidence to get his ideas across. He was sufficiently self-assured and did not back down too easily. While somewhat reserved and formal, he was both cooperative and prepared to follow the lead of others. In regards to service knowledge and administrative ability, he was found to be capable. The report concluded that he was 'a popular member of the officers' mess and was well thought of by all the ranks'. It is clear that 'leadership', 'mateship' and 'teamwork' had played a large part in Tom's war-time service. Interestingly, the report makes clear that Tom (like many other servicemen) was impatient to return to civilian life. This is not surprising given the fact that the war was at its end and his loving wife and children were waiting at home. Tom was finally demobilised on 7 May 1946. During his time in the RAAF he had forged a strong bond of friendship with many of his fellow servicemen especially Jock Ellis and Cec Hurley. Years later he continued to enjoy the company of those he had served with in the Second World War especially at the Anzac Day reunions.[5]

After returning home Tom was keen to renew his involvement in sport. His enlistment papers reveal something of his commitment in this area. In completing the section dealing with 'Sports and Games Most Proficient', Tom made the following notes: 'I have been an active football player and member of a surf club but at present non-competitive swimming is my only interest in sport'. Tom's involvement with the local Rugby League Football competition began in 1920 when he played for Broadmeadow. His ability as a forward, gained him a place in Central Newcastle's Reserve Grade team in 1921. While the Reserve Grade experienced mixed fortunes that year, the First Grade went on to win the Newcastle Premiership. This feat was not repeated until 1928, when Tom played his part in securing the First Grade Premiership for Central Newcastle. Although Tom played most of the 1928 season in Reserve Grade, it was his agility and speed in the forwards that won him a spot in First Grade. For example, on the 18 August Tom scored the second try of the match which saw Central Newcastle defeat Western Suburbs 24 to 9. While it was noted that 'it was generally expected that Central would prove fairly comfortable winners in this end of season match and the result confirmed expectation', the Football Correspondent for the *NMH* had much praise for Central's early attacking game and the decisive role of key players like Tom Farrell: 'Smith and Griffin paved the way for Central to advance, and following a vigorous rally, Hindle went across with a try which Bell augmented. Central 5-0. Within a few minutes Central were in again Farrell getting the try in the corner'. Tom also used his financial acumen to support the team being appointed 'Club Treasurer'. It was in

Tom (second row second from left) in team photograph (early 1920s)

this capacity that he watched Central defeat Northern Suburbs (11-8) in the First Grade Grand Final on 22 September before a capacity crowd at the Newcastle Sports Ground. Quite fittingly, Tom is listed among 'Central Newcastle's Senior Team' that won the Premiership (Crawford Cup) and Mullally Shield in 1928.[6]

Tom's purchase of a new home in Collaroy Road, New Lambton, at the beginning of 1929 brought his association with Central Newcastle to an end. As a resident of New Lambton he was obliged to play for Western Suburbs Rugby League Club. Tom would have eagerly complied with this requirement as it allowed him to begin a long and happy association with Western Suburbs Leagues Club. As a commentator later put it, '1929 – Tommy Farrell was back home in the Rosella fold after his stay with Central'. Although Tom had proven himself at Central, playing in the highly successful Seniors team, he was set to play in the Reserves for much of his career at Wests. The fact was that the Wests' First Grade side already had a formidable

Central Newcastle's Senior Team (1928) featured with the Crawford Cup and Mullally Shield. Tom is seated in the front row left.
Source: 'Central's Men of Yesteryear', *Newcastle Sun*, 20 November 1973

pack of forwards. Although the First Grade team had a poor 1929 season finishing in seventh position on the points table, the strength of the forwards was often commented on by various commentators. For example, the correspondent for the *NMH* reported on Wests' 30-4 loss to Northern Suburbs on 24 June, that 'Western Suburb's forwards were the equal of the opposing six, but all their energies were fritted away because of the moderate support in the back division'. As further evidence of their strength, four of the forwards (at various times) were selected to play for the Newcastle team in representative fixtures throughout the year. It is a testament to Tom's game skills that he secured a place in Wests' First Grade forward pack when the need arose. For example, on 29 August he featured in the team that defeated Maitland 5-4 at the Maitland Show Ground. This victory was one of only six wins throughout the season for Western Suburbs from sixteen matches. In reporting on the match 'The Forward' commented: 'on the whole the game was a very attractive one, both sides putting up good flashes of brilliant play, but luck was against Maitland'. No doubt the agile Tom Farrell featured in the match winning play.[7]

Mullally Shield Medallion presented to R E Farrell (1928)

The following season was an important one for Western Suburbs especially for the Reserve grade. Despite the ever increasing hardships of the Great Depression, supporters of the 'Rosellas' could take heart from the consistent success of the First and Reserve Grade sides. In the Mullaly Shield and Crawford Cup, First Grade made it to the final four only to be narrowly defeated (5-2) by Northern Suburbs in the semi-final. Reserve Grade had a most impressive season securing a place in the semi-finals after notching up a series of wins in closely contested matches. During the season Tom played a key attacking role for his team. For example, in the game on June 26, Tom was counted among the try scorers in Wests 10-6 victory over Morpeth East. In the semi-final, 'after a close interesting game Western Suburbs defeated Maitland United seven points to five'. In the final Wests came up against a strong South team. Although Tom was in the thick of play, scoring his team's only try, South defeated Wests 6-5. By all accounts it was an exciting game - 'The Forward' noted that: 'in the final of the Reserve Grade South Newcastle defeated Western Suburbs by six points to five. Stokes scoring the winning try in the last minute. For South, Bennett and Stokes tries, and for the losers Farrell scored a try and Kerr kicked a penalty goal'.[8]

Although Tom must have been disappointed by the close loss, he was keen to take his place in Reserve Grade the following season. In the 1931 season Wests' Reserve Grade won thirteen of its eighteen games. Tom was again a key player - for example, in the game against Central Newcastle on 2 July Tom scored one of the three tries. The result: Western Suburbs defeated Central Newcastle 12-3. Again on the 18 July 'Western Suburbs after a stern struggle defeated Maitland United at the Show Ground by the narrow margin of 3-0. The winning try scored by Farrell of Wests'. Wests went on to play Waratah in the semi-final on

12 September. Tom is listed among those who took the field for Wests in this hard fought match. In reporting on the game, 'The Forward' noted that 'Western Suburbs dominated the first half and led 3-2 at the interval. Play livened up considerably in the second half and both teams played football of a pleasing standard, but Wests retained its ascendancy and earned the right to play in the final. The game resulted in favour of Wests by 14-10'. In the final Wests came up against Norths who had remained undefeated throughout the season. Tom and his teammates played before a capacity crowd at the Newcastle Sports Ground on 19 September. Tom must have been caught up in the excitement as he observed thousands of supporters (particularly from the Cold-field areas) stream in to watch the First Grade final between Kurri Kurri and Cessnock. As a lead up event, the Reserve Grade final would have attracted its own supporters who added to the spectacle. One gets a sense of the excitement and expectation from the report of the correspondent from the *NMH*:

> Never in the history of the Rugby League has such a large and enthusiastic crowd been present to witness the final as that who attended the Newcastle Sports Ground on Saturday... Amid scenes of intense enthusiasm the Cessnock Municipal Band played the rival teams on to the ground and the game commenced before a record crowd of 10000 spectators. Streamers, rosettes, mascots and megaphones all bore the red, white and blue of Kurri Kurri or the black and gold of Cessnock. Coldfield's people made Saturday a gala day in Newcastle and from early morning, cars, buses and trains brought their quota of beribboned partisans down to witness the Rugby League final at the Sports Ground.

Unfortunately, once again Tom's team was not destined to come out on top. Despite this, it is apparent that it was a hard fought physical match - the same correspondent ('Penalty') reported:

> Northern Suburbs retained its undefeated record by scoring an easy victory over Western Suburbs in the Reserve Grade final at the Sports Ground 24-4. Wests tried to smother movements emanating from Norths by standing right up close and for a while it seemed as if its tactics might be successful, but nothing could keep Norths out. When Norths got its combination working, it raced through the gaps in magnificent passing rushes, and when stopped, reformed and attacked in another quarter. The game was hard throughout, there were no "beg pardons". Norths was the master of the situation for the whole of the game except for a few minutes at the beginning. Wests were certainly unfortunate to be pitted against so fine a team and performed meritoriously to hold Norths as well as it did. Wests team: Blunden, Hamilton, Williams(2), Harding, Mood, Bell, Gearing, Wivell, Pringle, Nesbitt, White, Farrell.

No doubt Tom was disappointed that he could not end his playing career for Wests on a higher note. A physical injury forced him out of the game at the end of the 1931 season. Despite this, he could be proud of his football achievements. He had played competitive football in the Newcastle competition for eleven years. Over his career he was a prominent member of the Reserve Grade team for both Central Newcastle and Western Suburbs featuring regularly on the list of try scorers.

Such was his agility on the field that he was promoted to First Grade when the need arose. He was counted among the 'Seniors' who secured the Crawford Cup and Mullally Shield for South Newcastle in 1928, the first time the Club had achieved this honour since 1921. Although he played First Grade, it was as a 'Rosella' Reserve Grader that Tom came to the fore. In successive seasons Tom played his part in ensuring that Western Suburb's Reserve Grade reached the finals of the football competition. In the 1930 final he was the only try scorer for Wests in its narrow loss to South Newcastle. Tom exhibited such a high level of sportsmanship and *esprit de corps* both on and off the field that he was able to count among his friends many of the leading footballers in the Newcastle region. These included Dew boy Rogers, Mo Harding, Pat Kirby, Jack Toovey, Keith Froome, Fatti Madison, Horry Banks, Ossie Screen, Mickie Freeman, Fred Welshman, Mo Wilson, Jack Wilson, Jack Harvey and Arthur Atchison. In all, Tom played 200 grade matches in his football career.[9]

Tom's decision to retire from the game did not prevent him from continuing his association with his beloved Western Suburb's Club. His business acumen and financial knowledge were much in demand during difficult financial times. For example, at the beginning of the 1932 season the balance sheet was looking pretty bleak. The accounts two shillings in arrears after the cost of the annual general meeting were taken into account. Tom worked with the management to bring the accounts back into the 'black'. The Committee decided to borrow money from the 'Juniors' and impose a levy on players for their guernseys. Such was the state of the finances that players only averaged three shillings and sixpence per game in payment throughout the season. As the Depression dragged on, matters only became worse. By the end of the 1933 season with gate receipts substantially down, Wests found that it had a revenue stream of about £100, an amount not sufficient to cover expenses and wages. Faced with financial ruin, the Club turned to prominent supporters to save the situation. Tom was one of the supporters who not only worked with the Committee to come up with a rescue plan but provided much needed funds to keep the club going. In May 1934, Mr Ott, the Club Secretary, undertook a recruitment drive writing 'to all citizens in the district with the object of obtaining as many members in the club as possible'. Prospective members were asked to pay an annual subscription of two schillings and sixpence 'to enable the club to carry on smoothly'. Although the Committee could guarantee the annual salary of the coach, there were insufficient funds to pay the players. Those whose contracts could not be honoured, were promised compensation when the club returned to profitability. Although such measures were far from popular, especially with the players, the Committee managed to secure the necessary finance to allow Wests to field teams in the 1934 competition. Despite its poor showing in the 1934 season the Committee could take heart that (after taking some tough decisions) it had ensured the survival of the Club. This was in part thanks to the financial assistance and sound business advice offered by prominent supporters like Tom Farrell.[10]

Given the role he had played in rescuing the Club, it is not surprising that Tom took up an active role as a member the Club Committee shortly after retiring as a player. In this capacity Tom regularly attended Wests' games (with members of his family) where he busied himself with administrative matters and the players' needs. His daughter recalls with pride how knowledgeable her father was about the game – 'how clever he was in telling everyone on the field what they should be doing'. His son remembers the fun he had attending football games with his father. While Tom attended to club business, his son (in the company of a minder) was free to enjoy the amenities of the football ground. John could recall the atmosphere in the dressing room as he father spoke to players – the pungent smell of 'oil of winter green' as the masseur (Sergeant Paddy Pender) went about his work. There were also the various culinary delights to tempt a young boy, the meat pies or pasties washed down with YY or NSW aerated waters. His son also recalls the post-match discussions his father would have with players and officials at the popular Sportsman's Arms Hotel in New Lambton. Here while waiting for his father the boy would enjoy a glass or two of raspberryade.

Farrell (second row, third from left) with the 1936 club delegates to the Newcastle Rugby League

Tom's efforts on behalf of the Club Committee did not go unrecognised – he was elected Vice-President, then President of Western Suburb League's Club in 1942 and again in 1946. His player background and administrative ability made him an ideal candidate to be appointed West's delegate to Newcastle Rugby League, the body that had overseen the Newcastle Rugby League competition since 1910. Throughout his long association with this body Tom used his base at Western Suburbs to promote the interests of the game throughout the region. In the late 1940s, for example, working in association with other delegates he was instrumental in establishing a Western Suburbs Associated Conference which was modelled on the second division competition which Wests had started in 1946. As President of the Western Suburbs Associated Clubs, Tom ran this competition from 1947 until it merged with the strong Second Division in the mid-1950s.

It is clear that Tom was an effective delegate for Wests. In 1964 the *NMH* carried the sports headline 'West cracking the whip on Newcastle Rugby League front'. In the article the correspondent 'broke into verse' to describe the effectiveness of the Wests' delegate:

> It's Tommy this and Tommy that
> They slap him on the back.
> But it's Master Tom who calls the tune
> When whips begin to crack.
> The reps come from North, down South and the Lakes,
> Sit around with VP's and give us the shakes.
> But the one who is feared most of them all
> Is Terrible Tom from the Big City Hall.
> So patrons take care, as you pass the West Club
> It's in Hobart Road, right next to the pub.
> Just bow down your head, don't give any lip
> For terrible Tom is there with his Whip.

Tom responded to such comments with modest good humour.

In reply he penned a few lines of his own which later were identified as 'Tom's Retort'.

Tom was also keen to promote the game throughout New South Wales. Long suspicious of power resting in the hands of a central authority based in Sydney, Tom was keen to see that all areas of the state had a role to play in the development of Rugby League. He worked to this end as a delegate for the Country Rugby League to the NSW Sydney Rugby League, the governing body for the sport of Rugby League in areas of New South Wales outside Sydney which had been formed in 1934. His administrative ability was once again demonstrated as he successfully managed touring teams around New South Wales. Such was his commitment to country rugby league that as late as 1978 he was still arguing against the dominance of the Sydney competition on the game. He objected strongly to the fact that talented Newcastle and country players found it difficult to secure selection in state or national teams because their metropolitan counterparts were preferred by the central authority. In his view it was yet another case of 'standards for the city and standards for the country'. Not one to let such partisanship go unchallenged, Tom wrote to the Rugby League Association to voice his disapproval.

Tom remained committed to Rugby League throughout his life. His son recalls with pleasure his trips to Sydney with his father and his mates to see the Rugby League Tests against France and England. He particularly recalls the Third Test against England in 1950 when fifty tons of sand were trucked in and spread on the 'Bulli Soil' cricket pitch at the Sydney Cricket Ground:

> The memories of the mud, the commitment of the
> likes of Matt McCoy, Doug Ritchie, Ben Purcell,

Dutchie Holland and their team mates and the thrill of Australia clinching victory in the dying moments of the game, when Lumsden dived over for a try in front of Tom and his Newcastle contingent. Tom let out a rare display of public excitement with a very vocal 'You Beauty', simultaneously hurling his precious hat high into the air. The hat was never recovered. He didn't care. 'You can always buy a new hat but you can't always beat the Poms'.

Such was Tom's interest in attending international football matches that he sought membership of the Sydney Cricket and Sports Ground Club from September 1966.

As his personal papers suggest Tom was an avid reader of football commentators in the press. He was keen to keep abreast of issues that affected the game in the local area. For example, in the 1950s he read closely articles dealing with the 'poaching' practices of certain Sydney teams, who secured talented local footballers for the Sydney competition. In the 1980s (now in his seventies) he considered the problems faced by local clubs when key players were absent due to state or national commitments. In considering these issues Tom would have been keenly aware that central football authorities did not always have the interests of the local area in mind when making such decisions. In whatever forum he found himself, he saw it as his duty to put forward the interests of Newcastle and the region as strongly as he could. In 1980 he argued that 'there is nothing wrong with the club standard of rugby league in Newcastle. Our own district competition is our life blood. Don't destroy it'. This did not mean that he had no interest outside of Newcastle. As noted Tom followed closely the successes of both state and national teams. And although wary of the Sydney football authorities, he was keen to know each week the results of the Sydney competition. Indeed, Tom's interest in football was not restricted to Rugby League – when other commitments permitted he attended Rugby Union and AFL matches as well.

Although his work for Rugby League involved him with various associations beyond the region, Tom remained true to the 'Rosellas'. No matter how lean the season, Tom's loyalty to Wests was unshakeable. This was made clear in 1968 when a friend noted: 'although your choice of the football team to win each year's competition is usually wrong and you have paid money out owing to your erring judgement, I figure you are loyal to the one club'. This club recognised such loyalty in 1975 by bestowing on Rolf Everist (Tom) Farrell Life Membership. His testimonial read:

> Joined Western Suburbs in 1929 and was a player in the years 1929, 1930, 1931 and 1932. Prior to this played with Broadmeadow Club in 1920 and then played with Central Newcastle in the years 1921, 1922, 1923, 1924, 1925, 1926, 1927 and 1928. In 1933 was on the Committee of the Club and from 1944 was a Delegate on the Newcastle Rugby League. In 1942 was President of West. Enlisted in 1942 and on return after the War was again President of West in 1946. During the years 1935 to 1939 was on the General Committee of the Country Rugby League. At the request of Western Suburbs accepted position of the West Macquarie League and held the position for 5 or 6 years. In about 1967 was again appointed Delegate for West on the Newcastle Rugby League and held this post for three years. Since 1929 has held continuous association with the Club either as Player,

an Official, a Financial Member or as nominated Vice President.

Tom enjoying an afternoon at the beach with some friends (1922)
– note the formal attire

He had also been made a Life Member of the Newcastle Rugby League in 1937. As noted in his testimonial, Tom not only played a significant role at Wests but gave of his services to Newcastle Rugby League and Country Rugby League throughout the State. This was noted by one Western Suburbs' commentator:

> He became a life member of Newcastle Rugby League in 1937. Played a leading role in Rugby League affairs as a delegate on the Newcastle League for many years to give both West Club and the District outstanding and valued representation in promoting the League code. An experienced and capable administrator Tom Farrell has been associated with the game as a player and official for 46 years and during that period has performed exceptional

service in the interests of followers of the great game of Rugby.

No wonder Tom was identified as one of 'West's prominent Personalities'. In 1979 Jack Mathews, a noted football commentator, reflecting on the contribution of Tom Farrell to Rugby League, concluded that:

> While his particular interest is now centred on the Western Suburbs Rugby League Club he has never been parochial, his unswerving belief being that the game, and its objects, are greater than the club or the individual…one has met many fine sporting administrators and gained much admiration for their dedication and selfless effort they have given to their causes. None has been more impressive as a splendid sportsman, an outstanding personality, both forthright and fair, objective in effort and far-seeing in thought than Tom Farrell. It is little wonder that he is so highly regarded and respected. He certainly deserves to be. He is the only one to down grade his many successful efforts to advance the standing and prestige of Rugby League wherever it is played. But that is in keeping with his insistence that he has been but one of a team. The game is fortunate to have had one such as Tom Farrell to do so much for it.

Such words are a fine tribute to one who did so much for the code of Rugby League not only in Newcastle but throughout New South Wales.[11]

While football took up much of his weekend interests during the winter period, it was swimming that occupied much of his leisure time during the summer months. Like many of his football mates, Tom found swimming an important means of maintaining fitness in the off-season. From 1920 to 1932 Tom was an active member of Cook's Hill Life Saving & Surf Club (CHLSSC), one of the leading surf clubs in the district. Although fitness was important, Tom understood that his club membership provided him an opportunity to serve the community. First and foremost the club's activities were aimed at protecting and saving human life. Regularly on weekends and public holidays, Tom and his brother, Charles, were to be found on Bar Beach discharging their duties as lifesavers. For example, on 29 November 1929 Charles and Tom Farrell were listed as one of the four members of the morning patrol at Bar Beach under the direction of Tom Wilkinson (Captain). In order to fulfil his duties as a lifesaver, Tom had to be a strong swimmer and proficient practitioner of search and rescue techniques. These included methods of lifesaving (belt, line and reel), resuscitation, promotion of warmth and hand carriage. Mastery of first aid was also a requirement.

Bronze medallion awarded to R E Farrell

Tom would have been kept busy on patrol as large crowds flocked to the beach over the summer months. The public came primarily from the densely populated inner suburb of Cook's Hill and from The Junction. The duties of a lifesaver carried with it some risk - for example, on 15 April 1928 a special committee meeting was held 'to deal with the shark fatality which had recently occurred'. Again in March 1931 the committee noted 'a recent fatality at a nearby beach'. It was the case that certain members failed to cooperate with the beach authorities – in late 1929 the committee complained that warnings were repeatedly ignored by bathers 'if they persisted in swimming in dangerous waters after being told to desist, they would be prosecuted'. Unfortunately, some lifesavers paid the ultimate price for their public service – on 13 February 1937 John Welsh, the popular sports secretary of Cook's Hill Club, lost his life in a shark attack. The number of fatalities, however, at Bar Beach was minimal. In fact, thanks to the proficiency and vigilance of its members, Cook's Hill Club had an impressive record of effecting the successful rescue of the public who found themselves in distress. For example the *NMH* reported on 14 February 1924 that 'at the Bar Beach on Sunday a bather named Warton got into a current and was carried out in a southerly direction for almost 200 yards. A member of Cook's Hill Life Saving Club donned the belt and the distressed swimmer was brought to safety. After being attended to by the Club's first aide patrol, Warton was able to walk home'.[12]

Already in possession of a Bronze Medallion (which he had achieved at school), Tom maintained his surfing fitness by becoming an active member of the Cook's Hill SLS Swimming Club which had been founded in 1919. Regularly on Wednesday evenings at the Ocean Baths and on weekends at Bar Beach the Swimming Club conducted a number of competitions with associated trophies and prizes donated by local dignitaries. Members could accrue points in these events for championship recognition at the end of the season. It is clear that for more than a decade, Tom and his brother were keen competitors. On 1 February 1922 C. Farrell is listed as one of the forty eight competitors in the 50 yards (Fred Markham) handicap. Charles came second in the first heat. On 11 January 1923 Charles and Tom Farrell were placed second and third in the First Heat of the 66 yards Sorby Ltd Handicap. On 9 January 1924 Charles and Tom Farrell are listed in the heats of the 50 yards handicap – both men finished second in their respective heats. On the 24 January 1924 the correspondent for the *NMH* reported:

> The Cook's Hill Surf Swimming Club held a 100 yards Stanley Wade handicap last night. This event is held to perpetuate the memory of a valued and respected member of the Cook's Hill Life Saving Club. Wintry conditions prevailed. First Heat: T.Farrell 18 seconds Time 1 minute 22 seconds… (details of three other heats)…Final: T.Farrel Time 1 minute 21.25 seconds. The Mahoney Shield was again advanced last weekend. The event was a single race (at the beach) in which A.Armitage was first, D.Bratter & T.Farrell dead heated for second.

No doubt the high level of fitness achieved by such regular competition greatly enhanced the club's ability to serve the local community by providing efficient and effective lifesaving in the surf at Bar Beach each weekend. This was explained by the Swimming Club's secretary: 'the objective of the competitive events conducted each week at the Ocean baths and in the surf is to improve the swimmer so that with the instruction in resuscitation method, each active member would be prepared when emergency called'. To this end, Tom continued to participate in swimming club events. On 12 February 1925 Tom was chosen to represent the club in the number three team at a surf carnival at Stockton Beach. Such was his success in the 1926-1927 season that Tom won the Green Cup for the most points scored in the season.

(Above) The Green Cup – engraving reads: Green Cup, Cooks Hill Amateur Swimming Club, For Point Score Competition for Season 1926-27. Won by R. Farrell.

(Left) Tom with the Green Cup – photograph taken at the Farrell home, 19 Collaroy Road, New Lambton in 1927.

On 14 December 1927 he was placed third behind his brother in the Fourth Heat of the J.Meighan Handicap. On 4 January 1928 Tom was placed second in the First Heat of the Dr Thompson Trophy Event. In the First Heat of the 150 yard Mark Howard Trophy Event on 11 January 1928 he was placed third. On 25 January 1928 Charles and Tom Farrell won their respective heats of the 66 yards Reg Pogonoski Trophy Event. In the final Charles was placed second behind W. Fitzgibbon. Tom was placed second in the final of the Alex Hodgson Trophy Event over 66 yards on 22 February 1928 with a time of 47.1 seconds. A week later he ran second in the 75 yard handicap with a time of 54 seconds. On the 3 January 1929 he repeated this feat with a time of 52 seconds. A week later in the 100 yards handicap Charles and Tom Farrell were placed second and third respectively behind M.Brown with a time of 1 minute and 24.25 seconds. On 15 January 1929 Charles and Tom were placed first and second in the Fourth Heat of the 150 yards handicap race. On 31 January 1929 the *NMH* reported:

> A 66 yards handicap for the trophy donated by Mr J.Carroll was conducted at the Ocean Baths last night in conjunction with the Thalberg, Joe Goldring and Bert Cook Memorial point score competitions. First Heat F.Neville (6 seconds) 1st , T.Farrell (8 seconds) 2nd , R. Hayman (1 second) 3rd, Time 43.15 seconds...(details of three other heats)...Final: Tom Farrell 1st, Jim Gibb and D.Brattan dead heat 2nd . Time 47 seconds.

On 7 November 1930 the Farrell brothers were again placed in the heats of the 100 yard handicap (Clive Hocquart Trophy). Further success followed in the heats of handicap races on 18 November and 2 December 1930.[13] Throughout their years of competitive involvement, Tom and his brother would have appreciated the level of fitness that swimming provided. Swimming proficiency (and associated activities) allowed them to carry out their lifeguard duties with confidence. This provided a direct benefit to the community. The Farrell brothers would have also taken great satisfaction from the strong comradeship that developed among the members. As with football, Tom forged life-long friendships with those he came into contact with through his association with Cook's Hill Life Saving Club. Chief among these was Arthur (Russ) Gow whose family first billeted Tom as an eighteen year old competitor in Sydney.

Cook's Hill Life Saving & Surf Club competing at Manly Beach (1920s)

As well as being prominent club competitors, Tom and Charles found time to assist with administration matters. The *NMH* reported on 12 February 1925 that Tom Farrell was elected secretary of the CHSLS Swimming Club. The minutes of 16ᵗʰ Annual Meeting of the CHLSSC include the name of C. Farrell among those holding the position of Vice-President. Membership was high and the competition for office was intense. In 1929-30 there were more than forty-five nominations for the limited positions vacant at the annual general meeting. It is an indication of the Farrell brothers' standing that they were chosen to hold such strongly contested positions.[14]

It was a great time to be involved with the club as a competitor or administrator. The period of the 1920s is regarded as 'truly the glory years of the Club'. As Ramsland points out, by the end of the 1920s:

> The Club held, for a time or permanently, more trophies than any other lifesaving club in the State. These included the Rundle Cup, the Resch Cup, the Tooth Cup, the Murdoch Shield, the Cecil Healy Memorial Shield, the Cornish Shield, Earp Shield, Vesper Shield, Spiers Cup, Whittaker Cup, Harris Cup, Bert Hones Nos 1 and 2 Cups, Thalberg Cup and Perpetual Forests Cup. But the most valuable trophy in their possession was the "Johnnie Walker" surf boat which became the Club's property in a competition lasting three summer seasons. It symbolised Cook's Hill's high status in the highly competitive world of surf carnivals.

While not regarded as 'swimming greats', it was recognised that Tom and his brother had brought honour to their club for over a decade. Consistently successful in club heats, both men were regularly selected to represent the club at various carnivals. It is clear that their consistent effort brought the club success. A photograph, entitled 'Trophies Galore' taken to commemorate the highly successful 1928 season, features the brothers. Seated in the middle row (in the company of six other club competitors and three officials) are Charles and Tom Farrell. Before them sit eight trophies acquired from local and state competitions. A fitting tribute to the contribution (both athletic and administrative) made by the Farrell brothers to the Cook's Hill Life Saving & Surf Club.[15]

Although Tom gave up competitive swimming in 1932, the same year he retired from competitive football, he did not give up his interest in swimming. It was an interest he passed on to his children as he taught them to swim. On many a weekend in summer Tom would accompany his children to the beach or Ocean Baths. Similar activities were pursued at the family's weekender at Fishing Point. Tom was keen to maintain his physical fitness throughout his life. He did not smoke and drank only in moderation. He found time during his working week to regularly undertake physical exercise. During the summer months, he and a group of work colleagues would swim at the Newcastle Baths during their lunch break. In winter the group met to walk to and from the City Hall to King Edward Park. During inclement weather the group sought an alternate route under the awnings of the shops along the CBD. In retirement he went to Merewether Beach every morning for a swim and to lie in the sun. He continued this habit well into his eighties. Such was his liking for the outdoors that he developed a great year-round tan. A friend recalled identifying him in the street by the shorts he was wearing and his mahogany knees. Tom's passion for physical exercise was one of the reasons he became so involved with establishing and protecting parks and recreational areas in the Newcastle region. Given his longevity, it is clear that Tom himself benefitted greatly by his life-long interest in physical activity.[16]

3: *Local Leader of Business*

From humble beginnings at Breckenridge & Co and the State Dockyard, Tom Farrell went on to become one of the Newcastle region's most respected business leaders. Having begun as a junior clerk at the Newcastle Abattoir in September 1921, he worked his way through the ranks achieving various senior management posts. In March 1966 he was appointed General Manager. A qualified accountant, he became a Fellow of the Australian Society of Accountants. His interest in home ownership and the Co-operative Movement, led him to become involved in The Hunter River Public Service Starr-Bowkett Building Cooperative Society, later The Greater Newcastle Cooperative Permanent Building and Investment Society. Such was his business acumen that he became a founding Director of the Greater Newcastle Permanent Building Society and Director of the NSW Permanent Building Association. Never neglectful of his civic responsibilities, Tom saw his position within the local business community as providing him a means of influencing public policy. As one commentator later noted Tom Farrell was able to use his prominence in business 'to campaign mightily on a range of issues'.[1]

The Newcastle Abattoir which came into being by virtue of an act of the NSW Parliament (1912) was charged with the responsibility of guaranteeing the quality of the meat supply in fourteen local councils and shires by means of establishing proper slaughtering, storage and transport processes. Given the lack of government control over hygiene, the previous system of relying on private slaughtering houses located throughout the district was deemed unsatisfactory. Under the Act, the Abattoir Board (later taken over by the Newcastle Council) had a statutory responsibility to ensure that the meat products supplied by the abattoir were of the highest hygiene (pure) quality. Primary responsibility in this area rested with the buyers and Meat Inspectors.[2]

Between 1921 and 1936 Tom worked as a junior, then senior clerk, in the bureaucracy that oversaw the operation of the abattoir. By November 1936 he was working in the 'accounts division', having qualified as an accountant. By this time Tom had also gained a full Meat Inspector's Certificate from the NSW Technical College. Promotion followed to that of 'Senior Accountant' in June 1940. At the instigation of the Greater Newcastle Council which took over the responsibility for the abattoir in this year, Tom was transferred to the Head Office in Mayfield West where he was charged with reorganising the clerical section in order to promote greater efficiency in administration. In his report to the Council regarding the administration of the abattoir, the Town Clerk found that Mr Farrell was a 'valuable officer'.

Over the next decade he went on to head the accounting division, being appointed 'Works Accountant' in April 1950. The following year in November 1951 he was appointed Assistant General Manager and moved office to the City Hall. At the time of his appointment the abattoir employed 350 persons, processed nearly 200,000 carcases (cattle, calves, sheep and pigs) per year and had an annual turnover of £1,250,000. Given his wide experience, Tom decided to apply for the position of General Manager of the Metropolitan Abattoir Board in Adelaide, South Australia. His letter of application outlined in detail his experience at the Newcastle Abattoir:

Head Office, Newcastle Abattoir (about 1930) –
original office at NDA Mayfield West (Warabrook)

Although my duties in the main have been administrative I have during my long association with the Newcastle abattoir had ample opportunity in obtaining experience in all phases of Meat Works activities. From 1921 to 1940 I was employed on the Abattoir Plant and have had experience in almost every department. I have worked in the Slaughtering Halls as a Meat Inspector, in the Export Department on the Grading Scales, in the Chilling and Freezing Rooms; at the Saleyards as Saleyards Attendant and have relieved in other Departments. For a number of years I regularly acted as Manager of the Abattoir Meat Department during the absence of the Manager on leave. Over a period of five years I attended Stock Sales in the Newcastle District and purchased pigs for the Abattoir Meat Department. For a period of ten years one of my duties included management of the Abattoir Butcher Shop, which was a separate entity, purchasing live stock on its own account for subsequent retail sale of meat to employees.

Although his application was not successful at this time, it is clear that Tom had all the necessary experience and expertise to manage an abattoir. It is not surprising, therefore, that in March 1966 he was appointed General Manager of Newcastle Abattoir. The appointment was a fitting climax to a most distinguished career in the Meat Industry. This was recognised by various commentators in the local area. One Newcastle businessman commented, 'your appointment is fully merited and it has been received with great satisfaction throughout the Newcastle region'. Two years later, Alderman Bell, commenting on the expertise of the General Manager stated, 'Mr Farrell was so well in touch with the industry that he was able to prepare any report for Council in thirty minutes'. He held this position until his retirement on 5 November 1968. In 1980 in recognition of his expertise in the meat industry, especially the export business, the *Newcastle Sun* identified him as one of 'The Men of the Meat World'. As a sign of his standing in the business community, he gained membership of the exclusive Newcastle Club where captains of industry and commerce regularly met. He was also appointed to the board of directors of Dark's Ice and Cold Storage Works in Wharf Road, Newcastle. As the General Manager of one of the ice-works major customers in the region, Tom was able to assist the growth and development of the enterprise.[3]

Both as a junior then senior manager, Tom worked to ensure the overall growth and development of the abattoir. By the time he headed the institution, Newcastle Abattoir was recognised as one of the largest and most efficient abattoirs in the state. Tom shared the vision of the abattoir's founders for an institution that could guarantee the delivery of 'wholesome and pure' meat supply while at the same time being financially independent and successful. Such a vision sat well with his concern for the local area and his belief in decentralisation. It was his view that Newcastle Abattoir operating as a regional public utility was 'the property of the people of the district'. His management approach involved financial prudence, ongoing staff development and constructive staff relations.

Management Group, Newcastle Abattoir (date unknown).
Tom front row second from left.

In the year he was appointed General Manager, the abattoir was 'big-business' with an annual turnover of eight million dollars. It had over three hundred employees and assets with a capital value of about four million dollars. It had a lucrative domestic and export trade with the capacity to produce a million 'killing-units' (cattle, calves, sheep, lamb and pig carcasses) per year. Slaughtering capacity per day was 500 cattle, 3600 sheep and 500 pigs which supplied 170 master butchers and operators in the district. Exports increased five-fold in ten years from 644 tons in 1956 to more than 3500 tons in 1965. Export markets had been established in the United Kingdom, the United States, Europe and Asia. Exports to Asia and Africa were on the increase particularly to the Philippines, Japan, Hong Kong and India. The by-products section was producing annually 5385 tons of edible tallow, lard, and dripping and 365 tons of fertilizers. In addition numerous products were made for various industries from hides, skins, hair, wool and blood. A number of vital pharmaceutical products were also manufactured from processed glands.

Courtesy of the *NMH* (8 November 1966)

In order to ensure that the abattoir was a modern facility, Tom was keen to adopt new techniques and machinery. He explained that it was the responsibility of his officers 'to carefully analyse new developments in methods, with special reference to hygiene, and economic presentation of meat to the public'. He counted among his successes the introduction of the 'on the rail dressing' system (where no part of the carcass touched the floor during the slaughtering process), the establishment of steam generated capacity which allowed the swifter transport of offal products especially in the by-product plant and the installation of larger chilling rooms (incorporating the latest materials and design) which increased capacity. By establishing new processes and ensuring that his officers were kept up-to-date with the latest trends, Tom ensured that the abattoir conformed to all modern practices. Not one to rest on his laurels, Tom was always

Tom adopts a 'hands-on approach' as General Manager, Newcastle Abattoir. Source: *NMH*, 8 November 1966

Tom inspects a 17-ton capacity refrigerated container at Darks Ice Works, Wharf Road, Newcastle. Also featured in the photograph (suited) are Mr R. Smith (Darks Ice) and Mr R. Tange (Boneless Meat Exporter). Source: *Newcastle Sun*, 3 October 1968

interested in improving working processes. He set as a target in his first year as General Manager to improve the handling of blood products by implementing modern methods which would prevent losses and improve the product.

In terms of training and innovation, Newcastle Abattoir led the way in the meat industry not only in New South Wales but throughout Australia. As one commentator put it, `the high standards that have been a consistent feature of the Newcastle Abattoir are recognised throughout the state'. This was achieved by 'encouraging personnel to train for higher positions to enable them to fill leading roles in abattoir conduct and management'. Personnel from Newcastle Abattoir went on to hold managerial positions at abattoirs at Homebush, Goulburn, Maitland, Gunnedah, Dubbo, Mudgee, Forbes, Aberdeen and Cootamundra. The Commonwealth Veterinary Officer in charge of the Department of Primary Industries, South Australian, the Senior Inspector in Charge, Illawarra Shire Council, the Manager of the Queensland County Abattoir and the Foreman of the Forbes Abattoir were all former employees of Newcastle Abattoir. In addition the abattoir could boast twenty five Commonwealth or State Meat Inspectors who had received their training on site.

It is clear that Tom developed a good working relationship with the employees at the abattoir. A journalist noted the strong bonds that existed between the personnel (professional and non-professional), commenting that for many 'it was more than a place of work – it was almost a way of life'. The strength of Tom's relationship with the work force is revealed in a letter sent by the Secretary of the Meat & Allied Trades' Federation of Australia, on the occasion of his retirement. The Secretary admitted that 'the Newcastle Branch Committee have always enjoyed good relationship and co-operation between Abattoir Management

Family network at abattoir

One of the most interesting aspects about the employees of the Newcastle abattoir is the widespread family ramifications.

Relationships are varied, ranging from sons and fathers to distant cousins, but all highlight the close connections the personnel have with the Abattoir.

It is more than a place to work — almost a way of life.

This close-knit feature of the Abattoirs makes for continuity of policy and dedication of service.

Manager

The present General Manager (Mr. R. E. Farrell) no longer has relatives working under him, but his father was a pig buyer and for many years his brother, the late C. W. Farrell, was bacon department manager. The late Mr. Eric Bell, previous general manager, was the son of the late deputy superintendent and chief inspector, and his cousin H. Bell is a slaughtering foreman. The close links are emphasised by the late Mr. J. Lance Lawson, the first secretary and general manager, whose daughter Mrs. B. Humphreys is now the chief female clerk and his nephew Nell Humble is the senior meat inspector.

Mr. A. W. Elliott, the assistant general manager and accountant has a brother and two cousins working at the Abattoir.

Brothers T. H. and E. H. Leece are senior staff members: T. H. Leece is the slaughtering manager, and his brother the senior stock buyer.

Mr. L. G. Hughes is the travelling inspector, and his brother A. L. Hughes is the chief clerk, while their nephew C. J. Barnier is a clerk.

Mr. H. Manson, senior inspector, has his twin sons John and Stephen working at the Abattoir. Other twins include Peter and Terry Evans.

There are a number of father-son combinations. R. W. Wright (meat inspector) and his brother, E. Wright (flower road foreman) are the sons of the late Mr. W. Wright, slaughterman.

Two sons

The late C. P. Johnson, a meat inspector, has two sons at the works—W. W. Johnson, hide and skin foreman, and C. P. Johnson, by-products foreman.

Mr. A. R. Tripp, the works accountant is the son of the first chief clerk, R. J. Tripp. An uncle was head stockman.

The father of J. Webster (inspector) was bacon department foreman. The two Bruniges brothers, both meat inspectors, were trained at the Abattoir.

Others

Other family connections include G. Gallagher, J. Webster, P. H. Mulhern, E. Smith, A. R. Bedford, Brian and Bernard Morrow, Aubrey and Bob Arnold, R. and P. Bradley, Reg and Ken Brown, G. and J. Bytheway, Terry and Clarrie Campbell, Eric and Horace Cook, Tom Maddison, Peter and Bryan Forbes, F. Franks, Gordon and Cecil Freeman, J. Tonks, Douglas and John Gardner, Allan, Bob and Harry Goldie, R. Gumb, Brian and Sidney Howard, Glen and Garry Johns, Rees and Wayne Jones, William, Percy and David Lloyd, Kevin and Ron Monagle, Noel and Earl O'Connor, C. and W. Partington, R. and D. Pounder, Allan and Kenneth Richardson, Don and Leonard Roberts, Philip Shedden and Stan, Ken, Victor and Fred Sullivan.

Courtesy of the *NMH* (8 November 1966)

and this organisation through the good offices of yourself. We feel you have earned this retirement after a long association with the Industry'. This is a telling comment from an organisation that did not always see 'eye-to-eye' with the management of the abattoir. The dedication of service by a significant number of employees also speaks of the positive work environment at the abattoir. At the time of his appointment as General Manager there were nineteen employees (including Tom himself) who had completed more than forty years of service. Tom was aware of the importance of staff morale – he therefore took decisive steps to improve the working conditions of his employees.

During his time as General Manager he overcame the shortage of change room and showering facilities by provided a much larger amenities block for workers. He was also keen to look after the welfare of managerial staff. In October 1968 one staff member wrote:

> I would like to take this opportunity of thanking you for all the assistance and advice given me since I commenced at the Abattoir. I would particularly like to thank you for your encouragement (and sympathy when failures occurred) during the time I was studying for my Accountancy Certificate. This encouragement was invaluable to me. I wish to thank you also for helping me with financial advice and assistance over the years when I was building my homes. Other instances of your assistance are too numerous to mention but for these I am truly grateful. I regret you have reached retiring age as I have always considered you to be a very competent manager and always treated your staff with respect and very fairly.

The same employee two years earlier had recalled Tom's sympathy, encouragement and assistance when he was downhearted and discouraged. He concluded by stating that Tom's intervention 'was material in enabling me to achieve my goal in becoming a qualified accountant'. Tom was always keen to put the interests of his employees and the community before that of bureaucracy. In short, he had a healthy mistrust of 'City Hall Bureaucrats'. This led him to oppose strongly the attempts by the Town Clerk to redirect profits from the abattoir to other city projects. It was Tom's view that all profits from the abattoir should be used to reduce killing charges and to improve workers' facilities. In this way profits were to be used to reduce costs to butcheries and consumers and improve the lot of the employees. On one occasion Tom personally intervened to prevent one client being declared bankrupt by the Town Clerk. The business concerned had come into financial difficulties due to embezzlement by a temporary manager. Tom placed faith in the owners, knowing them to be competent operators of a business. Using his authority, he reorganized the repayment schedule, allowing the business time to clear their debt. Although the Town Clerk was none too impressed, remarking 'it's on your head Tom Farrell', Tom's decision was vindicated – within two years the debt had been repaid and the business was flourishing.[4]

But Tom's working life was not without its difficulties. As a junior clerk he was involved with the preparation of the Board's submission to the Royal Commission charged with the responsibility of investigating the efficiency of the Abattoir, its fees, book-keeping methods, inspections and whether the Board was engaging in unfair competition with butchers, bacon curers and distributors. Tom had a personal interest in the Royal Commission's activities. Both his father and brother were involved with the Bacon Division, William as a buyer and Charles as a manager. The allegations against this division were made by a number of Sydney suppliers who were unhappy with the current arrangements, alleging that the Board paid too much for pigs, its bacon was sold at a reduced price and it showed preferential treatment to certain Master Butchers and businesses. It appears that a number of suppliers were particularly unhappy with the arrangements William Farrell had made with suppliers in the Northern Districts of New South Wales. After weeks of hearings, 1097 pages of typed evidence and 202 pages of advice by learned counsel, the

Royal Commission delivered its findings in March 1930. The Commission found all issues proved in favour of the Board. It was the view of the Commission that 'the undertaking as a whole is capably and efficiently managed'. However, despite this the Commission recommended that the Bacon Division be prohibited from trading due to certain deficiencies in book-keeping. It was the opinion of the Commission that 'the system in operation is deficient in respect of many primary essentials' and recommended that 'steps be taken to completely reorganise the system in order that department results may be readily ascertained and checked and brought into line with modern practice and requirements'. This obviously was an adverse finding for the Farrell family.

While Tom and his clerical colleagues were faced with a great deal of extra work as they updated the book-keeping system, Charles and William Farrell faced the real possibility of losing their employment. This was a cause of great concern, given the realities of the Great Depression. Fortunately for the Farrell family, a change of government in November 1930 brought a review of the Commission's findings. The following year the Lang Government fully validated the Board's actions, overturning the previous injunction. The Bacon Division was once again free to trade in pork meat and bacon. Both William and Charles continued to work for the abattoir until their retirement. Charles Farrell eventually became the Manager of the Bacon Division developing it into a highly profitable and successful section.[5]

As noted, Tom also experienced difficulties at times working with the Greater Newcastle City Council (NCC). Like many, he probably had some misgivings about the takeover of the abattoir by the Council in 1939. It was felt that the dissolution of the Board would have a detrimental effect on the standard of administration of the abattoir. Despite this, Tom throughout his managerial career, worked constructively with council officers. At times, however, the relationship became strained. In 1966, for example, Tom found himself at loggerheads with Mr Burges, the Town Clerk, when applications were called for in the press for the position of General Manager. Clearly, Tom was justly annoyed by the independent action of the Town Clerk – under the pre-existing arrangements he had the right of succession. Furthermore, he had the necessary qualifications and experience for the position. It is a testament to Tom's ability and his standing with the workforce that the Newcastle Abattoir Staff Officers' Union intervened on his behalf. In a long letter of protest to the Lord Mayor, the President pointed out that:

> we are all well aware of Mr Farrell's administrative ability and knowledge of the Meat Industry acquired over his 44 years of experience in practically all departments and through his regular promotions in the industry and his qualifications he had progressed to a high executive position. Mr Farrell's ability is widely recognised outside the Industry and it is the opinion of the Union he should have been automatically and immediately appointed to the position. We feel that by delaying and not making an immediate appointment that a reflection is being cast against Mr Farrell, and as members of a Union who have worked with Mr Farrell over the years we would like to remind the Council that in Mr Farrell, the Council has a most efficient and loyal servant, with the necessary qualifications, seniority and is fully conversant with all phases of the Meat Industry. It is the unanimous view of the Committee of the

Union that Council promote Mr Farrell forthwith to the position of General Manager.

With the backing of the Lord Mayor and the support of the Council, Tom was duly promoted to the position of General Manager. In April 1968, Tom again found himself at odds with the Town Clerk. Without consulting the General Manager, Burges had recommended to the Council that the Assistant General Manager, Mr Elliott, be sent overseas on an extensive study tour. The tour to America, England, Europe, Scandinavia and Japan was set to cost thousands of dollars. The decision met opposition within council – a number of aldermen were concerned that the General Manager had not been consulted. Given the lack of due process (and associated discourtesy), the Town Clerk moved that the decision be withdrawn until such time as Tom was properly consulted. The matter was resolved after Tom held a series of frank discussions with the Assistant General Manager and the Town Clerk. It was agreed that Mr Elliott would postpone his travel plans until after he assumed the position of General Manager. Tom's recommendation was received and adopted by the Council.[6]

Although tensions did arise from time to time, Tom maintained a good working relationship with the local government authorities. In 1966 Alderman McDougall, the Lord Mayor, congratulated the abattoir on its half-century of progress and service. He argued that its past growth and service would continue into the future under the stewardship of Mr Farrell. On his retirement the Council of the City of Newcastle thanked Tom for 'the contribution he had made to the welfare of the abattoir undertaking'. McDougall wrote, 'it has been a great pleasure to work with you and I sincerely hope that we will keep a close association in the city's interest in the future'.

Such sentiments were expressed at a federal level. It was the view of Senator McMullin, the President of the Senate, that the good work achieved by Tom Farrell at the abattoir would serve as a landmark. The captains of industry were also forthright with their praise. For example Mr R.D.Rumbold, General Manager of Unilever Australia Pty Ltd, commented 'we at Unilever are all sorry that the time has come for you to move out but I can assure you that nobody has earned our goodwill and good wishes more than you have'. Tom's interest in the abattoir was to continue after his retirement. He kept abreast of issues relevant to the meat industry and the development of the abattoir. He was particularly vocal in the 1980s as the State Government (with local government approval) put in place plans to close the abattoir.[7]

Tom's business acumen was not confined to his activities at the Newcastle Abattoir. As a prominent figure in a number of leading lending institutions, he worked to ensure the extension of home ownership to all sectors of the community in the Greater Newcastle and Hunter areas. He was particularly concerned that low income families had access to the necessary finance in order to buy a home. It is not surprising, therefore, that he became associated with The Newcastle Hunter River Public Service Starr Bowkett Society (NHRSBS) which began trading in 1924. Starr-Bocketts are 'cooperative non-profit organisations that provide interest free loans to their members and operate on the principles of mutual self-help'. Tom was attracted to Starr Bowketts because they were 'truly mutual' organisations that put people before profits. As he explained 'Starr Bowketts came into being by idealists to help people who had no earthly chance of ever owning their own houses by the ordinary means of existing finance'. In the 1920s housing finance was difficult to obtain - it was dependant on the borrower having access to a substantial equity and the means to meet high interest payments. Starr-Bowketts were particularly attractive to low income earners because they offered a compulsory saving element, the allotment of loans by ballot and the absence of the requirement to produce a sizeable deposit. The 1920s had seen a dramatic increase in the rate of mortgage lending (for all types of Building Societies including Starr Bowketts) stimulated by population growth and increasing confidence in the economy. To capitalise on such optimism the NHRSBS first operated out of a room at the rear of Ross Richardson Real Estate in Beaumont Street, Hamilton. The office was later moved to larger premises in the same street. The NHRSBS was the second cooperative in NSW formed after the Cooperation Act in 1923. By the time it was wound up in 1950, it had provided housing finance (from £100 to £600) to 168 Novocastrians. Tom and Kath Farrell were one of the couples who had benefited from membership of a Starr Bowkett Society. On 11 January 1924 Tom became the 77th member of the NHRSBS, later securing finance to purchase a property at 19 Colloroy Road, New Lambton.[8]

Office of the Newcastle & Hunter River Starr Bowkett Society
(Lindsay & Beaumont Street) Source: 'Photographs & History of the Greater
Newcastle & Hunter River Starr Bowkett Society', Rodd Papers, UNA

Due to the scarcity of archival material, it is difficult to determine when Tom Farrell became associated with NHRSBS. It is clear that he was not a member of the original committee. The first mention of Mr R E Farrell in the extant sources is in a 'List of Directors' of The Greater Newcastle Co-operative Building & Hunter River Starr-Bowkett Societies Limited' (Association) in 1946. This body was an association of the thirty three societies which had been established by the parent NHRSBS in the period 1924-1946. The association included 8 Starr Bowkett Societies, 12 Building Societies, one Permanent Building Society (Greater Building Society Ltd), one Savings & Loan Society (Greater Credit Union Ltd) and one Community Advancement Society. The Association had been incorporated in June 1944 as a means of better managing a group of like-minded cooperatives. Although no specific record has been found, it can be presumed that Tom was a founding director of the Association. Given this, it is also probable that he had been associated with the NHRSBS (and its associated entities) well before this date. A comment he made in 1986 (see below) suggest that he was one of the directors of No 2 Starr Bowkett which was incorporated in 1928.[9]

It is clear that in the twenty years after its establishment, the NHRSB had flourished. This was in large part due to Messrs Mathieson and Lean (founding members of the committee) and other directors including Tom who successfully guided the NHRSB (and its associated entities) through some difficult times. The Great Depression had witnessed a dramatic decline in dwelling construction and mortgage lending. The improvement witnessed in the second half of the 1930s was curtailed by the advent of World War II. During the war period lending for all types of Building Societies (including Starr Bowketts) fell sharply. It would have been evident to Tom on his return from active service in 1946 that the Greater Newcastle and Hunter areas were experiencing a desperate house shortage. This was an ongoing concern for the *NMH* which estimated in 1944 that Newcastle needed more than 6000 new homes. The house shortage in the Newcastle region was to remain a cause of concerns into the 1950s.[10]

It appears from later correspondence that Tom was so committed to the cooperative movement that he was quite prepared in difficult times to provide venture capital from his own funds. In 1986 he explained 'I would support an initial payment of $10000 to cover preliminary expenses. We did this originally to start the Permanent, there is no thanks for that now'. Later in the same document he commented 'start a Starr Bowkett by all means but first of all get a Board of young enthusiasts. No 2 Starr Bowkett carried on or struggled on with only 150 members in the Depression. In the Group we controlled the expenses'. Clearly Tom was one of these 'young enthusiasts' who steered the NHRSB (and its associated entities) to success despite the difficult times. In 1945 Mr Mathieson could report that 'the cooperative societies with which I am associated lent more than £700,000 and further money was available'. A year later the gross capital of the Association exceeded £1,500,000 with 6250 members (a six-fold increase in eight years). In advances the Association had loaned £1,250,000 in the period from 1924 with the expectation that working capital would exceed £1,500,00 when loan approvals were taken into consideration. In the same period Terminating Societies had advanced £578,487 and had secured a combined capital of £1,000,000. The No 1 Terminating Society which commenced operating in 1938 had provided finance for the construction of 107 new homes. The Nos 2-12 Building Societies had a combined capital of £900,000. These societies had loaned a total of £459,935 for the purpose of constructing new homes or purchase existing dwellings. The No 1 Starr Bowkett alone had provided 570 home loans to a total value of £207,500. The Nos 2-8 Starr Bowkett Societies with a combined membership of 3850 had provided a total of £377,638 of housing finance. Given the fact that the median house price in Sydney was about £750, it is clear that the Association had used its capital to provide a significant number of people with housing finance. With the basic wage set at about £400 per annum, Starr Bowketts nos 1-8 must have provided many low income earners the opportunity to purchase their own home. Such was their confidence in the cooperative that the directors hoped to establish new Starr Bowkett societies as soon as new members could be found. In addition the Permanent Building Society provided loans up to ninety percent of the value of the security offered and the Savings and Loan Society provided loans to members for personal purposes. The Community Advancement Society was in the process of purchasing an estate close to Newcastle where it was planned to construct 140 homes with modern design and all modern amenities. It was intended that tar sealed roads, formed footpaths, kerbing and guttering, street beautifications, park and garden areas would feature prominently in the estate. The project was regarded as marking a new era in the building society movement, an era that would provide 'improved housing, congenial surroundings and better citizens for Newcastle'. Given the achievements of the Association, it is little wonder that a partisan contemporary commentator remarked that 'miracles are performed by the Cooperation'.[11]

It is clear that the Starr-Bowkett Societies of the Association were particularly well run. In 1934 the Registrar of Cooperative Societies, had cause to hold an enquiry into Starr-Bowkett Societies in NSW after irregularities were found with certain institutions. In his findings, the Registrar commented that: 'it was no secret that it was only the good work done by Starr-Bowkett societies in the Newcastle district that stayed official action, in contemplation to follow England and ban the formation of further societies of this type'. High praise indeed for Nos 1-8 Starr Bowkett Societies of The Greater Newcastle Co-operative Building & Hunter River Starr-Bowkett Societies Limited and its rivals. Tom himself seems to have been particularly proud of the work achieved by the Starr Bowkett societies. He later explained that 'Newcastle had the highest percentage of home ownership in Australia because of the strong Starr Bowkett system'. He regarded Newcastle as 'the home of the Starr Bowkett system' in Australia. It is no surprise, therefore, that he regretted the decline of the system in the second half of the twentieth century. As noted, it was Tom's belief that they were the only building societies that were 'truly mutual'.[12]

Tom remained committed to the cooperative movement throughout his life. He served for long periods of time on the board of the various institutions which made up the Association. His involvement included long periods of time as Chairman of various boards. Over nearly fifty years of service to The Greater Newcastle Building Society Ltd, The Greater Co-operative Association Ltd, The Greater Credit Union Limited and affiliated entities, Tom was able to see the growth and development of a great financial institution which provided its members in Greater Newcastle, the Hunter Valley and throughout NSW a high level of financial security. This was something of which he was very proud. In 1973 in his twenty-sixth year as Chairman of the Board and thirtieth year as a Director, he reflected on the history of the Greater Newcastle Building Society Group: 'the Permanent Society was formed in 1945 and now has assets in excess of $65,000,000. It can be fairly assumed that

few of these gentlemen attending the meeting in 1923 realised
that they were taking a first step in forming an organisation
which today administers assets of nearly $100,000,000'. What
remained important to Tom was that The Greater Newcastle
Building Society Ltd continued to work for its members. He
remained committed to 'the consistent policy of the Society
since its inception to make finance available for home building
and purchase at the lowest possible (interest) rate'.[13]

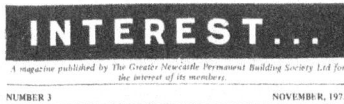

INTEREST...

A magazine published by The Greater Newcastle Permanent Building Society Ltd for
the interest of its members

NUMBER 3   NOVEMBER, 1973

FROM THE CHAIRMAN

The consistent policy of the Society since its inception has been to make
finance available for home building and purchase at the lowest possible rate.

Changes in the interest rate structure, however, do occur, and this dictates
that Building Societies must adjust their rates to the demands of the market
place.

The Australian Government, in September, 1973, initiated moves to raise
the level of interest rates throughout the economy, ostensibly to dampen
inflation. Building Societies, to maintain their existing funds and to attract
funds for future lending, had no alternative but to adjust the rates offered to
investors and, consequently, to increase interest rates to borrowers.

The rate now paid to investors – 7½% – is the highest ever, in the history
of the Australian Building Societies.

As yet, fortunately, they have not attained the rates applicable overseas –
particularly the United Kingdom – where the lending rate is up to 11¼%

Notwithstanding the narrow margin between the investment and lending
rates, which has remained constant over the years, the Greater Newcastle
Permanent Building Society has built up adequate reserves which are so
necessary to satisfy the confidence of the prudent investor.

It will continue to be the policy of this Society to maintain both rates at
the best possible figure consistent with money market conditions.

                                                              R.E. Farrell

Tom as Chairman of The Greater Newcastle Permanent
Building Society Ltd writes to members (1973)

Potential homeowners and investors continued to reap the
benefits of this commitment. The Greater Newcastle Building
Society Ltd continued to provide finance for housing in difficult
periods. For example, the Greater group emerged strongly from
the 1950s despite the ongoing problems associated with the lack
of housing. In 1964 Tom and his fellow directors were proud to
announce that:

increases in membership and share capital in the year ended July 1 were a record. Total assets were almost £4 million. The year had been the society's most successful and share capital and deposits had risen by £723,763. During the year loans totalling £979,359 were made, compared to £440,506 the previous year. The society had now loaned £5,186,580. Dividends of £164,190 were distributed and the board foreshadowed a dividend rate of 5½ per cent for 1964–65. Reserves stood at £124,472 and investment had increased to £326,935.

True to the founding principles of the institution, Mr Mathieson, the Chairman of Directors, reiterated that the main purpose of the Building Society was 'to lend money to wage and low salary earners, many of whom were not in a position to provide the initial high deposit requires by other lending institutions'. As if to underline the sound financial position of the cooperative and its plans for future expansion, it was announced that construction was to begin in the following year of a three storied air-conditioned office building in Tudor Street, Hamilton. The plan called for a redesign of the frontage in Tudor Street which included an arcade of shops on the ground floor and with office space on the second and third floors.[14]

Tom's involvement on various boards of the Greater Newcastle Building Society Group meant that he had to keep up to date with financial developments both here in Australia and overseas. To this end, as his personal papers reveal, Tom was an avid reader on financial matters. He was also an active member of The Association of Cooperative Building Societies. In 1952, for example, he worked closely with Mr W G Pooley, General Secretary of the association, to bring to the State

Government's attention the problem of revenue raising for Local Government. It was Tom's opinion that 'the burden of Local Government Rating on the individual homeowner is becoming intolerable' because 'the present method of rating cannot be regarded as equitable'. He proposed that the State Government levy a tax on behalf of Local Government which could then be distributed to local areas to provide necessary services. Mr Kelly writing on behalf of the General Secretary, informed Tom that the Association was keen for him to present his ideas at an upcoming conference. It was the view of Mr Kelly that Tom's presentation would be the 'news highlight' of the conference because 'it will be controversial; full of meat and of cogent concern to half the people in the State (homeowners) – hence its newsworthiness'. It was proposed, therefore, that Tom's speech would follow the Premier's so that 'it can come as a "hot potato" early up on the agenda while the Press boys are still there'. Tom followed up his appearance at the conference by organising (in conjunction with the Cardiff Heights & New Lambton Lookout Progress Association) a public meeting at the New Lambton Mechanical Institute on 8 October 1954. Here he agitated for the establishment of 'a permanent body of homeowners to fight to bring rates to a reasonable level and to bring about a return to smaller areas to control local affairs'. In 1965 Tom and Joe Richley appeared before a Parliamentary Committee in Sydney to make a submission in regard to the 'rating system'. Given Tom's standing in the Association, it is not surprising that he was also chosen as a delegate to International Conferences as well. Tom's interest in the 'Rating' issue was to remain with him throughout his life – he never missed an opportunity to agitate for a change in the 'rating system' to guarantee a fairer deal for home-owners.[15]

As noted, Tom remained a key board member throughout the 1970s and 1980s. This period witnessed a rapid expansion of the Greater Newcastle Building Society. In 1972 additions were made to the premises in Tudor Street, Hamilton costing over $300,000. The new structure comprised a six storey shopping arcade and office block. In keeping with his political philosophy, Tom was keen to ensure that decentralisation was a successful formula for the society. By the early 1980s the Greater had grown to become one of the biggest and most wide spread societies in the region. As a local journalist commented, 'first established at Hamilton in 1924, the Greater Newcastle Permanent Building Society, is the only locally based society with numerous branches throughout NSW. Of its 47 branches, 31 have been established to serve the Hunter Region. And with its decentralisation has come an increasing membership from a variety of areas throughout the state'. The 1980s also witnessed the expansion of the society's computerised systems. Starting in 1973 the society had pioneered the move to computerisation in the region, establishing an efficient on-line computer system which was available to all branches. Despite the modernisation, the focus remained the same - 'attracting a growing number of people to the traditional importance of the society as a home-lender'. As the Board Minutes make clear, the 1980s placed new demands on board members as they grappled with the challenges of a changing financial environment. Even though he was in his eighties, Tom met such challenges with enthusiasm. He remained committed to the ideals of cooperative finance up until his retirement from board responsibilities in the early 1990s. His enthusiasm and drive won him the respect of his fellow directors, even when they could not agree with him. As one retiring director noted in 1983:

Your ability to successfully direct the associated group with an all-round ability to advise on financial matters, has been an inspiration to endow the group with unequalled service throughout the building society movement, even state-wide. We have differed to agree on many occasions, but there has always been a common ground for the advancement of the respective societies.[16]

The growth and development of the Greater Newcastle Permanent Society is clearly evident in its headquarters located in Beaumont Street, Hamilton – photograph courtesy of the *NMH*.

Although Tom resigned from the Board of Directors of the Greater Newcastle Credit Union Limited in August 1990, he continued as a consultant. In this capacity he continued to attend Board meetings to discuss with Senior Officers items he felt were important to the future development of the Society. On his retirement from the Board, the General Manager of the Greater, Mr W.H.T. Prince, paid tribute to Tom's enduring service:

> The Board recorded in the minutes your long service both as Chairman and Director of All Societies of the Group and this Credit Union in particular. They acknowledged the unstinting time, work and efforts that you have given to the Group as a whole since 1937. Your direction and guidance over the years has been largely responsible for the growth and financial respect and standing this group of Societies enjoys with members and the public at large.

Fittings words for one who had delivered so much to those who aspired to home ownership in the Newcastle area by playing such a key role in ensuring the financial security of one of Newcastle's leading home-lending institutions. There were many in the Newcastle region who had obtained home ownership thanks to the assistance of Tom Farrell. As one colleague later recalled, what drove Tom Farrell throughout his long association with Starr Bowketts, Credit Unions and Cooperative Housing Societies was his passion 'for providing homes to the people of Newcastle and surrounding districts, not for profits for the organisation but simply to ensure people were 'looked after'. Tom was an extremely strong family man who had the strong belief that ordinary people deserved the chance to own their own home. In short, 'community and assisting people within the community was his great desire'. Tom left a lasting legacy at the 'Greater' – on the occasion of his death the following note appeared in the minutes of the Building Society:

> The passing of Tom Farrell brought to an end a

chapter in the history of Newcastle and in particular, this Building Society. Tom became involved with this Building Society through the Starr Bowkett Societies, one of the few ways in the early days for ordinary people to gather finance for the purchase of a home. He believed in this financing method to the end. He saw the benefits of a Building Society and its ability to fund many more housing loans than could be provided through Starr Bowkett systems and became a Director and then Chairman of the Board of the Greater Newcastle Permanent Building Society. He served this Society as a Director for 30 years and as Chairman for 26 of these years...the name Tom Farrell will always be linked to this Society through his devotion to the organisation. He spent many hours over many years giving commercial advice and offering assistance to improve the operation and performance. He will be sadly missed by those who remember his contribution and the manner in which it was given'. [17]

4: A University For Newcastle

By 1949 Tom was convinced that it was only a matter of time until a university college was established in Newcastle. In the previous decades he had witnessed a growing frustration in the local community as the State government prevaricated on the issue. On his return from the war, Tom was keen to become much more involved as an 'active citizen' in local issues. He regarded the failure of the Sydney authorities to provide Newcastle with an institution of higher learning as yet another example of the errant ways of centralisation. As he saw it, the denial of university facilities to the people of Newcastle was both an injustice and an obstacle to the growth and development of the region. In the service of his community, Tom struggled (with others) over the next two decades to address this issue.

Tom had no doubt that the Newcastle region could sustain a university college. It was a growing population centre with a strong education and industrial base. Technical schools provided training for future apprentices and two technical colleges provided advanced industrial training. A number of high schools catered for students with academic and professional ambitions. In 1949 the Newcastle Teachers' College began operation in rooms on the site of the Newcastle Technical High School. Despite being the largest provincial centre in New South Wales, the Newcastle region had failed to secure what its northern neighbour (the New England region) had achieved in 1938, namely a university college and before that a teachers college in 1928. Tom had grown increasingly frustrated by the level of disinterest shown by the State government in regards to this issue. He was particularly frustrated by the inactivity of Mr Heffron, the Labour Education Minister, who promised much in the press but failed to deliver any constructive plan to promote the project. As he later explained 'one night (in 1949) I listened to Mr Heffron at a Technical College presentation. I then formed the opinion that he was completely indifferent and had no intention of honouring past newspaper promises'. Tom's answer was to challenge the Minister in the press. One such letter clearly outlined the level of frustration parents, like Tom, faced when attempting to secure a tertiary education for their children:

> On Thursday 2 November I spent a pleasant evening at the father and son Annual Dinner sponsored by the Newcastle Boys High School. As I gazed around the throng of keen and alert Newcastle youth, I pondered and thought what these boys would be doing as a career. Here was assembled a large section of the most brilliant of the Newcastle youth. From their ranks should come the leaders of the future. During the course of several speeches I learned that many of these lads would be doing Primary School Teachers Courses at the Newcastle Teachers College. I also learned that only a meagre number would attend the University, mainly because of accommodation and financial difficulties. Why has Newcastle no Academic University? What is wrong with this City? Is it the people in it? The Press? Or our political representatives? Armidale secured a University College on a promise from the Government of the day that the people of that area would find £10,000. Cannot we do likewise?

Isn't it time we secured proper recognition from the
Government and other interested parties. No doubt
certain promises have been made by the Minister for
Education, but many promises in the past by Sydney
politicians have been repudiated. There is no reason
why University facilities could not be available in
1951.

Tom had first-hand experience of the difficulties involved in
securing a higher education for his children in Sydney. He
later explained that he was often attacked by his opponents for
'wasting his time' about this issue. But he remained convinced
that Newcastle could follow the lead of Armidale and establish
a university in a regional setting.[1]

In 1950 Tom had been approached by the recently formed
Liberal Party to stand as a candidate for the State seat of
Kahibah. Although he declined, Tom decided (with like-
minded residents) to form a branch of the Liberal Party in New
Lambton. Meeting regularly in the back shed of a member's
house in New Lambton, the group agitated for the establishment
of a university in Newcastle. Prominent members of the group
included Reg Ellis, Fred Welshman (in whose shed the group
met), Charlie Hopkins and Tom's sister and brother-in-law,
Mabel and George Whiley. Mabel Whiley (Science Mistress
of Newcastle Girls' High and later Headmistress of Hunter
Girls' High) was a committed high school teacher and strong
advocate for female education. Like her brother, she wanted
to ensure that the talented youth of the district, especially the
young women she encountered, had the opportunity to pursue
tertiary studies in Newcastle.

It was Mabel's idea to enlist the help of the New Lambton
Branch of the Liberal Party to reawaken political interest in

the university. With the support of the branch, she put forward a resolution to the 1950 State Convention that the Liberal Party strongly support and work toward the establishment of a university in Newcastle. The motion read as follows: 'that this committee recommend to the Executive, that the Liberal Party incorporate into its State Policy that it supports the opening of University Colleges in country areas and that it take the necessary steps to implement the establishment of a University College in Newcastle in 1951'. For the party's consideration Tom prepared a substantial document which outlined the structure, organisation and curriculum of the proposed university. This document clearly shows his commitment to the cause – his intelligence, foresight, dedication and capacity for sheer hard work. Tom envisaged that the university could begin operation within a year with the following faculties: Arts, Science, Medicine and Pharmacy. Medicine was included because of 'the status of the Royal Newcastle Hospital as a training hospital and the high standard of the staff'. Other faculties would follow 'with the growth of the university' including Engineering, Dentistry, Agricultural Science, Veterinary Science, Law, Agriculture and also Diploma of Education courses. Tom suggested that the following courses could be offered immediately: in the area of Arts - English, History, French, Psychology, Philosophy and Education; in the area of Science – Chemistry, Physics, Botany and Zoology. In addition Mathematics, Geography and Economic subjects could be offered. Tom believed that (with a few exceptions) suitable staff was already available in Newcastle:

> For all of these subjects, except French, Botany and Zoology, there are men already in Newcastle, lecturers either at Newcastle Teachers' College, Newcastle Technical College or Newcastle WEA Lecturers, who

could carry out the duties of lecturing to first years
– provided they were assisted by visiting lecturers,
had the benefit of frequent contacts with Sydney
University, could rely on it for syllabi, examination
papers, duplicated lists of examples, references to
text books and all the essential small details. In affect
have the support of the experienced staff of Sydney
University and be under its immediate control.

To facilitate the appointment of such staff, Tom included 'a
list of such men and their qualifications'. He also included
the proposed budget requirements of individual faculties, and
plans for proposed buildings such as laboratories and libraries.
The size of the student population and the range of text-books
required by individual faculties was also given due consideration.
Tom argued that his proposal showed 'the practicality of the
project' which would come to fruition with the support of
the University of Sydney and the Government authorities. He
closed with the following remarks: 'the extreme urgency of the
matter, and the opportunity for the Liberal Party to gain political
prestige from it, renders it essential for the plan to receive the
immediate support of the Executive'. No doubt as a practical
man Tom realised that his bold and ambitious proposal had little
chance of being fully implemented. Clearly on this issue Tom
was a visionary who saw the future potential of a university
college in Newcastle. As history would show (for example, in
regards to the Medical Faculty) key aspects of his vision were to
be eventually realised.

At the convention the motion was put by George Whiley and
seconded by Tom Farrell. The resolution met strong opposition
from the Sydney delegates led by McLaurin, a lecturer from
the University of Sydney. He argued that all available money

for tertiary education in New South Wales should be spent on the University of Sydney which was severely short of funds. When it appeared that the original motion would be lost, Tom's brother-in-law moved an amendment which resulted in the Liberal Party giving in principle support to the aims of the original proposal.[2]

Although the local press chose to report otherwise, Tom and his fellow members of the New Lambton Branch had succeeded in winning State Liberal Party support for the establishment of a university college in Newcastle. Tom clearly understood the importance of this support, particularly given the lack of progress to date. He later argued that 'it was from this branch that the first real shot came – there had been a committee of citizens in Newcastle for years advocating for a university but it was moribund'. The in-principle agreement of the State Liberal Party meant that Newcastle University was very much back on the political agenda.

The controversy in the press surrounding the Liberal Party's support brought the New Lambton branch into contact with Mr Harry Eddy who was responsible for the University of Sydney's extension classes in Newcastle. Eddy suggested that the members of the New Lambton Branch join forces with like-minded members of the community to advance the cause of the university. Although the exact membership of the group is not known, it included Reg Ellis (Chairman), Tom Farrell, Mabel Whiley, Griffith Duncan, the principal of the recently established Teachers' Training College and Max Pilgrim, a local architect. In all probability Eddy also joined the group.

Mabel Whiley, Tom's sister, became the driving force behind the group. She set out to convince the public and the governing authorities that a university college could be established immediately, at low cost, in the vacant Centaur Building in

Church Street. As Tom later explained ' my sister came out with a burst which received very good publicity and we continued to bombard all and sundry'. It was Mabel's husband, George Whiley, who had first come up with the idea. In defence of the scheme, she put forward her brother's detailed plans for the university (presented first at the State Liberal Party Convention) and a series of modified design drawings of the proposed site (supplied by Pilgrim Architects) which included the provision of a number of lecture rooms. Tom supported his sister with some political action of his own. He enlisted the assistance of Mr Douglas Darby, the Liberal and later Independent Member for Manly, who urged the Opposition Leader, Mr Vernon Treatt, to support the project. Tom invited Darby to Newcastle to visit the site and explain the intentions of the group. Darby, an ex-teacher, remained a key ally in the fight to establish a university college in Newcastle.

Despite Mabel's good efforts, the proposal of the 'Centaur Group' was destined to fail. The Minister of Education remained unconvinced that the Newcastle region could provide sufficient students for a university college. His department had already rejected the Centaur building as a suitable site for the establishment of the Teachers' Training College. His decision was also influenced by some local Labor aldermen who were convinced that the plan had been put forward by a group of 'political agitators' in the service of the Liberal Party. As Tom noted such opposition was effective because 'in a Labour stronghold such as Newcastle the people became suspicious of our motives'. [3]

The group's next move was to contact key organisations in Newcastle in the hope of galvanising public opinion in support of the university. These groups included The Chamber of Manufacturers, the Trades Hall Council, Rotary, Legacy, Apex, the Workers' Education Association (WEA) and the Return Services League (RSL). The group's efforts to establish a broad-based movement were successful - as Ellis later explained, 'you name it, we wrote to them and we had an excellent response'. Francis de Witt Batty, the Anglican Bishop of Newcastle, and Alderman Frank Purdue, the Lord Mayor, also threw their weight behind the project. With the knowledge they had wide community support, the group called a public meeting on the 15 December 1950 at the Chamber of Manufacturers' Office in Bolton Street. At this meeting Tom successfully moved a resolution that a committee be formed to work for the creation of university facilities in Newcastle. As a result the Newcastle University Establishment Group (NUEG) was created with the following executive members: Reg Ellis (President), Harry Eddy, Mabel Whiley, Beryl Anderson (WEA Secretary), H.V. Jackson, Jock Anderson and Jack Mead. Tom was asked to join the executive but declined. As he later explained he saw his role as 'taking an active part at regular group meetings'. This gave him the freedom to oppose executive decisions (if necessary) and argue for an alternate view. One gets the feeling that Tom valued his role as a 'noisy obstructionist', a person of strong conviction who was willing to put forward a dissenting view. Such a position did not always endear him to the executive of the NUEG – as he later explained 'I had a feeling often that members of the executive regarded me as a noisy fellow who should be kept out of the picture. I often brought up matters which were not agreed to by the Group'.

Given its broad base of support, it is not surprising that the NUEG was a non-political organisation – it was prepared to build on the past efforts of the now defunct Newcastle University Committee to advance the cause of the university. With renewed energy and impetus this 'strident and active organisation' was set (in Tom's words), 'to leave no stone unturned in propagating the need to establish a Newcastle University'.

The organisation was fortunate to have Reg Ellis, the first and only president of the NUEG, at the helm. A graduate of the University of Sydney, he had made Newcastle his home in the late 1930s when he gained employment as an industrial officer at Rylands Wire Works, a BHP subsidiary company. Over the next five decades, Ellis worked tirelessly for Newcastle, attempting to advance the cause of the region whenever he could. A later commentator identified him as 'a man of liberal and Liberal instincts with a strong sense of community…a steady, reliable man with a strong idealistic streak'. Although committed to a particular political view, he insisted that the NUEG remain non-political, attracting its support from as wide a circle as possible. Although at times enthusiastic, his calm, reasoned and gentlemanly approach won the NUEG the support of widely divergent political groups, including the Liberal Party, the ALP and even the Australian Communist Party.

Ellis would need his considerable powers of persuasion to keep in check some powerful identities within the NUEG. Chief among these was Harry Eddy who was instrumental in advancing the cause of the university. It was Ellis' opinion that Eddy was 'the one individual who was responsible above anyone else for the success of the NUEG'. From the start Eddy had very definite ideas about the type of university that needed to be established in Newcastle. First and foremost it needed to be an 'academic' rather than 'training' institution – an institution committed to core liberal values. Not surprisingly given his own academic affiliation, he believed that the University of Sydney was best placed to provide such an institution. It had already established a base in the region through its Department of Extension Classes with Eddy as a Senior Staff Tutor. In order to ensure the integrity of the university college (that is, as an academic institution) and the interests of the University of Sydney and its Department of Extension Classes, Eddy argued against the involvement of the University of New England and the foundation of an independent college. He was also vehemently opposed to the involvement of the recently founded University of Technology with its strong links to the Department of Technical Education. Eddy viewed the University of Technology as somewhat of a second-rate institution with its emphasis on 'technical training' and lack of autonomy, being under the control of the New South Wales Public Service Board. Eddy would have been aware that the Department of Technical Education already had a foothold in Newcastle offering diploma, trade and certificate courses through the Newcastle Technical College at Tighes Hill.

Eddy's considerable intellectual ability, his energy and capacity for hard work, meant that he tended to dominate the group. His commitment to a particular (some would say narrow) view of what a university should be, meant that he was closed to other members' ideas. He found it particularly difficult to engage with members like Tom Farrell who had a 'practical' rather than 'idealistic' approach to the issue. Tom was not so much concerned about the nature of the institution, he just wanted it established as quickly as possible. Tom's practical approach did not sit well with the idealism of Eddy and his supporters. Tom wanted action – it was his view that Eddy's position merely led to delay. From the start, Tom was frustrated by the group's tardy progress:

> our progress was slow – I always felt frustrated by the group and their attitude. There appeared to be a wish to float leisurely along and when I wanted action others just seemed to want to wait and see.

We lost valuable years early in the picture due to procrastination and tackling things which to me were unimportant.

Given the divisions within the group, Tom gave Ellis some sound practical advice:'it would have to be a quick campaign as we would never keep all of us together – divergent views and personalities'.[4]

While Tom may have had his misgivings about Eddy's position, he was encouraged by the overwhelming support the NUEG received from the local community. By mid-1951 over forty five organisations and 139 individuals were supporting the group. Thanks to Tom's sister the NUEG had collected 8000 signatures for a petition in support of the university. Mabel had utilised her pupils at Newcastle Girls' High, to conduct a series of street drives in support of the petition. Such was the positive response that it was decided to extend the drive to include towns like Maitland, Cessnock and Kurri Kurri. Mabel was pleased to report to the executive that she had identified about 175 students who intended to study at the university.

Despite the tensions, the NUEG executive met regularly, usually not

Canvas For University

Jane Campbell, captain of Newcastle Girls' High School, getting a supporter's signature for the establishment of a university in Newcastle. A street canvass for signatures to a petition for the university was held in Newcastle city streets yesterday.

Courtesy of the *NMH* (3 May 1951)

less than twice a month and sometimes as frequently as three times a week. The NUEG as a whole met once a month. There was no doubting the members' commitment to the cause. The group set out to convince the State Government that there were sufficient numbers of young people in Newcastle who were interested in pursuing university studies. The government would take some convincing since for the second time in 1950 the University of Technology had failed to find enough students to open its technological college in Newcastle. Tom was part of the delegation that travelled to Sydney on 7 May 1951 to meet with Mr Heffron, the Education Minister. As Tom had found in the past, Heffron was not that receptive to deputations from Newcastle:

> When they arrived they found that they were not expected. The telegram had given a mistaken date. They asked that since they had travelled over 200 miles, and it meant a whole day, the Minister should meet them…their request was not granted…they had to return to Newcastle, having achieved nothing except clarity on a new time for a deputation.

Given the fact that all members of the group had to gain leave from work to travel to Sydney on a Monday, the actions by the Minister must have been very frustrating. It was not until a week later (15 May), again on a work day, that the Minister agreed to see the delegation (Ellis, Tom, Mabel Whiley, Eddy and Anderson). This was the first of many frustrations Tom experienced dealing with politicians. As he later reported, 'there were many deputations to Premiers and Ministers but really we never got anywhere'. Despite of (or perhaps because of) his frustration, Tom found himself at odds with the views of leading politicians. This did not bother him – he was quite prepared to argue his case strongly. Such conviction did not win him friends in the halls of power – on one occasion, Tom was nearly thrown out of the Premier's (Mr McGirr) office after a heated debate. As Tom later explained he believed in maintaining the pressure on politicians: 'politicians are susceptible to attack…they will succumb more easily by outraged public opinion. Pressure and militancy they will run away from. If they feel the number are agin [*sic*] them they will support the side who kicks up the most noise'.

Heffron told the group that no government assistance would be forthcoming until the NUEG could produce a list of 200 'reasonably certain' students who intended to enrol at the university college. The Minister pointed out that such a list could not contain the names of any student seeking entry to the Teachers' Training College or classes offered by the University of Technology. Tom was not surprised by Heffron's position – he had already taken the Minister to task in the *Sydney Morning Herald* (*SMH*) for suggesting that there was no need for a university college in Newcastle because the youth were not interested. He now attacked the Minister for his subterfuge – writing under a pseudonym ('Evening Student') Tom vented his frustration about the Minister's decision. It was his view that:

> it is an impossible task and means that the Minister is stalling. I admire the sincere enthusiasm of the Newcastle University Establishment Group and the hard work it is doing to secure the best educational opportunities for the youth of the district. But it will be naïve if it accepts the Minister's imposed conditions. The only way Newcastle will get the

recognition for its needs is by making a protest that cannot be ignored. If Newcastle youth do not get the educational opportunities available to the metropolis, it will be the fault of the apathy of the Newcastle people. Newcastle should speak in no uncertain terms about the outrageous proposal of the Minister.

The letter clearly reveals the level of Tom's frustration with those who simply accepted the Minister's decision, including those on the executive of the NUEG. He pressed his point in a follow up letter (credited to 'Maitland'), arguing that the issue had wider implications:

> the lack of interest by the Minister for Education in either an agricultural college or an academic university in this area is typical of the customary indifference on important affairs affecting country districts. Sydney never goes short of attention on such matters. Newcastle and the Hunter Valley have an opportunity to assist themselves by supporting a new state. Greater benefits would accrue in this area. There would be no need to approach a Sydney politician for favours. Newcastle, the largest city in another State would be able to compete fairly with Sydney, Melbourne and Brisbane. Sydney has a population of 1,500,000 and 48 members of Parliament. Tomorrow, unless decentralisation becomes a fact and not a background phrase, it will have a population of three million and 80 members of Parliament.

Tom's commitment to decentralisation and the 'new state

movement' were central tenants of the political philosophy that guided his community action.

Although Ellis was disappointed that the Minister saw fit to impose conditions on Newcastle that were not expected of Armidale, he committed the NUEG to meeting the Minister's conditions. He made it clear that he did not accept the criticisms levelled by correspondents in the press:

> I disagree with the charge that the Minister has acted in bad faith. As a responsible public body, the Newcastle University Establishment Group cannot associate itself with this charge on such weak evidence. Administrating the task the Minister has set is difficult, but he has given a definite figure and pledged himself to take action if it is reached. We agree with Evening Student that Newcastle must bester itself to attain our objective but we know from the group's experience that this is happening. What is needed now is constructive action, not irrational charges against the Minister.

If Tom was the correspondent to the *NMH*, it is clear that from the start there was division among the members of the NUEG on how best to move forward. Given that Tom always valued 'action' over 'words', it is not surprising that he would find himself in the future at odds with the Executive of the NUEG who warned him ''to go steady'. Don't be a stormy petrel. Don't be forceful. Be discreet'. Tom, however, failed to be convinced – he remained committed to 'action' when 'a bit of vehemence' or 'a bit of a devil' was able to get things moving.

In contrast, the Editor of the *NMH* welcomed the news:

> Newcastle should welcome the assurance of the Minister of Education (Mr Heffron) that he would recommend to the University Senate that an academic university be established in Newcastle provided the Newcastle University Establishment Group could nominate 200 'reasonably certain students'. Because of failure to arouse interest when it was proposed to open a branch of the University of Technology in Newcastle, the Minister's qualification is understandable…Mr Heffron said he needed stronger support for the project from Newcastle. The group should see that this support was forthcoming.

Tom was not surprised by the position taken by the local press. It was his view that the *NMH* far too often toadied to the authorities in Sydney. As he later complained to Eddy, 'why we get so little in Newcastle is because of the quiet inoffensiveness of the *Newcastle Herald*. Take the leaders of the *Sydney Morning Herald* and *Telegraph* and compare it to the *Newcastle Herald*. If the *Telegraph* had been in Newcastle we would have had a university long ago'. [5]

Despite division among the membership regarding the Minister's motives, the NUEG lost no time in getting to work. One gets a sense of the workload involved in identifying the students required by the Minister from the Minutes of a NUEG meeting in May 1951. The minutes reveal that:

> there had been seven executive meetings in the month, a street drive to collect further signatures for a petition, the inspection of various possible sites for a temporary building and the preparation of recommendations on the matter to the Minister

after consulting with the Lord Mayor, arrangement of speakers…circulars to organisations asking them to receive speakers, statements prepared for press and radio sessions and completion of visits to Maitland, Cessnock and Dungog, address to various organisations, collection of donations to finance the Group's work. Fifteen letters had been received and fifty seven letters written apart from circulars and reports, posters had to be designed and produced.

But it was the collection of the student names that provided the greatest challenge. As one commentator reported:

> as names came in the person concerned had to be visited and the accuracy of the information checked. In the case of school students, some estimate of the chances of matriculation had to be obtained from teachers. Confirmation of serious intent was sought from parents. All of this was done by personal contact. For a group of volunteers the task was enormous.

Needless to say, Tom and Kath Farrell did their bit, making personal visits to as many prospective students as possible in Newcastle and the Hunter Valley. There was no doubting the couple's commitment to the cause – despite their busy home and work schedule, their allocated home visits were completed. It appears from a list contained in his papers that Tom and Kath Farrell visited more than twenty students in the Belmont area alone.

It must have been with a great deal of pride on 10 July 1951 that the NUEG handed the Minister a list of 357 students who intended to enrol in courses in the faculties of Arts, Economics,

Science, Pharmacy, Engineering, Dentistry, Law, Medicine, Physiotherapy, Veterinary Science, Agriculture Science and Architecture. The group also handed the Minister a petition with 14,500 signatures calling on the government to found a university college in Newcastle. In support of the petition the group submitted a document (no doubt put together by Eddy) arguing that the college should be established by the University of Sydney. It was argued that if the present response (prepared against a tradition of people not going to university) was any indication then the future of the university college (once established) was assured. Then the tradition would change and the institution would attract the support of 'the region's ablest persons' who at present sought higher studies outside the district. The NUEG recommended that the university college be established with the following faculties: Arts, Economics, Science, Engineering and Pharmacy.[6]

No doubt the Minister was surprised by the success of the NUEG in completing an almost impossible task. The evidence presented by the NUEG convinced him that there was a real need for the establishment of a university college in Newcastle. While the Minister may have been won over to the cause, Professor Stephen Roberts, the Vice-Chancellor of the University of Sydney, was far from convinced that there was a need to establish any further higher education institution outside of Sydney. Roberts was concerned that (given the money worries of the University of Sydney) such institutions would divert much needed funds from his institution. His concern was shared by the Editor of the *SMH* who had earlier stated that the idea of establishing more universities in New South Wales was 'out of the realm of realities'. Despite the Minister's interest in the project, Roberts put in place strategies to delay the project. Members of the NUEG delegation (including Tom) who met the Vice-Chancellor on the 8 August knew they were in trouble – all Roberts was prepared to talk about were the many difficulties (particularly financial) of establishing a university college. This was to be his response to the Minister and the University Senate.

In August Roberts asked the NUEG to submit a detailed costing and plans for temporary buildings. He also required details regarding the staffing and subjects to be taught. He told the group that such details were necessary in order to open the institution in 1952. By the end of October the Vice-Chancellor had the necessary documents. Ellis was pleased to inform the press that 'every time the Group has been set a major task, it has done it completely and quickly'. It was the case that the project continued to attract strong support. Despite this optimism it was clear that the cause lacked an advocate in Sydney prepared to push the project forward - Roberts was content to highlight the difficulties, Heffron (despite his enthusiasm) had little choice but to follow the lead of the University of Sydney. Faced with the realisation that it was most unlikely that classes would commence in 1952, Eddy proposed the establishment of an advisory committee (made up mostly of NUEG executive members) that would kick-start the process. In Eddy's plan administrative staff would be appointed when funding became available to oversee the establishment of the college. Teaching staff would follow in time for classes to commence in 1953. In early December Roberts put such a proposal to the University Senate – an Interim Advisory Council was appointed with an Acting Warden to follow when government funds allowed. While it was a step forward the problem remained that the University of Sydney was not prepared to do any more than was necessary. The matter was on hold until the government provided the necessary funding. This 'wait and see attitude' would have found little favour with Tom – he wanted action to benefit his community. Such procrastination only reinforced his belief in the cause of decentralisation.[7]

But a new player on the field was to provide the NUEG with new opportunities to advance the cause of the university college. On 12 November the Council of the University of Technology resolved to open a branch in Newcastle using the facilities of the Newcastle Technical College. With existing staff and students at hand, it proposed to offer higher courses in Technology and Science. It was also envisaged that the institution would offer Arts subjects for the University of Sydney. This decision was taken with the blessings of the Minister who had grown frustrated with the antics displayed by the University of Sydney in regards to the Newcastle University College (NUC). He was probably persuaded to take such a position by Professor Philip Baxter, the Acting Director of the University of Technology. Baxter's involvement was to be of major concern to certain members of the NUEG. The NUC duly opened on 3 December 1951 – classes in Applied Chemistry, Chemical Engineering and Metallurgy, Applied Physics, Civil Engineering, Electrical Engineering, Mathematics, Mechanical Engineering, and Mining Engineering (arranged into seven schools) commenced in March 1952. Humanities subjects were also taught from the start by staff from the University of Technology, Ultimo, or by staff from the Newcastle Teachers College.

While the NUEG welcomed the fact that university education had finally arrived in Newcastle, it remained wary of the involvement of the University of Technology. As noted, certain members of the group (particular Eddy) had set ideas about the nature of the university college to be established in Newcastle. It was their view that it should be an 'academic' rather than a 'training' institution. In certain minds the University of

Technology failed on this count. Critics of the arrangement argued that

> if there is any disposition here to accept the utilitarian view that a university should be a mere professional or technical school it must be discarded. The part of a university is that repository of knowledge and learning, a centre of the generalised culture which includes original inquiry and research into science and the arts. Its purpose is to keep the lamp of knowledge trimmed and burning brightly.

The NUEG was also wary of the relationship between Baxter and Heffron. It was their view that their academic college should remain completely independent of Government authorities, especially those involved with the Department of Education. On this count (in their opinion) the University of Technology failed. Their suspicions only grew further when the Minister refused to meet with them for the first three months of 1952. Although the NUEG had better luck with the Premier, Mr McGirr made it clear that the government had no money for the establishment of a university college in Newcastle. Tom believed that the Premier had adopted this position because he was driven by a desire to establish a Catholic University in New South Wales. Tom was not backward in challenging such a position - his defence of a secular institution led to some heated words being exchanged between himself and the Premier. McGirr's response was to threaten to throw the delegation out of his office. Tom's position was certainly not driven by sectarian concerns – he was on very favourable terms with many in the Catholic community, including his wife. It was motivated by his belief that a secular university was the best outcome for the people of Newcastle.

The NUEG's response to such government disinterest was further agitation. This took the form of 'continual pressure through the local members, through many local bodies, through approaches to the leaders of Government and the Opposition in State and Federal spheres, through the supply of information to the Hunter Press, through addresses to organisations and through larger gatherings'. For example the NUEG convened the Hunter Valley University Conference, under the Chairmanship of the Lord Mayor, on the 29 April at the Newcastle City Hall. It was reported that 'the room was completely filled and the conference unanimous and enthusiastic in support of the Group's policy'. Unfortunately, this enthusiasm was not shared by Mr Cahill, who succeeded McGirr as Premier in April 1952. When Cahill failed to commit to funding a university in Newcastle during the State election in February 1953, Tom vented his frustration in the press:

> Members of the University Establishment Group were dismayed that the Cahill Government made no reference to the Newcastle University in the policy speech. Local Parliamentarians had inferred that the policy speech would disclose some positive action. It is obvious that our Sydney-controlled legislature has no intentions of doing anything to assist the students of this district. Newcastle should support the creation of a new Parliamentary party to look after the interests of Newcastle as well as to faithfully serve the State as a whole... There is no logical reason why Newcastle has not a university. It is a vital link in our educational system. Sydney has enjoyed these facilities for more than 100 years. How much longer

will our Sydney – dominated Government deprive
us of a university?

In May, having won the election, Cahill only made matters
worse by announcing that the financial situation was so dire
that the government could not even commit to appointing a
warden to the Newcastle academic college. When the NUEG
finally got to see Heffron in March, two proposals were put
forward – the University of Sydney could operate a college
in the buildings of the Technical College or Newcastle could
offer tutorial classes supporting external teaching from the
University of New England. In the minds of the NUEG both
proposals were far from satisfactory. Tom for one saw the offer
of 'external studies' as a 'watering down' of possible full degree
courses which would be far more beneficial to the people of
Newcastle. He later explained:

> I believe it was better to study as an external student
> than not at all, but external studies were not the
> answer for Newcastle and did not constitute the
> essence of a true university education. I believed that
> we should not raise money to be used as a college to
> assist external studies. I believed it was better if we
> could raise money to found our own university'.

Tom once again vented his anger in the press – in a letter to the
Editor he pointed out that 'the refusal to establish a university in
Newcastle has been a severe rebuff to this city. The case which
the Premier (Mr Cahill) has repudiated promises made by the
Deputy Premier (Mr Heffron) is a sad commentary on the
sincerity of our political leaders'.[8]

By August 1952 the NUEG had had enough of the

government's subterfuge. Fully aware of the growing community discontent; the group decided to plan a mass demonstration at the Town Hall. Despite the teeming rain, over 500 attended the meeting on 7 August responding to the over 8000 letters of invitation that had been sent out. Members of the NUEG (including Tom and Kath) had been busy on the phones contacting key groups in Newcastle including the Teachers' Federation, the YMCA, employees of Cardiff Railway Workshops, the staff and students of Newcastle Teachers' College, the Housewives Association and the Businessmens' Forum. The organisational ability of the NUEG and the commitment of its members had once again come to the fore. Such was the enthusiasm for the cause that the meeting had to be prolonged by an hour to accommodate all the motions. The local press was also on side – the headline in the *NMH* read '500 In Demand For Varsity'. It reported the words of Ellis: 'all sections of the community are solidly behind this demand but each year hundreds are missing the opportunity for a university education for which they are justly entitled'. As a means of reinforcing this sentiment the paper included a series of photographs including one entitled 'Grammar Students at City Meeting'. These represented the young men and young women of the district that Tom and the other members of the NUEG were fighting for.

Despite the turnout, the government ignored the protest. As 1952 dragged on and the government stuck to its budget strategy, NUEG continued to press the issue. With a state election looming, the group had some success with the Leader of the Opposition, Mr Treatt, who came out in support of a university college in Newcastle. But the subsequent ALP victory in the 1953 election meant that matters remained the same. Eddy attempted to keep the momentum going by organising a conference in April 1953 which would bring together organisations which wanted to see an academic university college established in Newcastle. The *NMH* was pleased to report that the conference drew support from a wide-cross section of the community with 150 people and ninety-nine Newcastle and Hunter organisations in attendance. The message was a familiar one: 'every year scores of young men and women whose parents are unable to support them at the University of Sydney are forced to give up their ambitions to undertake further studies at such an institution thereby impoverishing not only themselves but the community'. The conference resolved unanimously that the ALP should fully support the establishment of an academic college, that an Advisory Council be established and that financial provision be made in the 1953-1954 State Budget to ensure that the institution commence operation in early 1954.

The government's response was to announce the introduction of a bill giving autonomy to the University of New England. Heffron informed the NUEG that the newly autonomous university would be asked to provide external studies in a number of centres including Newcastle. While not over enthusiastic about the scheme, the NUEG took some satisfaction in the fact that (while it continued to battle the government to establish a university college in Newcastle) the proposed tutorial scheme would be in the hands of an academic institution, not the University of Technology. Further frustration occurred when the University of New England announced in late August that it would not be able to commence its program in Newcastle until 1955 at the earliest.[9]

Matters took a turn for the better in October when a bi-election was called for the State seat of Kahibah. The government was under pressure to hold the seat with a strong Liberal candidate (Alderman Quinlan, former Lord Mayor of Newcastle) and Independent (Mr I.C. Alexander) contesting the election. The government's failure to establish a university college became a key election issue. As Tom explained 'we beat the Labour Government with their failure to do anything about a university during the campaign and it was obviously hurting'. Tom's lack of sympathy for the government's predicament must have been shared by many members of the NUEG, especially those who were also members of the New Lambton Branch of the Liberal Party, who had waited long and hard for the government to act in regard to this issue. It is clear that Tom, Kath and Mabel campaigned hard for Quinlan's election. One gets a sense of the pressure the government was under about the university from Liberal electoral pamphlets distributed in the Kahibah area. Under the headline '£500,000 for Sydney University Empty Site for Newcastle' the residents of Kahibah were informed:

Nothing will satisfy Newcastle but a full university. This year the State Government has allocated half a million to Sydney University, but did not allot one penny to help Newcastle obtain the higher educational facilities for its children for which it has fought so long. Newcastle has been brushed aside with empty assurances for years…it is clear that this district and its surrounding towns embracing the coalfields to Cessnock, should have its own university without any further delay. Is there a father so indifferent to his son's future that he does not want to give his son a better chance than he had, and surely there is no mother that does not want the best for her children. In the long years of false promises regarding the Newcastle University many brilliant boys and girls have been denied entry to a university because of the cost of board and travel in sending them away from home was beyond their parents means. Nothing drove the Government to do anything about this…Do not lose your hold now. Continue the shock treatment by supporting the Liberal candidate and you will see instant results…. This Government has been in power long enough to do much more for this district than it has done and it is high time they were told by the electorate that Newcastle is not prepared to sit down and take it any longer. A change for Kahibah will force the Government to consider Newcastle's needs. CONTINUE THE SHOCK TREATMENT. Vote HARRY QUINLAN.

An accompanying photograph read 'The Shortland Site… Empty as a Labour Politician's Promises'. While the author of the pamphlet is unknown, the sentiments expressed are very similar to those of Mr R.E. Farrell.

Under pressure and embarrassed by the University of New England's inability to provide the promised classes in Newcastle, Heffron announced two weeks out from the election that the government would inaugurate university courses in Arts and Economics at the NUC at the beginning of 1954. The courses would be taught by staff from the University of Technology with the University of New England providing the syllabus. The latter would set the examinations and determine the results.   It was Heffron's view that this arrangement provided the nucleus of the university college so long sought after by the people of Newcastle. He told the *NMH* on 23 October that 'Newcastle is now well on the road for the ultimate establishment of its own academic university'. More importantly for his party, he hoped that this announcement would silence the discontent in Newcastle and secure the bi-election for the ALP.

The plan certainly won the cautionary support of the Editor of the *NMH* who saw it as 'a start', an opportunity for Newcastle to build its own university. In a front page article entitled 'Arts, Economics Courses in Newcastle Next Year', the Editor informed his readers that: 'in the long agitation for the provision of a university to serve Newcastle and the Hunter Valley there has been repeated interest by the Minister of Education (Mr Heffron)…the judgement of those who retained the faith in the sincerity of the Minister is now partially vindicated'. Mention was made of Alderman Purdue, the Lord Mayor, who found the decision 'very heartening'. He went on to comment that 'the continued agitation of the NUEG, assisted by the people of Newcastle had obviously born some fruit'.

But the plan failed to win over the Executive of the NUEG who remained wary of the Minister's political motives and lack of consultation. Ellis told the *NHM* that the decision was a complete surprise to the NUEG which needed time to look at the detail. The President was particularly concerned about the nature of the courses that would be offered. Eddy's criticism was more deeply seeded – he was particular suspicious of the role of the University of Technology. He argued (as it turned out quite correctly) that under the terms of the proposal the University of Technology would eventually take over control of the degree program from the University of New England. This would place in jeopardy the plan to establish an autonomous academic university in Newcastle. Newcastle ran the risk of being left with an 'institute of technology' under the control of the State authorities. On 24 October Eddy told the *NMH* that 'placing the courses with the University of Technology was not satisfactory…because it was not set up for this purpose'.

Such a purpose could only be carried out within 'the scope an academic university'. Eddy must have also been annoyed that the University of Sydney had been sidelined leaving the Department of University Extension Classes with little hope of expansion in Newcastle.

Yet the Executive had to acknowledge that the government had made a gesture – to reject the proposal out of hand would have appeared churlish. The Executive of the NUEG, therefore, welcomed the establishment of an Arts Faculty at the Technical College and took comfort in the fact that the University of New England would maintain the high standards required. It noted the 'precarious' position of the University of New England in the arrangements and warned against any on-going interference by the Public Service Board particularly in the Council which was set to govern the college's activities. As if to underline its dis-satisfaction with the arrangements, the executive announced that the NUEG would continue its campaign to establish a fully independent academic university college in Newcastle.

The Executive found that not all members of the NUEG agreed with their position. Tom for one now found himself out of step with the Executive. As President of the Newcastle Branch of the New England New State Movement he had pointed out to the Editor of the *NMH* that he was 'delighted to hear the proposal by New England University to commence Full University Courses in Arts & Economics in 1954'. It is clear that Tom lacked Eddy's sensibilities about the nature of universities – from a practical point of view, he wanted a university college teaching Arts as well as Technology courses established in the city as soon a possible. Like Griffith Duncan, the Principal of the Teachers' College, he believed that the teaching of Arts at the Newcastle College was the first concrete step in Newcastle achieving its own autonomous university. It was in Tom's words, 'the toe hold we always wanted'. Unlike Eddy, Tom was not convinced that the University of Technology was set to dominate. He had been assured (as it turned out incorrectly) by George Booth, one of the local members, and Phillip Wright, later Chancellor of the University of New England, that the operation was to remain under Armidale's control. Tom, therefore, argued strongly that the NUEG should support the new arrangement and make it work. He pointed out that if the NUEG cooperated with the new arrangements, it may still be possible to work towards the outcome it desired – that is, an independent Academic University. Yet Eddy's position remained unchanged. Strong divisions were now to emerge in the NUEG as two strong personalities attempted to convince members of their position – Tom, 'the noisy obstructionist' versus Eddy, 'the man with the terrific ego'. Although Tom found that he often lacked the support of the group (with the exception of his wife), history would show that the position he took was the correct one. To Tom's satisfaction, Heffron honoured his commitment regarding the university college in Newcastle despite the ALP having lost the seat of Kahibah in the bi-election – with Liberal preferences the Independent candidate had secured the seat.[10]

The college duly opened on 4 March 1954 with Associate Professor Auchmuty taking charge of the Arts Faculty. Educated at Armagh Royal School and Trinity College, Dublin, where he won a Gold Medal for History and Politics, Auchmuty had held a professorial position at Farouk University, Alexandria, before taking up a position of senior lecturer in Humanities at the Ultimo campus, University of Technology. No doubt the authorities were impressed with his qualifications, but Auchmuty won his appointment on political grounds – he was seen as someone who would handle the situation in Newcastle. In his address to students Auchmuty stressed the importance

The opening of the Newcastle University College at Tighes Hill –
photograph courtesy of the *NMH*

of the event for Newcastle – it was the real beginning of
university education in the region. He was pleased to inform
the gathering that the Newcastle College had enrolled more
Arts students than any other institution in the country. In fact,
by the end of term one there were 302 students enrolled in

diploma and part-time degree programs, a further twenty eight in conversion courses (one year courses designed to upgrade qualifications from diploma to degree), thirty three in full time degree courses other than Arts and ninety eight in full or part-time Arts degrees. In stressing the importance of the links between the Newcastle College, the University of Technology and the University of New England, he was proud to point out that the Arts Faculty was entirely staffed with 'university' men with proper academic qualifications. One of the university men to accompany Auchmuty to Newcastle was Cyril Renwick who was an Associate Professor of Economics at the University of Technology (Kensington). It was under the leadership of these two associate professors that the Newcastle College was set to flourish.

The Newcastle University College Advisory Council met for the first time in June 1954. As a sign of the deep divisions within the NUEG the Executive failed to nominate any representatives. In a letter to Tom dated 23 December 1953 Eddy clearly outlined his position in regards to Baxter, the University of Technology and the new college. In Eddy's mind it was of the upmost importance that the NUEG and its supporters close ranks and oppose the new arrangements:

> There are people whose vanity or whose carelessness about what is going on right under their noses, could mean that they would go on to the Council and then they would regard everything said against the institution as something said against them. They would kid themselves that what they had was a genuine independent academic university. And their support (for the NUEG) would be lost. If Technology could detach sufficient big names from the Group

in that way, we would never re-assemble the Group. There would be no organized force of any weight to fight for a real academic University. Baxter knows that perfectly well. That is why he made a special effort to win Batty (Anglican Bishop of Newcastle) and Lingard (Editor of the *NHM*) when he was here…So long as he or his defenders continue to fight to smash the Group, we must take steps to hold it together. Its cohesion and the adherence of the "names" are just as important for the future fight as are the number of students.

It appears that Eddy had a deep personal mistrust of Professor Baxter. In his opinion; 'if you are to keep up with a bird like Baxter you MUST study your documents, you must be right on the ball all the time. The whole secret of the success of men like Baxter is that they never give you a clear cut issue to fight on. Not until they've got you where you can't fight. Every doubtful step is half and half'. He was later to remark, 'meetings with Baxter – Lies First Bunch, Second, Third'. He also had a mistrust of Auchmuty seeing him as 'Baxter's man'. Eddy's mistrust of Baxter was shared by other members of the Executive particularly by Charles Bentley, regional secretary of the WEA. It was his view that the NUC was 'a cuckoo in the nest of the Technology College'. It was 'the basis of Baxter's empire now firmly laid'. Bentley remained a loyal supporter of Eddy (thus an opponent of Tom) throughout the campaign.

The problem for Eddy was that there were 'rats in the ranks'. Without consulting the Executive, Baxter had approached members of the NUEG to take up a position on the Council. It was Eddy's opinion that Baxter had targeted members who would not be capable of mounting an effective challenge to the University of Technology: 'no one who takes things casually is going to deal with Baxter…he'll see its going to take forty hours a week or thereabouts to win the fight and he'll decide it is not worth it…obviously he is not going to make this a major interest. He is not going to be on the ball unless Baxter makes a bad blue'.

Eddy believed that it was up to him to save the situation and ensure that Newcastle achieved an academic university:

> Now who have we got, as a matter of objective fact, who knows the meaning of an academic university not only in general terms but also in a way it works out in detail, who in addition is prepared to give everything he's got, irrespective of the consequences to himself in order to get Newcastle an Academic University? Who is prepared to read everything, relevant, write everything necessary, never take his eye of the ball? He need not be fallible. Nobody is. But who is there? If you can point to such a person I'll be glad to unload as much of the burden as he'll take. Just now I feel sick and very, very tired through the work I've put into this. At the present rate I'm killing myself and I know it. But somebody must fight bureaucratic centralism or we'll find ourselves in a totalitarian dictatorship'.

While such comments clearly indicate Eddy's level of commitment, they also reveal a certain lack of balance.

Clearly Tom (who may have been identified by some as one of the 'rats') had continued to take Eddy to task for his dogmatic and inflexible stance. Eddy complained:

I take it very hard that you are continually hammering at my wanting my way. Whenever you are able to come up for that going over the minutes I'll show you case after case where I have yielded my opinions although it is all more work for me. Sometimes I have felt (and I realize this may be unjust and simply the product of tiredness) that you opposed things just because I put them up. I certainly have felt that it has added a terrible burden. That does not mean that I object to opposition but it has seemed to me often that you have not tried to enter into what the idea was but rather simply took a stand with the determination – no matter what anybody says I'm not going to budge from this. That may be unjust. If so I apologize. I'm merely trying to explain how I have felt'.

As Eddy's last comment indicates, he did not regard the dispute as personal – he closed the letter with the remark 'anyway we'd better have another beer'. The two men were certainly still on good terms in October 1953 when Eddy asked Tom to make a personal donation to the Workers' Educational Association. From its inception the NUEG had utilised the good services of Beryl Anderson, the Secretary of the WEA, to complete all its paperwork. With the WEA financially struggling, Eddy needed to ask members of the NUEG (including Tom) to contribute 'a couple of guineas' so that the WEA could continue to assist in 'the struggle for a university'.

Eddy kept the pressure up on Tom to change his mind through a series of letters in January. In a twenty six page (typed) letter dated 29 January 1954 Eddy returned to a familiar theme: 'by steam roll I mean fight for a single policy through thick and thin and irrespective of procedures. You say this when you say 'never have I given up on a cause'…you get an idea and you never give up. That makes group work impossible – at least if enough people do it. If I turned on this tactic I would have more success than you but we'd probably bust up the group'.[11]

Such criticism failed to move Tom – he remained convinced that Newcastle now had a university college which provided the young people of the region with Arts as well as Technology courses. He remained hopeful that this institution would one day develop into an autonomous university. Tom rejected Eddy's criticism – in a letter dated 26 January 1954 he pointed out:

> I have never tried to steam roll you or anyone else in the Group. Why should I? I have debated points and accepted defeat or victory – often I have changed my views but never have I given up on a good cause. Our Group is not the ALP. I don't belong to a clique or party in the Group. I cannot be expected to run along with others because of a mistaken sense of loyalty. You mention Churchill. Prior to 1939 did he accept the views of Cabinet? No he tried by his own free actions to awaken the people of the world to the impending peril. Surely I don't have to accept the views of the Chamberlains or the Asquiths because I pay my five bob.

In a further letter dated 22 February 1954 Tom pointed out that he regarded his dispute with Eddy as nothing more than a distraction. It was his opinion that 'we should be working with all our energies to try and achieve our final objective, not to waste so much energy on one another'. He restated his view that the current arrangements were a means to achieving that final objective, an autonomous academic university:

> I feel that the approach by the Group to the new
> state of affairs was wrong from the start…I still
> honestly believe that this is the commencement of a
> University for Newcastle. I feel we should have given
> it our complete blessing, got as many of our fellows as
> possible on the Council, made common cause with
> New England and given the impression to all and
> sundry that we <u>accepted</u> [*sic*] it was under the overall
> control of Armidale or New England should I say. If
> we had done this we might, only might but it was a
> possibility, have had a say in the show and we could
> then have tried to direct it on the lines of eventual
> autonomous control by the citizens of Newcastle.

Tom later admitted that such letters had little impact on him:
'Harry Eddy would write his 23 page letters to me which I had
difficulty in really understanding'. It remained Tom's view that
the NUC was 'the start of our university and that it depended
on the staff and students to carve out the type of university they
wanted'. As a result Tom 'wanted the NUEG to immediately
change its policies to recognise that the university had begun
and to alter our name to the Newcastle University Expansion
Group and to fight for money and eventually autonomy'. Tom
did not see Baxter or Auchmuty as 'bogey men'. In fact, he later
gave Auchmuty much of the credit for the future success of the
university.

But the Executive refused to listen to Tom, preferring to
follow Eddy's lead. When the issue of the NUC was raised at
the February (1954) meeting of the NUEG Eddy successfully
put forward a motion of non-cooperation. Tom (supported by

Kath) unsuccessfully attempted to amend this motion allowing members as individuals to accept a position on the Council. Tom then moved a second amendment 'that this Group actively favour the enrolment of students at the Newcastle University College'. In defence of his amendment Tom argued that:

> the crucial point was the gathering of students. He felt that, if the number of students was high, it would be possible to transfer the institution into what we want, but if the number was unsure, we might lose everything and our goal be put off for a further twenty years.

The minutes show that 'Mr Farrell's amendment was then put and defeated on a show of hands'. In general business Tom restated his position:

> He thought that the NUEG had broad Newcastle support in the past and that the path forward was to rally as many students as possible to the college, and press for as many additional facilities as possible and in this way transform it. A vigorous policy along these lines would command widespread support and would produce results.

Further discussion followed among Eddy, his supporters and Tom. The debate was carried over until the next meeting.

At the March meeting matters came to a head. Eddy put forward a motion (seconded by Batty) that:

> The NUEG shall not depart from its objective of a free Academic University or a College of an

Academic University. That it shall concentrate its own actions upon stating the facts about the existing set-up as forcibly, accurately, clearly and widely as it can. That since it is building for the centuries and not for today, it will carry through its pledges that it will not give up until it is satisfied that a genuine free Academic University has been firmly established.

Tom immediately moved an amendment 'that a decision be deferred until the next meeting when Professor Baxter and Professor Auchmuty could address the Group'. The motion lapsed for want of a seconder (Kath was not in attendance). A further amendment was put by Tom (seconded by the lawyer, Basil Helmore) that 'whilst adhering to its objective this Group is prepared actively to cooperate with the present set-up hoping it will lead to the independent Academic University it desires'. Tom then spoke for the amendment:

> There is no sense butting our heads against a brick wall. If we cooperate it may well be the best way through to our goal. Out of the existing institution may well develop an individual Academic University. This is a start. It is a major step forward. From this will grow a real university – Newcastle's own. Let us cooperate and support the project and bring about what we desire…It is time to end personalities and face realities. We should invite people from the University of Technology here and hear what they have to say…the Academic University belongs to Medieval Times. We must move with the times and ours is a Technological age to which a Technology University is appropriate.

Despite the logic of Tom's argument, his was a lone voice – as the minutes record 'this argument was used only by one speaker and was not supported by others'. The amendment was defeated 8 votes to three (Farrell, Helmore and Dr T. Hamilton). The original motion was put and 'carried on the voices'.[12]

The dye was now caste – as Wright points out 'the dominant NUEG ideology could never concede that the offspring of a hybrid 'technology university' might develop into a 'real university' in its own right'. Clearly Tom did not have the numbers to persuade Eddy and the Executive to take another course. A person of lesser character may have decided at this stage to walk away but not Tom Farrell. Tom decided to stay in the NUEG and fight on. As he later explained 'I then became a loner on the university group…but I stayed in the group, I stayed on to get the other view across'. Tom noted the unfailing support he received from his wife: 'I always had Kath sitting alongside me who would second my resolutions which, of course, were never carried'. It is clear that Tom blamed Eddy for the situation. Although he was quite prepared to acknowledge Eddy's important role in the NUEG, he argued that his rigidity, born of an unbalanced nature, severely compromised the achievements of the Group. He later commented: 'there is no doubt in my mind that if we had not had Harry Eddy on our side and in the group we probably would have never have had a University of Newcastle. His efforts were prestigious… (but) I felt myself that he was unstable with a tremendous amount of force and tremendous ego. On any issue, Harry Eddy believed that his view was paramount and no one else's view should be taken notice of'. Tom was saddened by the result: 'this was a great disappointment; I thought it a colossal blunder. What a pity that when Arts courses came to Tighes Hill, the group did not proclaim that we had won the battle, a victory for people's power'.

Kath & Tom Farrell (1960s) in the back yard of their home,
137 Russell Road, New Lambton.

Having been encouraged by his colleagues at the University
of Sydney, among them Professor John Anderson, Eddy moved
quickly to ensure that the contagion in Newcastle did not
spread to other possible university centres. In April 1954 he
organised a state-wide conference in Sydney to discuss the
development of universities in New South Wales. Needless
to say, Tom did not attend. A follow up convention held in
Sydney on 24-27 September 1954 only served to reaffirm the
NUEG's charter. Bishop de Witt Batty, Vice –President of the
NUEG, again came to Eddy's defence contributing an article to
The Newcastle Diocesan Churchman arguing that the institution
proposed for Newcastle would not meet the needs of the city
for an 'academic university'. Tom took the Bishop to task in
the *Herald* pointing out that 'the Bishop should remember
this is Newcastle, not Sydney, and if he waits for the type of
University we all aspire for then we will never get anything.

The suggestion for Technology to conduct Degree Courses on behalf of New England University should be quite acceptable as a start. It will give the poorer members of our community the right to attend and to do Academic University Degree Courses. What the Newcastle University will become depends on the future support and interest of the people of Newcastle'. Eddy got a further opportunity to restate his opposition to the arrangements when he was invited to contribute to the first edition of *Opus Tharunra*, the Official Journal of the Newcastle University College Students' Association.[13]

The battle positions were now pretty much set in stone. When Eddy moved back to Sydney at the end of 1954, Tom tried unsuccessfully to have him removed from his position as Secretary of the NUEG. He also tried unsuccessfully (in defence of freedom of expression) to question the decision by the Executive to restrict membership of the NUEG to those who agreed with the group's principles. Attempts at dialogue between NUEG and the staff of the NUC achieved very little. The NUEG's obstinate position did not prevent the NUC growing in strength as it continued to forge strong links with the community. During its first year of operation the students had achieved academic success particularly in the Arts courses where they outperformed their counterparts at the University of New England. The community recognised such academic achievement by the donation of a number of prizes. Plans were afoot to expand the curriculum with increased staff and facilities particularly in Architecture. 5000 people attended the college's first open day – Associate Professor Renwick (no doubt with the recent disastrous Maitland floods in mind) announced the establishment of the Hunter Valley Research Foundation. He was also instrumental in establishing in 1957 courses in the Bachelor of Commerce degree. In May 1955 Auchmuty (without advertising the position) was appointed to the Chair of History in Newcastle by the Council of the University of Technology. His power was further augmented by being appointed to the newly created position of Deputy Warden of the college. In 1956 Auchmuty with the help of Baxter had a significant win over the University of New England when NUC exerted its right to complete the work undertaken by fourth year honours student in Arts. Auchmuty pressed for the right of the University of Technology to award its own Arts degrees. In March 1956 the Newcastle University College Advisory Council established a subcommittee (with strong local membership) to discuss college development, autonomy and moving the institution to the site at Shortland. Things were happening.

While the college got on with its job, the NUEG continued its opposition. It accused Auchmuty of being part of a Baxter conspiracy to undermine the University of New England by achieving an Arts Faculty and degree for the University of Technology. It made a predictable submission to the Committee on Australian Universities (Murray Committee) established by the Menzies Government, attacking the University of Technology. When the Murray Report recommended that the University of Technology should retain its strong links to the NUC (as it established a Faculty of Arts in its own right as the University of New South Wales), the NUEG reaffirmed its plan to press for an independent university in Newcastle. It vented its anger at Auchmuty in 1958 when he admitted that he favoured the NUC severing its links with the University of New England when the University of Technology was able to award Arts degrees.

The University of Newcastle takes shape at Shortland –
photograph courtesy of the *NMH*

What did Tom think of all of this bickering? In his mind it merely served to emphasise that the position taken by the Executive of the NUEG was non-sustainable. As it continued to push for its idea of an ideal university education, the group ran the risk of becoming ever more irrelevant. It was self-evident that the majority of the community had accepted the NUC as a good outcome for Newcastle, a way forward for the young people of the district to receive a tertiary education. Writing to the *NMH* he pointed out:

> as an active member of the University Group, I cannot agree with the Executive. Criticism of universities can always be levelled and much may be justified, but it is one of those debating subjects dear to the heart of intellectuals and philosophers. There

is no result and often no answer…With people like Professor Auchmuty and Professor Renwick at the helm Newcastle has nothing to fear on standards. There is too much conservatism within the group. It is opposed to any change in tertiary education or innovation and refuses to involve itself in any risk or speculation. I am confident that the existing set up with all its deficiencies will prosper to a full-fledged, independent and autonomous university…It must be remembered that the group was formed primarily to establish a university, not to command it after it was formed. The group seems to be setting itself up as an authoritarian body to set standards for universities in Australia. Let us ask ourselves if the existing set up is an improvement on what we had previously. If it has anything to commend it let us cooperate and constructively suggest improvements. The inference that there is some diabolical plot to sabotage tertiary education in New South Wales could be true, but on the other hand it could be poppycock. I believe some people are trying to prejudice an issue still to be decided.

In his capacity as President of the Newcastle Branch of the New England New State Movement, Tom also found himself in a public spat with a group within the Executive he identified a 'the WEA clique'. Eddy and Bentley had taken it upon themselves to rebuke Tom for suggesting that the University of Technology should be encouraged to create branches in country centres as a means of improving decentralisation. In a series of letters to the *NMH* the protagonists exchanged blows – Tom having the final word when he pointed out 'my lone voice in the NUEG will continue to be heard, if my views are not parallel to those expressed by Messrs Eddy and Bentley, it doesn't worry me in the slightest'.

Tom's fear for the NUEG was that after doing so much good, it ran the risk of 'going out without getting any real credit'. The final meeting of the NUEG was held on 28 March 1958 – five members were in attendance (Ellis, Eddy, Bentley, Anderson and a Mrs E. Kirkwood). Baxter must have been pleased to see the group's demise – in February 1957 he had written to Harant, the Professor of Economic History at the University of Technology: 'this document is a continuation of the long campaign by a small and now largely discredited group of people in Newcastle who have been extraordinary hostile to the University, the Minister and everything connected with our activity in the city'. Others were kinder in their summation of the group. Ellis later wrote 'there is no doubt that Newcastle must have secured its own university eventually but it was equally certain that if it had not been for the NUEG that university would not have been secured as early as it was. We can feel very satisfied with the results off our endeavours'. Tom was one of those who could feel satisfied – although he did not always agree with the strategy applied by the Executive of the NUEG, he shared their goal. Together all members of the NUEG had worked for the establishment of a university college in Newcastle. This had been achieved. In Tom's words 'the group did a great service for Newcastle'. In summing up Tom's role in the NUEG Wright notes:

> Tom Farrell was a practical man with a limited education and with no intellectual pretensions. He knew what he wanted for Newcastle and was prepared to work very hard to get it. With the

advantage of hindsight, there can be little doubt that Farrell's practical instincts served him well.

There was, however, one last hooray for Tom and his colleagues on the Executive of the NUEG when the old opponents united to fight a common foe, Professor Baxter of the University of Technology. In June 1958 Baxter announced that he intended to divert £400,000 earmarked by the Federal Government for NUC to Wollongong. Once again Tom as President of the Newcastle Branch, New England New State Movement, prepared to rally the troops. He called on: 'the Newcastle University Establishment Group which did such a fine job in stimulating Newcastle opinion and which really established the university, to ask the Lord Mayor to convene a public meeting to protest emphatically to the Government if the £400,000 is taken away from this city'. It was his opinion that 'this is another shining example of the discrimination used against this city. It clearly reveals that, in comparison to Sydney, we are always at a disadvantage'. Tom's call to arms was effective. With the support of Ellis and Day (old comrades from the NUEG) Tom convinced the Lord Mayor, Alderman McDougall, to call a public meeting which was attended by over 500 people. At the meeting Professor Renwick put forward a motion (seconded by Tom) condemning the move by the University of Technology to divert funds to Wollongong. The motion was passed unanimously. Baxter's action once again raised the issue of the trustworthiness of the University of Technology. It was further resolved that the NUC should seek autonomy as soon as possible. To this end the Lord Mayor's Committee for the Establishment of an Autonomous University of Newcastle was established. Over the next few years, this body was to play a pivotal part in moving the NUC towards autonomy. Although Tom was asked to join the committee, he declined, no doubt confident that others (former members of NUEG, staff and students of the college) were better placed to guide the institution towards this goal. As it turned out, Baxter's plan came to nothing – the Federal Government intervened to ensure that the NUC received the money that had been allocated.[14]

Courtesy of the *NMH*. Tom must have felt a sense of achievement as the Foundation Stone of the Great Hall was laid (28 May 1971). The Farrells (Tom & Kath) were among the honoured guests at the grand opening

The Shortland Campus - photograph courtesy of the *NMH*

Over the next seven years Tom watched with interest as the NUC moved towards autonomy. The State Act which conferred independence on the University of Newcastle was signed and sealed on 23 December 1964. The University of Newcastle was constituted on 1 January 1965 by a Proclamation of His Excellency the Governor of New South Wales. Professor Auchmuty as Vice-Chancellor presided over a vibrant institution with an impressive number of students (1,460 undergraduates, forty post-graduates) situated at the campus at Shortland. It was an institution that was well resourced and well-staffed. Tom was pleased – the many years of hard work undertaken by him and many others had paid off. An autonomous university for Newcastle had been achieved. It was to bear much fruit – as Tom later pointed out 'one has only to go to the University of Newcastle now to know what an acquisition it has been to the city and to realise the number of our young people who have been able to avail themselves of Tertiary Education in their own region'. No doubt, given his environmental concerns, he was especially pleased how the campuses at Shortland developed.

THE UNIVERSITY OF NEWCASTLE

NEW SOUTH WALES 2308

FROM THE VICE-CHANCELLOR AND PRINCIPAL:
PROFESSOR J. J. AUCHMUTY.
M.A., Ph.D., M.R.I.A., F.R.Hist.S., F.I.A.L.

Telephone 68-0401

November 28, 1968.

Mr. T. Farrell,
137 Russell Road,
NEW LAMBTON, N.S.W. 2305.

Dear Mr. Farrell,

It was a wonderful gesture on your part to allocate the funds over from your Farewell function to our Great Hall rather than accepting a personal gift for yourself and your wife.

I can assure you the University appreciates not only this the latest of your helpful actions, but also the work you did in years gone by with the University Establishment Group and we who are now living and working on the Shortland site do hope that our founding fathers and the people of Newcastle are appreciative of what has been done in more recent years.

The party at the West Leagues Club was certainly a wonderful send-off, though I have no doubt that you intend to keep yourself in the public eye for many years to come. If only you could be sure of the votes of those present and their dependants all in one constituency, obviously you would romp home at the forthcoming Council Elections.

With every good wish for the future and with renewed thanks for your kindly gesture,

Yours sincerely,

J. J. Auchmuty.
Vice-Chancellor.

Letter from Professor Auchmuty, Vice Chancellor & President, University of Newcastle, thanking Tom and Kath Farrell for their donation to the Great Hall (28 November 1968)

In 1986 Tom's efforts were recognised by the University of Newcastle when he was awarded an Honorary Master of Arts Degree for his service to the local community. The letter of recommendation referred to 'the work Mr Rolf Everist Farrell performed in the community and particularly as it relates to the establishment of the University'. It supplied the following details for the consideration of the Degrees Committee:

> Rolf Everist Farrell, of 137 Russell Road, New Lambton was one of the Prime and Principal movers for the establishment of an autonomous University in Newcastle. He was the most actively and energetically involved from 1948 onwards – through the years of the University being a College of the University of Technology – then a College of New England University - and did not desist in his endeavours until 1964 when full autonomy was granted. Sixteen years of unselfish and dedicated service meant that Newcastle finally did achieve the initial goal of some of the first proponents for such an institution…Mr Farrell has and remains dedicated to Newcastle and the Hunter regions

On 24 April 1986 the Council of the University of Newcastle resolved to award Rolf Everist Farrell an Honorary Degree of Master of Arts in recognition of his contribution to the establishment of the university. The degree was conferred on 3 May 1986 as part of the Faculties of Arts and Medicine Graduation Ceremony. There to witness the event were Tom's family and friends – he was particularly pleased that he could share the day with his two grandsons (John and James Talty) who had received their Bachelor of Commerce degrees the day before. Six other grandchildren would successfully complete their degrees at the University of Newcastle in the years to come. In a real sense their success represented the fulfilment of his endeavours over so many years to secure for the young people of Newcastle and the Hunter region a tertiary education at an autonomous local university.[15]

Tom is congratulated by Sir Bede Callaghan,
Chancellor of the University of Newcastle, on receiving his Honorary degree

Tom with his wife on graduation day

5: A Champion of Blackbutt

Although Tom involved himself in many community activities after his return from the Second World War, the issue which remained closest to his heart was the promotion and protection of the environment by means of the establishment and development of urban green areas and National Parks. Tom was inspired to follow the example of the American naturalist, John Muir, who had been instrumental in having the Yosemite area in the Sierra Nevada Mountains of central California declared a national park in 1890. Although he was involved in many environmental campaigns, it was the establishment of Blackbutt Reserve that Tom regarded as his greatest achievement in this area. Blackbutt was, in his words, 'an environmental jewel that had been preserved for all future generations'. It was 'a wonderful thing for Newcastle'.

From a young age Tom had been struck by the beauty of the Blackbutt area. As a young man he often travelled on a privately-owned bus service (operated by Dutchy Arson) from New Lambton to Cardiff. He later recalled that 'as the bus travelled through the high area of New Lambton, this was all undeveloped bush land, he always thrilled at the wonderful view'. He was especially 'overwhelmed by the beauty of the view from the lookout'. Later he was to share these experiences with his wife and children; as the Farrell family spent many a Sunday afternoon picnicking and bushwalking in the area.[1]

Tom was quick to purchase some land in the area when an opportunity presented itself. In 1932 the Scottish-Australian

Mining Company, a London based company which originally owned much of Lambton, New Lambton and Kotara, released blocks of land for sale in what is now Blackbutt Reserve. In 1922 the company had sold a large number of subdivided blocks (either side of Kotara Railway Station) in what was later to become the suburb of Kotara. Despite the ideal location, the 1932 auction did not attract much interest. The harsh economic times brought about by the Great Depression ensured that only four of the blocks were sold. Two blocks were sold to The Returned Sailors and Soldiers Memorial Institute, one block to Mr Thomas Marshall, Superintendent of the Newcastle Abattoirs, and one block to Mr R. E. Farrell. Tom purchased an acre block (Lot 38) in Grinsell Street, Kotara, for £45.

In addition to being work colleagues, Thomas Marshall and Tom were members of the Cardiff Heights Progress Association a body which had pressed the local councils to establish the Blackbutt area as a national reserve. In particular, Tom enlisted the support of Alderman Edden, the Mayor of New Lambton, to call a municipal conference to discuss the issue. The New Lambton Council was keen to obtain land from the Scottish-Australian Mining Company to establish a reserve so that the area would not be quarried for its gravel or subdivided for housing. The council realised that any mining activity would 'undoubtedly contribute to the ruin of the natural environment'. At the municipal conference the proposal won the support of Hamilton, Newcastle, Wallsend, Carrington and Merewether Councils. Alderman Jenner of Hamilton spoke of the need 'to secure the spot for posterity'. Given the growth of the urban settlement in the Newcastle district, Alderman Skelton of Hamilton argued strongly that 'open spaces should be secured for future generations'. The municipal conference passed a unanimous motion that the various owners of the Blackbutt area be approached with a view of donating land for a national reserve.

Although the Scottish-Australian Mining Company (the major landholder) responded favourably, agreeing to make a free dedication of 75 acres of land in the Blackbutt area, the councils could not meet the conditions set down by the company due to the difficult economic conditions. A further conference in June 1932 failed to resolve the matter – the Mayor of New Lambton (no doubt urged on by Tom and the Cardiff Heights Progress Association) repeated the view that Blackbutt would make an excellent national park. He pointed out that 'all varieties of trees flourished there; ferns were in abundance and the country was in general in a virgin state'. The company had informed the newly formed Newcastle City Council (NCC) that it was willing to reserve land for this purpose (if certain conditions were met) but was under orders from its London office to subdivide the bulk of the Lambton Freehold Estate. But like the councils, the company was to find that the economic circumstances made it difficult to proceed. As a result, progress towards establishing Blackbutt as a national park was put on hold for a number of years. It did not help matters that the NCC, the most financially secure local body, was less than enthusiastic in regard to this issue. The Lake Macquarie Shire showed a similar disinterest. Tom was later to point out that:

we endeavoured to try to get the Newcastle City Council to resume the New Lambton Lookout area and Blackbutt…One interesting point which should always be remembered is that the Cardiff Heights Progress Association, prompted by myself, was responsible for getting the New Lambton Council to take up this matter to purchase Lot 51…Another interesting point which seems to be lost today, is that apart from myself, probably every member of the Cardiff Heights Lookout Progress Association was a resident of the Lake Macquarie Shire and at that time, there was no one within the Newcastle Municipality area who made any attempt to resume Blackbutt.

Despite the lack of interest shown by local government authorities, Tom and the Cardiff Heights Progress Association kept the issue alive by writing to respective Parliamentarians and Ministers 'calling on them to retain Blackbutt as a Public Reserve'.[2]

Tom also looked outside Newcastle to garner support. By 1925 he had become a member of the Parks and Playgrounds Movement of New South Wales. Although a Sydney based organisation, Tom decided to become its only non-metropolitan member, attending meetings while on business in Sydney. He found that the movement's goals complimented his own:

1. The preservation of ample space for recreation and nature conservation before the chance is lost, as it has been in many older lands.
2. The right of every Australian man, woman and child to healthy recreation.
3. The right of all Australians to enjoy the beauties and wonders of the Australian bush and the right of our flowers, trees and animals to preservation.
4. Recognition of the fact that field sports are a most powerful influence in building the national character, and that the wise use of leisure is a vital problem of our future.

5. The promotion of play leadership in the sports of the young and the provision of an ample playground for every school.
6. More players and fewer onlookers to build up the nation.
7. The principle that the beauties of our country should be the possession of our people.

Tom was able to persuade other members of the Cardiff Heights Progress Association to support the movement. In April 1936 Tom and Jim Marshall (the brother of Thomas Marshall) made a public statement on behalf of the group:

> The formation of a branch of the Parks and Playgrounds Movement of NSW is an excellent idea and one which we trust will come to fruition. Perhaps individual councils have done their best in the years gone by, but then you read that the Government has made available recreation areas of 66,000 acres during the past year, one can only come to the conclusion that the reason why none of these acres have been resumed in Newcastle is because there has been no local agitation. For many years the Cardiff Heights Progress Association has tried to get the Blackbutt area resumed. If a branch of this association was formed we would like to see our Councils take an interest in it. It might be possible for them to nominate representatives to help give the Association a district status. The trouble in the past has been that a financially powerful Council like Newcastle takes no interest in parks outside its own municipality, whereas if the New Lambton Lookout Area and Blackbutt, was resumed as recreational

grounds, Newcastle City ratepayers would receive just as much benefit from this beautiful area as would residents of New Lambton. Parks should be acquired for the District at the expense of the District, together with help from the Government...We know of no better way in which the District can express itself as a whole than by the formation of a Branch of the Parks and Playgrounds Movement of NSW.

Although a Newcastle Branch was not formed at this time, Tom (and other members of the Cardiff Heights Progress Association) saw that the Parks and Playgrounds Movement had an important role to play in reigniting interest in the Blackbutt area as a national reserve. They believed that such a group could successfully counter the lethargy displayed by the State Government and the NCC in regard to this matter.[3]

An opportunity to advance the cause came when the Return Sailors and Memorial Institute announced that it intended to dispose of its land (just below the lookout) at Blackbutt. Tom and Jim Marshall (on behalf of the Cardiff heights Progress Association) wrote to the New Lambton Council urging it to purchase Lot 51 for the purpose of public recreation. Alderman Dunkley, the Mayor of New Lambton, took up the initiative, urging the Constitute Councils to support the plan. Between them, NCC, New Lambton Council (contributing £250 each), Hamilton Council, Waratah Council (contributing £100 each), Adamstown Council, Wickham Council, Merewether Council and Wallsend Council (contributing £50 each) found the necessary funds (£900) to purchase the land. Clearly, the credit for securing the first section of land in the Blackbutt area for public recreational rested with Tom and the Cardiff Heights Progress Association. As Ramsland points out 'the 17 acres and 3 roods of Lot 51, which was the original part of Blackbutt Nature Reserve, was their achievement alone'. Tom would have been pleased that the land had been purchased as a result of a district initiative – it was his view that the resumption of Blackbutt as a national reserve was a matter for the whole district not just individual councils. It would have also pleased him that NCC had been involved – two years later (1938) it was to merge with the other district councils to form the Greater Newcastle City Council. The support of this body would be crucial for the development of the reserve at Blackbutt. On 4 March 1938 the area of 17 acres 3 roods (Lot 51) was officially gazetted as Blackbutt Lookout Reserve.[4]

Tom's effort was to bear further fruit. Boyed on by their decision, the district councils decided to purchase land adjoining Blackbutt Lookout Reserve in order 'to establish a National Park for Newcastle and its district'. In order to meet the total cost of £3500 the councils sought the assistance of the Department of Lands which agreed to contribute £2500 towards the project. The 144 acre 2 roods and 13 perches area was to be purchased from the Scottish-Australian Mining Company (lots 48, 49, 50 and 52) and two private individuals (parts 6-7 of lot 47). In supporting the project the *NMH* pointed out that Blackbutt was an 'ideal' area for a National Park with its 'wide stretch of virgin bush country, with hills and valleys and ample growth of native flora'. The paper was of the opinion that if afforded the proper protection, ensuring an abundance of flora and fauna, the area would one day 'become one of the district's finest assets'. It was not until March 1940 that the final payment of £730 was paid by the Greater Newcastle Council. On 11 October 1940 the *Government Gazette* recorded that Reserve No 69,539 at Cardiff Heights area (143 acres no roods 39 perches) was notified on 13 September 1940 for Public Recreation. Eighteen months later the Council successfully negotiated with the Scottish-Australian Company to add a further three acres of bushland (fronting Grinsell Street, Kotara) to the reserve. This brought the total size of the Blackbutt Lookout Reserve to 146 acres no roods 39 perches. Tom's vision had now taken shape – he had ensured that the beauty that was Blackbutt would forever be in the possession of the people of Newcastle. It would be his task now to protect and expand this vision.[5]

Although plans were drawn up by the Greater Newcastle Council in 1943 to make Blackbutt 'the show place of the district' by constructing easy-grade walks, removing dead timber and planting numerous Australian flora, the Second World War ensured that little was achieved in developing the reserve. A further plan was put forward in 1949

LAST PAYMENT FOR BLACKBUTT

The final payment of £750 for the redemption of the Blackbutt lookout reserve at New Lambton was authorised by the Greater Newcastle Council last night. The total cost of the acquisition was £3,731, of which £2500 was contributed by the Department of Lands.

The area of 144 acres 2 roods 13 perches will be reserved as a national park for Newcastle and district. In 1937 eight of the former councils agreed to contribute £200 towards the cost of acquiring the reserve. The department promised £2500, provided the councils undertook to meet all costs above that amount. This was agreed to. Last night the Finance Committee recommended that the final contribution by the council be made.

Courtesy of the *NMH*
(28 March 1940)

which included the construction of a tar-sealed access road, a caretaker's cottage, a series of picnic areas and clearing of the undergrowth 'to increase the sites natural beauty'. Once again little came of the scheme as Council deferred any action on the advice of its Finance Committee. As a concession the Council agreed to the formation of a committee made up of five members from the Kotara Progress Association and five private householders to control and manage Blackbutt Reserve. Alderman Boa agreed to represent the Council when the Blackbutt Reserve Special Committee met for the first time in November 1949.

Tom (who knew most of the committee members) no doubt

welcomed the formation of this group – it might yet prove the catalyst to kick start some development in the reserve. He had been working with the Cardiff Heights Progress Association to examine the possibility of establishing a zoo at Blackbutt Reserve. In an article dated 15 October 1950, the *NMH* reported that 'Mr T. Farrell successfully moved that Mr Brown (Secretary of the Taronga Zoological Park Trust) be asked for a copy of the annual report and statement of accounts'. It was the intention of the Association 'to collate information of the procedure for establishing a zoo at the reserve and present a practicable scheme to the Northumberland County Council'. Working through the Blackbutt Reserve Special Committee Tom sought funding from the Joint Coal Board 'to establish a zoo to serve the Northern Coalfields'. In response to an offer of two lionesses from Taronga Zoo, the Progress Association set about organising a conference of interested bodies to discuss the matter. The Blackbutt Reserve Special Committee was called upon to bring pressure on the State Government to provide public funding for the project on equal terms to that offered to Taronga Zoo in its first three decades of operation. For its first thirty-six years of operation Taronga Zoo had relied heavily on government support. As ever Tom was keen to see that Newcastle secured its fair share of State revenue for worthwhile community projects. Given his misgivings about the Sydney authorities, it would have not surprised him that the Premier, Mr McGirr, informed the Association early in 1950 that there would be no state funds available for the proposed zoological gardens at Blackbutt.

Further bad news was to come. In February 1950 the Blackbutt Special Reserve Committee's proposal for the comprehensive development of Blackbutt was rejected by the NCC. At a cost of £35,000 the Committee's plan envisaged road construction, picnic and other leisure areas including a swimming pool, aviaries and fishponds, a kangaroo park and a caretaker's cottage. Frustrated by the inaction of the Council, Alderman Boa recommended the establishment of a trust to control Blackbutt as a means of attracting adequate funding for the project. Although this won the support of the Council, it was not until 1954 that the Trust was finally established. The Blackbutt Reserve Special Committee also received little support from Council when a mine was established by the Scottish-Australian Mining Company on land adjacent to the reserve. All that could be done was to ask the Minister of Mines 'to ensure that the coal company preserve the beauty of the area'.[6]

It was against this background that the Northern Parks and Playgrounds Movement (NPPM) was established. In August 1951, Tom persuaded the Lord Mayor to call a public meeting to endorse the establishment of NPPM. The movement's designation, 'Northern' rather than 'Newcastle', indicated that the group intended to involve itself in issues beyond the Newcastle region. By November 1951 the movement's constitution, modelled on that of its Sydney parent, had been written. After examining the plans of the Northumberland County Council, it was decided to adopt as the movement's objectives, its recommendations in regards to parks and recreation areas. As Mr Hay, the Acting Secretary, pointed out 'the NPPM will set standards by this blueprint, we will accept nothing less and will oppose any attempt to whittle away these areas'. The Northumberland County Council was constituted by an Act of State Parliament in 1948 to organise town planning in the County Districts of the City of Greater Newcastle, the City of Maitland, the Municipality of Cessnock, the Shire of Kearsley, the Shire of Lake Macquarie, the Shire of Lower Hunter and the Shire of Port Stephens. It had similar powers to the Cumberland

County Council which oversaw town planning in the sixty one municipalities and eight shires in Sydney. Both the Cumberland County Council and the Northumberland County Council were dissolved on 19 December 1963 and were replaced by The State Planning Authority in accordance with the State Planning Authority Act 1963. The objectives of the movement were publically outlined in 1953:

> The main objectives were the preservation and development of present recreation and playground spaces in Newcastle and the North, the development of additional reservations for parks and playgrounds and the encouragement of the beautification of streets, highways, and public lands. Importantly, the movement is also interested in the care, development and establishment of National Parks and Reserves.

In Tom's mind the objectives were always clear and simple: 'the NPPM was essentially a great citizen organisation which protected and cared for Parks and Playgrounds'. In its second Annual Report the President put the relevant authorities on notice: 'every effort is being made to let the authorities know that there is a live and articulate body in the community which is prepared to fight against any encroachment on the all too few parklands available to the public'.

Tom sought the assistance of the Newcastle Business Men's Club and Newcastle Rotary to secure suitable office holders for the NPPM – Mr Stan O'Shea became the first President and Alderman Joe Richley, a local alderman and member of the Blackbutt Reserve Special Committee, became the first Secretary. Joe Richley served on Newcastle Council between 1953-1956 as an alderman representing the Mid-West Ward. As

Tom noted, Joe Richley was to become a very important figure in the movement:

> From the time Joe Richley came in, that's when the Northern Parks and Playgrounds Movement really bloomed. Joe Richley was a bloke who had tremendous energy and go – he was the fellow who could call a public meeting, and we called plenty of them – and he'll fill it up. You'd get knocked over, but Joe would come up smiling and he had access to Ministers, the Lord Mayor or Aldermen – he was very highly respected, and he gave this Movement a tremendous reputation.

Taking their lead from Joe Richley and Tom Farrell, other leading professionals (lawyers, architects, teachers and businessmen) were set to join the movement. This was to be important to the NPPM as it increased its standing in the community and gave it greater access to local planning authorities. Another advantage for the movement was that its members were drawn from various community groups including sporting bodies, P&C Associations and Progress Associations (including Cardiff Heights Progress Association). It was the view of Mr Hay that this made the movement a 'really representative group able to speak on matters without being subjected to a charge of partisanship'.[7]

The first priority of the NPPM was the extension and development of Blackbutt Reserve. Having successfully blocked a proposal to establish a bowling club in the lookout area, the movement turned its attention to making the plans for a zoological garden at Blackbutt a reality. Relying on the previous plan put forward by Tom and the Cardiff Heights Progress

Association, and working closely with the Blackbutt Reserve Trust and Taronga Park Trust, Alderman Richley proposed the establishment of a city zoo (without large animals) and aviary on a ten acre site at Blackbutt. It was envisaged that the zoo would eventually become self-funding but in the short term would need to be fully supported by the NCC. The project would involve the construction of a care-takers lodge, possible tearooms, fencing, animal pens, cages and the layout of lawn and pavements. A manager with 'a love of animals and birds' would be employed to run the enterprise as a ongoing business concern. Alderman Richley proposed establishing the zoo on a 'natural area of bushland ' opposite Grinsell Street, Kotara. He assured the public that:

> using this area in this way would not mean taking away any section of the reserve from the people. The natural beauty of the site would be preserved. People could not only take their children to see the zoo and aviary but should be encouraged to use the reserve itself more extensively for hiking and picnic excursions. The zoo would provide a focal point for further development.

Clearly Joe Richley shared Tom Farrell's vision for the Blackbutt area – it was to be an 'environmental jewel' preserved for the benefit of all people in the Newcastle region.

Spurred on by the NPPM, the Blackbutt Reserve Trust finalised its plan for a zoological garden in mid-1956 at a cost of £45000-£50000. Although the plan was based on that put forward by Richley (now President of the NPPM), it proposed a larger area for the zoo of approximately forty acres. Mr Stone, the Town Planning Consultant of Northumberland County

Council and Honorary Architect to the Reserve Trust, advised that with the addition of a further area under the County Scheme, the zoological gardens would take up no more than eighteen percent of the total acreage (222 acres) of the reserve. Given the maintenance of natural bushland between the various exhibits, Alderman Nesbitt, Chairman of the Trust, recommended the plan as 'one of the most progressive put forward for many years'. Alderman McDougall, the Lord Mayor, promised to support the scheme when it came before the Council. On 17 July 1956 the Greater Newcastle Council approved the plan in principle for the establishment of a zoological garden at Blackbutt Reserve to be completed within five years and sought additional funding from the State Government.[8]

The Council, however, was less enthusiastic about enlarging the reserve. In 1954 the NCC had objected strongly to proposals by the Northumberland County Council and the Blackbutt Reserve Trust to add an additional 106 acres to the reserve. At the time the existing viable area of the reserve was 131 acres. While the matter was eventually referred to the Minister of Lands, the plan came to nothing. Richley made it clear to the members of the NPPM that he was not going to allow the matter to rest:

> The present small area of 131 acres is completely inadequate. The opposition of the City Council to the addition of another 106 acres to the reserve is difficult to understand. Large parks in Sydney and Perth are considered too small and soon the area of the reserve will be unable to cope with the increase population as Newcastle expands. It could be the lungs of the city. We will continue to fight for the retention of the area as a public reserve.

In September 1957 NCC showed its unwillingness to work with the Blackbutt Reserve Trust and the NPPM to extend Blackbutt Reserve when it announced its intention to subdivide a 266 acre parcel of land it had recently purchased from the Scottish Australian Mining Company in an area of New Lambton Heights adjacent to the reserve. Of the 266 acres, only 27 acres was set aside for park land, the rest was to be subdivided into residential blocks. The NPPM's response was to stir up community opposition – those organisations that rallied against the plan included the Hunter-Manning National Parks Association, Rotary Clubs, Apex, Newcastle Trades Hall Council, YWCA, District Councils of the P&C Association, Progress Associations and the Newcastle Bowling Associations. There is no doubt where Tom stood on this issue – he consistently opposed the proposition that councils (even in debt) should raise revenue by means of the disposal of public land. He was later to comment:

the NPPM has fought very strenuously over a long period. And one of the main difficulties with us is that if we just had the job of holding what we've got and acquiring new park land that would be alright, but our greatest enemy is the damned councils. You can't get past that…the Town Clerk would draw up a schedule to show that all this land (set aside for park land) is worth one million pounds – two million pounds – it was going to cause a tremendous financial impost on the Council (if land was assigned as park land)…I would say to them, for God's sake (in regard to Council debt) borrow the money and let posterity pay for it.

He later recalled the fight the NPPM had to stop the NCC subdividing land adjacent to the reserve:

> I just turned up an old map here. It is a subdivision which the Council adopted – that is what Blackbutt was going to be – all subdivided, except the original area. That was all the council freehold land and they had the power to subdivide it and the tremendous fight by the NPPM and other parties to save Blackbutt, and eventually we achieved practically the lot – it was an absolute miracle.

Tom was set to play a key role in ensuring that this miracle came about.

Throughout 1958 the NPPM continued to agitate for the expansion of the reserve at Blackbutt. Among its strategies was a campaign to enlist the support of the State Government. To this end Tom successfully moved at the August meeting of the NPPM that letters be sent to the Premier and the local members. It was clear that Tom was not going to take 'no' for an answer – when the Premier replied that 'no funds were available', Tom immediately replied (on behalf of the NPPM) advising the Premier 'we deplore the neglect of Newcastle and its area and we consider that a proportion of the moneys available should be allocated to Newcastle instead of it all being spent in Sydney'. At the January meeting Tom successfully moved that letters be sent to the Northumberland County Council and Blackbutt Reserve Trust calling on them to bring pressure to bear on the NCC. Tom was particularly keen that the Town Clerk ensure that an engineering report on the Blackbutt proposal (prepared some six months earlier) be presented to Council. In December 1958 Tom attended a 'Special Conference' at Joe Richley's residence

'to discuss the problems arising from the short sighted policy of
NCC in disposing of Crown Land from time to time without
giving due consideration to the future needs of the City for
land for civic development, parks and sporting activities'. The
meeting which was attended by representatives of the Newcastle
Business Chamber and the NCC supported unanimously the
motion put forward by Tom that a 'Land Usage Committee be
formed as a Select Committee of the NPPM'. It was further
moved that the members of this committee should be selected
from 'those present at this conference with the power to make
additions'.

Tom and the other members of the Land Usage Committee
met with the Works Committee of the NCC in April 1959
to discuss the future of Blackbutt Reserve. As a result of this
meeting the Works Committee resolved that no subdivision
or other action should be taken until the Northumberland
County Council plan was prescribed. Despite this, a number of
aldermen (supported by the Town Clerk) continued to oppose
the reservation of the land at Blackbutt as a civic park. As a
result Tom successfully moved that a public meeting be called
to garner community support for the project.

In June 1959 the NPPM called a public meeting at the New
Lambton Mechanics' Institute to galvanize public opinion. Mr
R. Earp, the President of the National Parks Association of New
South Wales, addressed the meeting attended by about 130
people. It was his view that 'we think this land (the Council's
270 acres) should be used as a park and recreation grounds…
it will enhance the natural beauty of the area and provide a
parkland that is badly needed'. Alderman Alder moved a
motion that 'the meeting call on the council to make the land
adjacent to Blackbutt Reserve available for park and recreation
purposes, and that a limited area be subdivided and 70 per

cent of the net proceeds allocated for the development of a park'. An amendment was moved by Alderman Richley that 'the council be asked to reserve the whole of the 270 acres for park land'. He pointed out that 'subdividing some of the land was 'the thin end of the wedge' and more subdivision would easily follow if and when allowed'. Tom spoke in favour of the amendment pointing out the revenue raised from council rates – 'twenty years ago about £150,000 was collected in rates from the New Lambton area. Now it is about £1 million and in 20 years probably £2 million would be collected. Some of this could be used to develop the park'. The amendment was carried unanimously. On the motion of Tom Farrell (seconded by Donnelly) it was further resolved that:

> The State Government be asked to contribute the sum of £5000 as an initial advance to the development of the proposed park and that a similar approach be made to the Joint Coal Board which also makes contributions to community projects. Further that all delegates be asked to take back a request to their organisations to communicate with the Council and their parliamentary representatives their support of the resolution carried at this meeting.

Clearly Tom was keen to keep up the public pressure.[9]

Joe Richley (on behalf of the NPPM and the Blackbutt Reserve Trust) tried to win over some opponents on the Council by proposing a compromise plan – he put forward two alternate schemes which allowed for some part subdivision of the 270 acres (150 or 450 blocks) but retained the majority of the land as park reserve. Richley envisaged that the area would be developed as a large national park with botanic gardens, lakes and scenic thoroughfares. This compromise, however, failed to convince the Lord Mayor, Alderman Dunkley, who pushed on with his plan to subdivide most of the area. Under his proposal 500 home sites and a school block would be established with 400 chains of new roads including extensions into several existing streets. Only 117 acres would be set aside for recreation and open space. Dunkley envisaged the area as a 'residential dress circle' for Newcastle which would prevent the dangers of summer bushfires. It was his opinion that 'overall public use of large parks' was a thing of the past. The Lord Mayor's proposal was supported by Mr Baddeley, the City Engineer, who put

Blackbutt Area Plans Deferred

Three plans for the development of Blackbutt Reserve area were discussed at a special meeting of Newcastle City Council Works Committee last night.

The committee deferred consideration and sought further details on the three proposals.

The Lord Mayor (Ald. Dunkley), the City Engineer (Mr. Baddeley) and the Blackbutt Reserve Special Committee submitted separate plans.

The plans of Ald. Dunkley and Mr. Baddeley envisaged residential development of about half the area, leaving the remainder for parkland.

The Blackbutt committee wants most of the land specially developed as a park and picnic area, with some housing development.

The plans of Ald. Dunkley and Mr. Baddeley showed the present Blackbutt reserve as parkland with a series of wide strips of park intermingled with residential.

Building Lots

Ald. Dunkley said there would be 126 acres of the existing reserve and 124 acres of separate park areas, leaving room for 440 building lots with a 75ft. frontage.

Mr. Baddeley said his plan was similar, with about 400 lots with a 75ft. frontage.

The Blackbutt committee is urging 390 acres of park and 150 building lots.

cil could get up to £450,000 from a sale of building lots in the area. This could be allocated to provide a swimming pool, construct Carnley-avenue to a cost of £100,000 and leave another £100,000 for emergency implementation of the County Plan, which, he said, could cost the council £2 million.

The Blackbutt committee's beautification plan would cost up to £150,000, Ald. Dunkley said.

Ald. Jones said he would prefer to see only a limited number of residential lots sold and the rest remain as a park.

Ald. Sheedy felt that the park development should be in one section, not scattered over the areas.

A map showing undermining of the area was submitted by the Blackbutt committee.

The Works Committee recommended that a report on the cover over the undermining, photostat copies of the three plans and aerial photographs of the area be submitted to another committee meeting.

Ald. Edwards and Ald. Dunkley agreed that use of parkland was not the modern trend, but Ald. Sheedy said Newcastle deserved a park similar to the Sydney Centennial Park.

Courtesy of the *NMH*
(25 June 1959, 22 July 1959)

New Blackbutt Land Plan

A layout plan envisaging about 500 home sites on land next to Blackbutt Reserve has been drawn up by the Lord Mayor (Ald. Dunkley).

The plan also incorporates an extra 117 acres of recreational and open space, a school site and 400 chains of new roads, including extensions to several existing streets in New Lambton Heights.

The Lord Mayor will place the plan before the council as part of efforts to oppose a scheme submitted by Blackbutt Reserve Special Committee.

He wants his scheme approved by the council so that the revenue from the sub division can be reserved to help meet the cost of works proposed under the County Plan.

The Blackbutt committee has suggested that the bush land area of 270 acres next to Blackbutt Reserve be developed for a national park, including botanical gardens. About 150 building blocks, it claims, could be provided on the fringe to finance the park proposal.

The committee's plan, supported by more than 130 people at a public meeting early this month, and Ald. Dunkley's drawings will be submitted to a special meeting of the City Council Works Committee on July 21.

F.I.A. 'On Alert' For Infiltration

The Federated Ironworkers' Association in Newcastle

Ald. Dunkley said yesterday that the area was the residential "dress circle" of Newcastle.

"The provision of home sites would also beautify an area which at present constitutes a fire hazard in summer," he said.

"Mr. J. Richley, of the Northern Parks and Playgrounds Movement, and other devotees of the parkland scheme can't convince me there would be any advantage in the area becoming a national park. I know Blackbutt Reserve and the adjoining land like the back of my hand because I played there as a boy."

"Overall public use of large parks went out of fashion 20 years ago. There has been a big reduction in the number of people who visit the Botanic Gardens in Sydney and make use of the long, scenic walks in the Blue Mountains," he said.

The Lord Mayor's layout plan for the area next to Blackbutt Reserve allows for home lots about 66 by 150 feet.

Roads Extended

Grandview, Queens and Addison Roads and Dunkley-avenue have been extended. Queen's-road and Dunkley-avenue to join with Lookout-road and Addison-road to meet Ridgeway-road.

Ald. Dunkley said he had planned six new parks in the subdivision, the largest being about 41 acres. A park fronting the proposed arterial road to be extended from Carnley-avenue would increase Blackbutt Reserve from 123 acres to 153 acres.

The school site was 7½ acres and next to one of the recreation areas, he said.

forward a third plan arguing for about 400 home sites with a seventy-five foot frontage.

Proposals To Develop Blackbutt Area

Development of Blackbutt reserve was the biggest sole proposition to be put before any council in the history of local government in Newcastle, Mr. J. Richley said last night.

Mr. Richley, who is President of the Northern Parks and Playgrounds Movement, was addressing Newcastle Council Works Committee.

He submitted two proposals for the area, which allowed for subdivision of part, but left the remainder as park space.

"I think you all know what we have been doing there in the past 18 months," he said. "This move seems to have the support of many organisations as a means of making Newcastle comparable to any oversea city, with its parks.

"It is important for its tourist attraction, for entertainment of the citizens, and the opening up of the health of the city," he said.

Mr. Richley's proposals provided for a subdivision of 150 blocks, which could sell for about £97,000, leaving a balance of £92,000 for development of the area, or a subdivision of 450 blocks, to sell at an estimated £247,000 which would leave some £215,500 for development.

Ald. McDougall said those who had prepared the plan should be congratulated on their work. They had gone among the citizens and inspired the city with the project. If more citizens had taken action such as this in the past, the City Council could have done mighty things.

"We have mucked about on this for years and years and got nowhere. We cannot go on procrastinating. A committee should be appointed to go into this."

Ald. Myers said it should be the responsibility of the Works Committee to do something, and then coopt others to reach finality.

The Lord Mayor (Ald. Dunkley) said he had a plan in preparation which was almost completed.

Special Meeting

The committee Chairman (Ald. Sheedy) said the committee should get all plans and hold a special meeting in a fortnight to go into them.

The City Engineer (Mr. Baddeley): This is not urgent enough to have men taken off other planning to have something ready in a fortnight.

Ald. McDougall: The people want to know what we are going to do, and it is their right to know.

Ald. Dunkley: Not even a half per cent. of the population of this city is interested. We sent out 6000 circulars for a meeting on this and 140 turned up.

Ald. McDougall: This has never been urgent.

Ald. Edwards: This has been frustrated all along. Let's have some action and do something.

Big Proposition

The Town Clerk (Mr. Burges) said that 270 acres next to the reserve was acquired only three years ago, and the council had adopted in principle a plan that envisaged extensive subdivision.

"We must consider this calmly and rationally. The council has a big proposition here. There are many difficulties on this proposition here to-night, including zoning."

Ald. Jones said he supported the idea in principle, but wanted to see enough land subdivided to ensure the development of the area. This was not the only park in Newcastle that required development and money spent on it.

The committee decided to hold a special meeting in a month to discuss all plans on the area.

Courtesy of the *NMH* (24 July 1959)

On 21 July 1959 the different plans were discussed at a special meeting of the NCC Works Committee. The members of the committee remained divided on the issue. Alderman Edwards agreed with the Lord Mayor that 'use of parkland was not the modern trend'. Alderman Sheedy argued that while he believed 'Newcastle deserved a park similar to the Sydney Centennial Park development', he felt that 'park development should be in one section not scattered over the area'. Alderman Jones' position was that 'he preferred to see only a limited number of residential lots sold and the rest remain as park'. Not surprisingly, given the divisions, the Committee decided to defer its decision. It argued that no decision should be made until after a council inspection. While the aldermen dithered, Tom kept up the pressure. In September he successfully moved a motion at the monthly meeting of the NPPM that 'failing a decision being reached by Council at the Works Council Meeting the executive of the Parks and Playgrounds Movement be empowered to reconvene the public meeting originally held in New Lambton on 4 June'. Tom was aware of the importance of public pressure on public officials especially with a council election set down for later in the year.

Clearly, the NPPM had to step up its efforts to win over various aldermen if its cause was to succeed. While there is no doubt that all members contributed, the task seems to have been left mainly to Joe Richley and Tom Farrell. In regards to the situation in 1959 Tom later recalled that:

> Joe Richley at one stage gave me a piece of paper with the aldermen's names to try and change the voting – and he has written down here 'it is necessary to get this alderman or that to support or be absent' – what we wanted was only a vote or two, and I've written on it – this alderman was interviewed and he will change his mind at the next meeting. These things had to be done on many occasions.

It appears that the men's efforts did not go unrewarded. By April 1959 all the Labour Aldermen were on side. But still the matter was not assured – one or two votes remained in the balance.

Finally on 17 November 1959 the NCC accepted in principle the proposal put forward by the Blackbutt Special

Committee that the whole of the 270 acres next to the existing reserve be put aside for a city park and botanical gardens. The vote had been close – the motion was carried by nine votes to eight. It was clear the matter was not over. Alderman Edwards, a supporter of Alderman Dunkley, immediately gave notice that he would move a rescission motion at the next council meeting. Alderman Myers supported the Lord Mayor's unsuccessful motion that 'the Flaggy Creek, Glenrock Lagoon area be developed as an alternative to Blackbutt'. Next an attempt was made to involve the Lands Minister asking him to use his statutory power to set aside the decision. He declined, clearly indicating that the State Government was in a mind to approve the proposal. On 1 December 1959 the Council after a long and acrimonious debate confirmed by eleven votes to nine its decision on principle to adopt the Blackbutt Reserve Special Committee's plan. In reporting the success to the members of the NPPM, Joe Richley expressed his deep gratitude for 'the strong support accorded our activities by the public in general and the citizen organisations in the Newcastle district'. Blackbutt Reserve, now 400 acres in size, had been achieved thanks to community action inspired by men like Joe Richley and Tom Farrell. Not one to rest on his laurels Joe Richley attempted unsuccessfully to regain his position as an alderman on NCC in the upcoming Local Government Elections. Running as an independent he advocated (among other things) 'the retention of Blackbutt Reserve'. He argued that 'it would be a tragedy if this glorious stretch of bushland is chopped down and cleared. It is at present owned by the people and should be retained for their use and enjoyment'.[10]

Over the next four years the new plan for the development of Blackbutt took shape guided by a Works Committee consisting of members from the Blackbutt Reserve Special

Blackbutt Extension Plan

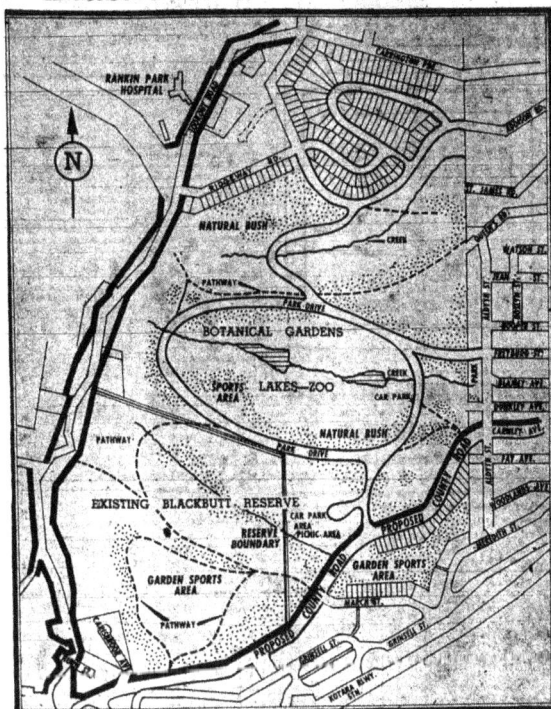

Courtesy of the *NMH* (24 October 1959)

Committee, the NPPM (including Joe Richley) and the Newcastle Division of the Town Planning Institute. Advice was sought from specialists and a number of permanent employees were appointed. Efforts were made to clear the scrub and plant a wide variety of Australian natives. In 1963 a more comprehensive plan was drawn up to examine the use of this 'extensive city park of great value' by various groups. It was envisaged that a series of sealed roads would link the various features including the botanic garden, open parkland, picnic area and animal enclosures featuring a koala breeding section. It was the opinion of Mr Earp, a member of the NPPM, that 'the new plan is comprehensive and almost visionary in its scope'.

Alderman Purdue, the Lord Mayor, believed that 'the reserve would be made available and enjoyed by and made attractive for hundreds of visitors as well as Newcastle citizens'. Tom would have been well pleased – his vision had now been realised. The natural beauty of Blackbutt Reserve was now preserved for all sections of the community to enjoy.

During this time Tom had acted as the Vice-President of the NPPM and an active member of the Management Committee. In June 1960 he joined Joe Richley on the Blackbutt Reserve Special Committee as a NPPM representative. In January 1961 when road work was proposed in the reserve, Tom quickly got on to the Council to ensure that 'before any action be taken in respect of the proposed road, the matter be referred to the Blackbutt Reserve Committee and also to the Special Committee set up by the Council to consider the overall plan for the development of Blackbutt'. As it turned out the gravel road was to be used to give workmen access to the reserve to clear

Good Progress At Blackbutt

Blackbutt Reserve would be a delightful leisure area for Newcastle citizens and visitors after a year, the Lord Mayor (Ald. Purdue) predicted yesterday.

In an inspection of the reserve yesterday, he showed progress being made on underscrubbing and burning off and the planting of native trees.

Newcastle City Council has planted 150 trees of different varieties in the reserve, including wattle, eucalypt and jacaranda.

In addition, berry-bearing trees, crabapples, lilly-pillies and others, have been placed in scattered positions to attract more birds.

At points accessible to the public, such as The Lookout and Grinsell-street, the council has cleared lantana and other undesirable undergrowth, burned off and planted young trees.

The new trees include several flowering shrubs to add colour to the natural bushland area.

Access Road

Ald. Purdue said that at the lookout in Charlestown-road lantana had been removed from the cliff face to enable steps to be built to permit people to reach an attractive cleared area.

The gravel road from The Lookout to Grinsell - street would be tarsealed next year and opened to provide public access to the middle of Blackbutt Reserve. Passing lanes would be provided to save the expense of a two-lane road.

The road would enable people to visit picnic areas to be provided at small dams built across natural watercourses.

The council proposed to erect a cottage in the future to accommodate a caretaker for the reserve.

"One of the caretaker's jobs will be to protect staghorns and elkhorns which we will put in the reserve. There used to be many in the bush, but people have pinched all but those on the highest trees," Ald. Purdue said.

Courtesy of the *NMH* (18 August 1961)

lantana bush. He also pressured the Council Management Committee to appoint a Parks Director as soon as possible so that one individual would be responsible for overseeing the development of all parks and playgrounds in the Newcastle region. Busy though he was with family and work, Tom did not shirk his responsibility to the community.[11]

Having fought so hard to make Blackbutt a reality, Tom was to be ever vigilant in defending what he and others had achieved. A further effort would be required in May 1963 when the Department of Education proposed to build a high school on twenty acres of the established reserve in an area between March and Aldyth Streets, Kotara. Mr Gelfius, the Newcastle Director of Education, informed the Council that 'he had been advised that an alternative site for a high school had been sought in vain'. The proposed area was the only site which was suitable in terms of its size, location and access to public transport. It was also well placed for feeder schools. Although the plan was opposed by

School Site In Reserve

The Department of Education says it has not been able to find an alternative high school site to land on the eastern edge of Blackbutt Reserve.

Map shows the area off March and Meredith Streets, Kotara, selected by the department for the proposed high school and playing fields.

The department told Newcastle City Council Works Committee this week that it could not find a second site as suitable in size, location and public transport services.

Council Against

The City Council does not want any part of Blackbutt Reserve used for purposes apart from open space.

It has strongly opposed the Department of Education's proposal and has asked that an alternative site for the high school be found.

The council Works Committee recommended a conference between Blackbutt Reserve Development Committee, the Department of Education and itself to discuss the school scheme.

Blackbutt Reserve Development Committee consists of the Works Committee and representatives of Blackbutt Reserve Special Committee, the Northern Parks and Playgrounds Movement, Newcastle Division of the Australian Planning Institute and Newcastle Flora and Fauna Protection Society.

The Town Clerk (Mr. Burges) told the Works Committee two questions involving Blackbutt Reserve had to be considered.—

● The council's attitude towards the Education Department's proposal to acquire land for a high school and sports areas.

● The scheme for overall development of the reserve.

Mr. Burges said the reserve development plan had been prepared by a sub-committee appointed by Blackbutt Reserve Development Committee.

Hard To Find

The Newcastle Director of Education (Mr. Gelfius) had advised that an alternative high school site had been sought in vain.

"You will appreciate the difficulty in securing such a large area of land with suitable terrain for a large secondary school and necessary playing fields.

"The Blackbutt Reserve site was chosen only after careful search," Mr. Gelfius said. "Because of advice received the department was encouraged to believe the proposed site might be made available for school purposes."

Though in Blackbutt Reserve, the area would be severed from the main reserve by a proposed extension of Carnley-avenue. In addition, the site was excellently placed for feeder schools and transport.

Mr. Burges said the layout plan for the development of Blackbutt Reserve was adopted in principle by the Works Committee last December.

The committee has suggested July 16 as the date for the conference.

BLACKBUTT RESERVE

PROPOSED HIGH SCHOOL SITE

Courtesy of the *NMH*
(5 July 1963)

the Council, the NPPM left nothing to chance – it immediately notified the Northumberland County Council that it opposed in principle 'the filching of parkland' by the Department of Education. Working in conjunction with Newcastle Flora and Fauna Protection Society, the NSW National Park Association, the Northumberland Council of Progress Associations, the NPPM pressured the Lord Mayor, Alderman Purdue, to call a public meeting at the Town Hall on 31 July 1963. At the meeting attended by about 200 people, Joe Richley called into question the Department of Education's efforts to find an alternate site – he advised the group that 'representatives of the NPPM and the Department of Education had inspected three alternative sites. Two were satisfactory and were being further investigated by the department'. While most speakers (including the Lord Mayor) supported the stand taken by NPPM, Mr Wheeler, the President of the Newcastle Parents & Citizens Associations (P & Cs), was strongly opposed. He spoke at length in defence of the Department of Education's actions arguing that: 'people at the meeting should represent human beings – children – and not koala bears, insects and birds'. He went on to challenge Joe Richley 'to tell us how many people he saw in Blackbutt Reserve last time he inspected it?' He concluded 'a high school will be used for the advancement of 1000 children'. Despite such opposition, the meeting overwhelmingly supported a motion that the NCC protest to the Minister of Local Government about the proposal of the Department of Education. Tom followed up this initiative by successfully moving a motion at the next monthly meeting of the NPPM that the group write 'to individual P & Cs asking their views in regard to the construction of schools, either Private or State Schools on Public Park Lands. Also advising P & Cs that this Movement would send representatives to their meetings to address them on this subject'. Clearly Tom had not been impressed by the position taken by Mr Wheeler at the public meeting and saw that direct action was the way to educate P & C Associations about the importance of public parkland. The stand taken by the NPPM was vindicated – in September 1963 the Minister of Education, Mr Wetherell, announced that no part of Blackbutt Reserve would be used for a secondary school and that another site would be found for the proposed Kotara High School. The response from Joe Richley, on behalf of the NPPM, was that 'the Minister's decision was welcomed; it justified the many protests made against the move to site a high school in Blackbutt Reserve'.[12]

Although there was still much to be done, it was clear that steps had been taken to implement a development program for Blackbutt Reserve. There was a degree of optimism about Blackbutt - Mr Bob Power, a member of the NPPM, told the *Newcastle Sun* in January 1964:

> Speaking personally I believe in the future of Blackbutt and it should be the common aim of all citizens to guard this prized heritage for in future years such a magnificent open space will play an important part in the cultural and recreational advancement of our city. Past history indicates that many overseas industrial cities are regretting the fact that trees have been removed over previous years and are now busily engaged in extensive regeneration schemes to compensate for past errors. Let our policy then be 'hands off Blackbutt'.

Like Joe Richley, Bob Power was a good mate of Tom Farrell who worked tirelessly for the 'Save Blackbutt' movement. A member of the New Lambton Branch of the ALP, Power was later identified by Tom as a figure who played an important part in frustrating the subdivision of the reserve by the council.

The development program at Blackbutt had resulted in the removal of much of the lantana, 'the pestiferous weed', that had spread throughout the four valleys and intervening ridges that made up Blackbutt. As Philipp Short later pointed out, this restoration work proved to be a great success – by 1966 even the experts were surprised how much ground cover and natural brush had been restored. In the southern section a native plant valley had been established with provision for graded walking trails. Native bush species had been reintroduced including red ash, rosewoods, hibiscus and omalanthus. A five acre rain forest had also been established with a section devoted to Hunter Valley brush trees and another to North Coast and Queensland brush species. A third area of twenty five acres contained a dry scherophyll forest with mostly spotted gums and smooth barked angophoras. The fourth natural vegetation area featured Blackbutt trees among ferns and other plants common to coastal bush gullies. The adjoining valley had been set aside for natural bush which was only disturbed by a number of fire trails. The third valley with an open area with a small mine was intended as the site for the botanical gardens and koala regeneration park. The rest of Blackbutt was intended as open forest with provision for watering facilities, public utilities and a caretaker's cottage. Such was the beauty of the area that it was described in 1966 as a 'Little Eden, an enchanting bushland which could be counted as one of the city's blessings'. It is clear that Tom and the other members of the NPPM took their role in ensuring the proper development of Blackbutt Reserve very seriously. The NPPM Minute Book contains various Commonwealth and State reports which provided information on current best practice in national parks. The group was also keen to regularly invite expert guest speakers to their meetings. In this way the membership became better informed on a range of issues and better able to engage in the public debate. It was this expertise that allowed Tom and the other members of the NPPM to speak with such authority in defence of the environment for so many years. Throughout 1965-1966 the NPPM continued to pressure the Council to fully implement its development plan for Blackbutt. [13]

Such expertise would be needed in 1966 when Blackbutt Reserve came under direct threat from the NSW Department of Main Roads (DMR). In August of this year the NCC agreed in principle to the construction of a six-lane expressway through part of Blackbutt Reserve. It is clear that Tom had identified a year earlier that the expansion of main roads in the Newcastle region could pose a threat to public park land. The minutes of the March 1965 NPPM Meeting detail a report given by Tom on 'The Position Regarding Main Roads Through Speers Point Park'. Two successful motions (both put forward by Tom) resulted from the tabling of this report – the first (seconded by Doug Lithgow) dealt with the calling of a public meeting to oppose the construction of main roads through Speers Point Park, the second (seconded by Sladen) involved the NPPM 'writing to the Main Roads Board asking them to supply the details of all proposed roads which encroach on land zoned as park land in the County of Cumberland'. An unidentified source made an annotation in the minutes regarding this motion – it reads 'this is the first blow by NPPM re the Expressway through Blackbutt Reserve proposal which surfaced publicly in August 1966'. It was Tom Farrell who delivered this first blow with the unanimous support of the NPPM. He did not have long to wait to find that his suspicions about the DMR were warranted.

The NCC had agreed to a five year plan (costing $3 million) which would result in a twenty acre area of Blackbutt Reserve being taken up by the proposed road running for three quarters of a mile through its western quarter. The road linking Tickhole Tunnel to the New Lambton area near Rankin Park Hospital, was to cut through three of the four main valleys which made up the reserve. While not all aldermen had approved of the Council's decision, the Lord Mayor, Alderman McDougall, was a strong advocate. It was his opinion that the motorway through Blackbutt (which only affected 'a relative small section of the reserve') would result in much quicker travel times between various suburbs in Newcastle. Furthermore, it would prevent the demolition of a large number of homes if an alternate route was found and it would open the city up to further tourism development. Clearly, the Lord Mayor had been successful in convincing the majority of the aldermen that the motorway project was 'in the city's interest'.

It was clear Tom and the other members of the NPPM had a real fight on their hands. The NPPM made it clear from the outset that it opposed the DMR's proposal because it contravened the road system proposed by the Northumberland Planning Scheme in 1955. The Northumberland County District Planning Scheme maps had been proclaimed by the Minister for Local Government in December 1960. Under this scheme County Road 23 was not a six-lane expressway carving its way through the reserve but an arterial road running along the escarpment. As Tom later explained, the proposed County Road 23 was 'accepted without protest by the citizens of Newcastle' because it only impinged on the perimeter of the reserve rather than destroying its main features. Throughout the controversy Tom and the NPPM did not deviated from their resolve to see a return to the original County Scheme. As Tom stated publically in 1974 before the House of Representatives Standing Committee 'I have always supported the legal and proclaimed existing road'. It was his view that over fifteen years of planning and preparation, road design, property resumptions and advice to developers it had understood that this would be the route.

Doug Lithgow, Secretary of the NPPM, announced that 'the movement would resist the proposed destruction of the reserve'. It was the view of the NPPM that the motorway was nothing more than 'a scar' which would cut through the Blackbutt area totally destroying its environment. The NPPM supported the view of Alderman May (who announced his intention to put forward a rescission motion) that the Council had betrayed the city by simply 'rubber-stamping' the DMR's proposal without proper consideration of the alternatives. In support of this conclusion Alderman Bassan later argued that the Council had made a 'deal' with the DMR 'so that the scheme was "bulldozed through" with only four aldermen dissenting'. Lithgow summed up the view of the NPPM: 'I am very disappointed that the City Council backed the proposal instead of leading the fight against the proposal on behalf of the citizens – but there will be one'. To this end, the NPPM joined forces with the recently formed Blackbutt Reserve Action Committee (BAC) to organise public opposition to the motorway. Joe Richley told the *NMH* that:

> The Northern Parks and Playgrounds Movement would use all its resources to oppose the Main Roads Department proposal. The department should find an alternative proposal instead of proceeding to cut a 180ft gash deep through three prominent ridges and the rich flora heads of three valleys. The reserve must be preserved because in the future it would

act as 'fresh air lungs' of the city and thus have an immeasurable benefit from a health viewpoint. The people would prefer to have it as such an asset than have a highway creating atmospheric pollution.

The NPPM was quick to enlist the assistance of other state bodies. Mr Rod Earp, past President of the National Parks Association of NSW, told the *Herald* that 'just how would the motorway affect the scheme? One may as well ask what Venus would look like if you replaced her vital statistics with a bag of cement'. It was his view that 'this is not a case of just another piece of parkland being used for roadway purposes, it is a case of the destruction of an asset that is of the highest value and is irreplaceable'.

At a public protest meeting held on the 21 September attended by 500 people Alderman May, the Chairman of the BAC, told the crowd that he was 'gaged' when he attempted to discuss the proposal at the recent council meeting. It was his view that when the aldermen took into account the alternate routes, there would be enough support on the Council to overturn the recent decision. Mr Dick Woodgate, Secretary of the Action Committee, reported that several hundred people had signed a petition opposing the proposal. Mr G. Duncan, President of Newcastle Teachers' College, unanimously moved a motion that 'the reserve be retained undisturbed as parkland'. It was Duncan's view that 'we want the whole of Blackbutt. It is a precious heritage for our children'. Joe Richley pointed out that 'a motorway would destroy the visual effects of the reserve'. Doug Lithgow argued that 'there is too much confusion about what is proposed for Blackbutt'. Although Alderman McDougall's attempted to persuade the crowd to his position, he did not succeed – a motion was carried to establish a Standing Committee from the BAC, NPPM, Flora and Fauna Society and the Planning Institute 'to carry out the resolutions and report back to another public meeting'. The battle had been joined.

At the September meeting of the NPPM Tom was keen to keep the momentum going. He successfully moved a motion (seconded by Lithgow) that 'the Blackbutt Reserve Action Committee arrange a deputation of a representative body of Newcastle citizens to wait on the Premier regarding the threatened destruction of Blackbutt Reserve by a motorway proposal by the Department of Main Roads'. As always Tom saw the value of political action in furthering a cause. Messrs Munro, Lithgow and Richley were the representatives of the NPPM on the BAC. He also successfully moved a motion (seconded by Davies) that the NPPM invite all the members of the Council to visit the reserve the following Sunday. No doubt he hoped that the aldermen could be persuaded to reverse their decision when they confronted the beauty of the area. When the aldermen and the DMR divisional engineer, Mr Hope, did visit in October Tom made clear that there were plenty of 'Save Blackbutt' supporters to greet them. At the same time the NPPM joined forces with the Northumberland Council of Progress Associations and East Lakes Council of Progress Associations to lobby the Premier, Mr Askin, to oppose the plan. It is clear that Tom felt betrayed by the political pundits in Sydney. In a strongly worded letter to the *SMH* which the paper refused to publish Tom vented his anger against the Premier:

> preoccupied as Mr Askin may be he would be unwise
> to lightly disregard a massive protest meeting held in
> Newcastle on 21 September…It is well known that
> Mr Askin does not usually attach much importance

to public opinion north of Hornsby, but the manifestation of wrath and disapproval of the people of Newcastle against a stupid act of vandalism in the destruction of their botanical gardens should be carefully looked at…Blackbutt is Newcastle's most prized natural possession. If the land had not been purchased by the Councils it would have now all be covered with homes, schools and churches. If this had been the case the highway would have been routed elsewhere. It looks as though Newcastle people have been keeping their reserve in trust for the Main Roads Board. The whole proposal is preposterous. Sydney would not tolerate the destruction of their botanical gardens. Why should Newcastle suffer this fate?

The political action seems to have had some effect. In December 1966 the Minister of Local Government and Highways informed his colleagues in the Legislative Assembly that he had instructed the DMR to review its road planning in Newcastle. He had reached this decision after receiving a large number of protests about the proposed motorway. While the news was welcomed by the BAC and the NPPM there was to be no let-up in the protest action. The DMR and the Lord Mayor seemed far from convinced that an alternate route needed to be found. At a special meeting of the NPPM held in March 1967 Tom and the other members present reaffirmed the view that 'Blackbutt Reserve was so important that it must be preserved in its entirety as shown in the Blackbutt Plan adopted by Council in 1963'. The battle was to continue.[14]

In May 1967 the BAC put forward an alternative route which had the motorway skirting the western edge of the reserve with only slight encroachment passing under Lookout Road. As Messrs Barnett and Woodgate, representatives of the BAC, pointed out 'the proposed route would take the motorway above the cliff face overlooking Blackbutt and keep it out of the best part of the reserve'. They conceded that 'encroachment could occur on the existing lookout and parking area if it had to, so long as the road was generally above the reserve and could be screened with trees from valleys within the reserve'. At the same time Mr Hope reported that the DMR was examining up to thirteen different routes and methods of construction. Included in these was the Marshall Street Route which involved the demolition of seventy-nine houses, a church, two schools and a hall in Garden Suburb. Although much more expensive than the proposed route it had significantly less impact on the reserve. Another involved a tunnel under the existing Hunter District Water Board reservoir costing $20.7 million. However, Mr Hope made it clear that the alternate routes (including the Marshall Street Route) were 'out of the question because of the unsatisfactory gradients, excessive costs and the large number of houses to be demolished'. The DMR remained of the view that 'the route it preferred went through the middle of the reserve gave good gradients and would cost only $3.3 million'.

In light of the Minister's announcement and the subsequent investigations of the DMR, the Council was now under increasing pressure to reconsider its position. At an acrimonious Council meeting in March 1967 the aldermen voted 11-10 to allow further discussion of the issue. The vote was taken only after Aldermen McDougal, the Lord Mayor, threaten to clear the packed public gallery if the interjections did not stop. The decisive vote took place on 4 July 1967. Before a packed public gallery and after a long two hour debate the aldermen voted 15-4 against an amendment that would have seen the Council support the alternate proposal put forward by the BAC. The aldermen then reaffirmed (on the voices) their support for the original DMR proposal. The 'stunned 'Save Blackbutt' supporters' (including Tom) were soon to realise the significance of this vote. It served to shield the Minister and the DMR from criticism – both could argue that the motorway would go through with the approval of the NCC. Far from defeated, the NPPM's responded by mustering as much political pressure as possible. The group went back to the Minister to argue its case. By August 1968 there was at least some positive news – Richley reported to his members that 'at the moment the issue is at Ministerial level and the Minister for Local Government and Highways, Hon. Mr Morton, is showing real interest and has assured us that no decision will be made until he has discussed the matter with a joint deputation of the Newcastle Chamber of Commerce, the Blackbutt Action Committee and the Movement'. As Watson points out, the scene was now set for the next two and a half years with 'the controversy over the future of Blackbutt waging on with alternate proposals, inspections and discussions'.[15]

As a means of increasing the political pressure the BAC canvassed all the candidates in the upcoming Local Government election set for November 1968 as to their position in regard to the proposed motorway. One of the candidates was Mr R. E. Farrell who had decided to run as a 'Citizen Group' candidate for Central Ward. Clearly Tom was hoping to influence public policy (particularly in regard to Blackbutt Reserve) by having a voice on council. His election would also strengthen Alderman Bassan's stand within the 'Citizen Group' in favour of an alternate route and hopefully persuade other aldermen within the group like the Lord Mayor, Alderman McDougall, and

Alderman Purdue to their position. As the second candidate on the 'Citizen Group' ticket for Central Ward Tom explained to the voters that 'the main reason for submitting myself as a candidate is my concern with the attempt by the Department of Main Roads to destroy Blackbutt Reserve'. He made it clear that he would resist 'to the full' any attempt by the DMR to alienate Blackbutt '. Although his candidature was supported by a number of eminent citizens including Joe Richley and Griffith Duncan, Tom failed to be elected (see Chapter 7). It would be left to Alderman Bassan to try to muster support against the proposed motorway among his fellow 'Citizen Group' aldermen on the Newcastle Council. Tom would continue his activism as a private citizen.

Matters took a turn for the worse in April 1970 when the DMR announced that it was reconsidering the Marshall Street Route. Faced with the possibility of losing their homes, a number of supporters of the 'Save Blackbutt' campaign formed a splinter group which effectively divided the protest movement. The Motorway 23 Protest Committee took as their slogan 'Houses Before Trees!'. The Editor of the NMH highlighted the dilemma facing the protest movement:

> The motorway must either cut through the western section of the Blackbutt Reserve or, according to an alternate proposal now revealed, cut a swath through one of Newcastle's best residential areas. The hostile reaction of property owners was predictable. That plan can be dismissed. Blackbutt Reserve is an oasis in metropolitan Newcastle. That will be its function as it develops as a northern capital. Year by year appreciation intensifies as the idyllic contrast to the nearby city is identified. It would be unfair to

charge planning officers of the Department of Main
Roads with lack of appreciation of the reserve…
If the reserve is to be sacrosanct – and for this its
potential through the distinctive foliage and trees
of its valleys has to be appreciated – the conflict of
wishes between the Department and the community
would be at a deadlock.

The Editor's solution was that 'a compromise might have to
be by acceptance of a motorway, following approximately
the present route with a widening of established roads but
without allowance for a 60-mile-an-hour traffic flow. Since
road traffic will double in approximately a decade, an expedient
solution would not be entirely satisfactory. Newcastle might be
compelled to accept judgement by an independent authority,
worthy of respect in investigation and determination'.

Despite the *Herald's* best efforts, the matter dragged on. In
October 1970 the Council considered once again a rescission
motion on the original 1966 proposal. It responded by deferring
any further consideration of the motorway until a further date.
This led to further protest meetings – in December 1970 a
meeting of New Lambton Heights' residents condemned the
proposed route demanding that the motorway be rerouted
around the western side of Lake Macquarie. Later that month Mr
Morton bowed to public pressure announcing that no decision
would be made on the highway before a public meeting was
called to discuss the matter. In February 1971 Tom (writing
as a member of the Blackbutt Reserve Committee and the
NPPM) felt compelled to enter the fray again. In a long letter
to the *NMH* he attacked those who supported the DMR's plan
questioning 'whether they have any real interest in protecting
a small part of the natural beauty of Newcastle'. Referring to

Blackbutt as 'the most prized natural asset in Newcastle' Tom made an impassioned plea:

> We have had to resist many efforts to subdivide and build schools at Blackbutt. It is understandable that this free area in the heart of Newcastle should be looked upon greedily by public authorities or other vested interests…The curious attitude of the Main Roads Board that parklands in Newcastle are fair game for them must be curbed and the only person who can do this is the Premier (Mr Askin). We know he does not relish spending money in Newcastle, but surely if he was prepared to find $25 million for the three miles of the Warringah Expressway he could find the relatively small amount to pay for one of the alternate routes and thus retain for Newcastle one of its most prized possessions.

This was vintage Tom returning to a familiar theme – attacking the Sydney authorities for their centralism while reminding them of their civic duty to Newcastle.   In June 1971 Tom joined with 800 fellow protestors to let Mr Morton know their view – at a meeting at the Town Hall organised by the NPPM it was unanimously resolved that 'no expressway should enter Blackbutt or the land owned by the NCC contiguous to it'. Mr Walker, the Director of the National Trust, commented that he found it incredible that the people of Newcastle would contemplate allowing an expressway through Blackbutt Reserve. The Secretary of the BAC, Mr Woodgate, told the assembled crowd that 'the proposed highway would be a monstrosity that would cut Newcastle like a river'. It appeared the Minister had had his answer. The Secretary of the NPPM, Doug Lithgow, said that 'only constant vigilance would save Blackbutt'. Given that this was the fifth meeting to protest at proposals to reduce the area of public recreation land in Blackbutt, the NPPM posed the following question 'how many more meetings must there be before our local government representatives get the message that this is one of the most valuable assets the city has and its value increases by leeps and bounds as time passes?'.[16]

Throughout 1972-1973 the NPPM continued to apply pressure. Tom provided an insight into his role as a lobbyist when he gave evidence to the Select Committee in 1974. When asked 'Have you made representations to the Council?', he responded 'Dozens of times'. Asked about the Council's response to his representations on behalf of the Blackbutt Reserve Committee he responded 'we have been ignored and I think some of us resented it. We feel that there should be greater consultation between the Council and ourselves, in view of the fact that we are appointed under a special provision of the Greater Newcastle Act'. Although clearly frustrated by the response of the Council, Tom explained that he remained on the Committee 'for one purpose only, to act as a sort of watch dog'. He did so because 'we are absolutely opposed to through traffic going through the reserve. There has been a lot of excellent development in the reserve that we applaud and are very happy about, but being citizens of worth, we think, we would like the Council to consult us and talk to us about it. We feel this is a very good thing for everybody'. Tom was not shy about putting forward his views to the Council. His papers contain the following strongly worded letter to an alderman dated 28 May 1972:

> What you are doing is setting up this city for the
> Labour boys to take over. In deference to public

opinion you should reconsider your attitude. You represent us in the Council and surely your views should be at least considered by you. Have you thoroughly looked into the Blackbutt question or have you been guided entirely by the engineer? I, in all my experience have never witnessed such strength in any public issue. I don't think the people of Newcastle are in the mood to accept the situation where you give Blackbutt away without a thorough reappraisal and get together of the citizens and the Council. Think it over quietly, you are in a position that your vote will either save or destroy Blackbutt.

Tom did not just single out the Labour aldermen for criticism. He later pointed out that the 'Save Blackbutt' campaign had received very little help from the aldermen whatever their political affiliation. Tom was not alone in his criticism of the NCC. The Editor of the *NMH* pointed out:

Most of the public's disquiet about Blackbutt has been directed to Newcastle City Council. But the DMR is making most of the rules, bowling the tricky balls, hitting the opposition out of the ground and keeping score. Not surprisingly it is winning on points. Not so the council – revealed as initially hasty, indecisive in the middle term and finally bereft of incentive or initiative. The council had the opportunity to search out more public information from the DMR. It has not done so. It had the opportunity to temper and mollify public disquiet. It has found only enmity. Given the opportunity to demonstrate leadership and generate respect, it has acted petulantly at times and with scant respect for the intelligence of its critics.

In spite of his misgivings, Tom had no choice but to work with the Council to find a solution to the Blackbutt issue. By the end of 1972 there were seventeen different proposals that the DMR had investigated. Included among these was a plan by the Resident Action Committee to abolish the motorway in its entirety. Mr Brown, the Hunter Divisional Engineer, rather ironically told the NMH that 'no two miles of road anywhere in Australia had been investigated as thoroughly'.

Tom and the other members of the NPPM Management Committee continued to battle away. In Joe Richley's words, 'they pursued a vigorous campaign to convince the custodians of public reserves of the need for the highest moral obligation in the care and use of public reserves'. Such effort brought some success – on 28 March 1972 the Council passed a rescission motion opposing the Blackbutt route. But the deep divisions within the Council were soon evident. On 8 May 1972 Alderman Purdue, a former Lord Mayor, expressed his disappointment with the 28 March decision:

> Now the 'tumult and the shouting' have subsided I think it is appropriate to review dispassionately the amazing 15 votes to 6 decision on March 28 by Newcastle Council apparently with the object of pandering to a very large pressure group…in the interests of the city and its people and those who have to visit it daily with excessive delays and unnecessary accidents, I hope the Minister for Local Government with his usual sound judgement will decide to proceed with the only satisfactory route

so thoroughly planned and commenced by the Department of Main Roads.

Not surprisingly, Tom felt that Alderman Purdue's comments should not go unanswered. In a strongly worded letter he pointed out that:

No one can deny that Alderman Purdue has had a tremendous influence on civic leadership in Newcastle for many years. It is a great pity however at this stage of his career he is intent on the destruction of Blackbutt. Instead of castigating citizens as pressure groups would it not be more correct to say that they are people with a vision for the future. The County Plan proclaimed and accepted years ago by the Council has now been endorsed by a big majority. Why not accept the situation? Is Alderman Purdue setting himself up as a 'Pressure Group? The discredited intrusion into Blackbutt provides for a 65 mile an hour road instead of a 45 hour road as per the County Plan. Alderman Purdue would agree that the main killers on the road are alcohol and speed. Peats Ridge is a shining example. Main Roads experts gave a 65 miles per hour speed. Many people lost their lives. Common sense and pressure made them bring the permitted speed back to 45 and of consequence a great reduction (was made) in accidents and deaths. Alderman Purdue says the proposed motorway caters primarily for motorists between Swansea and Charlestown whose destination is the city or industrial centres. It is absurd to consider that the destruction of Blackbutt would assist these folks…

The argument put forward that to destroy Blackbutt will permit the free flow of traffic to the Industries and the City is nonsense. The savings in time of the short journey through Blackbutt would save one minute in time whether you are going to the City, to the Industries or to Brisbane.

Unfortunately for Tom there were a significant number of aldermen who shared Alderman Purdue's misgivings. At the Council meeting on the 15 May 1973, notice was given that a motion to rescind the rescission motion of the 28 March would be put at the next meeting. This effectively would put the Blackbutt Route back on the agenda. Tom immediately made his views known:

> Newcastle Council holds Blackbutt in trust for the citizens. It should respect our wishes. The deplorable and questionable tactics as evidenced at the council meeting on May 15 fills us with dismay...It is rubbish to say that the route through Blackbutt is the practicable one. If this part of Newcastle was completely undeveloped, if there was no Blackbutt Reserve and no homes or industries, the proposed route through the heart of Blackbutt would be the last one considered. It still would not be considered if it contained an industry or supermarket. It is filched because it is parkland. How absurd is it that civic minded citizens in having Blackbutt reserved almost 40 years ago now find all they achieved was to keep it on ice for the DMR. Alderman Dalton no doubt speaking with tongue in cheek stated that a decision should be made in the interest of

the majority of citizens. If he really feels that way, I challenge Alderman Dalton to admit the subject to referendum. This is a democracy in its true form. No one has fought harder than I to retain this haven for the people of Newcastle, but I would accept without question the decision of the people of Newcastle.

Tom, however, was not to get his plebiscite. On the 30 May 1973 the Council voted 11-10 to reverse the rescission motion, confirming its previous 1966 decision to support the motorway through Blackbutt. Within a week of this setback Tom and Joe Richley were back at Blackbutt with the Lord Mayor pressing the case for an alternate route. This strategy seems to have had an impact - Alderman McDougall told the press that 'we were especially looking at alternate routes to the one suggested and it is pretty obvious that it is not impossible to adopt an alternate route'. In order to keep the momentum going, the NPPM produced a 'Save Blackbutt' pamphlet in July 1973 which was distributed widely. In it the group argued that 'for many city and suburban people whose daily lives are enmeshed in an urban existence, the Reserve provides an easily accessible source of Australiana – the bushland, with its trees and flowers, birdlife and insects, ferns and fungi. It is a peaceful escape from the noise and rush of a city – a place of recreation and relaxation for humans. For these reasons alone Blackbutt Reserve should remain inviolate'.

In September 1972 Tom's partner in arms, Joe Richley, retired from the presidency of the NPPM. In recognition of his mate's years of service Tom moved a motion that 'Mr Joe Richley be appointed a life member of the movement'. This motion was carried by acclamation. It was in this position that Joe Richley was to continue the fight to save Blackbutt. The Minutes of the

September Meeting of the NPPM record the following details: 'Mr Rolf Farrell then made a presentation to Mr Richley as a token of the esteem in which he was held by the membership. Mr Farrell remarks were supported by Messer Shields, Lithgow and Dews. Mr Richley then replied, expressing his appreciation of the presentation and the complimentary remarks. He was given a standing ovation by the members present'. This was a fitting tribute for a man who was one of the founding fathers of the conservation movement in Newcastle.

The equivocation and vacillation of the council did little to settle public disquiet. Blackbutt Reserve remained under threat. With the Marshall Street Route still on the table, the opponents to the motorway remained divided. The DMR with its ongoing support on Council, its emphasis on cost-savings and its ability to play one group off against the other, was still in a position to finally win the day. This was the view of Philipp Short, Staff Writer for the *NMH*, in March 1973. In a long opinion piece he argued:

> Over the running of things the aldermen managed to whip up perhaps the biggest local government hullabaloo in Newcastle this century, nobody would answer the public's questions, nobody would show them plans, nobody (of any importance) would let them talk about the motorway as a whole... The conservation forces gathered two groups, the Northern Parks and Playgrounds Movement (ironically formed to safeguard open space under the Northumberland scheme) and the Blackbutt Preservation Society, set up to oversee the development of the area. Until 1970 the Blackbutt Action Committee (as the combined group was

called) battled on bravely. Then in a brilliant political manoeuvre, the DMR came up with the old Marshall Street alternative and its threat to about 50 homes. Immediately another group appeared intent on the preservation of homes and for two crucial years the conservation and anti-motorway forces were split. With the introduction of the Resident Action Committee's more contemporary opposition to the motorway in its entirety, the conservation forces were further fragmented. In fact, the Save Blackbutt forces were perhaps the most luckless of all. Their battle was fought at a time when progress was still measured entirely in dollars and concrete, expressways and cars. If the matter was introduced for the first time tomorrow they would have some chance of winning. Current theories by many planners suggest that the age of expressways is past. Given another six years to fight the battle, the conservationists would win. But it would seem in 1973 that only an act of God or a Federal move will stop Motorway 23 going through Blackbutt. Newcastle is about to enter the expressway era as most modern cities are looking for a way out. It has not exactly been a painless entry.

Such comments clearly show how close Newcastle came to losing 'the jewel' that was Blackbutt. It survived because 'citizens of worth' like Tom Farrell refused to give up the struggle despite the many difficulties involved. Such determination was to be finally rewarded.

Shortly after meeting Tom and Joe Richley in May 1973, the Lord Mayor announced that he welcomed a Federal Government study into Blackbutt and the motorway. Alderman

McDougall was responding to the announcement by the Federal Minister for Urban and Regional Development, Mr Uren, that he had made a strong case to the Federal Minister for the Environment and Conservation that there should be an inquiry into the matter. Uren had informed the local Federal Member, Alderman Peter Morris, that it was necessary to refer the Blackbutt matter to a Standing Committee of the House of Representatives 'to provide the necessary nucleus for a study of the social and environmental impact of freeway development'. If the findings of the committee were adverse then the future of the motorway through Blackbutt would be in doubt. Alderman McDougall explained to the press that the Federal Government was legally entitled to hold such an enquiry if it was providing funds for the project. As Short predicted it was a 'Federal move' that now held out some hope that Blackbutt could be saved.[17]

Blackbutt study welcome, says McDougall

An environmental inquiry on the route of Motorway 23 through Blackbutt Reserve would be welcomed, the Lord Mayor (Ald McDougall) said yesterday.

"I would definitely like to see a study made of the route and its alternatives — and the sooner the better," he said.

"I made a study of the reserve myself this morning," he said. "I went with Mr R. E. Farrell and Mr Joe Richley, of the Northern Parks and Playgrounds Movement.

"We were specially looking at alternative routes to the one suggested and it is pretty obvious it is not impossible to adopt an alternative route," he said.

Ald McDougall was commeting on a statement that the Federal Government was likely to make the Motorway 23 route through Blackbutt a test case on the future of urban expressways.

The Minister for Urban and Regional Development (Mr Uren) has made a strong plea to the Minister for Environment and Conservation (Dr Cass) for an inquiry.

In a letter to Ald Morris, MHR, Mr Uren said by referring Blackbutt to the standing committee on en-

vironment and conservation the Government would provide the necessary nucleus for a study of the social and environmental impact of freeway development.

Ald McDougall said he understood the Commonwealth could make an inquiry into the motorway route if it were providing funds for the project.

"Otherwise, I understand it is up to the State Government," he said.

"I am sure those opposed to the motorway route

would welcome any inquiry.

"Further consideration will be given to the matter by Mr Richley and his group following our inspection today.

"I can assure the public that our minds are not closed one way or another. We want to know that the right thing is being done for the reserve," Ald McDougall said.

Ald McDougall said the "we" referred to those people inside and outside Newcastle City Council who were not satisfied with the DMR route through the reserve.

Ald McDougall made his statement in face of the council decision on May 30 to allow the Motorway 23 route through the reserve. The decision, by 11 votes to 10, reversed a rescission motion of March 28, 1972, opposing the Blackbutt route and confirmed an original 1966 decision by the council.

ALD McDOUGALL

Courtesy of the *NMH* (2 June 1973)

The House of Representatives Standing Committee on Environment and Conservation began its hearings at the University of Newcastle on 16 March 1974. On behalf of the Blackbutt Reserve Committee Mr J. Richley and Mr R.E. Farrell made the following submission:

> Blackbutt is our major park; it has been preserved for decades for public recreation. The NSW Gazette No. 36 of 4 March 1938 set out clearly that the area is resumed under the Public Works Act 1912 for the following public purpose as a Public Recreation Ground at Blackbutt, Cardiff Heights. This set the seal on the area for retention as a Public Reserve.
>
> Blackbutt is unique. Three quarters or more of Blackbutt Reserve contains about sixteen native tree species. In the special zones with less than one quarter of the total area, a further sixty-six native grown trees species are listed. This specialised forest community cannot be replaced just anywhere.
>
> The Reserve is used extensively by school children as far afield as Armidale, Denman and Wahronga for study purposed in Biology, Botany, Geology and general ecology. Approximately 1200 children attend on average each week.
>
> Large numbers of people and smaller children frequent the Reserve particularly during the winter months. For example, one Sunday approximately eighteen months ago, the Blackbutt Action Committee took up a petition to present to the Councils and some 6000 signatures were obtained in the Reserve that day. This type of attendance is

not uncommon. So there is no question as to its popularity by young and old alike…

Without the action of citizens and sympathetic local councils of 40 years ago, the whole of this area would now be covered with homes and industry. It was saved for posterity, why at this late hour does the Main Roads Board want to change a road plan to drive deep into the heart of Blackbutt.

We strongly urge that the area known as Blackbutt be retained for all time for the citizens, not only of Newcastle, but the whole of Australia.

In support of this submission, the Blackbutt Action Committee published a lengthy treatise entitled 'Save Blackbutt: The Case Against State Highway 23 Violating Blackbutt Reserve' which argued that the proposed motorway would have an adverse impact on the social and environmental fabric of the Newcastle region:

Cities should be designed for people to live in and emphasis must be given to the varied and many interests of the citizens. Transport is important but the emphasis and type of transport changes from time to time. Parks have always been very important and at no time has there been any change or reduction in the need for parks. The trend is, in fact, in the other direction, and, as cities become more and more congested the need for parks becomes more and more pressing, particularly as leisure time grows more extensive. Accordingly, it should be a principle that nothing should be allowed to interfere with any park.

We have shown you what a long and intense

struggle it has been to acquire Blackbutt Reserve and to keep it. We have explained what the proposal means and how it was introduced to Newcastle Council in an unusual manner. We have shown the defects of the Expressway and the absence of town planning information and planning required for such an expressway. We have shown something of the information which is required. We have shown, and in this respect we have weighty support from town planners, that the proper route for the Expressway is west of Lake Macquarie and Newcastle. We trust that what has been said in this case will result in much deeper consideration being given to the proposed Expressway and to other expressways which may be constructed in the future in New South Wales.

The Blackbutt Reserve Committee submitted that the new road should be built according to the original approved roadway (Highway 23) as set out in the Northumberland Planning Scheme, to which there had been no objections. As Richley and Farrell pointed out in their submission:

> Included in this Planning Scheme were details of State Highway 23. The DHR in 1945 produced an atlas which provided for an arterial road system mainly for Newcastle and Lake Macquarie. SH 23 was shown in this as part of the system and both the Newcastle City Council and the Shire Council concurred with the plan. Again when the County Scheme was being prepared between 1949 and 1952 the DHR scheme was incorporated and placed on Public Exhibition in July 1952. After dealing with

objections it was again placed on exhibition in 1955 no objections to the route of SH 23 were received from any source.

The Blackbutt Reserve Committee never at any time made any objection to the SH 23 as included in the County Plan. SH 23 did take certain areas of Blackbutt on the perimeter.

The Blackbutt Reserve Committee opposed the alternate route now proposed by the Main Roads Board. It is a great departure from the original plan and deviates deep into the prime section of Blackbutt Reserve.

Tom was not only involved with the writing of the Blackbutt Reserve Committee's submission; he also agreed to appear before the Select Committee to give evidence. Over a number of hours Tom presented a cogent argument against the proposed route based on eight main points:

1. No consultation was ever made by the Newcastle Council to the Blackbutt Reserve Committee when the legally prescribed County Road 23 was changed to the alternate scheme now proposed by the Main Roads Board.
2. The final decision of Council was carried by only one vote. If Council had refused the Main Roads Department they would have found another route.
3. There are misgivings about the Main Roads Board ability and commitment to public consultation.
4. If Blackbutt had not been designated as a park, intensity of residential development in the area would have made it virtually impossible for the Main Roads Board to

build the road in the position that they now say there is no alternative.

5. Given the Newcastle Council's dependence on the Main Roads Department for financial support, it is really only a faint echo of the Main Roads Department. The Council is so dependent on the financial support to keep their work force engaged that the Main Roads Board influence on the Council might cause them to not be masters of their own destiny. The relationship between the Council and the Main Roads Board needs to be examined.

6. Citizens should not be placed in a position of plotting alternative routes. What the Council and the Main Roads Board should be doing is to justify without question why the provision of the County Roads as pertaining to Route 23 should be so dramatically changed. The changing of the Plan was done in a most secretive and peculiar manner. No one was informed or consulted outside official channels. The first indication the citizens of Newcastle had was that the Council had agreed unanimously to endorse the new route proposed by the Main Roads Board as a matter of 'URGENCY'. And that was in 1967. Many aldermen have since changed their thinking. Council is far from unanimous now.

7. Upgrading of Route 23 as it concerned Lookout Road and Charlestown Road is now put forward as a reason for rejection.

8. Council opposed the use of underpasses and tunnels as a means of preserving Blackbutt but this is a common practice throughout the world as seen in Bergen, London and Sydney.

Given the environmental and social importance of Blackbutt (as outlined in the written submission) Tom made an impassioned plea: 'if Newcastle wants to hold this area in perpetuity not only for this generation but for those that follow, it will need to be ever vigilant'. Tom had certainly kept his watch – he had been ever vigilant in defending Blackbutt for the people of Newcastle.[18]

Not willing to await the outcome of the Select Committee's deliberations, the NPPM continued to apply political pressure. As it had done on previous occasions, the NPPM canvassed the prospective candidates for the upcoming Local Government elections set down for December 1974 as to their position in regard to the motorway through Blackbutt and other environmental issues. But as Ramsland points out by the end of 1974 'the wind was definitely blowing in the favour of the 'Save Blackbutt' supporters and against the intrusion of the proposed expressway into the reserve'. It was the unanimous finding of the Select Committee that 'in no circumstances should Motorway 23 enter or cross Blackbutt Reserve'. It recommended instead that planning and construction of a freeway should commence on the western side of Lake Macquarie as soon as possible. The Select Committee made it clear the Federal Government was prepared to withhold funding if necessary to prevent the proposed motorway through the Blackbutt area. Unlike his predecessor, the recently sworn in State Minister for Transport and Highways, Mr Fife, had no wish to take on the Federal Government over an environmental issue. Like his Federal counterpart, it was his view that the environment needed to take precedence over motorway development. Faced with potential opposition at both a Federal and State level, the NCC on 22 October 1974 rescinded all previous decisions made regarding Blackbutt. Although the DMR remained belligerent to the end, the Federal Minister for Transport, Mr Jones, delivered the death blow to the motorway project when on 28 October 1974 he stated unequivocally that Motorway 23 would not be built through Blackbutt Reserve. The stance by Tom, the NPPM and the Blackbutt Reserve Committee had been vindicated. Blackbutt Reserve had been saved! In yet another letter to the *NMH* Tom took time to reflect on the outcome:

> The unanimous report by the House of Representatives' Standing Committee on the expressway through Blackbutt Reserve vindicated those who over the years have staged a vigorous campaign to preserve Blackbutt. The Standing Committee comprising one Labor and two Liberal members, commented in their findings that Newcastle City Council had not previously given the public an adequate opportunity to express their views either for or against the route of the expressway. Thirty-four witnesses appeared before this impartial committee. The opportunity was appreciated. It is hoped that the Department of Main Roads will dismiss the idea of an expressway through the suburbs of Newcastle and will return to the idea of the construction of an arterial road to serve the industries and local requirements. The type of road design by the DMR and accepted by them until 1966 and as shown in the County Plan would come within this category.

Tom was also keen to acknowledge the assistance of Mr Peter Morris, Federal Member for Shortland, 'who was mainly instrumental in having the case study of Blackbutt placed before the House of Representatives committee for their consideration'. It was the same Peter Morris who later as the Federal Minister for Lands and Forests made 'a graphic promise to stop parks being grabbed for motorcars'. Interestingly, in his maiden speech to Federal Parliament Morris had made the following observation: 'local government and other authorities have for too long accepted the principle of pinching pieces of public park as the most economic course for so called progress. The public is no longer prepared to sit back and take whatever is dished out to them in the name of progress'. No doubt with the recent Blackbutt Reserve and Birdwood Park protests in mind, he added 'in staid old Newcastle people were coming together spontaneously to protect natural beauty'.[19]

Although the battle had been won, the NPPM did not rest – it worked to ensure that any future threats to Blackbutt from the DMR were removed. The first priority was to ensure that Highway 23 was constructed as soon as possible in line with the route set down by the Northumberland County Plan. The longer term goal was to ensure that the proposed National Highway was built west of Lake Macquarie. Clearly Tom saw he had a role to play in promoting both projects. He once again used the press to apply political pressure – he wrote to the Editor of the *NMH* in November 1976:

> The Lord Mayor, Alderman Anderson, is to be complimented. It was heartening to read that he supported the national highway west of Lake Macquarie (we all do)…He also added that it was urgent for a wide route for traffic to move from the southern to the northern side of Newcastle… Alderman Anderson's views coincide with the oft-expressed opinions of Mr J. Richley and the Northern Parks and Playground Movement. The

county road designed by competent engineers of the Main Roads Department and at the time supported by the Newcastle City Council and Lake Macquarie Shire Council provided an arterial road of six lanes at satisfactory speeds...It is to be hoped that the other aldermen who have always opposed the construction of particular road on the original route set down by the Main Roads Department will get behind the Lord Mayor and press for the construction of Highway 23 set out in the Northumberland County Plan.

While Tom would have to wait some time to see the construction of a National Highway west of Lake Macquarie, he would have been pleased by the DMR's announcement in June 1979 that it intended to construct Highway 23, more or less, along the route outlined by the original county plan. Tom's only regret was that Joe Richley did not live to see this event. On reflecting on this decision, Tom commented 'Newcastle has achieved a notable victory because of the combined efforts of many. The new plan as it affects Blackbutt should be accepted without equivocation'. Tom continued to apply pressure on the Council right up until the time Highway 23 was constructed. In May 1979 he moved a motion (seconded by Lithgow) at the monthly meeting of the NPPM that 'the Newcastle City Council be advised that we approve of the plan for the widening of Highway 23 as it affects Blackbutt and consider that it confirms with the plans which we have consistently advocated that it lies within the proposed alignment in the County scheme'.[20]

Another key issue to concern the NPPM was the operation of a coal mine in close proximity to the reserve. Since the end of the nineteenth century coal mining had been a prominent

Blackbutt highway

From R. E. Farrell

THE Main Roads Department in 1945 produced an atlas which provided an arterial road system mainly for Newcastle and Lake Macquarie.

State Highway 23 was shown on this as part of the system and both Newcastle and Lake Macquarie councils concurred. Again when the County Scheme was being prepared between 1949 and 1952 it was adopted substantially and together with minor amendments incorporated in the scheme and placed on exhibition in July 1952 by the Northumberland County Council.

After determination of objections the scheme was again on exhibition in 1955. No objection to the route of State Highway 23 was received at either of these exhibitions.

The route did impinge to a degree on the perimeter of Blackbutt Reserve but this was accepted without protest by the citizens of Newcastle.

This route required some resumption of houses. The new proposal does not take as much of Blackbutt and also no house has to be resumed.

The furore on Blackbutt really began in 1966 when as a matter of urgency the council was foolishly stampeded into a new proposal to construct an expressway which would have destroyed the main features of the Blackbutt Reserve.

Right through the Blackbutt controversy the Northern Parks and Playgrounds Movement and the Blackbutt Reserve Committee have never deviated from the resolve to return to the country road.

The late Mr Joe Richley and I were deputed by the Blackbutt Reserve Committee to make a submission to the House of Representatives Standing Committee on Environment and the whole emphasis of our submission was to return to the country road as exhibited in 1955.

The new route as proposed by the Main Roads Board has finally, more or less, returned to the original country road.

Newcastle has achieved a notable victory because of the combined effort of many.

The new plan as it affects Blackbutt Reserve should be accepted without equivocation.

R. E. FARRELL,
Russell Rd, New Lambton.

Courtesy of the *NMH*
(12 June 1979)

feature of the area. Of the six mines that operated close to Blackbutt in 1945, Borehill Colliery was the most significant. Situated to the north of the reserve, the colliery worked an underground coal seam producing on average eighty to one hundred tons of coal per year specifically for Newcastle Steel Works. The NCC effectively became the landlord of the mine when it purchased the land adjoining the reserve in 1956. By the mid-1960s the colliery, like its competitors, was facing closure due to poor mechanisation and falling levels of production. Buchanan Borehole Collieries came to the rescue, however, negotiating an extension of the lease and introducing widespread mechanisation to the plant. As the size of the mine increased it produced about 900 tons of coal making it one of the largest collieries in the Newcastle district.

Given its potential for environmental damage, the NPPM was keen to see the mine closed. One way of achieving this was to persuade

"WELL! THEY'VE GOT **NOTHING** TO COMPLAIN ABOUT NOW!"

Courtesy of the *NMH* (12 May 1971)

the NCC not to extend the lease. This was the objective of a motion Tom seconded (moved by Dick Woodgate) at the monthly meeting of the NPPM in July 1970. Some months later the NPPM strongly opposed the move by the mine to increase its operation by leasing a further thirty acres of reserve land. In a delegation to Mr Fife, now Minister for Mines, the NPPM argued that the mine should be restricted to its original lease. Furthermore, strict conditions should be imposed regarding the restoration of the land at the end of the lease. Mr Dick Woodgate, the Secretary of the BAC, made it clear to the press that there were concerns about the status of the 250 acres regarded as part of Blackbutt but not yet formally declared. Suspicions were further raised when permission was not obtained from the NCC or the Company to photograph the coal operations at Blackbutt. Joe Richley in the 1971 Annual Report of the NPPM informed his members that the movement would do all in its power to prevent the destruction of Blackbutt 'caused by the extension of mining activities'. In order to get its message across the NPPM called a series of public meetings. These meetings seem to have raised the level of public concern about the mine. On 12 May 1971 a Lumsdon cartoon featured in the *NMH* showed a desolate Blackbutt Reserve with a denuded landscape. At the front of the scene, two smartly dressed figures stood in close proximity to the mine - the caption reads 'well, they've got nothing to complain about now'. Lumsdon's clever use of irony may well have been intended to sound a public warning bell. The NPPM kept the pressure up by contacting all the prospective candidates in the upcoming 1974 Local Government election asking them their position on the issue. Mr Don Barnett, the President of the NPPM, informed the candidates that 'should you reply indicate strong support for the Movement's aims we will accordingly notify our members and affiliated organisations and seriously consider your merit as a candidate'. This was a not so subtle way of exerting political pressure on the aldermen in the hope of winning support on the Council for key environmental issues.

This sort of pressure resulted in the NCC agreeing not to increase the amount of land available to the mine under the terms of the lease. As a result, in August 1976 the Company announced that it intended to close the mine within two and a half years. Mr McLean, the colliery manager, informed the press that 'the Company had an agreement with NCC to restore the land to its natural state when operations finished'. To this end the Company had already planted more than 1000 trees. Mr McLean assured the public that the mine had not affected the park – the stockpiled coal would be removed before the mine's closure. This announcement was well received by the NPPM. Lithgow explained that 'the cessation of work at the mine would give Newcastle Council a real chance to rehabilitate the area as a major centre in the reserve'. The NPPM continued to keep the pressure up. In 1978 at the August meeting Mr Barnett, the President of the NPPM, moved a motion (seconded by Jo Shields) that 'the Newcastle City Council be asked when the mining lease is due to expire and to enquire as to what plans have been made to remove buildings associated with the mine and for the restoration of the area'. At least the issue which had worried Mr Woodgate some seven years earlier had now been resolved. Mr Barnett was pleased to report to the members that all, except two small pockets of Blackbutt had finally been dedicated as public reserve. In the Annual Report the President paid particular homage to Joe Richley and Tom Farrell 'who fought for almost twenty years to achieve the dedication of the majority of Blackbutt Reserve'. As a sign of his standing in the movement, Mr R. E. Farrell was appointed (unopposed) to the position of 'Life Patron', a position Joe Richley had held up to the time of his death in July 1978. To this was added a 'Life Membership of the NPPM' in December 1987.

The mine finally closed in March 1979. As the *NMH* indicated the company had fulfilled its obligations under the terms of the lease: 'when mining operations ceased the company had promised that as part of CSR's good citizen policy, it would restore the site to a plan drawn up for the Council by Sydney landscape architects, Bruce Mackenzie and Associates'. At a cost of $250,000 the Company had removed surface buildings, coal stockpiles and sludge pools, replacing them with grass and native trees. The mine site was officially handed over to the NCC on 26 March 1980. Three years later on the 13 November 1983 the old mine site was formally opened to the public by Alderman Joy Cummings, the Lord Mayor, having been transformed into a landscaped recreation area attached to Blackbutt Reserve. As Tom delivered the address at the opening, he would have been very pleased that the reserve had been named after his old mate Joe Richley, a man who had worked tirelessly for the conservation of the environment in the Newcastle region. As the local press reported 'the Joe Richley Reserve had been landscaped using the natural contours left by the mine as well as the ponds which were part of the site. A watercourse meanders through the reserve and children's play areas and picnic tables and barbecues have been built at distances to invite privacy'. In reflecting on the opening of the Richley Reserve, Doug Lithgow, the new President of the NPPM, commented:

THE STAR · May 5, 2010 7

>> International Year of Biodiversity

One man's legacy

Tom Farrell at Green Point, Belmont, in 1985. He fought for a reserve at Green Point to preserve its important environmental and cultural heritages for future generations.

Green pockets of lush tress and thriving wildlife can be found throughout the suburbs of Newcastle and Lake Macquarie.

Blackbutt Reserve, Mount Sugarloaf and Green Point Reserve, in particular, are good examples of public space and nature coming together.

The conservation of many of these sites was due to the efforts of one man – Tom Farrell (1904 – 1996).

He has also left a legacy in the form of the Tom Farrell Institute for the Environment at the University of Newcastle.

Institute director Tim Roberts said the legacy was two-fold, as a patron of the Northern Parks and Playground Movement and through his donations of money.

"The family has left behind a financial legacy to allow ongoing funds to be awarded to PhD students to do environmental research," he said.

Professor Roberts said Tom Farrell also fought for the conservation of many reserves in the Hunter region.

Proudly supported by

2010 International Year of Biodiversity

star★

NEWCASTLE & LAKE MACQUARIE
Your community newspaper

"He was instrumental in Blackbutt Reserve being established, in particular during the 1930s and 40s, he lobbied New Lambton Council to keep the site," Professor Roberts said.

"At the time the council wanted to sell bits off and put a roadway through it."

Professor Roberts said reserves make up an important part of the environment.

"People need them to get back to nature," he said.

"They also show, on a relatively large scale, what the area would have looked like 100 years ago.

"A place like Blackbutt Reserve showcases our endangered species but it also allows native animals to have a place of refuge."

The Tom Farrell Institute was formed in 2006, and holds public forums, specialist workshops and creates online educational resources.

To find out more about the Tom Farrell Institute, go to www.newcastle.edu.au/foundation or phone 4921 7453.

Professor Tim Roberts reflects on the legacy of Tom Farrell
Source: *The Star*, 5 May 2010

I was particularly pleased to have been present in Blackbutt Reserve on Sunday, 13 November when the Rt. Worshipful the Lord Mayor of Newcastle, Alderman Joy Cummings unveiled a plaque giving recognition to our long-time leader and parks campaigner, Joe Richley. The memory of Joe lives on in our hearts and the work of his committees is embodied in every park that has been saved from alienation, and in the general improvement of the environment that has been achieved…It is ironic but satisfying that Joe's name should embellish that bit of Blackbutt that was alienated for the coal washery and colliery that we fought so hard to stop. Thankfully we now see a blighted part of the reserve restored in a way that enhances the reserve and serve an important role in the total management of the park…Our work has always been voluntary and done in the name of the Movement and I take this opportunity to mention the names of the others beside Joe who have contributed greatly to the work of the Movement, Rod Earp, Tom Farrell, Dick Woodgate, Don Morris, Arthur Munro, Joan Wilson, Don Barnett and Jack Shields to mention a few. There are many others like Miss Pendleton, Peter Podmore, Brigadier Corlette and the indomitable Wilf Dews who have also made very significant contributions.

What these words serve to illustrate is that Tom's significant role in the establishment of Blackbutt Reserve was played not as an individual but as part of a team. Doug Lithgow's name would also have to be added to the list of those who had 'contributed greatly to the movement'. It was Tom's view that Doug Lithgow was mainly responsible for the success of the NPPM in the period after Joe Richley's death. Doug 'was the bloke' who ensured that the NPPM did not suffer the same fate as the NSW Parks and Playgrounds Movement which folded through lack of interest in the late 1970s. At one stage Tom feared that the NPPM would also disappear but 'fortunately there we got a bloke whose name is Doug Lithgow and it's terribly important that these organisations such as the NPPM be kept operating especially in Newcastle'.[21]

Having secured Blackbutt Reserve, Tom and the NPPM worked to ensure that the Council adopted a proper management plan for the area. As Lithgow later explained 'it's not just getting a reserve set aside, it's a matter of seeing that it's managed effectively so that its natural features aren't destroyed'. In 1976 the President was pleased to report that

> The publication of the study prepared by Bruce Mackenzie had been one of the highlights of the year. A number of years ago we proposed that he be asked to prepare such a study and in fact offered to provide money to assist. At long last we have a broad outline plan which outlines what can be done to preserve the naturalness of Blackbutt. A number of the recommendations such as the removal of cages for birds and animals and the future development of the coal mine site have already provoked comment. I hope the city council will now authorise the Local Committee to arrange for detailed plans to be prepared.

Tom was particularly keen to ensure that no sectional interest in the community was allowed to alienate any part of the reserve for a purpose it was not intended. From an early date he had consistently opposed the handing over of any public land to private organisations so that it could remain for the enjoyment of all members of the public. It was for this reason that he opposed the use of the pond in Richley Reserve by the local Model Boating Club. At the May 1987 meeting of the NPPM he successful moved a motion (seconded by Tate) that 'we write to the Mayor requesting that this activity cease...we suggest the Model Boating Club finds an alternative site'. By August the issue had been resolved – the Secretary of the NPPM was pleased to report that he had received a reply from the Town Clerk who had informed him that 'the Modellers had sought another venue and that this would not be Blackbutt'. In a further motion (seconded by Shields) at the May 1988 meeting of the NPPM, Tom stressed his 'continued opposition to any alienation of the reserve for any sectional interest'.

Throughout 1977 the NPPM pressured the Council to be more pro-active in securing the State Government funding to which it was entitled. It was the view of the NPPM that one of the main reasons that the park land held in trust by the Council was not adequately developed was that the Council failed to secure the necessary funding from the State Government. The 1977 Annual Report points out 'we have recently found that the Newcastle City Council has not requested funds of which it is entitled from the State Government for the development of parkland held in trust. We are currently pursuing the matter'. In 1979 the President was pleased to report that there had been 'welcomed signs of support from Local Government' when the Council finally appointed landscape architects to develop Blackbutt Reserve. In the following year's annual report the President commented 'we have continued our interest in the area'. One of those to maintain his interest was Tom Farrell – the

June 1982 issue of *The Northern Parks and Playgrounds Movement Quarterly Review* commented on Tom's input at recent meetings and acknowledged 'all the help, advice and assistance that he has given since 1952'. This sustained effort by the membership (and other interested bodies) produced a significant dividend in 1989 when a comprehensive 'Blackbutt Reserve Plan of Management' was produced. It provided NCC with a blueprint to properly manage into the future the 182 hectare-site for the benefit of the whole community. Further improvements were made to the wildlife and aviary exhibits from 1992 onwards.[22]

In 1988 the City of Newcastle recognised Tom Farrell's years of service to the community especially in regard to his defence of the environment. He received an Australia Day award for his 'outstanding citizenship, not only as a Novocastrian but as an Australian'. Tom was happy to identify the establishment of Blackbutt Reserve as his greatest achievement. The following year Bob Power recognised this when he referred to Tom as 'a great Blackbutt supporter and originator'. There is no doubt that Tom had played a key role (as part of a team) in the establishment of what remains today as one of Newcastle's great treasures. As Lithgow pointed out 'Tom Farrell is the man we must thank for Blackbutt today'. Tom was certainly proud to have played his part in establishing Blackbutt and then ensuring that it remained intact for the benefit of the whole community. The struggle by the NPPM and other organisations to save Blackbutt had been long and hard. The fact that 'practically the lot' was achieved was nothing short of 'an absolute miracle'. He explained later in life that Blackbutt remained a very special place – 'you've only to go down into Blackbutt – it's just an absolute inspiration, to go down into this beautiful area, right in the heart of Newcastle, and feel you've played some part in retaining it. It certainly gives you a thrill'.[23]

Aerial photograph of Blackbutt Reserve, Blackbutt
Reserve Plan of Management.
Courtesy of The City of Newcastle

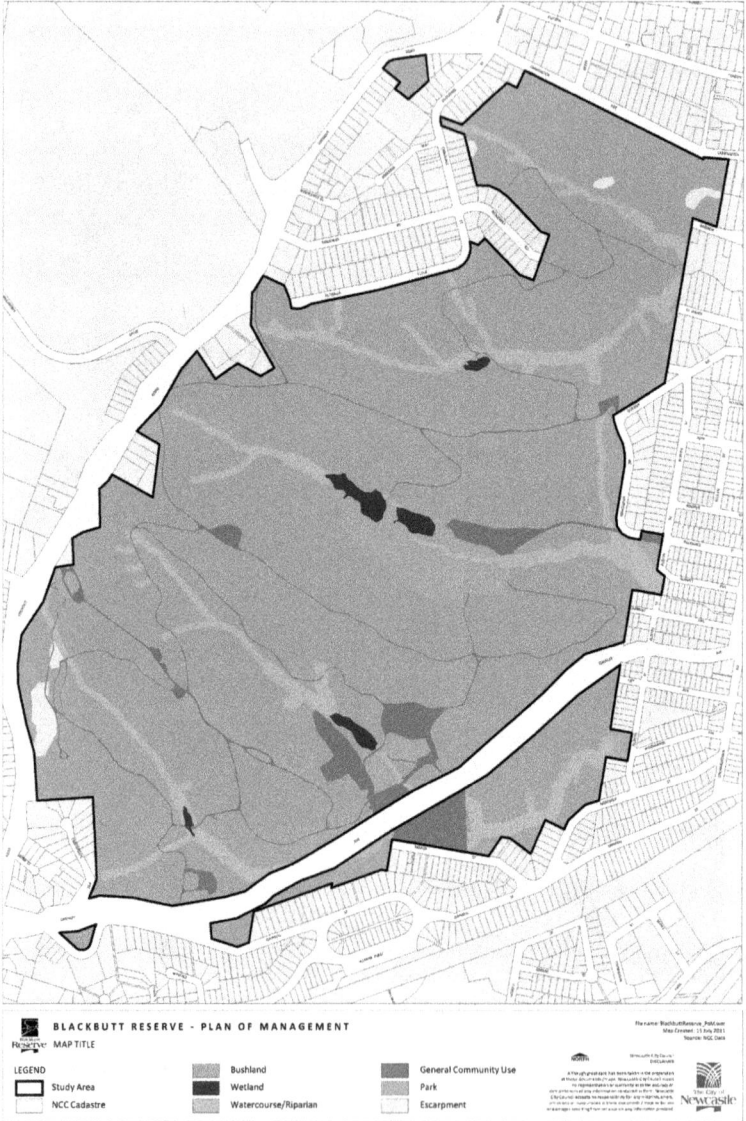

Map Title of Blackbutt Reserve, Blackbutt Reserve Plan of Management. Courtesy of The City of Newcastle

6: A Great Park Man

In a speech to the NPPM in 1984 Tom Farrell made this remark: 'I've always been interested in trees and parks'. Given this, it is not surprising that Tom wanted his own children to develop an appreciation for the Australian bush. This was one of the reasons why the Farrell family so frequently visited the Blackbutt area on weekends. But this appreciation was not just for the Farrell family. Tom believed that the whole Australian community benefited from being exposed to open spaces. It was for this reason that he became a member of the Parks and Playgrounds Movement of New South Wales and subsequently founded the NPPM in Newcastle in 1952. The maxim that drove him was 'our citizens want parks, they want recreation areas and they want open spaces'. Tom believed that public parks were important to each successive generation. National Parks served to preserve the nation's natural heritage. Local parks served to preserve areas where families could escape the hustle and bustle of everyday life by enjoying recreational activities in a natural setting. As Tom and his fellow members of the NPPM were to find out, their struggle to establish and preserve public parks, recreation areas and open spaces had both disappointments and successes. But as significant areas of Blackbutt, Barrington Tops, Glenrock Lagoon, Lake Macquarie, Mount Sugarloaf, the Myall Lakes, and inner Newcastle became identified as preserved public land the NPPM delivered great benefits to the community.

Tom's interest in 'open space and parks' was driven by a goal to ensure that as many people as possible could enjoy living

The Northumberland
County District
Scheme Map,
City of Newcastle –
note the provision of
'green areas'.
Source: NUA.

in the urban environment. It was this desire that led him to become so involved in town planning. Taking his lead from the Northumberland County Plan, Tom believed that towns and cities should be designed for the benefit of the community. This meant that towns should be divided into distinct residential, commercial and industrial areas, that public parks, recreational and playground spaces should be incorporated into the overall design and that an effort should be made to beautify streets, roads, avenues, highways and public areas. Urban communities should also have easy access to national parks, reserves and 'green belt' areas, that is, spaces of wild bush or open uncultivated farmland. These standards (as outlined by the Northumberland County Plan) were to become the town planning blueprint for Tom and the NPPM from which there would be no deviation. As noted, the NPPM from the outset made it clear that 'we will accept nothing less and will oppose any attempt to whittle away these areas'. In words reminiscent of Rousseau, the President of the NPPM, Joe Richley, outlined the importance of parks and gardens to the movement. It was his opinion that parks were essential to the development of the nation:

> What are parks for? Are they pretty places to look at? Are they of historic and scientific interest? Are they open spaces for active recreation? Are they places for quiet and solitude? Are they places for the enjoyment of nature? Parks include all of these things. The over-all purpose of any park system as I see it, is to fill a need of the people. Automation, labour saving devices in the home, faster transportation, the shorter working week, longer and more frequent vocations, longer life expectancy means increased leisure time. The way people use this leisure time will determine

the kind of nation we will become. A properly developed national program of parks at all levels of government is an essential element in the building of the character of our nation for the future...Urban communities are changing rapidly, they are growing actually exploding into fantastic patterns of urban sprawl, bringing great pressure on all agencies of government. All open lands are at a premium and at the very time when we should be expending all our energies to acquire new park land, we are fighting a constant battle against encroachment...Park men are trustees and custodians of public lands for recreational use: land essential to the spiritual and physical well-being of the people. It was no easy job to acquire these lands, it took foresight, courage, money. Now they are irreplaceable and priceless, they are intrinsic to freedom itself.

It is clear from these words that 'park men' like Joe Richley and Tom Farrell held a deep, almost spiritual appreciation for 'green areas'. Their interest in parks, playgrounds and reserves was driven by an altruistic desire – both men believed that the wider community benefitted greatly by its exposure to parks and gardens. In short, parks and gardens were essential to the well-being of any urban community. It was, therefore, in Joe Richley's words 'our job to preserve parks, protect them from encroachment or dissipation and add to them for the benefit of generations yet unborn'.[1]

As early as 1945 Tom came into conflict with the planning authorities over a zoning matter. He joined with other New Lambton residents to sign a petition objecting to the possible industrial use by a glass company of the Pit Paddock, near

Morehead Street and Durham Road, Lambton, by a local glass company. He had moved to Russell Road in 1926 after being assured by the Municipal Authorities that 'New Lambton was gazetted a residential district'. Despite this, by 1947 the company had occupied a number of the old pit buildings. Tom working with the New Lambton Progress Association received assurances from the Northumberland County Council that 'the glass company was a non-conforming industry in a residential district'. In 1950 Alderman Boa, a member of the County Council, assured the residents that 'the area in question was zoned for open space and residential purposes'. In 1952 and 1953 the company applied unsuccessfully to the County Council to have the area rezoned 'industrial'. In an attempt to have the decision overturned the company appealed to the Minister for Local Government. Tom now a member of Cardiff Heights-New Lambton Lookout Progress Association swung into action organising local opposition to the plan. As head of a delegation to the Minister he argued a strong case against allowing the company's plans to proceed. He pointed out to the Minister that:

it must be clearly understood that this area has been proclaimed a residential district since 1924. In 1945 when there was no industry and all could take a detached view of the issue, the Newcastle Council advised that this was a residential area. Also in 1951 when the (Leonara) Glass Company was in existence the County Council zoned it as residential. It was only in 1952, following representations from the Glass Company, the pressure was brought to bear on the County Council to establish industry in the Pitt Paddock… It is a serious matter for the Minister to contemplate the alteration of the zoning to suit one particular company and to cause hardship and loss to hundreds of residents by depreciation of the value of their individual homes…Taking into consideration the present residential development…it would appear that the industrial area will run a deep salient right into the residential area. Why permit the intrusion of industry into one of the most beautiful and purely residential areas of Newcastle? Surely no one would contemplate a Glass Company in Killara.

It was Tom's view that the glass works should be relocated to Jesmond where there was adequate industrial land available. It appears that the Minister took some notice of Tom's detailed and well-argued submission. In allowing the project to go ahead, he limited the glass works to the area of the old pit buildings. The majority of the Lambton-New Lambton area was to retain its 'residential' zoning status.

The Fight to Prevent the Alienation of Public Land

Although he was involved in many issues, Tom never lost sight of the importance of protecting his local area. In 1965 he worked with Joe Richley and the NPPM to formulate plans for the consideration of the City Council to establish and maintain park land in the Cardiff Heights, New Lambton and Lambton areas. In 1968 at the March meeting of the NPPM he successfully put forward a motion (seconded by Pepperall) opposing a public housing development on land at Alexander Park, Lambton. At the same meeting he successfully moved a second motion (seconded by Barnett) that the movement write to Mr G. Whitlam, the Federal Leader of the Opposition, opposing the alienation of parkland in Alexander Park for housing. In 1970 Tom (seconded by Barnett) successfully put forward a motion at the May meeting of the NPPM opposing the Newcastle Council's decision 'to use Lambton Park as a car park'. Tom was particularly concerned about the alienation of public parks by bowling clubs and other sectional interests. In 1984 he reflected on his unsuccessful efforts to save Tauranga Park in Lambton in the 1930s:

> Tauranga Park was a small uncared for area right near where Western Suburbs Leagues Club is today. The citizens of the area called a protest public meeting because the Mayor of New Lambton and the Council were going to construct a bowling club on this tiny little bit of park. We failed in that, couldn't stop it but it gave me the inspiration to try and establish a movement such as this (NPPM) to try and encourage people to hold on to the areas which we did have and to get other areas.

Tom was angered that some years later the NCC allowed the Bowling Club to move to a new area of New Lambton Park transferring their lease of the land in Tauranga Park to a ladies bowling club. Despite this, Tom and the NPPM 'took up the cudgels' to successfully block the construction of a library on what remained of the area of Tauranga Park.[2]

Such was Tom's concern about the alienation of public land in 1958 that he worked with Richley to establish a sub-committee of the NPPM entitled the 'Land Usage Committee'. Its task was to address the problems 'arising from the short sighted policy of the NCC in disposing of Crown Land'. Needless to say Tom was an active member of the committee. Such was the seriousness of the issue, that Richley in his Annual

Report felt the need 'to sound a warning about the alienation of our parks by the cancerous growth of bowling club houses and grounds (sometimes at the expense of children's play areas), and the attitude of some of our aldermen and councillors to the right of liquor club houses on parks'. The President was clear on the action that needed to be taken: 'this movement must oppose this trend with every available avenue of opposition'. Three years later the President again warned that 'there seems to be an accepted practice of Councils to foster licensed club houses on public land which is wrong in principle. It violates the meaning of the word public and it is morally wrong in that it encourages gambling and the dispensing of liquor on public parks; moreover it has created a most unsatisfactory precedent which unfortunately leads to further alienation of public parks'. This had become such a problem by 1965 that the NPPM formed a special sub-committee, the Anti-Park Alienation Committee' to deal with the matter. In the '1966 Annual Report' Richley reported that 'the Anti-Alienation Committee has a full time job in preventing the loss of parkland. A glance at the County map shows many park areas with the word 'suspended' across them. A major problem is that provision in the Local Government Act which allows Councils to accept money in lieu of park areas from subdividers'.

Tom needed no prompting to take action against the sectional interests that posed a threat to public land. Over the next thirty years he worked in conjunction with the NPPM to prevent local councils allowing the alienation of public parks in favour of sectional interests. For example, in 1958 Tom was one of the main figures who successfully defended Nesca Park, Cooks Hill, from being sold off by the Newcastle Council. By rezoning the area 'residential' the council had attempted to subdivide the land for building blocks. In October Tom and

Nesca Park bounded by Nesca Parade and Brookes Street, Newcastle.
Photograph courtesy of the *NMH*

the other members of the NPPM took direct action, appearing before a hearing in Newcastle and later writing directly to the Minister for Local Government. As the 'NPPM Annual Report 1964-1965' was pleased to report such action 'was responsible for the preservation of Nesca Park'. In 1961 Campbell Park, Adamstown, was 'saved from the filching by the Electricity Commission' and the integrity of Toronto Park was preserved when an application to construct a club house was refused. In 1963 Tom moved a motion (seconded by Munro) at the August meeting of the NPPM that a letter be sent to the Minister of Local Government 'protesting at the decision of Newcastle Council to lease public land at Waratah West'. At the October meeting in 1967 Tom moved a motion (seconded by Lithgow) that 'we request the Minister of Local Government and the Minister of Lands to enact legislation to protect public reserves from the increasing demands of professional sporting clubs'. This followed the encroachment of public land by a sporting club at Mula Street, Charlestown, and the suggestion by Newcastle Council that a car-park was needed to be built at Civic Park, Newcastle. In 1968 Tom opposed the sectional use of Harker Oval by Western Suburbs Leagues Club and Adamstown Park by Adamstown Rosebuds Football Club. In 1969 he urged Newcastle Council to reinstate Mitchell Park, Merewether, as a public open space by removing the embankment and fence. In 1970 he opposed the use of Flaggy Creek Reserve, Glenrock, for motorbike rallies and the construction of a road through Jefferson Park, Merewether. There was also a request to Lake Macquarie Shire Council (LMSC) to remove the fence at Charlestown Oval. Towards the end of the year Tom made representations to various politicians 'to deplore the suggested changes to the law which would make it easier for councils to permit the use of public reserves for sectional use'. In the January 1971 meeting of the NPPM he moved (seconded by Shields) that letters be sent to the leaders of the Australian Labour Party, the Democratic Labour Party and the Australia Party seeking changes to party policies making it more difficult for councils to alienate public lands. Tom was also concerned that the relevant authorities should do all in their power to beautify existing sites and parkland. Later that year, therefore, he took steps to have the Maritime Services Board plant Moreton Bay Figs at the west side of Throsby Creek and requested that the NCC seek expert advice regarding the Merewether Beach Front, sea wall and promenade. He was also given the task by the NPPM of investigating areas for open space in Tarro and Sandgate.

In the '1972 Annual Report of the NPPM' the President was pleased to report that 'the decision of one council in this State to grant a lease of public parkland for the construction of a clubhouse was challenged this year. In a momentous decision, the court upheld the challenge and the council's decision was found to be illegal'. Boyed on by this decision Tom continued to press Newcastle Council to oppose the fencing off of any area of parkland for sectional use. At the March meeting of the NPPM he moved a motion (seconded by Harris) that a letter be sent to the council protesting against extensions planned to Alder Park Bowling Club. This was followed by letters to LMSC and NCC requesting that the appropriate authorities prosecute those responsible for driving motor vehicles in public parks. At the July meeting of the NPPM in 1975 Tom moved (seconded by Shields) that a letter be sent to the NCC 'enquiring as to its policy on the provision of neighbourhood park areas as suitable play areas for children particularly in the older parts of Newcastle'. In 1976 action was taken to oppose the partial alienation of Halton Park, Croudace Bay, for the construction of a yacht club. In 1977 a letter was sent to the Minister for Local Government 'advising him that LMSC had acted contrary to consultants advice on the setting up of Rathmines Bowling Club and asking him to intervene in the matter and stop the despoliation of such an important area'. At the February 1978 meeting of the NPPM Tom moved a motion (seconded by Shields) that action should be taken to prevent further encroachment on public land by Valentine Bowling Club. At the same meeting it was moved by Farrell (seconded by Shields) that the Hunter District Water Board should carry out extensive landscaping and improvements at its head office.[3]

In his Annual Report of the NPPM in 1978 the President took stock of what had been achieved by the movement:

as members are aware the Movement has for many years vigorously opposed the use of public parkland for sectional use, such as bowling clubs, sporting bodies, etc. Many of these clubs whilst starting in a small and innocuous fashion eventually straddle the parkland with giant licensed premises and adjacent tar-covered parking areas. It is our movement's belief that this development is not in the best interest of the community. We have on a couple of rare occasions prevented this type of development where the land in question was dedicated public parkland. We are therefore greatly disturbed by the recent amendment to the act by the State Government permitting alienation of dedicated public parkland for public use. We will be confronting this issue head on with local politicians and we look for them for support.

Although the President foresaw political difficulties ahead, he had pleasure in reporting that the movement had achieved the removal of hoarding in Hunter Street, significant improvements to the harbour foreshore and the beautification of the highway into Newcastle from the West. A year later he could report that the movement had achieved landscaping of railway bridges, rehabilitation of quarry areas, tree planting in heavy industrial sites and landscaping of the highway from Tarro to Mayfield.

Another cause of concern was the councils' willingness to accept money from developers in lieu of park land. At the November 1978 meeting of the NPPM Tom successfully moved a motion (seconded by Shields) that 'a letter be sent to NCC asking what was the total amount of money paid to the Council by sub-dividers in lieu of providing open space over the past ten years together with an itemised list showing how the money was spent'. It is clear that the problem was widespread – in May of the following year Tom seconded a motion moved by Lithgow calling on the Minister of Planning and Environment to ensure that provisions were written into planning schemes that obliged local planning authorities to dedicate as park land those areas of land acquired for parks under the County Plan.[4]

The Northumberland County Plan

These motions make clear that the municipal authorities were not always interested in maintaining and extending the open space provisions of the Northumberland County Plan as prescribed in December 1960. At best the development of planning in the region was haphazard. In 1983 Lithgow summarised the planning in the region as 'a catalogue of lost opportunities, closed off options and miserable funding for implementation'. Successive State Governments had changed the rules on the organisational framework from County Councils, State Planning Authorities, Planning Commissions and Planning and Environment Departments. The municipal authorities had opposed from the start the proposed method of funding proposed by the County Scheme. The scheme provided for funding along the same lines as that which operated in the Sydney Cumberland Region with the cost of acquisitions for implementation being shared equally by the State Government and Local Government through a Development Fund on a county wide basis. While the scheme raised significant funds for the Cumberland County, the Northumberland County Scheme failed to raise any revenue because the local municipal authorities were not willing to meet the cost. In 1964 matters became worse when the State Planning Authority took over responsibility for the County Plan. Local councils were slow to adopt comprehensive local plans based on a regional framework. Instead individual councils adopted a piecemeal approach relying on Interim Development Orders. They were also slow to ensure that State Government authorities lived up to their responsibilities. It was Lithgow's opinion in 1985 that 'the Newcastle-Lake Macquarie Councils have been remiss in not co-operating over the past thirty years to bring pressure upon the State Government in Sydney to play a greater role in the provision and maintenance of regional open space in their areas'. In its efforts to maintain and extend open space in the Newcastle region, the NPPM continued to fight against this culture. But progress was slow due to the indifference of municipal and state authorities displayed by haphazard planning and inadequate funding. Despite this, the NPPM continued to battle away – in one year alone the Secretary of the NPPM handled over 1000 letters both inwards and outwards and produced a number of scientific and research articles.[5]

It is clear that Tom also played his part in attempting to over-come these problems. In the 1974 local government election, for example, he canvassed the prospective candidates to support the adoption of a planning scheme for Newcastle within three years. In an attempt to solicit greater interest from the Federal Government in regard to funding, he put forward a motion (seconded by Lithgow) at the May 1968 meeting of the NPPM that 'the Federal Government be approached for a grant of $10 million per annum for financing the acquisition of parks and reserves by local governments and the setting up of an expert advice service'. In regard to State Government funding he moved a motion (seconded by Dews) at the June 1985 meeting of the NPPM that 'we write to our local State members asking them to ask a question in the House trying to obtain information regarding comparative provisions of funding for open space and National Parks in the Northumberland

and Cumberland Counties'. In regard to local government he moved (seconded by Wright) at the February 1984 meeting of the NPPM that 'we write to NCC asking it to establish an Advisory Committee to go through all parks in Greater Newcastle to determine the active and passive priorities. This could be an advisory body of citizens and aldermen to prepare a study of appropriate uses for all parks'. At the August 1985 meeting Tom moved (seconded by Dulcie Hartley) that 'we ask the Planning and Environment Department to make a regional study of every parcel of land in the lower Hunter area with a view to having all Crown Land in the area considered for public recreation or open space'. At the same meeting he moved (seconded by Wright) that 'we write to Mr Carr and Mr Wran bringing attention to the great difficulties experienced in acquiring open space in the region and point out that Crown Land should be set aside for public parks'. Clearly despite the difficulties involved, Tom found the necessary energy to keep putting forward a cause he felt passionate about. Not only did he regularly attend the monthly meetings of the NPPM, he also was an active member of the management committee. Given his knowledge, interest and enthusiasm for parks and gardens it is not surprising that he regularly contributed to the discussion and put forward or seconded a series of motions during 'general business'. In fact, as the NPPM Minute Book attests, during his long association with the movement, he never attended a meeting without contributing in some form or other. Indeed, at some meetings he was responsible for moving or seconding all the motions that were carried in general business. When Tom combined his energy with that of other members of the NPPM things began to happen – this gave the people of Newcastle continued access to more parks and gardens in the region.[6]

Not only did the NPPM lobby local politicians and

government agencies, it provided assistance to other groups who were attempting to secure adequate open space in their local area. Although dismissed by their critics as nothing more than 'armchair theorists', the members of the NPPM led by example offering practical solutions to environmental issues. In his '1986 Annual Report' Lithgow commented that 'throughout the year hundreds of representations have been made to politicians, Councils and other organisations on a range of issues. We have also received countless requests for information and help and we have tried to keep the main issues before the public through the media'. Although there was little interest at first, the media became a vital tool for the Movement to get its message across. As Richley pointed out in his '1964-1965 Annual Report' 'we owe a great debt to the *Newcastle Herald*, the *Newcastle Sun* and local radio stations for their space, time and service in bringing our views before the public'. This opinion was supported by Doug Lithgow in his '1980 Annual Report' who acknowledged 'the assistance given throughout the year by the media and the *Newcastle Morning Herald* in particular, in bringing its views to the public and reporting environmental issues generally'. It appears from subsequent annual reports that the President's closing comments regarding the media were realised: 'we trust that we will be afforded similar treatment in the years ahead'. In the '1991-1992 Annual Report' Lithgow made the following point:

> your movement cannot give the service that is needed without help from its members and the wider community who enjoy and cherish all those things we have been actively involved with over our forty year struggle…there is so much done by your movement that is important but will never be

recorded. The letters that are written to the press by members to inform and help shape public opinion. The research, the help to other organisations and hundreds of telephone calls and enquiries. Indeed it is the knowledge that we are part of a broader community and that we share and help one another that makes the Northern Parks and Playgrounds Movement worthwhile.

Tom Farrell was one such member who was actively involved for over forty years. By the motions he put forward, the letters he wrote and the assistance he provided like-minded organisation, he ensured that there was much achieved by the NPPM that was important.

In Defence of Local Parks

Throughout the 1980s and 1990s Tom continued to fight to prevent the alienation of public land for sectional interests. Working with the NPPM he opposed the establishment or extension of club facilities in the following areas: Nobby's Beach, King Edward Park, Belmont, Charlestown and Speers Point. He also attempted to ensure that land occupied 'by insolvent bowling clubs or small clubs or for any other reason of alienation be returned to public open space and that the Local Government Act be strengthened regarding parks'.[7] Although he was not able to prevent a car-parking area being established on land at Reid Park, Newcastle, he had better luck regarding King Edward Park and Empire Park. He also opposed roads or off-road vehicles encroaching on park land in the Toronto Area or at Wangi Point.[8] He worked to ensure that park land remained accessible to the general public – for example, at the May 1986 meeting of the NPPM he put forward a motion (seconded by Wright) that 'we write to Newcastle City Council asking that West Park, Adamstown, be opened up for public use'. In a second motion (seconded by Parsons) he moved that 'Newcastle City Council be asked to remove the fence surrounding No 1 Sports Ground'. In 1988 he opposed further development at Bar Beach and the establishment of the Redhead Pumping Station because of 'its detrimental effect on the nearby swamp'. Tom also worked to increase the amount of park land available in the city by encouraging BHP to donate part of its holdings at the State Dockyard for community use. He also attempted to improve the aesthetic environment by encouraging landscaping projects at Wangi Point, Warners Bay and Eleebana; tree-planting programs at Westend Park, Adamstown, Speers Point and along the route from Hamilton to Hannell Street, Wickham.[9] He also worked over a number of years to ensure that areas such as Adamstown Park and the site of the old Adamstown rifle range were retained as recreational land. He also fought to ensure that the Shortland Wetlands Project was fully supported.[10] On a matter close to home, he fought unsuccessfully for the retention of the land at the old Abattoir site as a botanical garden or wooded parkland. The decision to subdivide a significant part of the site into residential blocks was keenly felt by Tom as it meant a significant loss of Newcastle's green-belt. He also fought unsuccessfully to prevent the land being alienated at Dixon Park for the construction of public-housing apartments. In the '1964-1965 Annual Report' of the NPPM the President commented that 'the major disappointment this year was the Movement's unsuccessful attempt to bring to the public's notice the importance of retaining all the City owned land adjacent to Dixon Park for public use. We convened a meeting on this issue which was well attended. The City Council, however, disregarded our suggestions and agreed to the sale of three acres of the land to the Housing Commission'.[11] Tom and the NPPM had better success from 1959 onwards in implementing a development plan for Braye Park, Waratah, which involved site restoration and extensive tree planting. Tom also visited sites in Stockton and Fern Bay on a number of occasions to investigate encroachment of public land by motor enthusiasts and local clubs. Further north, Tom and the NPPM worked with local resident groups to challenge the alienation of public land by sectional interests at Soldier's Point, Dutchman's Beach, One Mile Beach, Shoal Bay and Boat Harbour. In regard to the acquisition of park land, Tom made his position clear in 1985 when in a motion (seconded by Wright) at the August meeting of the NPPM he stated 'we must attempt to get every parcel of Crown Land in Port Stephens into reserve'. Among the Movement's successes was Tomaree National Park which was finally gazetted in 1984 after a twenty year effort. Commenting on this achievement in his '1983-1984 Annual Report' Lithgow made the following comment: 'here again a time lag from proposal to gazetting has been too long and great damage has been done to the area over the intervening years by no management, no care and no responsibility on the part of the Government at all levels'. These comments serve to underline the ongoing problems faced by Tom and the Movement as they battled to secure public open space for the community.[12]

District Park, National Park & Civic Park

Tom was also part of the NPPM's campaign to protect the integrity of District Park, National Park and Civic Park from sectional interest. Although the whole of District Park had been designated as a sport and recreation area by the Northumberland County Plan, between 1958-1963 the NPPM had to fight a long campaign (with varying degrees of success) to protect sections of the park being turned into a supermarket car park, a heliport, an aero-club, a bowling club and a sports stadium. It was the view of the Movement that the whole area needed to be maintained as a sport and recreation area as 'there would be a dearth of these areas as the city developed'. As late as 1985 Tom was still attempting to exert some pressure on the development of this open space – at the June meeting of the NPPM Tom with the support of Adamthwaite moved a motion that 'we ascertain who controls District Park to see if it can be developed as unfenced open space to take off some playground pressure from National Park and further that we bring pressure to bear on those investigating parklands under a grant from the Federal Government (per NCC) to ensure that NPPM input in a search to find alternative sites for active recreation'. Tom's motion alluded to another pressing issue – the protection of National Park situated on the common boundary of Cooks Hill and Hamilton South. Originally a public park and recreation ground with an area of 27.1 hectares, much of National Park had been fenced off or alienated from public use and given over to the exclusive use of a club or other sectional interest group. The remaining open sports fields and netball courts were cramped together in a space leaving only a limited area for general public recreation. It was the view of the NPPM that National Park had the potential to provide the local surrounding suburbs which had limited open space with sufficient rest parks, recreational areas and children's playgrounds. The NPPM joined forces with Carl Boyd, a local solicitor, and the Hamilton South Residents Group to form the Save National Park Committee. In the face of NCC's decision to hard-surface a large area of open land at National Park, the Save National Park Committee advocated the preparation of a Plan of Management for the park. It was the opinion of the NPPM that 'National Park had been seriously alienated over the years and is too heavily used on those open areas that are commonly available. The Park is characterised by ugly fences and sterile hard surfaces without landscape relief and too many buildings. The most recent removal of the green sward in the remaining common access and replacement with hard paving has created another loss of amenity to the Cooks Hill – Hamilton South area'. Despite the setback, it was an issue that Tom and the NPPM persisted with – at the May 1986 meeting of the NPPM it was unanimously moved that the Council produce its Management Plan for National Park. Tom added his voice moving a motion (seconded by Parsons) that NCC be informed that the Movement was opposed to any fence or structure being established around No 1 Sports Ground or in the vicinity of National Park.[13]

Civic Park used as a car-park
(early 1960s) – photographs
courtesy of the *NMH*

Tom and the NPPM were also keen to ensure that the Civic precinct was also properly developed. In 1968 Lithgow put forward a proposal to the NCC for the establishment of a 'Civic Square' which included, 'Newcastle's most important park', the major civic buildings (The Town Hall, Cultural Centre and Nesca House) and the 'architectural gem', James Menken's Presbyterian Church of St Andrew. An important feature of the proposal was an extensive tree planting program in the park and its surrounds. It was proposed that consideration be given to the closure of Wheeler Place, Burwood Streets and Laman Streets. It was hoped that the scheme would 'assist in the creation of a Civic Square worthy of the City'. Tom was keen on the project – at the May meeting of the NPPM he put forward a motion (seconded by Woodgate) that the Council (in light of the proposal) begin its replanning of Civic centre as soon as possible. Although progress was slow there was optimism in the 1976 'Annual Report' that the construction of the Administration Block and the Art Gallery and the partial closure of Wheeler Place created 'ideal conditions for the creation of a Civic Square based on the park'. A year later the President reported 'of great satisfaction to our membership is the development of the Civic Square between Newcastle City Hall and the New Administration Building. This project was first suggested by one of our members some years ago and we can take a certain amount of pride in seeing the development come to fruition'. As the NPPM Minute Book reveals Tom remained fully supportive of Lithgow's efforts to see the plan through to its end. At the January 1989 meeting of the NPPM Tom put forwarded a motion (seconded by Shields) that 'the President's submission to the NCC's Civic Management Plan be endorsed'. Three years later Lithgow was pleased to report that 'progress is at last being made with the planning of redevelopment of the

Civic area'. Part of this progress was a city square concept based on Civic Park with preparations for an overall strategy for a redevelopment from Darby Street through to Auckland Street with provision for a plaza in Wheeler Place. The President was pleased to report that the improvements to Civic Park had taken place 'without the costs and the need for the unreal projects that had been floated in recent years'. Among the 'unreal projects' which the NPPM had opposed was the construction of a multi-storey tower within the civic precinct. By supporting proposals like that put forward by Lithgow, Tom and the other members of the NPPM ensured that Civic Park continued to play an important part in the city's community life.[14]

Civic Park Precinct – photograph courtesy of the NMH

Birdwood Park

Unfortunately not all inner-city parks could be saved. As Tom pointed out in 1981, 'Newcastle has lost many recreational areas, Jefferson Park, Birdwood Park, Shortland Park and Alexander

Park, that's just in the city area alone. You will see great swathes of your public land filled in with asphalt to park cars on it and that's absolutely wrong'. Birdwood Park had come under threat in 1971 when it was announced by the Department of Main Roads that King Street was to be widened to accommodate a six-lane dual carriageway. The road works were to come at the cost of Birdwood Park which was to have its total area of two and a half acres drastically reduced. Like Jefferson and King Street Parks, Birdwood Park had been allowed to deteriorate to a point where one commentator referred to the area as a 'derelict paddock'. The NPPM believed that this was a deliberate plan by the State Government so that neglected parkland could be excised for road works. At the May 1971 meeting of the NPPM Tom voiced his concern putting forward a motion (seconded by Jones) 'that we request that the Council retain Birdwood as a park and give details of the work to be carried out on Stewart Avenue'. The matter was again raised at the November meeting when the NPPM produced a report critical of the plan. It reminded the relevant authorities that 'a park with gardens and trees enhances the appearance of the city and provides psychological and aesthetic satisfaction amidst the noise, hustle and stress of inner city areas'.

Response to the DMR's plan was immediate – the NPPM joined forces with other like-minded community groups to organise a number of protest meetings. A large crowd holding placards reading 'Find another way for the Motorway', 'Keep the Woods in Birdwood' and 'By-pass Birdwood for a better road plan', heard Mr Suters, representing the Newcastle Division of the Australian Institute of Architects, point out that 'the proposal is a classic example of the amenities of the park being sacrificed for the needs of the car. We must recognise the value of the parks and open space. The destruction of parks for roadways has accelerated in the Newcastle area. We must take stock now or it will be too late'. In his 'Annual Report' later in the year, the President of the NPPM, Joe Richley, was pleased to report that 'the plan provoked considerable public criticism and was almost universally condemned by the public'. The protest, however, failed to deter the Council from proceeding with the project. It argued (rather fancifully) that there would be minimal loss to the total area of the park by the widening of King Street – the road would simply divide Birdwood Park into three separate areas. Richley's response was to the point – 'scarred and disfigured already by parked motor cars, Birdwood Park is finally to succumb to these mechanical monsters in the name of progress…The park will now become three large traffic islands but to the Council it will still be a park'.

By means of a petition and letters to the Editor the Council was pressured to change its position. By July 1972 the campaign appeared to be having some success – Alderman McDougall, the Lord Mayor, announced that he would raise objections to the plan at the next Council meeting. He argued that 'parkland in this vicinity is at a premium and I feel that the largest possible area of Birdwood Park should be preserved and intensively beautified'. Although it appeared the Lord Mayor was onside, the Council was far from united on the issue. During a debate which lasted one and a half hours, several key aldermen spoke strongly in favour of the project. As a result the matter was referred to the Works Committee which reported back within two weeks that (without any satisfactory alternative) it unanimously supported the original proposal. The Council at its next meeting endorsed the recommendation of the Works Committee.

In December 1972 it was reported that 'the plans to build a road through Birdwood Park' were set to go ahead the following year. It was also announced that the Council planned to remove a row of trees in Stewart Avenue in order to widen the road. This evoked an immediate response from local residents organised by Norm Barnwell, a local high-school teacher, who formed the Stewart Avenue Preservation Society (SAPS). This group immediately placed a series of placards in Birdwood Park and along Stewart Avenue that read 'Save This Tree' and 'Don't Axe Me'. Although the Lord Mayor and the City Engineer attempted to assure local residents that no trees were earmarked for removal in Stewart Avenue, the rumoured threat to the arboreal shield in the area had galvanised opposition to the proposed road through Birdwood Park. SAPS next produced an engineering report that put forward an alternate route for the road extension which maintained the integrity of Birdwood Park. When the Council failed to respond, SAPS announced that it intended to take direct action by chaining people to trees in Birdwood Park. The NPPM, the Newcastle Resident Action Committee and Newcastle Trades Hall Council joined with SAPS to organise a protest meeting in Birdwood Park on 24 February. At the meeting attended by about 250 people Barnwell called on people 'to attend the council meeting the following night and do all they could to embarrass the Works Committee'. At the Council meeting on 25 February before a packed public gallery, the Council reiterated its support for the proposal. Although a petition 'with a great many signatures' was tabled, a motion to have the matter deferred failed to get a seconder. It was made clear that the majority view of the aldermen that the protestors 'were engaged in a belligerent attempt to embarrass people who were doing their best for the city'. One alderman went so far as to describe Birdwood Park as an area 'only used by five people or circuses'.

In the early morning of the following day Council workers

moved in to begin clearing trees in Birdwood Park. They were met by Barnwell and about twenty protestors who proceeded to obstruct the heavy machinery by leaning against the trees. Police arrived and removed the protestors (including Barnwell) by force. Within hours it was all over – seventeen trees in Birdwood Park had been felled and removed. Lithgow echoed the sentiment of many in the community when he said 'it was appalling that work should have gone ahead before the decisions of last Sunday's public meeting had been considered by the council. This was a wilful act of premeditated vandalism'. The next day the Editor of the *NMH* observed that, "Newcastle has rarely felt the official boot-heel across the cheek of its good conscience as it did in Birdwood Park yesterday. The council's mechanised invasion of the park was high-handed, provocative and disgraceful'.

Courtesy of the *NMH* (3 July 1973).
Even a visiting circus troupe joined the protest to save Birdwood Park.

At the next Council meeting, amidst howls of protest from the public gallery, the Council formally rejected the plan submitted by SAPS – with the trees removed the road widening program could now proceed unabated. It is clear that Tom was angered by what had occurred. At the March meeting of the NPPM he moved a motion (seconded by Richley) that 'the Minister of Local Government be approached to receive a deputation to show the Movement's disapproval over Birdwood Park'. Years later he complained to a Parliamentary Select Committee about the heavy handed tactics of the Council and the DMR's failure to comply with proper due process: 'the destruction of Birdwood Park by the Main Roads Board did not give us the opportunity to lodge objections. The County Plan was changed, there was no public exhibition and the Council proceeded to destroy trees and construct a road notwithstanding vehement protests of citizens and civic bodies'. With the integrity of the park now lost, Tom took steps to ensure that the Council kept its word that it would replace the lost area of parkland with other dedications of parkland in the area. In June 1974 he moved a motion (seconded by Dews) 'that we ask Newcastle City Council and the Minister for Highways to acquire vacant land adjacent to Stewart Avenue and Parry Street and develop it as park land as compensation for the loss of land in Birdwood Park'. In 1981 he was still waiting for the Council to fulfil its commitment – at the July meeting of the NPPM he moved a motion (seconded by Wright) that 'the Council be requested to honour their promise to compensate the people of Newcastle with another park area for that part of Birdwood Park that was vested in the Department of Main Roads'. Although he found little joy in the Council, Tom must have derived some satisfaction in the fact that many of the aldermen who had supported the destruction of Birdwood Park, were not re-elected in the Council elections

A section of Birdwood Park before
and after the destruction –
photographs courtesy of the *NMH*

in 1974. In the lead up to that election Tom had drawn up a letter from the NPPM asking the prospective candidates to declare their position in regard to the Council's pledge to compensate the community for the loss of open space in Birdwood Park. Clearly the Newcastle community had not appreciated the Council's heavy handed approach. The election issued in a new era for

Newcastle with Alderman Joy Cummings being elected mayor. It was Tom's view that 'Joy Cummings was the only alderman who was really solid'. Lithgow went further: 'I must pay tribute to Newcastle's great Lord Mayor, Joy Cummings, whose support for conservation and the Newcastle environment will ensure her memory in the hearts and minds of Newcastle people in the future'. Under Cummings' able leadership the Council was set to adopt a more enlightened approach to environmental issues. The first fruit of this new approach was the decision by Council and the DMR to shelve plans to convert King Street into four lanes through to Darby Street. This would have resulted in a the removal of a substantial section of Civic Park. It appears that the Council had learnt a lesson from its poor handling of the Birdwood case – at least in this case 'trees' were given greater priority than 'roads'. It appeared that the Council was becoming more aware of the environmental concerns of the community.[15]

Kooragang Island Nature Reserve

It was such an environmental awareness that led some elderly Stockton residents to complain to their State member about the impact of coal dust in their suburb. In particular, the residents were concerned about the pollution which originated from Kooragang Island, a composite island situated in the Hunter River estuary. Almost a quarter of the island (704 hectares out of a total of 2600 hectares) had been partly or wholly developed for industrial use. Such was the effects of air and water pollution (not only on Stockton) that the State Pollution Control Commission was forced to act. It was aware that in 1972 the National Trust had listed the area as 'classified landscape worthy of preservation' in its *Hunter 2000 Report*. The report which followed made a number of recommendations including that 'a fairly large part of the presently undisturbed area of the island should be preserved in its natural state'. The Coffey Report (1973) was to become the NPPM's blueprint in its attempt to preserve the habitat of the river estuary and establish a nature reserve on the island. Working with the National Trust Landscape Committee the executive of the NPPM worked to establish development plans for Kooragang's unspoilt areas based on the Coffey Report. Tom was fully supportive of the executive's handling of this matter – at the June 1974 meeting of the NPPM he moved a motion (seconded by Munro) that 'the Newcastle City Council be asked to supply its plans for recreation areas on Kooragang Island'. At the July meeting he moved a motion (seconded by Shields) that 'the matter be left in the hands of the executive concerning the landscaping of Walsh Point'. It was clear from the comments of the President that Walsh Point was in a pretty poor state. This would have been of particular concern to Tom who had worked here in the 1920s.

By June 1976 there had been some progress. Lithgow (seconded by Tom) received support from the members to send a letter to the Premier regarding Kooragang. The letter:

> noted with great interest the Council's proposals for planning for Industry and for the establishment of a Natural Area under the control of the National Parks & Wildlife Service on Kooragang Island. We complement the Council on its underlying concept and general strategy and we strongly support Council's initiative. We believe that the Natural Area proposed should include all the area recommended by the Coffey Report regarding the development of Kooragang Island and we hope that Council will reconsider the finding of the Commission in this

regard and resolve to include all the Natural Area proposed by the Coffey Report, in its control plan.

A second motion put forward by Lithgow (seconded by Tom) resolved that 'this motion be conveyed to the Newcastle City Council without delay'. Despite the commitment by Council, progress in establishing a nature reserve was slow. In his '1978 Annual Report' the President of the NPPM, Don Barnett, commented 'we have pursued many and varied subjects during the previous twelve months. Amongst these has been Kooragang Island – and the adoption of the Coffey Report'. The following year the President reported: 'in February this year the Movement organised a meeting which was addressed by the Senior Projects Officer of the Australian Conservation Foundation on the Kooragang Island Conservation Area. Despite the excellent and inspiring address little action has developed on this issue and perhaps our attention might be directed on this matter in the ensuing year'. What was particularly frustrating was the fact that during the year the area had been nominated and accepted for inclusion on the interim 'Register of the National Estate' by the Australian Heritage Commission. Furthermore, the Kooragang Island Advisory Committee had commissioned a report to determine the boundaries of the proposed nature reserve. Major studies were also been undertaken by the Department of Public Works, the Newcastle Flora and Fauna Society, National Parks and Wildlife Service, the Department of Environment and Planning and the NSW Fisheries Department. What was now needed was government action. The next year, Lithgow, the new President of the NPPM, reported that action on the proposed reserve was becoming urgent – the government needed to implement as quickly as possible the Coffey Report. He noted that the NPPM had received a sympathetic letter from the Minister of

Planning and the Environment but nothing had eventuated. Pressure continued to be exerted by various groups including the NPPM until finally the State Government announced its intention to establish a nature reserve in 1981. The Kooragang Nature Reserve was finally gazetted by the National Parks and Wildlife in 1983. But as the '1983–1984 Annual Report' of the NPPM pointed out that the task was not yet complete: 'the Kooragang Nature Reserve is another important step but much is still needed if the Hunter estuary is to remain a viable and living entity providing a diverse habitat for birds, fish and crustaceans'. It was not until 1985 that a State Environmental Protection Policy (SEPP) was promulgated for fourteen established wetlands in NSW including Kooragang Island. Tom continued to seek government assurances that the community would have the greatest possible access to the protected areas on Kooragang. At the June 1985 meeting of the NPPM he moved (seconded by Adamthwaite) that 'we apply pressure on those who control Kooragang to see if it can be developed as unfenced open space'. At the October 1987 meeting Tom moved another motion (seconded by Kennedy) that 'a suitable area should be set aside on Kooragang for sporting activities and recreation'. The importance of Kooragang for conservation purposes was reflected in a major rehabilitation project undertaken by the Hunter Catchment Management Trust in the Hunter River estuary, Ash Island, Tomago and Stockton Sand Spit. The aims of this project were to rehabilitate, restore and create fishery and other wildlife habitats. The importance of the work undertaken by the NPPM and other organisations to preserve and protect this area is underlined by the fact that Kooragang Island Reserve is the largest single estuary reserve in NSW.[16]

The Myall Lakes

In his '1970 Annual Report' Richley referred to his optimism for the future. It was his view that 'the climate of public opinion is changing and that people are becoming more aware of the importance of the environment in our day to day life'. It was such an awareness that led to local residents opposing the ongoing sand mining operation within the Myall Lakes area. From 1956 onwards various mining companies had operated in the outer dune barrier of the Myall Lakes extracting mineral sands such as rutile and zircon. In 1965 in response to intense public opposition to sand mining along the NSW coast, the government established the Sim Committee to provide recommendations regarding sand mining and conservation. In 1967 the committee recommended the establishment of a national park between Broadwater and Kataway Bay, to the east of the lake system, which would, however still allow the continuation of sand mining in the rest of the area. Richley worked closely with Rod Earp, the President of the Hunter Manning National Parks Association (later the National Parks Association of NSW) to convince the government authorities to establish the National Park and exclude sand mining from the entire area of the Myall Lakes. In August 1970 Lithgow released the following statement to the media:

> the Northern Parks and Playgrounds Movement fully supports the proposal for the establishment of a coastal National Park in the Hunter Valley Region at the Myall Lakes. The Myall Lakes and their surroundings are well known for their outstanding natural beauty and the area is well situated to serve the expanding urban and industrial area of the lower Hunter as a worthwhile national park, equal in quality

to the Royal National Park or the Kuring-Gai Chase in the Sydney Region. The Myall Lakes Committee representing leading conservation organisations and a wide body of community opinion has prepared a viable National Park proposal which will ensure the balanced development of the Myall Lakes system... The Myall Lakes National Park will establish a firm basis for the continued development of the tourist and sea food industries in the Port Stephens and Stroud Shires and as such will make a positive contribution to the overall potential of the Hunter Valley region.

Scenes of the Myall Lakes (1970s)
Photographs courtesy of the *NMH*

Concerning the ongoing mining operation in the area, the Secretary clearly spelt out the NPPM's total opposition:

> all the north coast beaches and their hinterlands are threatened with systematic despoliation over the next twenty years by rutile mining and the Government proposes to withhold only four miles of the coastline for scientific research. The narrow coastal strip adjacent to the Myall Lakes should be withheld from sand mining while it still remains intact. The destruction of the area could jeopardise the viability of the entire Lakes' system.

The work of the Myall Lakes Committee, the Hunter Manning National Parks Association and the NPPM was finally rewarded in 1970 when the NSW Cabinet approved the establishment of the Myall Lakes National Park which included Broughton Island and the bed of the lake system. Two years later the Myall Lakes National Park was gazetted. Despite this success, sand mining was to continue for another five years in the high sand dunes along the eastern edge of the lake. The NPPM continued to pressure the government to bring all such activity to an end – in his '1977 Annual Report' the President was pleased to point out that 'the Movement has supported other conservation bodies in their efforts to prevent further sand mining in the Myall Lakes National Park. We are, therefore, pleased to report that the State Government recent decision on this area goes most of the way to fulfilling this need'.

In 1977 the State Government banned all sand mining in existing National Parks and began to phase out mining in areas proposed for national parks. Tom was clear that Richley had played an important role in seeing this matter through to a successful conclusion – he later referred to his friend as 'the right hand man in the Myall Lakes'. But Tom and the other members of the NPPM had also played their part, as had the members of various other conservation groups. When reflecting on the struggle to establish the Myall Lakes National Park in 1984, Tom remarked 'we've got a very proud record in respect to things of this nature'.[17]

The Myall Lakes National Park. Courtesy of *NMH*.

The Barrington Tops National Park

In conjunction with the Hunter Manning National Parks Association, the NPPM also took the lead on working for the establishment of a national park at Barrington Tops. In the 1950s there was a push from local councils and business interests to establish an extensive resort and holiday village in the Barrington Tops area. Richley and Earp once again joined forces to oppose the development arguing that it would destroy the area. Public pressure resulted in the State Government in 1959 setting aside as nature reserves two small areas, one on Gloucester Tops, the other in the Williams River. The next ten years saw the government under increasing pressure to protect the whole Barrington area. Finally in 1969 the government announced that it would establish the Barrington Tops National Park consisting of 14,000 hectares including the areas of Mount Barrington, Mount Royal and the Gloucester Tops.

Barrington Tops National Park, Gloucester, NSW –
photographs courtesy of the National Parks & Wildlife Service, NSW.

Views of Barrington Tops National Park, Gloucester, NSW – photographs courtesy of the National Parks & Wildlife Service, NSW.

In the 1970s and 1980s the Movement took part in the debates concerning the use of native forests for timber production. As forest areas were progressively withdrawn from logging (rainforests first then eucalypt forest) the size of the national park grew. The park was enlarged to a size of 62,980 hectares by major additions in 1984, 1997 and 1999. In 1986 the Barrington Tops National Park gained World Heritage listing. In 1993 Lithgow reminded the members of the NPPM 'of the Movement's long and active interest in the Barrington Tops area since 1952'. He pointed out that 'the Movement supports the declaration of a Wilderness Area over those lands at Barrington Tops which were assessed by the National Parks and Wildlife Service as meeting the criteria for wilderness'. He urged all members 'to write to all local members of parliament and to the NSW Premier demanding that the wilderness be declared'. One can be sure that Tom was one of the members who wrote often to the government authorities regarding the Barrington area. In 1996 the Editor of the *NMH* had cause to reflect on Tom's role in the establishment of the Barrington Tops National Park. He concluded that 'without people like Tom Farrell who through their actions, persistence and courage, this public place would not have become a reality'. The Barrington Wilderness was declared in 1999[18]

Mount Sugarloaf

Richley, Tom and the NPPM also played a significant role in establishing the Mt Sugarloaf State Park. Mt Sugarloaf is a mountain in the lower region of the Hunter Valley overlooking Newcastle, Lake Macquarie, Cessnock and Maitland. From its summit, spectacular 360 degree views can be obtained of the surrounding area. A plan for a park was first put forward by the NPPM in 1961. At the June meeting Dews (seconded by Cartwright) put forward a motion that 'fifty to sixty acres including the summit be sought as a reserve'. Richley informed the members that only a 'very small area in such an outstanding beauty spot was available for public use'. Over the next four years Don Morris worked on a much grander proposal which envisaged a park area of 1500 acres consisting of 1400 acres of land at the northern end of the Sugarloaf Range adjacent to the Heaton State Forest and a State Forest Park of 100 acres at the summit point. In submitting the proposal to the Minister for Lands, the Forestry Commission, the State Planning Authority and the Minister for Conservation for their consideration the NPPM argued that:

> with the likely expansion of Newcastle towards the west around the northern end of Lake Macquarie and the amalgamation of the present isolated communities from West Wallsend south, the Sugarloaf Range forms a natural separation between this major urban complex and the cities of Maitland, Cessnock and Kurri Kurri. It is very fortunate that major forest reserves exist over most of the range, thus protecting it from undesirable development. We feel that a park proposal at Mount Sugarloaf should accept these reserves and attempt to supplement them, as the Forestry Commission's policy of development of tourist roads, provision of fireplaces and other facilities in State Forests, would seem eminently suitable to the development of this area.

Clearly the NPPM saw that the Mt Sugarloaf Range, if properly managed, could provide a significant green belt area for the cities of the lower Hunter.

At the end of the following year, Richley made clear his appreciation of the support the proposal had received from the Minister of Lands and Mines, Mr T. Lewis, MLA and the Member for Kurri Kurri, Mr Ken Booth MLA. Due to this political support he was confident that 'the proposal to establish a State Park of 1400 acres at the northern end of Mt Sugarloaf appears certain to be brought to fruition in the near future'. Unfortunately, LMSC was not as supportive of the scheme. In 1967 Mr Lewis made clear that the State Government supported the acquisition of 1120 acre park at Mt Sugarloaf on the condition that LMSC found the money to compensate Coal & Allied Industries, the company who owned the mining rights for the underlying coal deposits. In what Richley described as 'a wonderfully public spirited gesture' the company had offered to sell the land at a much reduced rate. Despite this, the LMSC had failed to act. It is clear that Lewis was frustrated by the response – he told the members of the NPPM at the 1968 Annual General Meeting that he was keen to proceed with action sanctioned under Section 197 of the Crowns Lands Consolidation Act 1917. He envisaged that with the company's agreement the land could be resumed under the terms of the Public Works Act 1912. In July 1969 the company announced that it was not satisfied with the amount of money on offer. Lewis then referred the matter to the Lands Board. In response the NPPM working with Dews on the Mt Sugarloaf Trust, increased its pressure on the LMSC to commit more money to the project. Tom and Richley prepared to give evidence before the Lands Board. It is clear from a later statement that Tom had been involved with the Mt Sugarloaf proposal from an early date. In reference to the struggle Tom commented that 'you don't know the bloody fight we (Joe Richley and I) had to give to get Sugarloaf'. As the President was pleased to report in his

'1970 Annual Report' the efforts of the two men did not go unrewarded:

> This year has seen the campaign for a reasonably large park at Mount Sugarloaf brought to a successful conclusion. Messrs J. Richley and R. Farell [*sic*] attended a Lands Board hearing and gave evidence in support of the Movement's proposal for a reserve of 1,120 acres. The Board's decision was in the affirmative. The Hon. T. Lewis, Minister for Lands has agreed to provide fifty per cent of the cost of acquisition if the Lake Macquarie Shire Council and the Cessnock City Council would provide twenty-five per cent each. This they agreed to do.

Clearly Tom and Richley's appearance before the Lands Board had done the trick. The efforts of the NPPM to persuade the LMSC to throw its financial weight behind the project had also born fruit. Although the size of the State Park was not as large as had been first proposed, it was as Richley pointed out 'an achievement of which the Movement can be justly proud'. Quite fittingly, in 1979 a row of trees was planted in the Mt Sugarloaf Reserve to honour the memory of Joe Richley. Among the participants was Tom Farrell who had done his part to secure the area for the community. Tom would have been pleased that over the next ten years the scope of the project grew as Crown Land and State Forests were joined to create the 3937 hectare Sugarloaf State Conservation Area. This area was located within the catchment of the lower Hunter River and the small watercourses that flowed directly into Lake Macquarie adjacent to the towns of Awaba, Freeman's Waterhole, Killingworth, Mulbring, Seahampton, Wakefield and West Wallsend. It remains today an area of significant environmental importance. [19]

Glenrock Lagoon State Recreation Area

Another key area of Newcastle that Tom was active in preserving was Glenrock Lagoon. This area only ten minutes-drive from the Newcastle City centre contains the last surviving pocket of coastal rainforest in the region. It is an area steeped in Aboriginal culture and rich in fauna and flora. Nearby on forty hectares of land the Scout Association of Australia had been granted a lease to pursue scouting activities. Shortly after its formation the NPPM and the Newcastle Flora and Fauna Protection Society began to lobby the State Government to protect the area. The Northumberland County Plan had recommended that the area be reserved for open space and recreation. It was clear under the county plan that the area was considered part of the city's natural green belt. However, the local councils showed little interest. In 1950 some progress was made when the LMSC dedicated as reserve land eighty-nine hectares of Crown Land at Flaggy Creek, a watercourse about 4 kilometres long that rises about 3 kilometres South of Kotara and flows into Glenrock Lagoon. The Flaggy Creek Reserve included two waterfalls, Little Flaggy Creek, Flaggy Creek and the area up to Kahibah and Highfields. Little Flaggy Creek is a tributary of Flaggy Creek – both creeks flow into Glenrock Lagoon. Throughout the 1950s the NPPM pressured the relevant authorities to produce a proper development plan for Flaggy Creek Reserve. As Tom later recalled it was the Movement that 'pressed the State Government to financially support the development of this area'. As a result a trust was established to administer the area in 1952. In 1960 the Flaggy Creek Reserve was zoned open space under the terms of the Northumberland County Plan. The adjacent areas were zoned non-urban being set aside for special uses and open space.

By the mid-1960s the NPPM was interested in creating a large area of coastal land bounded by Glenrock Lagoon, Burwood Road and Dudley declared a wild-life refuge. Much of this land was owned by BHP who operated the New Burwood Colliery at Whitebridge and the Old Burwood Colliery near Glenrock. Although the surface works at Old Burwood Colliery were now redundant, its shafts provided access and ventilation for the New Burwood Colliery. Given that much of this land was owned by BHP, Tom was keen to make contact with the company. As early as March 1965 Tom was attempting to organise a meeting between Mr Wilkinson, the Manager of BHP Colliery, and a delegation from the NPPM regarding land at Glenrock. At the October 1970 meeting of the NPPM Tom moved a motion (seconded by Munro) that 'we ask BHP to apply to have the area bounded by Glenrock Lagoon, Burwood Road, Flaggy Creek Reserve and Dudley declared a wild life refuge'. At the January 1971 meeting he moved a further motion (seconded by Shields) that 'the General Superintendent of Collieries BHP be asked what was the company's intended use of the Dudley area and is this in conflict with the intended dedication of a wild-life sanctuary'. Although BHP was slow to respond, the President was confident of a positive outcome due to the fact that 'the company had already dedicated similar areas in the Wollongong region for this purpose'.

Such optimism may have been misplaced as the idea of a coastal park came under serious challenge from certain quarters in the years that followed. The NPPM working with various other organisations had to oppose the establishment of a coal-loader off Burwood Beach and the push for residential development on Merewether Ridge in the 1970s. Working with the Newcastle Fauna & Flora Association, Lithgow undertook extensive research into the natural history of the area. The published findings recommended that the area should be declared a State Recreation Area. At the same time the NCC and LMSC had initiated a major study into the possibility of setting up a major reserve based on the Glenrock area which would include all uncommitted foreshore lands from Blacksmiths to Merewether. The study found that the area was of great conservation and recreational significance and recommended that it be considered as a major recreational area. Tom had kept a watchful eye on developments. In November 1978 in response to a proposal by the Hunter District Water Board to expand its sewage treatment facility at Burwood Beach, Tom had moved a motion (seconded by Shields) that 'a letter be sent to the Planning and Environment Commission informing them of the proposal by the Hunter District water Board and requesting them to ensure that the whole of the land is retained as open space'. Tom put forward a second motion that letters be sent to the Minister for Public Works, Hunter District Water Board, NCC and Richard Face, the local State member. The on-going operation of the sewage plant was a problem as leaking mains had polluted Glenrock Lagoon.

In his '1980 Annual Report' the President of the NPPM explained that the Movement had spent a great deal of time working for the proper management of the Flaggy Creek Reserve which was a central element in the Newcastle-Lake Macquarie Coastal Study. To this end the NPPM had worked closely with Richard Face, the State Member for Charlestown, to ensure that a trust is established made up of citizens and representatives from Local Government to manage the existing Reserve and other Crown Lands in the area and work for the acquisition of the remaining open space recommended in the Newcastle-Lake Macquarie Coastal Study. In the 'NPPM

Annual Report 1981' the President was pleased to point out that 'one of the most important proposals developed this year was the proposal by the NSW Department of Planning and Environment for a State Recreation Area encompassing lands designated for a major recreation area within Newcastle –Lake Macquarie Coastal Study'. This matter had been first raised with the NPPM by Mr John Paynter, the Assistant Director of the NSW Department of Planning and Environment, when he addressed members at the Annual General Meeting the year before. The proposal recommended that land between Merewether and Dudley and around Jewells Swamp be established as a State Recreation Area in conjunction with an extension of the Awabakal Nature Reserve at Dudley. The President urged that 'the areas which are existing open space or Crown Land should be immediately dedicated and the Government make a commitment to the acquisition of the adjacent areas'. Throughout 1982 the NPPM worked with the Newcastle Flora and Fauna Society and various local Progress Associations to advance the issue. Efforts to establish an ad hoc committee to work for the Glenrock State Recreation Area proved frustrating as meetings were held irregularly. Despite the slow progress, Lithgow, in his '1982 Annual Report' rallied the troops, reminding them that 'it is vital to the urban area of Lake Macquarie and Newcastle that this project be brought to fruition in the near future'. Tom did his part to move the cause forward – at the July meeting of the NPPM he moved a motion (seconded by Wright) that 'through Richard Face we write to the Minister for Planning and Environment asking that a parcel of land be purchased from BHP to be secured as part of a coastal land reserve and that all of the Coastal Lands Study proposal that is not presently public reserve should be acquired for that purpose'. As Tom's motion makes clear the NPPM appreciated the support it received from the local member, Richard Face. As Lithgow was later to comment 'Richard Face got right behind us and was a great help in the formation of the State Recreation Area'.

In line with Tom's suggestion the State Government and the LMSC began to acquire small but significant areas of freehold land that was vital for the implementation of the Newcastle-Lake Macquarie Coastal Study. Tom, however, was opposed to land exchanges that might be agreed to between the State Government and BHP. He wanted the government to acquire the land outright. At the October 1984 meeting of the NPPM Tom moved a motion (seconded by Wright) that 'we write to the Lands Department objecting to land swaps with areas of Flaggy Creek Reserve with BHP and we urge that the Government should take steps to acquire it'. Tom moved a second motion (seconded by Wright) that 'we write to the Premier, Neville Wran, asking him to make a firm commitment to the Glenrock State Recreation Area and to make a statement about the stage that has been reached'. In 1984 the NPPM placed a submission before the Bicentennial Authority for the funding of the Glenrock State Recreation Area. The submission was based on the work Lithgow had completed in conjunction with the Newcastle Fauna and Flora Association.

Tom did not have to wait long for a reply. On 29 March 1985, Bob Carr, the Minister for Planning and Environment, announced that the land would be preserved as the Glenrock State Recreation Area. Later that year BHP and the State Government agreed on the transfer of 130 hectares of coastal land between Glenrock Lagoon and the northern end of Dudley Beach. In return BHP received freehold title of several areas of Crown Land in the northern section of Lake Macquarie. Although Tom would not have been happy with this arrangement, he would have appreciated what had been achieved. In July 1986 the core area of the Glenrock State Recreation Area (150 hectares) was finally gazetted. Significantly, the protection of the area was vested in the NSW Parks and Wildlife Service, a statutory body charged by an Act of Parliament with the responsibility of guarding the natural heritage.

In his '1984–1985 Annual Report' Lithgow emphasised the significance of what had been achieved:

> the proposed Glenrock State Recreation Area between Merewether and Dudley will be the first State Recreation Area in our region and will cover nearly 500 hectares of distinctive coastal scenery and attractive bushland. Its potential for passive recreation and nature conservation, for bushwalking and surfside activities, in a relatively natural setting, is greatly enhanced by its proximity to the largest population density of the lower Hunter.

The President's only regret was that 'this was not secured thirty years ago when it was first proposed by the Northumberland County Council, for it has suffered scars from insensitive development, particularly over the last twenty years'. The President closed his report by paying special tribute to Richard Face and Ken Booth, the Treasurer, 'for their untiring efforts to secure the Glenrock State Recreation Area which will be of great significance to the region as a whole'. It is clear that Tom shared these sentiments – at the January 1986 meeting of the NPPM he supported a motion (moved by Ron Jackson) that 'we write to Richard Face congratulating him on the hard work done on our behalf'.

In order to build on what had been achieved, the Glenrock

Community Advisory Committee was formed with members being drawn from eighteen different conservation groups. Key members included the NPPM, the Newcastle Fauna and Flora Society and the Australian Conservation Foundation. Ongoing issues for the committee included the continued quarrying of the area by Newcastle Council, potential environmental damage by plans of the Hunter District Water Board to upgrade sewerage facilities at Burwood Beach and a mining proposal for Burwood Beach. Other issues included indiscriminate dumping of rubbish in the area, four wheel drive and trail-bike damage, erosion and mine subsidence. Tom was ever vigilant in his efforts to protect the area. At the May 1986 meeting of the NPPM Tom moved a motion (seconded by Dews) that 'we protest against any mining at Burwood Beach on Hunter Water Board land and demand that the land be included in the proposed Glenrock State Recreation Park forthwith'. In a second motion (seconded by Adamthwaite) Tom moved that 'the NPPM support the publication of the Glenrock Management Document'. At the May 1987 meeting Tom moved a motion (seconded by Jackson) that 'we make representations to Minister Carr, Crosio and the NCC, the Hunter District Water Board and the LMSC supporting the action of the Glenrock Community Advisory Committee in seeking the closure and rehabilitation of quarry lands and the inclusion of all adjacent lands as part of the State Recreation Area'. It is clear that Tom and the Glenrock Community Advisory Committee spoke with one voice. In his '1986 Annual Report' Lithgow clearly articulated the challenges faced by those working to preserve the Glenrock State Recreation Reserve:

> the proper management of the partly gazetted Glenrock State Recreation area is of paramount

importance if the natural and archaeological value of the area are to be maintained. There is certainly great public interest and support for Glenrock... The surplus Water Board land must be brought under proper management within the park at the earliest possible date. The Council gravel quarry must be rehabilitated and this suggested sand mining of the area blocked. The work of the soil conservation service on erosion control has been unfortunate. Great damage has been done not only to a large amount of vegetation, but to archaeological remains before they have been properly documented. The main problem is that there can be no positive design control until a management strategy has been decided and goals and standards set. There is a great need for attractive development that is sympathetically carried out towards clear management goals. Many of the bulldozed four wheel tracks should be closed. A graded peripheral walking trail from Merewether Heights to Dudley along the higher land could be established as part of the Bicentennial.

The President reassured members that 'we are working with the other conservation and resident groups who have an interest in the Recreation Area to achieve these goals'.

It is clear that Tom was keen to keep up the pressure. At the May 1987 meeting of the NPPM he moved a motion (seconded by Wright) that 'we reaffirm our previous position that all workings of the quarry cease immediately and that the runoff be contained as per the Coastal Lands Study'. In June 1987 he supported a NPPM's initiative to call a Public Protest Meeting to bring an end to all quarry activities in the Glenrock area.

But the relevant authorities proved obstinate. By the end of the year the President had to report that the Hunter District Water Board and the NCC wanted to continue to quarry Glenrock Buff, 'the State Recreation Area's most scenic headland', for another fifteen years. This decision had been taken without the benefit of an Environmental Impact Statement. In response the NPPM called on the Minister to immediately close the quarry and gazette the Water Board Land within the reserve. At the very least the NPPM called on the Minister to prepare a management strategy for the whole of Glenrock State Recreation Area that demonstrated how the existing quarry is to be incorporated and rehabilitated within the future reserve. Furthermore, the NPPM demanded that an Environmental Impact Statement be prepared to show the quarry's impact on the reserve and its effect on its surroundings. The NPPM's efforts to have the quarry closed and establish a Management Plan for the area continued into the 1990s. The NPPM also applied pressure on the District Water Board (Water Corporation) to limit the impact of its Burwood Beach Waste Water Plant on the surrounding area. It was a busy time for the NPPM - a change of State government in 1988 had brought its own difficulties – in his '1993-1994 Annual Report' the President referred to 'the horrendous attacks on the environment' that had occurred in the year. It was the opinion of the President that 'the Government had lost its way with the wilderness declarations… planning in our own region has become a sort of alchemy where the statutory process is hidden and bypassed with bureaucratic procedures employed to confuse rather than elucidate'. This led to a degree of frustration – in his '1994-1995 Annual Report' Lithgow commented 'we are confronted with a conservation backlog in our region and environmental quality is eroded each day we excuse ourselves from finding solutions. It is intolerable that the main reservation issues near our urban areas have not been resolved. The major regional reservations identified for the lower Hunter need to be dedicated in the life of the present parliament or they may never be acquired'.

Despite the difficulties, significant progress regarding the Glenrock State Recreation Area was achieved during the 1990s. A plan to rezone as 'residential' seven hectares of land on the northern side of Glenrock Reserve had been blocked by a number of local resident and environment groups (including the NPPM). Additional land was purchased by the State Labour Government in the late 1980s and added to the reserve. After long and protracted negotiations the Merewether quarry closed and significant improvements were made to the Burwood Beach Wastewater Treatment Works. Lithgow later pointed out 'we've had to force the issue on the quarry. The potential of the quarry was to destroy a very important part of the State Recreation Area. And there's been other things happen, like the sewage outfall that made a hell of a mess there'. Finally, the long awaited Plan of Management for Glenrock State Recreation Area was adopted by the Carr Labor Government in 1997. An additional forty hectares of land was added to the Recreation Area consisting of two parcels of land, one along the oceanfront at Burwood Beach and another on the southern side of the Pacific Highway between Highfields and Merewether Heights. In 1999 when the former Bailey's farm off Scenic Drive at Merewether Heights was donated to the Glenrock State Recreation Park, the National Parks and Wildlife Service, with the help of local volunteers put in place a weed eradication program.

Today Glenrock State Conservation Area covers an area of 534 hectares which stretches along the coastline between the residential suburbs of Dudley and Merewether. The area contains ten significant vegetation communities, two endangered

Glenrock State Conservation Area, located adjacent to Kahibah
and Highfields between Merewether Beach and Dudley Bluff.
Photographs courtesy of the *NMH*

ecological communities and five threatened flora species.
There are more than 145 historic sites in the area including the
oldest road/tram and rail tunnel remains in Australia and the
remnants of Burwood Colliery, one of the oldest coal-mining

sites in the Hunter. While the preservation of this significant area was achieved thanks to the efforts of many groups and individuals – Tom Farrell and the other members of the NPPM had played their part. In commenting on the role of the NPPM Lithgow made the following remarks: 'so things happen in the public arena in fits and starts. It's terribly important for the community to realise that there's nobody up there looking after you. Absolutely, the community has to really tune in and get cracking. And that's what the Parks and Playgrounds Movement has been doing all this time I suppose'. There is no doubt that Tom Farrell was one of those who had been 'tuned in' and 'got cracking' on the Glenrock issue.[20]

Hunter Region Botanical Gardens

Another issue close to Tom's heart was the establishment of a Botanical Garden in the Newcastle region. He had raised this issue as early as 1958 when Mr Cahill, the Premier, had informed the NPPM that no funds were available for such a project. In response Tom moved a motion (seconded by Tate) at the November 1958 meeting of the NPPM that 'the Premier be advised that we deplore the neglect of Newcastle and its area and we consider that a proportion of the moneys available should be allocated to Newcastle instead of it all been spent in Sydney'. Although little progress was made in the next twenty years, it was not an issue that the NPPM was prepared to ignore. In his '1977 Annual Report', Barnett informed members that 'we have pursued with the Planning and Environment Commission the need to set aside in future planning an area for Newcastle & District Zoological Gardens'. At the June 1980 meeting of the NPPM Tom moved a motion (seconded by Barnett) that 'we write to the Minister of Agriculture asking him to establish a Botanic Gardens in the Newcastle region for the people of the Hunter Valley'. Tom made clear to the Minister that 'when possible sites are being investigated the Movement should be consulted'. As Lithgow pointed out in the '1980 Annual Report' over $2 million dollars each year was spent managing Sydney's Botanic Gardens. The Movement expected 'a similar per capita expenditure to be made on a Botanic Garden for the Hunter Region'. By 1981 a special subcommittee, the Botanic Gardens Steering Committee (headed by Barnett) had been established. It set out to enlist the support of the public for the project by holding a series of meetings. In the '1982 Annual Report 1982' the President was pleased to report that

> The Botanic Gardens Steering Committee has completed its work and on 9 June 1982 a public meeting was held and a Botanic Gardens Committee formally established, again under the leadership of Don Barnett. They are continuing the work and have already set up a Friends of the Botanic Gardens organisation. We wish them well and will continue in our support for this important facility in the Hunter region.

Hunter Region Botanic Gardens located north of the Hexham Bridge at Tomago. Courtesy of the *NMH*

The Hunter Botanic Gardens, north of the Hexham Bridge, Tomago.
Photographs courtesy of the *NMH*

In the following year's 'Annual Report' the President reported that 'we have continued to support the Botanic Gardens Committee and our Vice President, Don Barnett'. The Committee after visiting the Botanic Gardens in Sydney and Coffs Harbour had developed its proposal and developed a constitution. By the end of 1984 matters were progressing with the President of the NPPM reporting that 'Don Barnett and his Botanic Gardens Committee have made an important contribution and proposals for a Botanic Gardens at Tomago are nearing fruition'. In 1986 the Hunter Region Botanic Gardens were opened to the public at Heatherbrae near Raymond Terrace. The 140 hectares site (much of it bushland) was leased to the Hunter Region Botanic Gardens Ltd, a non-profit company of volunteers, by Hunter Water Corporation. The company of volunteers was charged with the responsibility of designing, developing and managing the Gardens. In his address to the Annual General Meeting of the NPPM in 1996, Don Barnett paid tribute to the Movement which he described as 'the father of conservation and environmental organisations in Newcastle'. He acknowledged that the establishment of the Botanic Gardens would not have been possible without the support of the NPPM. One of the catalysts had been Tom Farrell who continued to advocate for the Botanic Gardens in the years ahead.[21]

Newcastle East

Tom also maintained a keen interest in the inner-city area of Newcastle, particularly in the East end. Over a number of decades he supported the efforts of Lithgow and other members of the NPPM to ensure that the heritage value of this area was protected. Of particular interest were Nobby's Island and the breakwater, Fort Scratchley, the area around Shortland Esplanade, inner city commons like Pacific Park and the Harbour Foreshore. The aim of Lithgow and the NPPM was to oppose any piecemeal development of the East End by ensuring that a proper town-planning approach was adopted. Tom's interest in the area can be dated back to 1966 when at the January meeting of the NPPM he moved a motion (seconded by Jones) that 'we seek a meeting with Mr Morris, the Minister for Transport, regarding the release of the railway land at the East of the City for parkland'.

At the October 1969 meeting of the NPPM Tom moved a further motion (seconded by Lithgow) that 'we ask the Newcastle City Council to request the planning officer to complete an open space study for the city area which was commenced by the Northumberland County Council and prepare a balanced functional classification of the New Park system'. Between 1966 and 1970 Tom displayed a keen interest in the East End of the inner-city area by putting forward a number of motions at various meetings of the NPPM. These motions dealt with the release of railway land associated with the Zaara Street Power Station for parkland, the area of Fort Scratchley becoming parkland and the development of Pacific Park in accordance with the County Plan. At the June 1969 meeting of the NPPM Tom seconded a motion put forward by Lithgow that 'a letter be sent to the State Planning Authority to investigate the preservation of the Nobby's Scratchley area and its recommendations be forwarded to the Minister of Lands'. This motion followed a presentation by Lithgow at the previous meeting entitled 'Historic Sites of Newcastle East'. In his presentation Lithgow referred to a *SMH* article which commented that 'to think of Newcastle without Nobby's is to try to think of Sydney without the Harbour Bridge'. Action in this area was necessary because in February 1969 the Works Committee of the NCC had inspected a site for a parking area near Nobby's breakwater. At the February meeting of the NPPM Tom was quick to condemn the proposal moving a motion (seconded by Lithgow) that 'we oppose the Newcastle City Council's proposal to turn the sand dunes into a parking area'. The NPPM joined forces with other groups including the Newcastle Trades Hall Council, the Communist Party of Australia and the Newcastle Principals' Association to successfully block the Council's plan. Clearly the proposed action by Council had showed that the site was vulnerable to poor development decisions.

In 1970 Lithgow submitted a proposal to the National Parks and Wildlife Service that significant areas of the East End such as Lieutenant Shortland's landing area, Governor Macquarie's Promenade and Fort Scratchley be declared Historic Sites. Despite a 'vigorous campaign' by the NPPM and the support of key aldermen like Joy Cummings, the proposal was rejected. The Movement took some solace in the fact that an enlarged version of the proposal was included in the City Engineer's Development Scheme for Newcastle East. In 1974 the NPPM joined forces with the Newcastle East Residents Group to put forward a proposal for the revitalisation of the area which included the establishment of an extensive recreation area on the site of the existing railway marshalling yards, a tourist road encircling the harbour foreshore and beachfront and a one way traffic area bounded by Scott, Pacific and King Street. The NPPM sought representation on the Newcastle East Development Committee and its landscaping subcommittee. Lithgow used this forum to put forward the strong view that any proposal for the East End (which he described as 'this most important area of Newcastle') must make adequate provisions for open space. The Movement wanted to ensure that its voice was heard in any proposal put forward to the Planning and Environment Commission. It strongly supported the Interim Development Order which NCC had prepared in line with the County Plan. It would oppose any attempt to fundamentally alter this concept.

Tom did his best to ensure that the County Plan was followed. When the Council proposed to build a car park on land at Pacific Park in 1975, he mustered the troops. At the July meeting of the NPPM he put forward a proposal (seconded by

Shields) that 'this movement support the Pacific Park proposal as contained in the County Plan and oppose the construction of a car park as proposed in the Pacific Park area'. At the June 1976 meeting Tom put forward a further motion (seconded by Lithgow) that 'the Newcastle City Council be asked to do all in its power to establish Pacific Park in accordance with the Northumberland County Plan'. At the same meeting Lithgow put forward a motion (seconded by Tom) that:

> letters be sent to the Minister for Planning and the Minister for Local Government and the Newcastle City Council to bring to their attention our concern at the long drawn out process of acquisition and development of the area of Pacific Park at Newcastle East. The area was zoned for park in 1952 by Northumberland County Council shown as park in the Minister for Lands Government Scheme in 1955. It was the subject of ministerial inquiry and included in the 1960 prescribed scheme. The Movement asks that all authorities with interests in the area make strenuous efforts to bring the park to fruition. We are particularly adamant that all lands acquired by Newcastle City Council in pursuance of its planning powers must be developed as parkland'.

Despite the lobbying efforts of the NPPM, progress in this area was slow. The President in the '1976 Annual Report' remained hopeful that the recent closure of the Zaara Street Power Station would expedite matters. However, a year later the President could only report that he continued to hope that a solution could be found 'to the many social and physical problems in the area'. In the '1979 Annual Report' the President reiterated the Movement's opposition to the Council's initial proposal for the harbour foreshore. It was the view of the NPPM that the plan was 'simply another development dedicated to the motor car with no real thought to landscaping or beautification to a very important area of Newcastle'. The NPPM argued that the harbour foreshore area could not be considered in isolation – it had to be seen as part of the East End Plan which was under consideration by the Planning and Environment Commission. Tom continued to lobby for this position – at the May meeting of the NPPM he seconded a motion put forward by Lithgow that 'we ask Newcastle City Council to dedicate as parkland the area of land which has been acquired by the Council under the provisions of the Northumberland County Plan'. [22]

The following year brought much better news. The President was pleased to report that:

> the Movement's involvement with community interest in an effort to secure a comprehensive planning scheme for Newcastle East that was based on cultural, historic and economic potential was brought a step closer this year when the Minister for Planning and Environment, the Hon. E.L. Bedford, gazetted the Newcastle East Interim Development Order'. This order replaces the old Northumberland County Planning Scheme for Newcastle East. We have been deeply and continuously involved with the project since 1962 but have been confronted with the herculean task which could not have been overcome without banding together with other community groups for mutual support'.

Progress had also been made in regard to Pacific Park, Fort

Scratchley and the Harbour Foreshore. The City Council had at long last begun the establishment of an enlarged park and had adopted an imaginative landscape plan prepared by Bruce McKenzie. Although the NPPM was disappointed that the Government did not see fit to demolish the old hospital site in order to create a full park (as envisaged in the 1960 plan), it was pleased that Pacific Park would take its place as 'the centrepiece for the redevelopment of the East End'. In regard to the harbour foreshore an agreement had been reached between the local and State authorities that the obsolete railway marshalling yards would be relocated to allow the development of foreshore parklands and some medium density housing. Furthermore, in line with the NPPM's push for the beautification of the harbour foreshore from Nobby's to Merewether Street Wharf, the Council had decided to conduct a nationwide architectural competition to find a suitable design for the area which is 'the gateway to the Hunter region'. In regards to Fort Scratchley, the NPPM had made representations to the Heritage Commission and the Commonwealth Department of Services to have a management and landscaping plan considered for the area. It was hoped that the Commonwealth Government would fund the restoration of the tunnel complex and fortifications because 'the area is not only important to the history of Newcastle but to the heritage of the Commonwealth as a whole'. As Lithgow pointed out 'it is twelve years since this Movement began agitating for the Fort to be made open to the public as an important part of the historic site which included Nobby's Headland, Governor Macquarie's breakwater and Lt. Shortland's landing site when he discovered the Hunter River and its coal deposits'.

The winner of the Newcastle Harbour Foreshore Competition was announced in 1981. The NPPM was pleased that the winning design provided a strong link between the commercial heart of the city and the harbour front as well as featuring the historic areas of the East End. Not one to miss an opportunity Tom attempted to persuade the Council to consider additional open space along the foreshore. At the July meeting of the NPPM he moved a motion (seconded by Molesworth) that 'the City Council consider the resumption of the site of Dark's Ice Works (in Wharf Road) for a public park'. Although nothing came of this proposal, the NPPM could take heart in the fact that restoration work on Fort Scratchley had finally begun. While this was a step in the right direction, the NPPM encouraged the NCC's Fort Scratchley Steering Committee to press the Federal Government for more adequate funding. In regard to Pacific Park, the NPPM used its place on the Newcastle East Task Force to ensure that the recommended extension of the park would proceed in line with the landscape plan.

In 1983 the State Government announced the release of land at Newcastle East for development as parklands and housing. In addition the foreshore project received combined government funding in excess of $8 million. At the July meeting of the NPPM Tom moved a motion (seconded by Jackson) that 'a working party be established towards having the historic East End site fully developed and we bring the submission and the results of our working party to the attention of all appropriate bodies'. Tom's strategy was part of a plan by the NPPM to revitalise the proposal for a Historic Site at Newcastle East which had been first put forward in 1969. At the October meeting he moved (seconded by Jackson) that the Discussion Paper on the East End Historic Site, prepared by Lithgow, be submitted to the Fort Scratchley Trust Committee. He also moved (seconded by Adamthwaite) that 'the whole of the area comprising the old Teachers College (Scott Street) be retained for public space and community facilities'. In regards to Pacific Park Plan significant progress had been made with the construction of a new surf pavilion and underpass which linked the green to the beach front. As if to mark its significance, Pacific Park was chosen by the *NMH* as the site of a memorial fountain marking the newspaper's 125 years of service to the community.[23]

Pacific Park, Newcastle
Photographs courtesy of the NMH

In 1984 the NCC agreed to establish a Newcastle East Historic Site Working Party with Alwyn Adamthwaite as President and Lithgow as Secretary. A submission was made by the Council to the Heritage Council of NSW for a $10,000 grant for a Newcastle East Management Study under the National Estate Grants. It was hoped that the area would be brought under professional management preferably under the National Parks Act which provided the proper statutory framework for Historic Sites in New South Wales. It was the opinion of the President of the NPPM that 'the harbour foreshore project is moving…the community should come together to ensure that all projects – Newcastle East Historic Site, the foreshores and promenade – are fully funded and the total concept is brought to fruition within the next two years'. Despite such optimism, the next year was to bring further frustration and disappointment. In 1985 it was announced by an inter-departmental committee that significant changes were to be made to the winning landscape design. The foreshore landscaping area was to be dramatically reduced by a Housing Commission development against Nobby's Road and the construction of a large car park adjacent to Newcastle Railway Station. It was the view of the NPPM that 'the resulting landscape will only be a shadow of the scheme that won the competition'. At the July 1985 meeting of the NPPM Tom let his frustration be known – he moved (seconded by Adamthwaite) that 'we inform the authorities of our strong disapproval of the Newcastle East Housing Commission development as inappropriate in the area. We insist that the Harbour Foreshore scheme be followed'. At the January 1986 meeting he seconded a motion by Wright that 'this Movement has absolute and utter support for the winning tract design (Foreshore Newcastle) which should not be deviated from in any way whatsoever as it was the winner of an international competition. Any proposal to alter it must require the Council to bring the judges back who must then determine a decision'. At the next meeting Tom responded sharply to the letter from Bob Carr, the Minister for Planning and the Environment, regarding funding for Fort Scratchley – he moved a motion (seconded by Parsons) that 'we disagree with his attitude to our submission and that we inform him that because there are two other fortified historic sites elsewhere in Australia does not justify the fact that the oldest fortified locality and historic defence site in Australia is being neglected for consideration'. Clearly the Movement was dealing with a number of setbacks in this period.

Fort Scratchley
Courtesy of the *NMH*

Tom, however, did not allow these setbacks to curtail his activism. At the May 1986 meeting of the NPPM he moved (seconded by Bryce Gaudry) that 'we call for a public competition to create an effective form of monument for Lieutenant Shortland'. At the same meeting he seconded the motion by Joyce Bond that 'we support the Hills Residents Group proposal to add to Cathedral Park'. At the July meeting he moved a motion (seconded by Jackson) that 'we obtain a legal opinion regarding the legality of the Commission Building Approval without an environmental impact study'. To assist with the legal costs, Tom donated $500 to the fighting fund. Despite this effort, nothing much had changed by the end of the year. In the 'Annual Report' the President of the NPPM informed members that 'the outlook is not bright for the implementation of the Newcastle Harbour Foreshore Scheme'. It was the opinion of the President that 'the Housing Commission and the State Rail Authority have destroyed the principles of the scheme':

> Notwithstanding the fact that the foreshore, including Nobbys and Fort Scratchley, is registered as a National Estate conservation zone, and that the area has a unique historical association and contains buildings on the National Estate Register, the State Government pushed ahead with the building of housing flats in spite of widespread concern and opposition. This is doubly disconcerting because there is just no reason at all why the housing development in the Nobbys Road area was not set back in accord with the Tract design that won the competition, or in compliance with Map 14 of the Inner Area Conservation Study (Newcastle City Council).

The Northern Parks and Playgrounds Movement and the National Trust of Australia proposed the area now being built out as part of the proposed Historic Site at Newcastle East...the area covered by the Housing Commission is probably the site of the first coal mine in Australia...It is deplorable that the Housing Commission's report on the area made no real investigation of the early history of the area. The Movement is not amused, nor are we convinced that a full investigation has been made of this historic area. It is an insult to our intelligence and to our City that it should be left to the Housing Commission to conduct an historical survey! The Movement does not see itself as the arbiter of the history of the city, but we are adamant that further investigations must be made to uncover all the evidence.

Other matters of concern included the rail easement and Wharf Road alignment, overhead rail gantries, over-building of the Queens Wharf project, removal of the Market Street pedestrian concourse, the fenced railway car park at the Watt Street intersection and the restoration of the Customs House. In the President's view: 'now that the original winning scheme has been so badly ravaged, it is important to call for a review of the uses of the residue of the old railway marshalling yards. The parkland proposals at the end of Telford Street must be restored to the plan, so that this important vista through to the harbour is not built out, and more public space is provided around the Bond Store'. In closing the President paid tribute to the former Lord Mayor, Joy Cummings, 'the City's most popular and articulate spokesperson for the foreshore scheme'.

Newcastle East End Precinct
Courtesy of the *NMH*

During 1987 Tom tried to rally support for the NPPM's position. At the June meeting of the NPPM he moved a motion (seconded by Molesworth) that the group contact Tim Moore, Shadow Minister for the Environment, pointing out that the East End would be a 'big issue' for the Liberal Party in the upcoming State election. At the same meeting Tom supported a motion moved by Wright that the Movement enlist the support of the Trades Hall Council in regard to secure State Rail Authority land at the East End for open space. At the July meeting Tom moved a motion (seconded by Wright) that 'we write a follow up letter to Tim Moore and update him on issues relating to SRA land and East End matters'. The same motion suggested writing to Virginia Chadwick, the local Member of the Legislative Council and Opposition Whip, to inform her of these issues. At the September meeting Tom seconded a motion by Wright that Bob Brown, Green Member of the Tasmanian Parliament, be asked to address the Annual General Meeting

Doug Lithgow with Tom – photograph courtesy of the *NMH*

of the NPPM. Clearly Tom was attempting to rally political support for the campaign. At the October meeting he spoke at length about the Southside Park at Newcastle Harbour arguing that 'there should be a parkland area established in the woolshed environs'. Tom was no doubt pleased that in this trying year two members of the NPPM were publically recognised for their environmental work – Doug Lithgow received The Newcastle University's Board of Environmental Studies Environmental Achievement Award and Joy Cummings was honoured with a Civic Reception for her outstanding contribution to the protection of the Newcastle environment. The following year Doug Lithgow was to receive the Dunphy Award for the most outstanding environmental effort by an individual.[24]

Harbour Foreshore Park under construction.
Courtesy of the *NMH*

When the State Rail Authority announced that it intended to auction off its lands at Newcastle East, the NPPM in coordination with other organisations organised a public protest meeting at the City hall on the 5 August 1987. The growing public discontent led to the State Government withdrawing the land from sale and transferring it to the City Council for addition to the Harbour Foreshore Park. At the February 1989 meeting of the NPPM Tom put pressure on the new State Government to honour the previous government's commitment – he seconded a motion put forward by Wright that the Greiner Government confirm that SRA land in Newcastle East would be set aside for open space. The efforts, however, to prevent the overbuilding on the foreshore by stopping the Housing Commission project came to nothing. The NPPM continued to put forward its proposal for a Coal River Historic Site and the establishment of a working party to establish the heritage value of the site. At the March 1989 meeting of the NPPM Tom made his view clear – he put forward a motion (seconded by Shields) that a letter be sent to the relevant State authorities 'expressing our total opposition to any proposal which would see any alienation of public land or of historic sites at Newcastle East'.

In the aftermath of the earthquake the Movement quickly developed a proposal to complete the Newcastle Harbour Foreshore Scheme. It was felt that this would give the city centre the lift it needed. The proposal which included a narrowed rail easement with a parkland corridor was at odds with the Newcastle Transport and Development Study (1990) which advocated the removal of the rail corridor from Civic. It was now the task of the NPPM to save the foreshore as well as the railway. As noted, Tom was a strong supporter of an integrated public transport system which included the retention of the railway through to Newcastle Station. There was positive news on the establishment of a Historic Site in Newcastle East. In conjunction with other groups, the NPPM was finalising its submission to the State Government. There was hope that the State Government and the City Council would at last promote and develop the site as an important historic cultural and recreation attraction.

Harbour Foreshore Park, Newcastle
Courtesy of the *NMH*

Throughout the 1990s the NPPM continued to place before the relevant authorities its vision for the East End Historic Site and the Harbour Foreshore Park. It was not until 24 June 1998 that the Fort Scratchley site was listed on the National Trust Register. In December 2003 The Coal River Precinct was finally gazetted and listed under the NSW Heritage Act. The Foreshore Plan of Management was formally adopted by NCC in 2003 – some fifteen years after Queen Elizabeth II had officially opened the Bicentennial Foreshore Park. The fight to retain the rail corridor continues to this day. Lithgow in particular, but also Tom and the other members of the NPPM, could be justly proud of the role they had played in preserving these areas for the people of Newcastle. The East End including the Pacific Park area would remain a historic focal point for the city. The Foreshore Park would remain a large open space for recreation and a green edge base to the CBD. Both areas served as a visual gateway to Newcastle and the Hunter Region.[25]

Lake Macquarie

Tom's interest in establishing green open spaces in the heart of Newcastle, did not prevent him seeking to establish significant park lands in the Lake Macquarie area. As early as 1959 Tom had moved a motion (seconded by Munro) at the September meeting of the NPPM that 'a letter be sent to the Minister for Mines asking if he would be prepared to receive a deputation in Newcastle to discuss the matter of the reservation of 500 acres (the area now known as Green Point) between Valentine and Belmont as a public reserve'. Twenty-five years later Tom reflected on the long struggle to establish State parkland in Lake Macquarie which included Green Point:

> The area was available then and the Minister for Lands at the time…we took him out and showed him the area and there were no firm promises made but we always felt that we'd get the land (from Valentine to Belmont) when the mine finished. Well the mine is finished now and of course you've seen what they're going to do they're going to commercialise it, subdivide and sell it. Lake Macquarie – when you go around the world, you can go the Killarney or you can go to Lucerne or you can go to many of these other lakes…Lake Macquarie is one of the

most beautiful spots in the world. And there is hardly
a bit of it that is kept for public recreation.

Tom put the slow progress down to the 'damned councils' who
were 'our worst enemies'. By 1984 he had to acknowledge that
the NPPM's objective to establish a National Park in the Lake
Macquarie area was not going to be a realised. He conceded
after twenty-five years of agitation that 'there is not one yet
and there never will be'. But despite this Tom and the other
members of the NPPM could be justly proud of having worked
in conjunction with other groups to successfully establish
significant park lands in the Lake Macquarie area. Among these
were Rathmines State Recreation Area and Green Point. The
movement could also be proud that it had played its part in
limiting the amount of pollution in the lake.

As it had done in the Greater Newcastle area, the NPPM
looked to the Northumberland County Plan to provide
a blueprint for future park lands and reserves in the Lake
Macquarie area. Tom made this clear when he successfully
moved a motion (seconded by Suters) at the June 1967
meeting of the NPPM that 'the movement strongly object to
the proposed development of Black Ned's Bay (Swansea). That
we lodge objection with all appropriate authorities stating that
the zoning remain as shown in the County Plan'. At the same
meeting Tom moved successfully (seconded by Dews) that
'we seek a deputation to the Minister for Local Government
regarding public reserves in the Lake Macquarie area'. It was the
view of the NPPM that the LMSC should purchase the land
prescribed by the Northumberland County Plan by imposing
a levy of fifty cents on every rate payer. Additional funds could
be acquired by approaching the State and Federal Governments
for subsidies.

As noted over a thirty year period Tom and the NPPM took direct action to establish and protect park and recreational land in the Lake Macquarie area. Areas to benefit from this action included Belmont, Black Ned's Bay, Charlestown, Croudace Bay, Speers Point, Sulphide, Swansea, Toronto, Wangi Point and Warners Bay. Tom regularly raised matters regarding the Lake Macquarie area at the monthly meetings of the NPPM. For example, during 'General Business' at the June 1976 meeting Tom moved or seconded eight of the twelve motions. Of these, four dealt with matters relevant to Lake Macquarie:

(Farrell/Richley) letters be sent to the Chief Secretary and Minister for Lands protesting against the action of the Lake Macquarie Shire Council in filling areas of Lake Macquarie at Belmont and Warners Bay.

(Farrell/Richley) that a letter be sent Newcastle City Council asking that Cernley Avenue be extended to Cardiff Road in accordance with the County Plan.

(Richley/Farrell) that the Minister for Local Government be complemented on his statement regarding the future of Black Ned's Bay and we seek his guidance as to a method by which the area can be best protected against further attacks by developers.

(Lithgow/Farrell) that the NPPM is opposed to the destruction of the naturalness of Winding Creek and that the Lake Macquarie Shire Council, the State Planning & Environment Commission and the Lands Department be approached with the aim of establishing a stream control plan for Winding Creek which acknowledges all uses and values relating to Winding Creek including: public values, wildlife values, private flooding problems, channelled areas, scenic and urban conservation values, educational values, recreational values and development of open space and broad area values.

In their efforts to preserve and protect as large an area of Lake Macquarie as possible, Tom and the other members of the NPPM certainly kept the Secretary busy over a number of decades. In the '1985 Annual Report' the President reported 'throughout this year hundreds of representations have been made to politicians, Councils, and other organisations on issues ranging from Speers Point Park to Black Ned's Bay. We have received countless requests for information and help and we have tried to keep the main issues before the public through the media'.

Tom and the NPPM also worked to maintain the pristine nature of the lake by limiting the impact of pollution from sources such as sewerage effluent and erosion. In regard to the latter, the NPPM argued that much of the pollution in the lake was caused by siltation, brought about by developers removing trees from various housing estates. It proposed that the costs involved in correcting the problem should be passed on to developers. In this way there would be an incentive for developers to protect the top soil by preserving trees thus reducing the problem of siltation. The NPPM also welcomed the Council's decision in 1968 to significantly increase its tree planting program. At the January 1971 meeting of the NPPM Tom moved a successful motion (seconded by Shields) that 'we investigate the possibility of having a committee to investigate pollution in Lake Macquarie'. By October 1972 in cooperation with the LMSC and other groups, a public meeting had been called to establish a committee to work for the preservation of Lake Macquarie and to identify suitable large areas of lake-frontage for recreational purposes. This large and representative citizen committee immediately took action to protect the Jewell's Swamp area from unsympathetic development. In 1977 it reported the LMSC to the State Pollution Control Commission for work it had carried out on reclaimed areas of Warners Bay. It was the opinion of the committee that the development had had a detrimental effect on fish life and weed growth in the area. In 1987 after a series of public meetings the United Residents Group for the Environment of Lake Macquarie (URGE) was formed. Two years later the President of the NPPM reported on the progress of this committee: 'there has been a number of issues that have come up and URGE have been quite busy. It has been very important that they've been operating'. It was clear Tom was fully behind the activities of URGE. At the October 1987 meeting of the NPPM he seconded a motion put forward by Molesworth that 'we support all URGE proposals'. It is clear from the press clippings that he collected that Tom maintained a keen interest in the environment of Lake Macquarie.[26]

Rathmines Recreation Park

One area of lake-frontage that Tom was keen to see preserved as park land was the RAAF base at Rathmines. This area was close to Fishing Point where the Farrell family had their holiday house. At the May 1970 meeting of the NPPM Tom moved (seconded by Barnett) that a delegation be sent to the Works Committee of the LMSC 'to discuss the establishment of a park on the site of the Rathmines RAAF Base'. Two months later at the NPPM meeting Tom moved a further motion (seconded by Woodgate) that 'an approach be made to the National Parks

Fund asking for financial assistance to retain the whole of the (Rathmines) area for park land'. Taking its lead from Tom, the whole of the NPPM got behind the proposal. In the end of 1970 the President reported:

> a project which has occupied a lot of your committee's time has been a campaign to persuade the Federal Government to cancel the balance of debt owed by the LMSC for the purchase of the former RAAF base at Rathmines. This area is ideally suited for the development of a regional lakeside park. The Council's financial position makes it difficult for it to repay the debt without disposing of the greater part of this land. If this campaign is to be successful it needs the widest possible public support.

At the June 1971 meeting of the NPPM Tom put forward a motion (seconded by Shields) that 'a letter be sent to LMSC outlining our concerns about the type of development proposed for Rathmines'. In the 1971 Annual Report the President of the NPPM made clear the movement's position in regard to the RAAF base:

> the Movement's aim is to have the whole of the former base dedicated for public parkland. Largely through the local Progress Association, a considerable portion has been set aside and the boating facilities are outstanding. Over the years, the Movement has sought unsuccessfully to have the Commonwealth Government cancel the outstanding part of a debt owed by the Council which had purchased the land in the early 1960s for $200,000. We have also sought

financial assistance from the State Government and have approached the Council to seek their cooperation in making a joint approach, again unsuccessfully.

Despite the setbacks, the President was confident that given the increasing importance of environmental matters in political circles 'the time should soon be ripe to make further approaches because it was most important to obtain as much parkland as possible in this area'.

In May 1972 Tom was active in opposing a proposal put forward by LMSC to establish a large caravan park on the site at Rathmines. He supported a motion put forward by Shields (seconded by Stranton) at the monthly NPPM meeting that the movement object to the proposal pointing out 'the need to preserve the whole area for public use and the need to preserve the tree cover'. The agitation continued throughout the year. The President reported to members at the end of the year:

> the movement is persisting with its attempts to have the Lake Macquarie Shire Council relieved of the burden of the remainder of its debt to the Commonwealth. We believe that if the Commonwealth Government can give the people of Sydney considerable areas of harbour side land which must have a real estate value of millions of dollars, it should cancel the remaining $120,000 owed by the Council so that this magnificent area of land can be preserved in its entirety for the whole of the Hunter Valley.

The President informed members that the fight would continue – 'we have some very staunch allies and we will push this matter with all means at our disposal'.

Tom continued to be part of this fight. By 1975 the Commonwealth Government had been persuaded to forego further payment for the site. At the July meeting of the NPPM Tom moved a motion (seconded by Shields) calling on the Federal Government to bring this matter to a conclusion. He further moved (seconded by Shields) that the movement write to the LMSC asking that a proper plan for the area be implemented. This was necessary to limit the site's exposure to possible damage. Immediate action was necessary to protect the grassed areas from the negative impact of unauthorised parking. By the end of 1976 the NPPM had achieved a successful outcome – the financial position of LMSC was secure and a development plan had been implemented for the area. The President of the NPPM was pleased to report: 'the plan for Rathmines Recreation Area was welcomed by the members and when one thinks back over the years it is clear that sustained pressure from community groups has produced a plan in which almost the whole area is now to be used for recreational purposes'. In the ensuing years Tom and the NPPM continued to monitor the implementation of the plan for the Rathmines Recreation Area. As noted, in July 1977 Tom worked to prevent the nearby bowling club encroaching on the area. At the October 1982 meeting of the NPPM Tom moved a motion (seconded by Jones) that 'we request that LMSC look at all aspects of use of Rathmines Park so that damage to the park may be stopped'. It was by such vigilance that Tom, the NPPM and other community groups worked to ensure that Rathmines remained a wonderful recreational asset for the whole region.[27]

Green Point Foreshore Reserve

Another area that Tom fought long and hard to preserve was Green Point on the northern shore of Lake Macquarie between Belmont and Valentine. Much of the two hundred hectare site had remained relatively untouched by development due to its long association with coal mining which came to an end in 1984. It was this fact that led local residents in 1929 to petition the State Government to set aside the area as a foreshore park. Although nothing came of the measure, Tom was not deterred from raising the issue again with the State Government in 1957. As noted, Tom was part of a NPPM delegation that met with Mr Tom Lewis, the Minister for Lands, to secure State Government support for the establishment of a park in the area. Despite the Minister's lack of commitment, the NPPM pressed ahead – by 1965 there was optimism within the NPPM that the State Government could be won over. In the Annual Report the President noted:

> negotiations following our representations over many years to have 500 acres of water front land between Belmont and Valentine (including Green Point) set aside for public parks and recreation have progressed to a point where the Lake Macquarie Shire Council has taken the necessary action as advised by the NSW State Planning Authority in accordance with the Local Government Act to preserve the area for public reserve.

A year later the President thanked Tom and the other members of the NPPM New Parks Subcommittee for the work they had carried out on 'the Cardiff Point (Green Point) Park Proposal'. Interestingly, the President pointed out that progress to bring the plan to fruition had been slow:

> this proposal is a good example of the time and persistence required to bring a Park Plan to finality. The Cardiff Point Proposal has been progressively pursued since 1957 and in spite of the obvious necessity for this park, it will take further efforts to secure it. All members are asked to support us in this matter.

One member keen to continue the fight was Tom Farrell. At the September 1966 meeting of the NPPM Tom successfully put forwarded a motion (seconded by Lithgow) that 'we take the matter up with the local member and ask his advice regarding representations to the Premier and the Mines Department'. At the June 1967 meeting of the NPPM Tom put forward a motion (seconded by Dews) that 'we seek a deputation to the Minister for Local Government regarding public reserves'. Shortly after this meeting Tom was part of the NPPM delegation that met with the President of LMSC to discuss Black Ned's Bay, Cara Ville Reserve, Cardiff Point, Hudson's land reservoir near Charlestown and Belmont Yacht Club. At the January 1969 meeting of the NPPM Tom moved a motion (seconded by Barnett) that 'the President and the Secretary of the Movement call upon the new President of LMSC to discuss parks and reserves in the shire'. At the February 1969 meeting of the NPPM Tom moved a motion (seconded by Suters) that 'the siltation of Lake Macquarie at Green Point be referred to the Chief Secretary's Department'. At the same meeting he put forward a further motion (also seconded by Suters) that 'we write to the Minister for Lands requesting government assistance for LMSC to acquire land adjacent to Lake Macquarie for parkland'.[28]

Clearly the optimism of 1965 had begun to dissipate. The President had been correct when he pointed out that the struggle to save Green Point was to be a long and protracted fight. In fact, local government inactivity coupled with State Government indifference left Green Point vulnerable to development for the next two decades. The failure of various government authorities to protect this important area came to a head in 1984 when mining operations ceased. At this time an application was made for the land to be rezoned to allow for a residential, tourist and marine development. Under the terms of this development plan fifty percent of the land would be set aside for residential sub-division, thirty percent for parks and recreation and twenty percent for tourist and business activities. Regarding the latter, a marina and shopping centre were to be situated at Green Point. Less than one third of the total two hundred hectare site (sixty hectares) was to be set aside for public open space – the remainder was to provide 1750 housing sites, a commercial district and a caravan park (including holiday cabins).[29]

Faced with the permanent loss of the site, the NPPM sprang into action. Once again Tom took a leading role. In May 1983 he put forward a proposal (supported by the NPPM) that LMSC seek financial assistance from the Bicentennial Authority to secure Green Point area as parkland. At the same time Tom advocated that the LMSC should do all in its power to pressure the State and Federal Governments to keep the area 'in its natural state'. It was Tom's view that any proposal for Green Point 'should reveal a clear understanding of the area's relationship to the lake as a whole and the foreshore system in particular'. It was essential (in Tom's view) that 'any policy put forward should ensure that Green Point was regarded as an integral and not separate part of a well-planned overall strategy for the lake'.[30] In February 1984 Tom was part of the NPPM delegation that met with Mr Ken Booth, the State Treasurer and Member for Wallsend, to discuss the future of Green Point. Booth was sympathetic with the park proposal – he promised to raise the issue with his parliamentary colleagues.[31] In order to drive home the point the NPPM urged the relevant authorities to undertake an environmental audit of Lake Macquarie. As Lithgow pointed out it was 'an absolute necessity that the remaining naturalness of the lake (including the parcels of land fronting the lake at Green Point) be preserved in every possible way'.[32]

Tom at Green Point in 1985 – courtesy of the *NMH*

Always one to understand the power of public opinion, Tom put forward a motion (seconded by Jackson) at the February 1985 meeting of the NPPM that 'we call a public protest meeting against the proposal (Green Point Estate) to rezone the Cardiff Point area'. At the same meeting he proposed (seconded by

Scobie) that a special sub-committee of the NPPM be establish to coordinate the public protest and (seconded by Wright) that the NPPM should enlist the support of the National Trust, NSW Flora & Fauna Society, the Botanical Gardens Committee and Tocal Youth Council.[33] Clearly once again Tom was mobilising the troops. Working with local community groups including the Green Point Action Committee, the NPPM galvanised opposition to the proposed development. The objective was to preserve for future generations an area with 'distinct natural systems and unique industrial archaeological features left over from its coal mining past'.[34] In the longer term the NPPM had not given up hope of establishing a large National Park in the Lake Macquarie area in line with those established in Sydney (Royal National Park and Kuring-gai National Park).[35] Tom continued to support this concept. At the August 1987 meeting of the NPPM he proposed a motion (seconded by Kennedy) that 'we publicise the concept of a Lake Macquarie National Park in connection with the upcoming local elections'. At the same meeting he moved a further motion (seconded by Jackson) that 'we write to every candidate and ask them to support the National Park idea'.[36]

In response to the growing public opposition, the LMSC agreed to an environmental impact study. Following up on its earlier work, the NPPM continued to pressure the Council to secure funding for a park at Green Point from the Bicentennial Authority. It was proposed that the Green Point project could form part of a landscape and urban design competition similar to that which had been proposed by Newcastle Council. Unfortunately, this proposal failed to win bipartisan support in the upcoming local government elections. The candidates remained divided on the issue. However, the newly elected Council did announce that it intended to set aside a significant proportion of its Bicentennial Grant ($1 million out of a total $2.5 million) to establish an eighty hectare park at Green Point. Although questions remained about funding, the movement threw its weight behind the Green Point Bicentennial Park.[37] At the October 1987 meeting of the NPPM Tom successfully put forward four motions (all seconded by Wright):

1. That NPPM fully support the concept of a Bicentennial Lakeside Park between Valentine and Belmont.
2. That we ask the LMSC and the NSW Government to take immediate steps to acquire the (specified) sections of land we nominate as appropriate for parkland.
3. If there is any rezoning proposal other than open space recreation, the proposal must be subject to a planning study and inquiry as approved by Lake Macquarie Council.
4. The Movement ask the LMSC to engage a qualified landscape architect, Bruce McKenzie, to design and prepare an immediate assessment of the area for open space.

At the same meeting he proposed a further motion (seconded by Molesworth) that 'we write to every local member, sending a photocopy of Bicentennial Park (Sydney) report, asking them what Newcastle is getting in comparison'. In a further motion (seconded by Molesworth) he won the support of the meeting to enlist the assistance of Chris Puplick, Liberal Senator for NSW.[38] At the following meeting, Tom moved a motion (seconded by Wright) that 'we write to Alan Morris and Peter Morris (both local ALP Federal Members) pointing out that $27 million has been spent in the Sydney area in the last seven years in the acquiring of regional parks. Unfortunately, not one hectare of land has been acquired in Lake Macquarie'. Tom had such an understanding of the issues regarding Green Point that he was asked by the NPPM to prepare a history of the site to assist the ongoing campaign. It is clear that the NPPM did not regard the establishment of the bicentennial park as the end in itself. While it was an important first step, the NPPM intended to push on with its campaign to have the whole two hundred hectare site set aside as reserve. This included Tom writing to the Newcastle Trades Hall Council to enlist its support.[39]

Faced with growing public opposition, the developer put forward a modified proposal which set aside up to one hundred hectares for open space and approximately 130 hectares for housing. This was also rejected by the NPPM and the Green Point Action Committee as much of the significant environmental areas ended up as low density housing.[40] The campaign suffered a major setback when the Mayor, a candidate for the Seat of Swansea in the upcoming State election, announced his intention to withdraw his support for the acquisition of Green Point. This *volte-face* seemed to place the whole campaign in jeopardy. Despite the NPPM's opposition, the Mayor was duly elected.[41] It appeared certain that funding for parkland at Green Point was not going to be achieved anytime soon.

Despite this setback, the NPPM attempted to convince the new Greiner government of the merit of its cause. At the April 1988 meeting of the NPPM Tom put forward a motion (seconded by Shields) that 'we congratulate the Liberals on gaining Government and congratulate Mr Moore on being elected as Minister for the Environment…we are now looking forward to the rapid implementation of the promise for an Environmental and Open Space Study into the needs of Lake Macquarie and its foreshores'. In another motion (seconded by

Parsons) Tom returned to a familiar theme – 'we reply to the letter from Mr Hay and send a copy to every member of the Cabinet drawing attention to the comparative spending in the last seven years (Sydney-Newcastle) suggesting we should have a fairer share'. At Tom's suggestion the NPPM issued a 'press release' informing the public that key members of the Cabinet including the Minister for the Environment and the Opposition Leader (now Bob Carr) had been invited on a ferry trip of Lake Macquarie.[42] No doubt Tom hoped that when confronted by the natural beauty of the area, the politicians would agree that it needed to be protected.

Tom at Green Point, a place of natural beauty –
Courtesy of the *NMH*

At the next meeting of the NPPM Tom tried to maintain the momentum – he moved a motion (seconded by Shields) that 'we write to Mr Clarke, the Secretary of the Mines' Subsidence

Board, that we wish the whole of the area of Green Point to be given to public parkland as proposed by the Northumberland County Council'. At the same meeting Tom seconded a motion put forward by Shields that 'a map of the proposed Lake Macquarie National Park be sent to Mr Richard Jones MLC'.[43] Jones was a newly elected member of the Legislative Council, a Democrat with environmental credentials. Clearly Tom was keen to win support for the national park and Green Point from across the political spectrum. At the July meeting of the NPPM Tom returned to a familiar theme. He moved a motion (seconded by Shields) that a letter be written to the Minister for Local Government and the Minister for Planning regarding Green Point:

> that the Minister be told that we are aware of the Sydney Development Fund in the County of Cumberland and are at a loss that no similar fund exists in the County of Northumberland. We ask how much has been contributed by the SDF in the purchase of the $35 million spent on recreation areas in Sydney and how much has come from the State Government?[44]

Tom was keen that the Leader of the Opposition, Mr Jones MLC and Mr George Keegan, the newly elected Independent Member for Newcastle, should question the government about the ongoing disparity that existed between Sydney and Newcastle in regard to the funding of parks and recreation areas. In a series of motions (all seconded by Shields) Tom won the support of the members 'to write to Mr Carr asking him the same questions about funding. We should also write to Mr Jones MLC asking him to ask a question in the Parliament on the same matter' and 'to Mr Keegan MP seeking details of the operation of the SDF and ask him why a similar fund does not operate in the County of Northumberland?'.[45] Tom was also keen to keep the pressure on the local councillors – he moved a motion (seconded by Shields) that the Mayor of LMSC be fully informed of the correspondence received from the Mine's Subsidence Board regarding Green Point and seconded a motion (put forward by Shields) that 'personal approaches be made to all aldermen on this issue'.[46] In support Lithgow moved a motion (seconded by Shields) that 'the members of the NPPM be asked to write to the Minister for the environment and their local MPs asking for funding from the State Government to acquire Green Point for public open space' – CARRIED UNANIMOUSLY.[47] Clearly, despite the disappointments of the year, Tom and the NPPM were not going to give up - for the rest of the year the movement kept the issue of Green Point in the public spot light. Tom wrote again to the *Herald* arguing that 'Green Point should be retained for public recreation as it was in the 1950s'. He urged LMCC to immediately 'rezone the land as a flora and fauna reserve'. Tom's children also wanted action on the issue – in a series of letters Tom's son and daughters urged the authorities to properly manage the lake.[48] In December 1988 the NPPM in conjunction with other organisations organised an onsite campaign meeting which was broadcast live on local radio stations, 2HD and 2NC.[49] The issue was not going to go away any time soon.

Tom would have taken heart that the *NMH* seemed to be on side. On 15 December 1988 the paper published an opinion piece headed 'Green Point by name and look' in which it argued that 'Lake Macquarie City Council has only one option when it meets to consider the application for rezoning of the Green Point estate. And that is to reject the application as a first step to having at least the bulk of the estate's 224ha rezoned as a flora and fauna reserve'. The paper went on to urge the LMCC 'to take the only responsible course and put the recreational needs of scores of thousands, now and in the future, before the profits of a few'.[50] Over the next few years, the paper kept up its pressure on the local authorities to find a proper resolution to the Green Point issue.[51]

Lewis' view of the ongoing saga of Green Point.
Courtesy of the *NMH*.

The following year Tom continued his efforts to secure funding for the adequate provision of parks and recreation areas around Lake Macquarie. At the January 1989 meeting of the NPPM he successfully moved a motion (seconded by Shields) that:

a letter be sent to the Lord Mayor of Newcastle saying that we consider that the time is appropriate for the establishment of a fund similar to the Sydney

Development Fund in this region and ask him to call a meeting of all the mayors of the region to discuss the issue and that a similar letter be sent to Virginia Chadwick asking that the same matter be discussed at a meeting of Hunter parliamentarians.

He also continued to press for the acquisition of Green Point as open space. At the same meeting of the NPPM he moved (seconded by Shields) that 'a letter be written to the Minister for the Environment regarding Green Point asking what funds have been made available in the Sydney region for open space acquisition in the last ten years compared to Lake Macquarie'. In a further motion (seconded by Shields) Tom asked that a letter be sent to 'the Secretary of the Charlestown Branch of the ALP complimenting the branch for their support for the acquisition of Green Point for public recreation and that a copy be sent to every branch of the ALP in Newcastle'. Tom also moved a third motion (seconded by Shields) that 'we write to Mayor of LMSC saying that we fully support his endeavours to secure the whole of Green Point for public recreation'. At the February 1989 meeting of the NPPM Tom reported on the discussions he had had with Alderman Hanley regarding Green Point. He also moved a motion (seconded by Wright) that 'we prepare (after public consultation) an updated version of the Lake Macquarie National Park proposal and remind the relevant authorities that they have had the proposal in the past'.[52] He wrote again to the paper urging the authorities to buy Green Point. He pointed out in the letter that 'the retention of Green Point is far more important for the region than Blackbutt or the East End. It is imperative it be saved for future generations'.[53] Tom's efforts did not go unrecognised. In March 1989 a concerned resident wrote to the paper 'congratulating Mr Tom Farrell and the

Northern Parks and Playgrounds Movement on their enormous contribution to the welfare of residents of the Hunter Valley over the years'. It was the opinion of this correspondent that 'without the vision and foresight of such people our standard of living and recreational facilities would be severely limited'.[54]

The problem for those who wanted to retain Green Point as open space was that the land was privately owned by a number of parties. In 1990 estimates put the total cost of purchasing the land at $5 million. Without a commitment from the State Government or Council to provide such funding it was difficult to find a way forward. The Greiner Government proved reticent to commit to projects in what was a safe Labor area, the LMSC ran hot and cold on the issue.[55] There were, however, some break throughs – in 1990 the Green Point Task Force was established and the State Government offered $1 million dollars (later withdrawn) to help the LMSC to purchase the property. The Council later acquired part of the estate (Portion 37A) for the cost of $1 million dollars.[56] Furthermore, the Green Park Action Committee won the support of the Newcastle Trades Hall Council to place green bans on the area.[57]

Matters became more complicated in 1992 when the major landholder sold 170 hectares of the site to a new development company.[58] Further protests followed as new development applications were lodged. Over the next few years the matter dragged on with each side putting forward a series of claims and counterclaims.[59] Tom did what he could to remain involved but in the years after his wife's death (1988), his declining health meant that he left it to others to take the lead. The matter was finally resolved in May 1995 when a formal settlement was struck between the LMSC and the developer. With State Government approval, the Green Point estate was rezoned to allow for the development of 120 hectares of regional park and fifty-eight hectares for residential development. The State Government gave a commitment to provide $500,000 funding for the next three years to develop the foreshore park.[60]

Although the compromise was far from ideal, the NPPM could take heart that a significant proportion of the Green Point estate had been secured as open space. One of the key players to achieve this outcome was Tom Farrell. Over four decades he had pursued his dream to secure for the residents of Greater Newcastle and Lake Macquarie a foreshore park of great natural beauty. In 1966 Richley had reminded the members of the NPPM that Green Point would not be won without 'time and persistence'. While there were many (both within and outside the NPPM) who had devoted the necessary time and persistence to secure a large area of open space at Green Point, Tom Farrell had shown the way. Despite the many disappointments he had faced over the years, Tom doggedly pursued the matter to its end. As he had done in so many other environmental campaigns, Tom's determination over Green Point had been an inspiration to others.

Young local residents enjoying the view of Green Point Foreshore Reserve.
Courtesy of *NMH*

7: *A Matter of Civic Duty*

As recounted, Tom was keen to resume his community involvement soon after his return from the war. Although much of his time was taken up with environmental issues, he maintained a keen interest in the public transport needs of his community. His commitment to public service led him at first to join the Liberal Party, as a local member, then take an active part in the New England New State Movement. He finally attempted to assume a more direct role running for an aldermanic position on NCC. What drove him in each of these enterprises was a strong sense of civic duty – a belief that he could make a difference – a belief that he could make his community a better place. In 1965 Tom rather modestly stated 'I have taken an above interest in public affairs'. In fact, his interest in public affairs led him to live a life of continual service for his community.

In 1950 as a member of the Cardiff Heights-Lookout Progress Association, Tom pressed the Northumberland District Council of Progress Associations to agitate for the electrification of the Newcastle suburban rail system. He argued that the bus network was incapable of serving the growing population in Newcastle. This led him to oppose the State Government's decision to disband the Newcastle tram network in favour of buses. To register his protest he had called a public protest meeting and completed a bus survey (undertaken by Joe Richley and himself) in the Cardiff Heights-New Lambton area. He followed this up with writing to the Commissioner of Transport on behalf of the Cardiff Heights-Lookout Progress Association complaining of the overcrowding on the buses. The protest action had received some coverage in the press:

> Mr T. Farrell said that more than 300 people had been left behind at four stops between 8 am and 9 am since schools reopened. Tabling a series of daily check sheets prepared by the association, Mr Farrell said on February 8, people left at Croudace Street were nine, at Brett Street five, at Wickham Road eighteen, and at Baker Street twelve, between 8.05 am and 8.45 am.

It was Tom's view that 'transport is chaotic. It is time the Department admitted it is not capable of handling the district traffic'. His solution was to press for the electrification of the train line: 'Mr Farrell said buses could not shift the population now. They could be efficient only as feeders to electric trains. The resumption of necessary land and planning of the future electric service was urgent'. Tom argued that the electrification of the line would be of great benefit to commuters. He informed his friend, Douglas Darby, the Liberal Member for Manly, that 'it would cut travelling time by at least fifty per cent'. Despite Tom's efforts, the State Government showed little interest – efforts to electrify the line between Sydney and Newcastle were not put in place for another thirty years.

Tom did not allow this to dampen his enthusiasm for public transport or trains. He later declared that 'I have always been a great train man'. He continued to argue for an efficient and comprehensive public transport system for the Newcastle region. As he pointed out in 1978 'the city cannot survive unless it has proper transport'. Part of his plan was to maintain the passenger rail line into Newcastle Station. It was his view that 'if you finish the train line at civic – the top of Newcastle will just die like a rotten pear. Whatever is there now will just die'. Clearly Tom was a man of vision – his words continue to resonate today in a debate that still perplexes the city.[1]

Given his local profile, it is not surprising that Tom was approached by the Liberal Party in 1950 to stand as a candidate for the State seat of Kahibah. Although he declined the invitation, he joined with other likeminded residents to form a branch of the Liberal Party in New Lambton. As noted, from this platform the group agitated for the formation of a university college in Newcastle. While this remained a key priority, it is clear the New Lambton Branch remained active on a number of issues including 'decentralisation', parks and gardens, public transport and State Education. In was with this policy platform that the New Lambton Branch attempted to win for the Liberal Party the safe Labor seat of Kahibah. Although their efforts proved unsuccessful in two general elections and one bi-election between 1950-1956, Tom's close friend, Joe Richley decided to contest the seat for the Liberal Party in the 1956 State Election. Alderman Richley's stated objectives provide a valuable insight into the policies which were important to Tom and his fellow members of the New Lambton Branch. Alderman Richley's objectives for Newcastle were:

Decentralisation – the creation of effective LOCAL authorities for all Government Departments.

Transport – the new deal throughout this major economic factor of the city, including an electric suburban railway system and efficient co-ordination of all road transport, under LOCAL control.

Flood Control – immediate implementation of the full schemes for prevention of serious floods.

Water Supply and Sewerage – extension of these essential services to all settled and potential areas, as urgent work.

Pensioners – creation of Eventide villages, with their own humane hospitalisation, for voluntary admission of old age pensioners.

Like Tom, Richley saw 'the holding of public office' as a means of 'community service'. Inspired by a belief in 'decentralisation', he advocated that the needs of the local community should be met by local not 'Sydney' authorities. Like Tom, Richley argued that Newcastle had been neglected for far too long by the 'central authorities' located in Sydney. He told electors that:

It is because I am convinced that Newcastle can well do with a change that I am standing for election to the State Parliament. The affairs of this city (the third port and sixth city of importance in the Commonwealth) are in a really deplorable state. The consequences of neglect over many years must be obvious to all...The people of this city should be enjoying in greater degree the progress which has come to the Commonwealth, but we still have to put up with antiquated train services, inefficient wharf and coal loading facilities, level railway crossings, just to mention a few examples of our backwardness. I wish to bring an enlightened Newcastle point of view into the State Parliament. If given a majority

vote by the people I shall not let up in my persistence
for a new deal for Newcastle.

Like Richley, Tom would also attempt to deliver 'a new deal for
Newcastle' by his persistent community action over many years.
Despite his support for important local issues, Richley failed
to win the seat attracting only 27.63 per cent of the formal
primary vote. The seat was won by the sitting Independent
Labor Member who attracted 57.2 per cent of the vote from
the Labor Party candidate with 42.8 per of the vote after
preferences. It was clear that the New Lambton Branch of the
Liberal Party would find it difficult to contest this 'blue-ribbon'
Labor seat.

The driving force behind the New Lambton Branch at this
time was Reg Ellis, another friend of Tom, who remained the
Chairman throughout the 1950s. Like Tom, Ellis was a man of
principle who had little time for political expediency. He was
keen to ensure that the principles of the Liberal Party were not
put aside for some pragmatic political advantage. In 1959 this
position led Ellis and the New Lambton Branch to come into
conflict with the Federal and State Executive of the Liberal Party.
In this year the New Lambton Branch had made its position
clear to the Richardson Inquiry that it opposed the payment
of salaries to parliamentarians. The Richardson Committee was
one of three public inquiries into parliamentarians' salaries and
allowances in the 1950s which found (contrary to the view
of the New Lambton Branch) that parliamentarian should be
entitled to a publically funded salary as their position was closer
to a full-time occupation, a job or profession. This conclusion
challenged the widely accepted notion that political life was not
a job or profession but a vocation undertaken out of a sense of
duty, a sense of community service. As a result the Richardson

Report received wide spread criticism with many in the community attacking politicians, their salaries and their 'perks'. When parliamentarians on both sides of politics ignored the public opposition and indicated their support for the findings of the Richardson Commission, the New Lambton Branch at its May meeting moved to disband. Although some members had doubts regarding the wisdom of this action with one questioning the constitutional legality of the move, the Chairman carried the day persuading the majority of the members to support the resolution. It was clear that Tom supported this move – he later explained that this action 'gave the game away with a feeling of contempt to our Parliamentarians who had ignored the feelings of the electorate'. Tom singled Ellis out for particular praise: 'may I record my admiration for our Chairman who had refused to be deviated from his firm and courageous resolve on the Richardson salary grab – the final conclusion which could be summarised as a victory for greed and hypocrisy'. Clearly this incident provides an insight into what drove Tom and others to participate in public life. For Tom and many of his contemporaries, involvement in public life was not about personal gain or financial advantage – it was about a commitment to civic duty, being able to return something to the community. It was this commitment to civic duty which was to remain with Tom throughout his public life.

The condemnation of the New Lambton Branch did not go unchallenged by the Liberal Party machine. On receipt of a letter explaining the action, a number of Liberal Federal luminaries took it upon themselves to attack the members of the branch. For example, George Pearce, the Deputy Government Whip, went so far as to argue that the action was a threat to 'freedom itself: 'I suppose your members have expressed themselves to their satisfaction. I could not help thinking though, when I read your letter that if every Liberal Party Branch took the same action, the next Federal Election would be most satisfactory for the Socialists, the Communists and those others who seek to extinguish the flame of freedom'. Adam Holmes, the Acting Minister for the Army, was of the view that 'surely the members of the Branch, whilst entitled to their own individual opinions, would accept the principles determined by the Federal executive for the guidance of all members of the Party'. Francis Bland, Chairman of the Commonwealth Joint Committee of Public Accounts, pointed out that 'I have never found that throwing in the towel accomplishes anything except defeat. Once you get outside a Movement and start criticising you are regarded as throwing stones and being disgruntled, and you accomplish nothing except your own frustration. I think you have been in politics long enough to know that you can't always get your own way however strongly you hold your opinions'.

When this criticism failed to move the members of the now defunct New Lambton Branch, the State Executive decided to take a more direct tack. The executive held a 'special' annual meeting outside the electorate with only selected members invited to attend. The past chairman and 'the really active members' (including Tom) were excluded. It was hoped that by denying the principle office holders the right to vote, the executive could ensure that the motion to disband the branch could be overturned. The plan was discovered, however, when news of the meeting reached the ears of the principle office holders. Ellis made sure that the majority of members (including Tom) were present at the 'special' meeting of the disbanded branch attended the 'Annual General Meeting'. The matter received some coverage in the press. Under the heading 'Liberal's Unit Re-Formed', the *NMH* reported that 'New Lambton branch of the Liberal Party was re-formed at a meeting of some former members and supporters at the Liberal Party Centre, Hamilton, last night'. The paper pointed out that former members including Ellis, attended the meeting for a brief period but failed to join the re-formed branch. There is no doubt that the action of the now defunct New Lambton Branch had caught the attention of the State Executive. The paper reported that the meeting was attended by key members of the Liberal Party machine including the State Field Supervisor (Mr A. T. Lenchan), Mr Fraser MLA, Mr Morris MLA, Mr Fairhall MHR, the Northern Regional Supervisor (Mr A. Waugh) and Mr Saddington MLC'. It appears that Mr Fraser was particularly upset by the actions of the New Lambton Branch. Labelling the action to disband the branch as 'unconstitutional', Fraser told the gathering 'if there is something wrong in our party's policy, let's get at it – not resign or disband. Let's go to our State Council and fight for our views'. Given the presence of the Liberal 'heavy-weights', it is not surprising that the few members present complied with the wishes of the State Executive and reformed the branch.

It is clear that Tom was disappointed with the State Executive and the members who supported it. He argued that it was hypocritical of the State Executive to reform the branch against the wishes of the majority of its members – Tom likened this action to that taken by the Labor Party when it forced its members to put party before principle. He regarded it as yet another example of the evils of centralisation when 'the Sydney Steam Roller comes into commission to stifle the censure from the local area'. The words and deeds of the Liberal 'heavy-weights' did not move Tom Farrell – he left the party to continue his fight for his local area in another forum.[2]

Tom's mistrust of centralised power led him to embrace the 'New State Movement'. Plans to divide New South Wales into a number of new states had had a long history. Of particular importance were the movements in Northern NSW and in the Riverina which had strong regional support. Royal Commissions were set up in the 1920s and the 1930s to investigate the matter. The Nicholson Royal Commission (1935) recommended that three new states be created within the boundaries of NSW, including a northern area that took in Newcastle. Although the Country Party (through key figures like Earl Page and David Henry Drummond) was the main promoter of the movement, the idea of establishing new states drew some support at times from elements within the Labor and Liberal Party.

Prior to 1959 Tom and other members of the New Lambton Branch had done all in their power to promote 'decentralisation' within the Liberal Party. When Douglas Darby MLA, was asked to speak in Newcastle in 1950, Tom prepared a series of notes for his friend on the topic of 'decentralisation'. Matters which Tom felt needed to be addressed included: a university (not in the future but now), electrification of the suburban railways, national parks within easy access to the city, botanical gardens, zoological gardens, art galleries, a conservatorium, museum, public lending libraries, elimination of railway crossings in the city centre, regular steamship services direct to and from Newcastle, immediate completion of the Sandy Hollow Railway, reconstruction of roads throughout the district, autonomous control of suburban transport, stamp duties and an improvement in Taxation Department facilities. In short, Tom explained 'we want amenities on a smaller scale to those applicable in Sydney, Melbourne, Adelaide and Hobart'. Tom added a cautionary note:

> I am satisfied that the Liberal Party approach to the things that count in this city has not yet created much enthusiasm in the minds of the ordinary Newcastle

people, and speaking now to you as a Liberal member I would say that it is essential for the Liberal Party to take a more active interest in matters pertaining to Newcastle of a local and perhaps parochial nature. Within 50 miles of Newcastle there is a population of 320,000 people. Newcastle should have more Liberal representation in Parliament.

Here Tom provides a clear insight into what motivated him to join the Liberal Party. He believed that by actively promoting the issue of 'decentralisation' within the party he could win for Newcastle its proper share of State infrastructure spending. This in turn would lead to greater access to a wide range of local amenities and services. In short, Tom was prompted to join a political party so that he could better serve his local community.

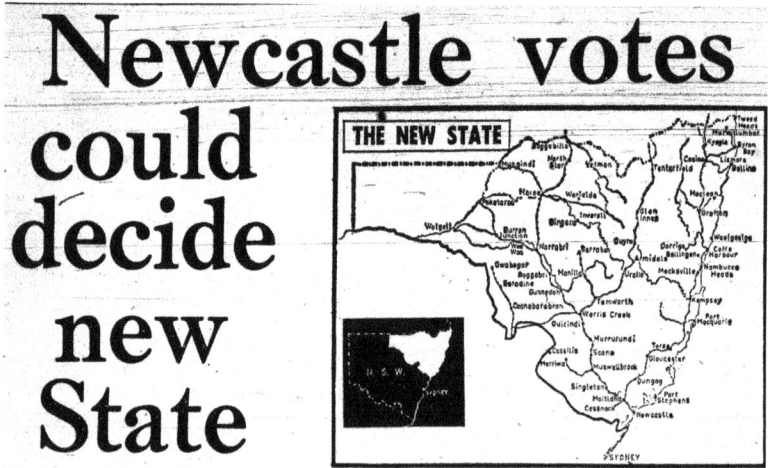

Suggested boundaries for the 'New State' – courtesy of the *NMH*

At the heart of his push for 'decentralisation', Tom believed that the interests of Newcastle would be better served by the establishment of a new state. It was logical, therefore, that at the

1951 NSW State Conference of the Liberal Party he joined with other members of the New Lambton Branch to put forward a resolution that 'this Conference support the principle of the creation of New States in Australia'. To the branch's surprise, given the dominance of the 'Sydney' delegates, the motion was passed by a majority of three to one. In the light of the resolution's success, Tom was called upon to speak to the press explaining the branch's 'unqualified support for the New England New State Movement'.[3]

In 1952 Tom explained his enthusiasm for the New State Movement with its 'constant advocacy for decentralisation and localised autonomous government within the Federal Constitution'. It was his opinion that under the present system 'the Hunter Valley area and many other country areas have been sadly neglected'. This had been brought about because 'the control of our major political parties is tightly held by Sydney interests'. The 'Sydney interests' ignore the fact that much of the State's wealth is derived from the hinterland. Such is their drive for centralisation that they allow Sydney 'to bleed the country to build up its own magnificent buildings and improvements'. Tom noted that while the Hunter Valley in the last few years had received limited state funding for infrastructure projects, Sydney had received £60 million for the construction of the Eastern Suburbs Railway, Warrangamba Dam, Kingsford Smith Airport, New Spit Bridge, Botany Bay Seaport and the Electrification of the Railway from Sydney to the Blue Mountains. He regarded this as evidence of 'the systematic exploitation of the country over decades'. He argued that this exploitation was set to continue 'while we have the spectacle of Sydney politicians with a sizeable majority in the State Legislature'. He regarded it as nothing short of stupidity that 'one city had more representatives than all the rest of NSW'. It was Tom's opinion that the establishment of a new state in Northern New South Wales would overcome the difficulties of centralisation with its sectional interests... The politicians representing the new 'New England State' at both a State and Federal level would be intimately aware of the needs of their own local districts. As a result the 'wasteful extravagance in and around Sydney' would be brought to an end as the 'expenditure of funds and decent amenities would come to the Northern areas (including cities like Newcastle)'. Given Tom's strong commitment to the local area, his interest in the New State Movement is not surprising. It was his belief that Newcastle and the Hunter would only receive the proper amenities and services they deserved (given their wealth) if a new state was established in Northern NSW.[4]

Tom remained committed to this cause after he resigned from the Liberal Party. The members of the (disbanded) New Lambton Branch formed the nucleus of the Newcastle Branch of the New England New State Movement (NBNENSM) with Tom Farrell as its president. In this role Tom worked closely over many years with Ulrich Ruegg Ellis who was later described as the 'arch-priest' of the New State Movement. Ellis was a journalist, author, political organiser and activist who had become Earl Page's private secretary in 1928. In 1936 Ellis had joined the Commonwealth Public Service holding a number of important positions including Deputy-Director of Public Relations in the Department of Post-War Reconstruction. Not always on good terms with various ministerial heads, he resigned from the Public Service in 1947 to establish a rural lobby group, the Office of Rural Research & Development, working closely with the Country Party. From 1933 onwards he was active in the New State Movement, working at first as publicity officer for the Riverina Secessionist Movement. He went on to write a number of polemical works arguing the case for constitutional review and further decentralisation. He was one of the key presenters at the Nicholas Royal Commission becoming a member of the executive of the New England New State Movement in 1948.

Ellis clearly valued Tom's views on the New State Movement. In 1952 when working on the booklet 'The Case for New States', Ellis wrote to Tom (through the Organising Secretary of the New England New State Movement) requesting information regarding the support for new states in the Newcastle area and the exact terms of the resolution which the New Lambton Branch had put before the Liberal Party Conference. As noted, in his reply Tom assured Ellis of his 'unqualified support for the New England New State Movement'. It was such enthusiasm which led Tom and the other members of the NBNENSM to work tirelessly in the 1950s and 1960s for the success of 'Operation Seventh State'. Ellis explained the objectives of this movement:

> the immediate purpose of Operation Seventh State is to secure substantial personal support and establish an impressive fighting fund for a spectacular assault on the obstacles to decentralised government and development. Operation Seventh State offers to everyone interested in building a great Australia the opportunity of supporting the crusade by making generous annual contributions, over a period of five years, in accordance with their means. The Movement will welcome enquiries and will be pleased to supply information on all aspects of the fight to extend democratic self-government in the interests of national advancement, individual welfare and defence security in a troubled world.

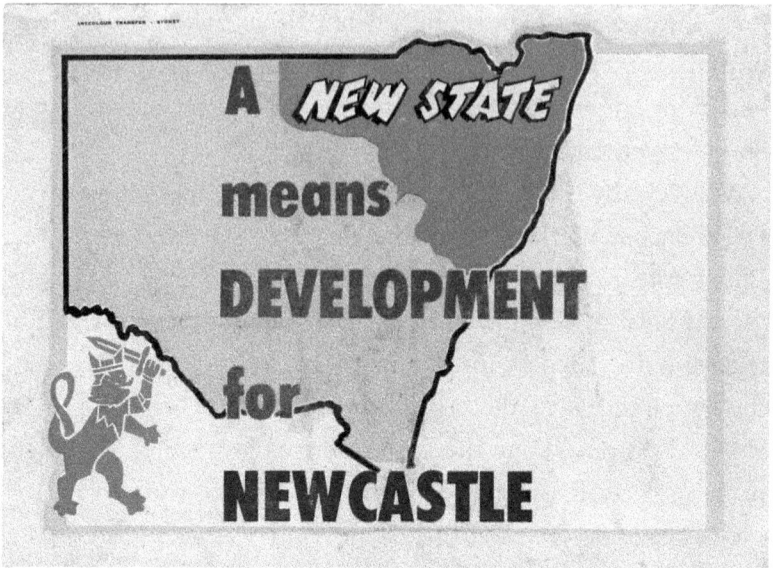

Car bumper or window sticker promoting a Seventh State

As President of the NBNENSM, Tom worked hand in hand
with Ellis and the Seventh State Executive to ensure that the
movement's action program was implemented in the Hunter
region. Under the movement's slogan 'Victory Goes to the
Bold and not the Timid', the NBNENSM set about conducting
an education campaign which involved the distribution of
educational materials and the holding of public meetings.
Examples of the educational materials held in the Farrell Papers
include a car bumper or window sticker entitled 'A New State
Means Development for Newcastle', a pamphlet entitled 'Self-
Government for New England' and a flyer based on an article
reprinted from the *Australian Country Magazine*. Delegations
were also organised to canvass the support of key political figures.
For example, in a letter (dated 1952) the Organising Secretary
of the New England New State Movement discussed with Tom
tactics to be employed at an upcoming meeting with the Federal

Labor Leader, Dr. Evatt. Tom later claimed that a delegation of which he was a member had successfully persuaded Mr Askin, the Premier of New South Wales, to support the cause.

NEW ENGLAND NEW STATE MOVEMENT
NEWCASTLE BRANCH

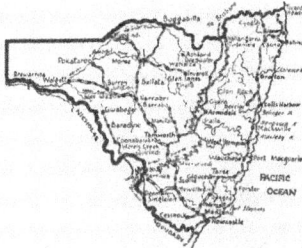

THE SEVENTH STATE

DEAR SIR,

YOU ARE CORDIALLY INVITED TO ATTEND THE NEW STATE CONVENTION AT THE CITY HALL, NEWCASTLE, AT 7.30 P.M., THURSDAY, 20TH MARCH, 1958. YOU WILL THUS HAVE THE OPPORTUNITY OF LISTENING TO SPEAKERS SETTING OUT THE AIMS AND ASPIRATIONS OF THE MOVEMENT.

NEWCASTLE HAS MUCH TO GAIN BY ITS INCLUSION IN THE PROPOSED NEW STATE. JUST PRIOR TO THE WORLD WAR II A ROYAL COMMISSION RECOMMENDED TO THE GOVERNMENT THAT A PLEBISCITE BE HELD IN THE AREA TO ASCERTAIN THE WISHES OF THE INHABITANTS. OUR MOVEMENT IS PRESSING FOR THE HOLDING OF SUCH A REFERENDUM. TO ACHIEVE ECONOMIC DECENTRALISATION, IT IS NECESSARY TO HAVE POLITICAL DECENTRALISATION.

MAKE NEWCASTLE INDEPENDENT OF SYDNEY THE SAME AS MELBOURNE AND BRISBANE HAVE DONE!

YOURS SINCERELY,

R. E. FARRELL, PRESIDENT.
L. SADDINGTON, M.L.C., VICE PRESIDENT.
A. McWILLIAMS, VICE PRESIDENT.
W. HUTCHINSON, HON. SECRETARY.
J. RICHLEY, HON. TREASURER.

Flyer issued by the NBNENSM inviting residents to hear Ulrich Ellis speak in Newcastle in March 1958.

As a member of the Seventh State Executive Committee, Tom attended regional representative conventions to clarify ideas and extend support. It was out of these conventions that a Constitution for the New State was drafted. He also did his part to ensure that two petitions were presented to the NSW Parliament and two petitions to the Federal Parliament and helped to persuade the Federal and State Parliaments to appoint All Party Committees to review the Constitution. The petition presented to the NSW Parliament in 1950 was signed by 13,000 people; the 1959 petition was signed by 32,000 people.

As President of the NBNENSM and Member of the Executive of the New England New State Movement Tom had the pleasure in welcoming Ulrich Ellis to address the Twelfth Convention of the New England New State Movement in Newcastle in 1958. The local branch produced a flyer (signed by R. E. Farrell, President) inviting concerned citizens to hear Ellis speak. The flyer explained that 'Newcastle has much to gain by its inclusion in the proposed new state'. In his speech Ellis took up a familiar theme - he argued that 'Newcastle shared with the people of the northern districts a sense of frustration and irritation arising from the failure of the Sydney Government to recognise its needs'. But he went a step further reminding delegates that:

> having in mind past obstacles to the creation of New States erected by the Sydney Parliament, the New England Movement has devised means to facilitate the establishment of New States in the future. We have drawn up a Draft Constitution as a guide to those who, in elected constitutional Conventions, will determine the form of government required by the people of the State of New England. This Draft

Constitution contains provisions designed to permit electors in substantial areas to initiate the formation of a further State. Fifteen per cent of the people in an area with actual or potential resources equivalent to those of Tasmania – the smallest State today – may petition the legislature for Statehood. On receipt of the petition a referendum must be held. If the referendum is carried then the legislature is bound to take the necessary steps to carry out the wishes of the people. The Hunter Valley already contains a total population approximate to that of Tasmania which has enjoyed self-government since 1826 and has been a Federal State in its own right since 1901. As Tasmania can function as a State and provide full public services on an unusually high standard, there is nothing to prevent the Hunter, with even richer resources, from doing likewise. The first step towards the State of the Hunter is the achievement of New England's aims…Their sole hope is successful participation in the New England separation movement, knowing that New Englanders already look forward to the day when they themselves will concede the right of the Hunter to control its own local affairs when it wishes to go alone.

Such a notion must have been music to the ears of a decentralist like Tom. Not only would the New State Movement free Newcastle from the shackles of Sydney domination but hold out the possibility of statehood for the Hunter in the future.

It is clear that Tom had played his part in the formulation of this policy. This was later acknowledged by the President of the Seventh State Movement, Dr P. A. Wright, when he thanked

Tom for 'his forthright opinions'. Wright also made clear that Tom had made significant financial contributions to the cause – reference is made to the 'practical support' which Tom had given 'in such generous terms'. In 1968 Ellis also acknowledged the work of the NBNENSM as a whole commenting that 'a branch of the Movement has functioned at Newcastle and Newcastle representatives are on the Executive. They have always displayed the greatest understanding of the viewpoints of those other parts of the Seventh State and have cooperated in every way'. Clearly Tom's vigor and capacity for hard work on behalf of the New England New State Movement was appreciated. It was the same level of application and diligence that he displayed when involved in any community group.

<pre>
                              1,7 Russell Road,
                              New Lambton,
                                           N. S. W.
                              AUSTRALIA.
                              23rd May, 1957.

The Prime Minister,
   INDIA.

Sir,

       The Australian Press has published a report that you
are anxious to dispose of British Monuments in India - mainly
Statuary such as sculptured models.   The New England New
State Movement which aims at achieving a decentralised autonomous
Sovereign State within the Commonwealth of Australia by
constitutional methods is very interested and would be pleased to
have details of your offer.

           It is expected you would convey such works to us by
gift - a little Colombo Plan in reverse.

           The New England New State Movement would re erect these
monuments, if suitable, in many of the provincial cities of our
area; Newcastle, Maitland, Tamworth, Grafton, Armidale, Lismore,
Inverell.   In Australia is has been customary for such
monuments to be confined to Capital Cities, but we are anxious
for Country Towns to benefit likewise.

                   Yours faithfully,

                   PRESIDENT.
</pre>

As President of the NBNENSM, Tom wrote to the Mr Nehru,
the Prime Minister of India, requesting British Statuary (23 May 1957).

BY AIR MAIL

F. 44/1/57 - PMP

K. Ram, I.C.S.,
Principal Private Secretary
to the Prime Minister

PRIME MINISTER'S SECRETARIAT
NEW DELHI
May 29, 1957.

Dear Sir,

I am desired to acknowledge receipt of your letter dated May 23, 1957 and to say that the Government of India have not yet formulated any particular scheme for the disposal of statues etc. in India. So far, it has been stated that those statues, which are of historical and artistic value, will be kept in proper places such as museums etc. The main objection here has been to some particular statues which refer to persons who were very unpopular in India.

2.   However, if any particular statue, which is at present in India, is required in Australia, the Government of India would be prepared to consider the matter. These statues are mostly of British Viceroys, Governors, Generals, etc. who served in India during the last 150 years. Some of them have already been shifted to our museums.

Yours faithfully,

(K. Ram)

The President,
New England New State Movement,
137, Hussell Road,
New Lambton,
NEWCASTLE N.S.W.
(Australia)

Reply by the Principal Secretary to the Prime Minister of India (29 May 1957) to Tom's request for surplus British monuments.

As a measure of his standing in the movement Tom was charged in 1957 with the responsibility of writing to the Prime Minister of India to acquire British Monuments such as sculptured statuary models which were surplus to the requirements of the newly independent Indian Government. The Indian Government's intention to dispose of such items had received some coverage in the press. Tom informed the Indian Prime Minister, Mr Pundit Nehru, that:

> the New England New State Movement would erect these monuments in many of the provincial cities of our area: Newcastle, Maitland, Tamworth, Grafton, Armidale, Lismore and Inverell. In Australia it has been customary for such monuments to be confined to Capital Cities, but we are anxious for country areas to benefit likewise.

```
                                137 Russell Road,
                                New Lambton.
                                           N. S. W.
                                     23rd July, 1957.




K. Ram I. C. S.,
   Principal Private Secretary,
      Prime Minister,
         New Delhi.

Dear Sir,
               Thank you for your letter of May 29th, 1957,
Ref F 41/1/57.

               My Movement would be glad if you would offer a
Statue of King Edward Vll, for re erection in Newcastles glorious
King Edward Park.

               If you agree to this and advise us, we will then
approach the authorities concerned.

                    Yours faithfully,




                         PRESIDENT.
```

Tom's letter to the Principal Private Secretary, Prime Minister of India (23 July 1957) requesting a statue of King Edward VII for King Edward Park.

Mindful of the costs involved, Tom requested that the Government of India would 'convey such works to us by gift – a little Colombo Plan in reverse'. In his reply, Mr K. Ram, Principal Secretary to the Prime Minister of India, pointed out that:

> the Government of India had not yet formulated any particular scheme for the disposal of statues etc. in India. So far it has been stated that those statues which are of historical and artistic value, will be kept in proper places such as museums etc. The main objection here has been to some particular statues which refer to persons who were very unpopular in India. However, if any particular statue, which is at present in India, is required in Australia, the Government of India would be prepared to consider the matter. These statues were mostly of British Viceroys, Governors, Generals etc. who served in India during the last 150 years.

Encouraged by the letter Tom wrote again to the Indian Government requesting 'an offer of a Statue of King Edward VII, for re-erection in Newcastle's glorious King Edward Park'. No doubt Tom was aware that the king had undertaken an extensive tour of India in 1875. His interest in this imperial item reveals his strong connection to Australia's British heritage. Like many of his countrymen, Tom thought it appropriate that symbols of British monarchy and British imperialism should continue to adorn Australian cities. Given the conservative nature of Australian society at this time, it is not surprising that 'new staters' like Tom wanted to uphold the value of 'constitutional monarchy' by ensuring that the British Monarchy retained its position as 'Head of State' under the terms of the constitution of the newly formed states. Given this, Tom was no doubt disappointed that no statue of the Emperor of India arrived from the subcontinent to adorn King Edward Park. In fact, no statue was donated by the Government of India to adorn any city in the proposed new state of New England.[5]

By the end of the 1960s 'Operation Seventh State' had achieved some success. Thanks to a sustained fundraising and publicity campaign undertaken by groups like the NBNENSM the newly elected Liberal-Country Party Government had decided a referendum on new states would be held in the New England area as defined by the Nicholas Royal Commission. The referendum would test the feeling of the electors of the Northern Tablelands, the North Coast, the North Western Slopes and the Hunter Valley including Newcastle about separating from New South Wales and forming a new state. Tom was to play a key part in the campaign for the 'yes' vote in Newcastle. A series of letters from Ellis, the Campaign Director, attest to that.

While no doubt happy about this decision, Tom would have realised that the referendum in Newcastle would face a number of hurdles. A number of key members of the local Labor caucus had already voiced their opposition to the idea of a seventh state. When Newcastle Council proposed to send delegates to a New State Convention, Alderman Breen had referred to the movement as a 'joke'. It was the view of Alderman Wade that 'the council was wasting time, labor and money in sending delegates away'. Aldermen Jones agreed with his Labor colleague arguing that 'even if it costs nothing to the council but the wear and tear on the council's car and petrol, it was a waste of the council officers' time' It was Jones' view that 'the two main political parties – Labor and Liberal – were both opposed to the movement. Newcastle would not be the capital of the New

State. It would be Grafton. Newcastle would be left on its own'.

Such comments highlight the obstacles Tom and the members of the NBNENSM faced in winning support for the referendum in Newcastle (a Labor heartland and the largest demographic centre in the New England area). Not only were some local Labor luminaries opposed to the establishment of a new state – their position reflected that of the Labor Party as a whole. A further problem was that the coalition parties were not wholeheartedly in favour either. As Belshaw points out 'the Liberal Party had never been a strong supporter while even within the Country Party there was some opposition'. The referendum also faced opposition from the Dairy Industry, an influential force in the Northern Districts, which feared losing access to the Sydney milk markets.

Given the opposition, it is not surprising that 'The Referendum for New England Electors' held on 29 April 1967 failed to win the majority support of voters – 168, 103 votes were cast in favour and 198,812 votes against. The strongest 'no' vote was registered in Newcastle (72 per cent) and the Manning-Gloucester dairy districts (66 per cent).

Courtesy of the *NMH* (29 April 1967)

Although 67 per cent had voted in favour of the proposal in traditional new State areas – this was not enough to counter the total 'no' vote. The referendum was lost with the 'yes' vote totaling 46 per cent of the formal votes cast compared with 54 per cent for 'no'. As Farrell points out 'the New Staters had been outmaneuvered again and were unable to show the NSW Parliament that a majority of the electors in the area wanted to separate and form a new state'. On reflecting on the defeat of the referendum in Newcastle Tom later argued that 'if they had come out and said that Newcastle would have been the capital of the New State, the referendum would have been carried'. It may be the case that sectional interests within the movement itself had played a part in the referendum's defeat. The forces at play in Grafton were certainly something Alderman Jones had commented on. It appears that sectional interests were also at play in Newcastle – Tom commented 'Newcastle people didn't want these country bastards running it'.[6]

Lumsdon cartoon (29 April 1967) – courtesy of the *NMH*.
Figure to left (Newcastle's Hunter Valley) - caption reads 'YOU CAN HAVE YOUR NEW STATE, MATE, BUT WE DON'T WANT TO BE IN IT!!'

Despite their disappointment, Tom, the NBNENSM and the New England State Movement as a whole battled on. There must have been a high degree of frustration that the 'yes' campaign would have been successful if the 'no' vote could have been moderated in Newcastle. But with little prospect of the majority of the Newcastle electors changing their allegiance to the Labor Party and that party's continued opposition to the proposal, the Executive decided to change tact. It was decided to field 'New State' candidates in electorates that had shown strong support for the 'yes' case at the next State Election set for February 1968. This decision brought the New England New State Movement into direct conflict with its old ally, the Country Party, which campaigned against the position of the 'New State' candidates. Faced with strong opposition from both sides of politics and a lack of funds, the Movement attracted 15 to 20 per cent support across four electorates. No candidate was elected.

Although this defeat effectively marked the end of the New England New State Movement, Tom never gave up his support for 'decentralisation'. As his daughter later recalled when Tom mentioned the word 'Sydney' it was almost always prefaced by the word 'bloody'. In July 1968 he wrote to the President of the New England New State Movement pledging his continued support. The President assured him that 'we shall be keeping you posted of events when they start to happen'. In 1978 he remarked 'I don't make any apology – I am a decentralist'. The reason that he gave was – 'the only way Newcastle can truly prosper is to throw off the shackles of Sydney domination – it is as simple as that'. Clearly his sense of civic duty had not diminished. His position had not changed in 1988 when he wrote to the paper complaining of 'the broken promises and the abject neglect of Newcastle over decades'. He called both political parties to task:

> Mr Greiner and Mr Unsworth have had ample opportunity to give us a fair share of financial community projects compared with Sydney. Such projects are vital for a city as important as Newcastle. Why doesn't the Government give us an opera house, an entertainment centre, or a great sporting centre like at Homebush Bay or Moore Park? Why doesn't it give us a museum like the $50 million one at White Bay Power Station? Why doesn't it eliminate the troublesome Newcastle railway crossing? Why doesn't the Government give us a national park on the Hunter River or modernise our suburban railways? The Government is spending $650 million to modernise the Sydney network. Shouldn't we be entitled to something? We need an electrified railway to Maitland and Belmont. The electrification was to be completed 30 years ago. We need the reintroduction of a passenger train service to Singleton. A Government with an overwhelming majority of politicians from Sydney can hardly be called a NSW Government. In my view there is only one party in NSW, and that is the Sydney Party, Labor or Liberal. One thing Mr Greiner and Mr Unsworth have in common, as far as Newcastle is concerned, is that their vision does not extend north of Hornsby. Anyone who votes for the Sydney Labor Party or the Sydney Liberal Party in the Newcastle area is throwing their vote away.

Despite the demise of the New State Movement, there was still a lot of fight left in Tom Farrell. The sentiments expressed in 1988 owed much to the views formed in the 1950s and 1960s. Throughout the decades his adherence to 'decentralism' was based on his motivation to do his best for Newcastle and the Hunter Region.[7]

It was this fighting spirit that led him to seek election to the local council in 1965. Although he was Assistant General Manager of the Newcastle Abattoir at the time, Tom understood that he was entitled to nominate as a candidate even though Section 30 (2a) of the Local Government Act stated that 'a person is subject to a special disqualification within the meaning of the Act if he holds any position of profit under or in the gift of the Council'. Since it was his intention to resign his position to take up public office, he believed that he was compliant with Section 30 (2a) of the Act. As he pointed out 'I felt as a layman that there was little in the Act to stop me from nominating and then it was my intention to resign at some time between the election and/or accepting 'civic office'. It was his view that it would have been irresponsible to resign before the result of the election was known. Unfortunately for Tom the Returning Officer did not agree with his interpretation of the Act and therefore, disqualified him under Section 30. Being as he explained 'a person of enquiring disposition', Tom sought the assistance of Ulrich Ellis to clarify the matter. He asked Ellis to write personally to Davis Hughes, the Minister for Local Government 'with the idea of getting the information and the legal position of the reason of rejection'. Ellis was well acquainted with Hughes – he was once leader of the Country Party and State Member for Armidale. In his reply (personally signed 'with compliments Ulrich') Hughes upheld the decision of the Returning Officer on the grounds that 'Mr. Farrell was employed by the Newcastle City Council on Nomination Day and as such was disqualified under Section 30 and the Returning Officer had no alternative other than to decline to nominate Mr. Farrell as a candidate for election as an alderman of the Newcastle City Council'. Tom would have to wait until he left his employment with Newcastle Council before attempting to run for local government again.[8]

Such was his intrepid public spirit that a month after he retired as General Manager of Newcastle Abattoir, Tom sought election as an alderman for Central Ward of the Newcastle Council. Not surprisingly given his views about the 'Sydney Liberal Party' and 'Sydney Labor Party', he sought election as a candidate for the Citizens Group led by the Lord Mayor, Alderman Doug McDougall. It was the intention of this group 'to keep Newcastle free from the political caucus' by putting forward candidates 'who have been chosen for their ability and integrity'. In this way 'the Citizens Group would ensure non-party local government in Newcastle without political bias'. Running on a platform of 'sound, able local government administration Tom and the other candidates advocated improved child-minding facilities, improved council services to the public, continued protection and development of Blackbutt Reserve, more playing fields to cater for junior sport, an extension of library services, the provision of adequate and up-to-date facilities for Live Theatre, the sewering of all possible homes in the interest of public health, improved transport services including rail and ferry, better airport facilities, the construction of a new rail station in Newcastle, a new floating dock, replacement of existing rail-crossings, improvement of Stockton foreshore, improved caravan park facilities, control of litter, smoke abatement, air, river and beach pollution, support for the construction of a new Fruit and Vegetable Market at Shortland, the establishment of a Council sponsored Building Society to finance redevelopment, homes for the aged and the alleviation of the heavy burden of rates. Given that the preservation and development of parks and open space, improved public transport, pollution abatement and the control of rates were central to this platform, one can see the hand of Tom Farrell in the formation of the policies of the Citizens Group.[9]

NEWCASTLE COUNCIL ELECTION

SATURDAY, 7th DECEMBER, 1968

R. E. (TOM) FARRELL

A MEMBER OF THE INDEPENDENT CITIZEN'S
GROUP TEAM
VOTE STRICTLY IN ACCORDANCE WITH OFFICIAL
"HOW TO VOTE" TICKET

A ratepayer of CENTRAL WARD for 40 years
A resident of NEW LAMBTON for 40 years

THE LOCAL MAN

with

LOCAL KNOWLEDGE

and

LOCAL ENTHUSIASM

Support your own New Lambton resident.
VOTE in accordance with Citizen's Group
"How To Vote" Ticket

POINTS OF POLICY

Dear Voter,

On the 7th December, the Newcastle City Council election will take place to elect a new team of Aldermen.

I resigned from my employment recently, so that I could contest this election as I am emphatic that there are some things that MUST be done, and done quickly, to further the interests of all residents of Newcastle and particularly the householders of Central Ward where I have lived for 45 years.

Concern with the attempt by the Department of Main Roads to destroy the "BLACKBUTT RESERVE" is my MAIN REASON for submitting myself as a Candidate. I will RESIST to the full any attempt by the D.M.R. to alienate BLACKBUTT. This area was originally purchased by the Ratepayers of Newcastle. It is NOT, and never was Crown Land.

I intend to call upon the Government to replace Railway gates at Adamstown with a modern overbridge. Surely the Second City of N.S.W. can demand and receive better traffic flow. Newcastle has not had one overbridge over a main line constructed in 50 years.

I will press for the elimination of dirt approaches to proposed Donald Street overbridge — this must be of pleasing architectural design.

I will urge the creation of the Public Rest Park on the neglected area of Lambton and Tauranga Roads, New Lambton, by the planting of native Eucalypt Nicholli.

I will press forward with New Lambton's just claim for a community centre. Available funds amounting to $42,000 and contributed to the New Lambton ratepayer are being held by the Mines Subsidence Board for distribution.

During the present life of Council I will resist any attempt to increase rates to the home owner. Other sources of funds must be obtained from elsewhere, either from Federal or State Government Consolidated Revenue.

It is my belief and others agree, that the City Council should have its own separate planning section to assist speedily in carrying out the normal progressive functions of an expanding city.

Alarmed at the spread of disease by the poor standard of garbage collection I will press for the Garbage Container to be RETURNED to the homeowner's property as is the case in any modern city.

I will press for a proper authority to investigate and provide for the fixation of Council Salaries.

If my colleagues in the Citizen's Group and I can obtain solid electoral support in this election, I am confident that we can expect a marked improvement in the lot of the average resident of the City, and a revitalised status for its Council. Remember, vote in accordance with the official "How To Vote" ticket.

I will to the best of my ability try to achieve these objects. Thank you.

Yours sincerely,

R.E. (Tom) Farrell

137 Russell Rd., New Lambton

Electioneering material for Mr R. E. (Tom) Farrell

Under the slogan 'The Local Man with Local Knowledge and Local Enthusiasm' Tom introduced himself to the electors of his ward as 'an energetic fighter with the true interests of the people of Central Ward (embracing New Lambton, Broadmeadow, Hamilton) and Newcastle at heart, and a man with capable administrative experience'. The candidature of R. E. (Tom) Farrell was endorsed by twenty leading citizens including Ernie Dunkley, Joe Richley, Griff Duncan, Ann Von Bertouch, Glen Maloney, Neil Smith, Cedric Tate, Bill Curry, Jean Harris, Doug Lithgow, Bill Bond, Bob Hosking, Ken Mulholland, Kevin Moon, Jack Shields, Reg Ellis, Dick Woodgate, Jack Webb, Jim Lewis and S. Scobie. Such an endorsement was a testament to Tom's standing in the community. It is not surprising that his candidature would be supported by his old 'comrades' (Richley, Lithgow, Shields, Ellis, Woodgate and Curry) whom

VOTE CITIZENS GROUP
CENTRAL WARD

[1] GOSPER, Bernie L.

[2] FARRELL, R. E. (Tom)

[3] NORRIS, Keith W.

YOU MUST VOTE FOR ALL CANDIDATES
AND FOR ALL OTHER CANDIDATES IN THE ORDER OF YOUR PREFERENCE

ALD. BERNIE L. GOSPER Alderman Central Ward 3 years during which time promoted methods for and/or fostered :— Cancer Treatment Centre, Newcastle. Airport Newcastle. Home Nursing and Domestic Help for Aged and Infirm. Improved traffic control and safety. Deputy Sheriff Newcastle Staff Officer Civil Defence, (Newcastle). Returned Soldier, served over 6 years A.I.F. Rank Major — served C.M.F. 12 years. Actively engaged civic affairs including Legacy, Police & Citizens' Boys' Club. Officiated in Charity Appeals, Freedom from Hunger, Salvation Army Red Shield. Was President (twice). State Councillor of Australian-American Association. Was State Vice-President and President of Northern Districts, N.S.W. Amateur Athletic Association.

MR. R. E. (Tom) FARRELL Qualified Accountant. Fellow Australian Society of Accountants. Qualified Meat Inspector. Officer Newcastle Abattoir 47 years. Held General Managership three years. Returned Serviceman. Served R.A.A.F. 1942-46. F/Lt. Active member Cooks Hill Surf Club 1920-32. Played Rugby League, Central and Western Suburbs Clubs. Served on General Committee, Life Member, N'cle. Rugby League. For some time Pres. Western Suburbs Rugby League Club. Member General C'tee N.S.W. Country Rugby League. Vice President Northern Parks & Playgrounds Movement. Member Blackbutt Reserve C'tee. Actively interested Co-operative Movement mainly Building Societies and Insurance. Director N.S.W. Permanent Building Soc. Assn. Resided New Lambton since 1927.

MR. KEITH W. NORRIS O.B.E., ED. Age: 48. Occupation: Valuer — Hunter District Water Board. Member Commonwealth Institute of Valuers. Address: 75 Janet St., Merewether. I have resided in Merewether 45 years. Returned Soldier — 2nd A.I.F. Interested in Citizen Military Forces over 30 years. Squadron commander 14 Field Squadron, Royal Australian Engineers — Harriett St., Waratah — 14 years now retired. Appointed — Member of the Order of The British Empire — 1959. Awarded — Efficiency Decoration — 1964. Member — Merewether Sub-Branch RSL. By virtue of employment and family background possesses keen interest and understanding of local Government Affairs.

MEN of ABILITY and EXPERIENCE

Davies & Cannington, Printers, 137-139 King Street, Newcastle, 2300.

The Citizens Group candidates for Central Ward.

he had fought alongside on many a campaign. But he could also count on the support of a former Mayor (Dunkley), leaders of commerce and industry (Hosking, Mulholland, Scobie, Smith, Tate and Webb), leading academic figures (Duncan), patrons of the arts (von Bertouch and Harris) and leading sportsmen (Maloney). There is no doubt that Tom Farrell attracted support from a wide cross section of the community in Newcastle.[10]

Of the three Citizens Group candidates put forward for Central Ward Tom was listed second on the ballot paper after Alderman Bernie Gosper. The third candidate was Mr. Keith Norris OBE, ED. After listing his qualifications, work experience, war service and community service, Tom informed voters that he had 'resigned from his employment recently, so that he could contest this election as I am emphatic that there are some things that must be done, and done quickly, to further the interests of all residents of Newcastle and particularly the householders of Central Ward where I have lived for 45 years'. He explained that the main reason for his candidature was 'to resist to the full any attempt by the Department of Main Roads to destroy Blackbutt Reserve'. He then listed the main points of his policy as the replacement of the railway gates at Adamstown with a modern over-bridge, the elimination of dirt approaches to the proposed Donald Street over-bridge, the creation of a Public Park in neglected areas of Lambton and the establishment of a community centre in Lambton. Furthermore, he intended to resist any attempt by Council to increase rates, press for the establishment of a separate planning section within Council, improve the standard of garbage collection and place a cap on Council salaries. He promised the residents of Central Ward that if elected he and his colleagues in the Citizens Group would bring about a 'marked improvement in the lot of the average resident of the City and a revitalised status for its Council'.

Clearly Tom was motivated to hold public office for the benefit of the community.[11]

On polling day Tom attracted 8.6 per cent of the primary vote securing 314 of the 3634 formal votes in Central Ward. Clearly Tom was a well-known and respected resident of New Lambton with booths in this area providing him with his best result - 78 votes (New Lambton Scout Hall), 81 votes (New Lambton Public School) and 53 votes (Oster's Garage New Lambton). Having secured the third highest primary vote Tom needed to rely on preferences to secure the third aldermanic position for his ward – Henderson (Labor) and Gosper (Citizens Group) with 43.4 per cent and 34.8 per cent of the primary vote respectively had secured the other two positions. Although Tom received 420 preferences mainly from Norris (the third Citizens Group candidate) the majority of Labor preferences flowed to another candidate. As a result Tom failed in his bid to become an alderman for Central Ward in the Newcastle Council. Although disappointed, he could take heart from the fact that he had attracted 20.2 per cent of the total vote after preferences had been counted. As he later told a supporter he took great encouragement from the fact that the Citizens Group had achieved 'an overall majority of fifty-five per cent in the New Lambton area'. Much of this support could be put down to Tom Farrell.[12]

Although Tom did not seek public office again, he continued to be driven by a strong sense of civic duty. This led him in retirement to lend his support to a number of key community projects. This sense of civic duty had driven him throughout his life – as an ordinary citizen, a Liberal Party member, a 'new stater' and as a prospective candidate for public office. At its heart was a great sense of civic pride – that Newcastle and the Hunter region were places of boundless potential. Ultimately,

Tom was driven by a strong desire to help people – to unlock this potential for the benefit of all members of the community. Given this, it is little wonder that Tom was recognised as one of the great Novocastrians. As one commentator put it in 1996 'Newcastle has borne many fine children. Tom Farrell was one of the finest'.

Kath and Tom Farrell (1960s)

Conclusion

When asked in later life 'had he got things done?' Tom answered 'Oh yes!'. This was no idle boast. Through a succession of public campaigns Tom Farrell had achieved a great deal for his community. With others he had been instrumental in establishing a university college in Newcastle. He had worked tirelessly to secure for Newcastle and the Hunter Region key areas of open space and national parks. Of these Blackbutt Reserve remained for him 'an absolute inspiration'. But he also played his part in a whole hearted manner in preserving Green Point (Lake Macquarie), Mount Sugarloaf, Glenrock Lagoon, Barrington Tops, the Myall Lakes and numerous other small parks and reserves in and around Newcastle. A decentralist throughout his life, he never gave up his belief that local authorities were best placed to deliver essential services (including public transport) to the local community. It was this belief that saw him devote so much time and energy to the establishment of a seventh state in New South Wales. Tom, however, did not act alone – he was at his best when he worked as part of a team. He took an important role in a number of key groups including the Cardiff Heights Progress Association, the Newcastle University Establishment Group, the Northern Parks and Playgrounds Movement and the New England New State Movement. Not one to seek the limelight, he promoted the leadership of key individuals like Joe Richley, Reg Ellis, Rod Earp, Don Barnett, Doug Lithgow, Harry Eddy and Ulrich Ellis. He worked tirelessly alongside fellow activists like Mavis & Wilfred Dews, Don Morris, Arthur Munro, Peter Podmore, Jack

Shields, Dick Woodgate and Greg Wright. He brought to these groups a boundless energy, determination and enthusiasm, a high degree of intelligence and a tremendous ability to organise. Always driven by a strong sense of civic duty and community service, he worked tirelessly for the people of Newcastle and the Hunter. And this against a background of a successful career in business, having risen through the ranks to become the General Manager of the Newcastle Abattoir and a key figure in the establishment of the Greater Newcastle Building Society and other local financial institutions. His approach in the co-operative movement was practical and pragmatic. Tom would have been the first to admit that nothing he achieved would have been possible without the love, devotion and loyal support of his wife. Kathleen Farrell was the centre of Tom's world – she was his inspiration, his anchor. Tom devoted himself to his wife and his five children. Kath, his four daughters and his son meant everything to him.

Tom died on 20 July 1996. He was ninety-two years of age. In acknowledging the death of this 'tireless worker', this 'tireless campaigner', the Editor of the *NMH* wrote:

> When they made Tom Farrell, as the saying goes, they broke the mould. The loss of this extraordinary powerhouse of a man last week caused great sadness in Newcastle and beyond. Mr Farrell's long life was studded with achievements that will continue to benefit the region he loved for decades to come. In business he rose from a dockyard worker to general manager of Newcastle Abattoir, for many years an important enterprise. From that platform of relative prominence, he campaigned mightily on a range of public issues. Many of the major parks and reserves

that are taken for granted today by the people of the Hunter might never have come into existence were it not for Mr Farrell and those whom he inspired with his indomitable energy. Blackbutt Reserve, Mt Sugarloaf, Barrington Tops, the Myall lakes – all of these were wrested against great odds from reluctant authorities with the help of Tom Farrell's relentless insistence. Newcastle has borne many fine children. Tom Farrell was one of its finest.

A fitting eulogy for one of Newcastle's best. Tom was laid to rest next to his wife in Whitebridge Cemetery on 25 July 1996. The epitaph on his tombstone simply reads: 'An ever caring man of integrity and vision'.

Tom Farrell (1904-1996) – 'A Powerhouse of a Man'.

Endnotes

CHAPTER ONE

1. For family details see: N.McKey, *Pioneering Family: A History of the Warlters Family*, 1976, The Tom Farrell Papers (TFP), University of Newcastle Archives (NUA), A8288 (i), pp.32-34; Record of War Service, R.E. Farrell, Australian National Archives, Canberra, Series A9300/5243117. See also A.Hunt to W.Farrell, 'A Letter of Thanks from the Commonwealth of Australia Department of External Affairs', 19 January 1901, in McKey, *Pioneering Family*, p.47. For details of William Farrell's cinematographic enterprises see John Farrell, 'Tom Farrell Biography As Experienced By His Son', 17 February 2010. For details of Deborah Ann Farrell's death see 'Records of Katoomba Cemetery', accessed 23 March 2013, < http://www. bmcc.nsw.gov.au/cemetery_register/map/maps.cfm?rid=6350&s=1&tid=0.024007936772>. For the Farrell family's interest in the turf see J. Mathews, 'Man of Many Interests and Well Worth Knowing', *Newcastle Morning Herald* (NMH), 24 October 1979. It appears that Tom maintained his father's interest in horse racing – see B.Budden 'Air Force Mates Find a Winner', no date, Tom Farrell Papers in possession of John Farrell (TFPJF); see also Memorandum and Articles of Association Dungog Jockey Club Ltd, Elliott & Waller, 1912, TFPJF.

2. 'Entry for Charles Farrell', Cooks Hill Roll Book 1911-1920, NSW State Archives (Kingswood) NRS 19083/1/1. Charles Farrell (aged 10 years 9 months) enrolled into Class 4B, date of admission 28 June 1909. Unfortunately, the roll book is quite incomplete – no entry was found for Edward or Tom. A.Beavis (District Inspector) to P.Lollard (Chief Inspector), 3 January 1908, Cooks Hill School Administrative File 1905-1913, NSW State Archives (Kingswood) 5/15485A; on enrolment restrictions see Beavis to Lollard, 26 February 1908, Cooks Hill School Administrative File 1905-1913, NSWSA 5/15485A. The restriction had little impact on the growing school population, by December 1918 the effective enrolment was 489 students – see Faulkner to Lollard, 20 December 1918, NSWSA 5/15485A. For Board's remarks see *NMH*, 17 July 1913. On Cooks Hill Public School see R.A.Low, 'Cooks Hill Public School: A Brief History', Newcastle, 1994, Newcastle Region Library, Local Studies & Archives (NRLLSA), LHQ372/ PAM Box; S.Thornton, 'A Goodbye to Traditions', *NMH*, 12 December 1976.

3. See Board's comments on the curriculum at Cooks Hill Superior School in *NMH*, 17 July 1913; see also A. Barcan, *A Short History of Education in New South Wales*, Martindale Press, Sydney1965, pp.207-210; A. Barcan, *Two Centuries of Education in New South Wales*, UNSW Press, Sydney, 1988, pp.186-189. All three Farrell boys began their careers in commerce or industry – Charles and Edward at the BHP and Tom at the Brickenridge & Co Timber Merchants – see McKey, *Pioneering Family*, pp.33-34. For public exhibitions of school work see Clemens to Dawson, 22 March 1915, NSWSA 5/15485A. It should be noted that Clemens was far from an impartial commentator, he was in fact the teacher of the superior class.

4. For the activities of the swimming club see Back (School Principal) to Walsh (District Inspector), 12 March 1912, NSWSA 5/15485B, Clemens to Fraser (Life Saving Club), 23 March 1915, NSWSA 5/15485B. It is likely that Tom achieved his Bronze Medallion while at school. For details of the rifle club see "School Routine", 1 May 1914, NSWSA 5/15485A; for the school band see 'Repairs to Band Instruments', 'Memorandum to McLelland', 2 December 1918, NSWSA 5/15485A; for football club see Madden to Walsh, 7 December 1914, NSWSA 5/15485A. For details of Tom's introduction to rugby league see Mathews, 'Man of Many Interests'. For details of Tom's truancy see Farrell, 'Tom Farrell Biography', p.3.

5. For the recollections of the Farrell children about their parents see; Farrell, 'Tom Farrell Biography'; B. Hincks, 'Memories of My Father', 28 April 2012; C. Nelmes, 'Recollections of My Father', 28 February 2012; J. Manson, 'Memories, Perspectives and Recollections of Dad', 6 January 2012 and K. Talty, 'Memories of My Father', 13 April 2012. The recollections of the Farrell children are held by T. Roberts, Tom Farrell Institute for the Environment, University of Newcastle.

6. Quotation taken from Farrell, 'Tom Farrell Biography', p.3. For Tom's recollections of his childhood see V.Tripp, 'Open Foundation History Project Profile on a Successful Man Mr R.E. (Tom) Farrell', 1987, TFPJF, p.2; see also recollections of the Farrell children - Farrell, 'Tom Farrell Biography'; Hincks, 'Memories of My Father'; Nelmes, 'Recollections of My Father'; Manson, 'Memories, Persectives and Recollections of My Father'and Talty, 'Memories of My Father'.

7. For details of Tom's age and qualification gained on leaving school see Tripp, 'Profile on a Successful Man ', p.1. For information on Breckenrige's timber business in Newcastle see M.Breckenridge, *Mills, Merchants and Migrants*, Fastbooks, Sydney, 1992, pp.138-163; 'Breckenridgie's Timber Yard', accessed 21 May 2011, <http://newcastle.nsw.gov.au/about-newcastle/history-and-heritage/attractions-and-sites/civic-park> for an outline of Tom's career at the Newcastle Abattoir see *NMH*, 8 November 1966.

8. see; Farrell, 'Tom Farrell Biography'; Hincks, 'Memories of My Father'; Nelmes, 'Recollections of My Father'; Manson, 'Memories, Persectives and Recollections of My Father'and Talty, 'Memories of My Father'.

9. For details of Tom and Kath Farrell's early married life see Farrell, 'Tom Farrell Biography', p.4; Hincks, 'Memories of My Father'; Nelmes, 'Recollections of My Father'; Manson, 'Memories, Persectives and Recollections of My Father'and Talty, 'Memories of My Father'. For details of Tom's siblings see McKey, *Pioneering Family*, pp.33-34. Edward (Mick) Farrell married in 1929, Charles (Charlie) Farrell married in 1934, Mabel gained her Science Degree from the University of Sydney in 1927 – she then took up a country teaching post – see Farrell, 'Tom Farrell Biography', p.4. For the remark about Kath Farrell see Ellis to Farrell, 20 January 1984, TFP, A8289 (viii). For details of 'Rally Round' see Farrell, 'Tom Farrell Biography', p.4. For comments of Tom's niece and nephew see N. Boutillier, 'Memories of Tom Farrell', 24 April 2012; K. Maher, 'Details of Uncle Tom's Life', 3 April 2012. Both recollections are held by T. Roberts, Tom Farrell Institute (TFPTFI). See also material drawn from the recollections of the Farrell children.

CHAPTER TWO

1. For details of conditions in Australia in the 1930s see P.Grimshaw, M.Lake, A.McGrath & M.Quartly, *Creating a Nation 1788-1990*, Penguin Books, Melbourne, 1995, pp.231-255. For recollection of Tom's daughter see Hincks, 'Memories of My Father'. For details of the impact of the Japanese advance on South-East Asia on Australia see Peter Dennis et al., *The Oxford Companion to Australian Military History*, OUP, Melbourne, 1995. On the midget submarine attacks on Sydney and Newcastle see Richard Reid, *No Cause for Alarm : Submarine Attacks on Sydney and Newcastle, May-June 1942*, Department of Veterans Affairs, Canberra, 2002. For Tom's decision to enlist see Hincks, 'Memories of My Father'. Tom had to seek permission to enlist because he was employed in a 'restricted occupation', that is, an occupation considered vital to the welfare of the nation. Normally such employees were exempt from conscription and were forbidden to enlist voluntarily – see M. Johnson, 'The Civilians Who Joined Up', *Journal of the Australian War Memorial*, Issue 29, November 1996, accessed 27 March 2012, <http://www.awm.gov.au/journal/j29/>. For comment about sportsmen and servicemen see Australian War Memorial, 'Sport and War', accessed 17 October 2011, <http://www.awm.gov.au/exhibitions/sportandwar/>.

2. For details on enlistment and prior military service see 'Application for a Commission in Administrative Branch Royal Australian Air Force' in 'R. E. Farrell Citizen Air Force Recruitment Papers', Air Force Personnel, National Archives of Australia, A9300/5243117. For the period 1941-1942 and role of RAAF see Dennis et al., *Australian Military History*. For details on Militia and conscription see Australian War Memorial, 'Conscription during the Second World War, 1939–45', accessed 21 October 2011, <http://www.awm.gov.au/ encyclopedia/ conscription/ww2.asp>. For details of Tom's reaction to houses being commandeered by the military and his preparedness for war see Farrell, 'Tom Farrell Biography'; Hincks, 'Memories of My Father'. In regards to the financial difficulties the Farrell family faced as a result of his enlistment see Farrell to Hughes (Deputy Commissioner of Taxation), 28 March 1952, TFPJF; see also Farrell, 'Tom Farrell Biography' – John Farrell remembers his father telling his mother not to pay utility bills and council rates during his absence. Tom intended 'to fix that up when he got back'.

3. For the results of Tom's medical examination see 'Farrell Air Force Recruitment Papers'. The scars on the left thigh resulted from an earlier appendectomy. Harrison's Sulcus, a condition which causes a horizontal line at the lower margin of the thorax to develop where the diaphragm attaches to the ribs, is caused either by a childhood respiratory illness like asthma or rickets, a condition caused by a Vitamin D or mineral (calcium, phosphate) deficiency. Given Tom's active outdoor sporting life, it is more likely that he suffered from a mineral deficiency as a child. Whatever caused the condition, the evidence of Harrison's Sulcus, provides some insight into common childhood ailments in Australia in the early part of the twentieth century. For details of Tom's training at the Officer Training Facility at the University of Melbourne see Farrell to Storm, 19 February 1987 TFPJF – during the war the Air Force conducted its personnel training at the University of Melbourne; see also Farrell, 'Tom Farrell Biography'.

4. For details of Tom's war service see 'Record of Service Officers RAAF'; 'Personal Record of Service-Rolf Everist Farrell'; 'Enclosure No 222358 – A Certificate of Service & Discharge' in 'Farrell Air Force Recruitment Papers'. For details of '76 Squadron' see Australian War Memorial, '76 Squadron RAAF', accessed 15 July 2011,<http://www.awm.gov.au/units/unit 11103second world war.asp>; 'No 76 Squadron Online', accessed 15 July 2011,<http://no76.squadronassociation.org/>; see also 'Outstanding Wartime No 76 Fighter Squadron – On the Move Again', no date, TFPJF; 'No 76 SQN Fought The Air War From Milne Bay to Tokyo', *RAAF News*, October 1940, TFPJF. For Tom's service overseas see McKey, *Pioneering Family*, p. 34; 'Letter of Application', Farrell to Chairman, Metropolitan & Export Abattoirs Board, 19 August 1952, FP A8290 (viii). For Tom's recollections of his war service see Farrell to Storm, 19 February 1987. See also Farrell to Hughes, 28 March 1952 – Tom states in this letter that 'in 1944 I was posted overseas'. See also 'RAAF Daily Routine Orders by Flight Lieutenant P S Jones', 15 January 1945, TFPJF.

5. For an example of the letters Tom received from his wife see Kath Farrell to Tom, 16 August 1945, TFPJF; for examples of the children's letters see John Farrell to Tom, 5 August 1943, 2 September 1943 and 30 June 1945, TFPJF. For details of the report by Captain McLachlan see 'Confidential Report',14 November 1945, in 'Farrell Air Force Recruitment Papers' . For Tom's demobilisation see 'Enclosure No 222353' in 'Farrell Air Force Recruitment Papers'; see also 'Royal Australian Air Force Statement of Account', No 67155, 27 May 1946, TFPJF – balance due to Rolf Everist Farrell was £742.14.1. For details of the strong bonds of friendship Tom held with his fellow servicemen (especially Ellis and Hurley) see Hincks, 'Memories of My Father'. See also Farrell to Storm, 19 February 1987; B. Budden,'Air Force Mates Find a Winner', no date, TFPJF – the article records that the Merriwa racing identity, Harold Baldwin, 'raced the two year old colt (Prince of Mates) in partnership with Tom Farrell, a retired Newcastle businessman and a former Sydney bank manager, Ron Wicks'. The colt won the Merriwa Combined Agents First Maiden Handicap over 1000 metres. See also Algie (Secretary of 76th Squadron Association) to Farrell, 26 March 1976 TFPJF; Quoy (President of the Fighter Squadrons' Branch) to Farrell, 1 September 1976 TFPJF.

6. For details of Tom's early football career see B.Power, *The Saga of the Western Men: Story of Western Suburbs (Newcastle) RLFC*, Western Suburbs Leagues Club, 1966, p.132. For details of Tom's career with Central Newcastle see T.Bryden & T. Bunn, *Butcher Boy Barrackers: A Brief History of Central Charlestown Rugby League Football Club 1910-2001*, Central Newcastle Rugby League Football Club, Charlestown, 2001, pp.4-8, p.65, p.95. See also B.Quinn, *Legends of League: A History of the Newcastle Rugby League 1908-1999*, Newcastle Newspaper Ltd, 1999, pp. 12-14. For details of First Grade match see *NMH*, 20 August 1928. For details of Grand Final see *NMH*, 24 September 1928. For details of Tom's listing among 'Senior Players' see 'Team Photograph' in Bryden & Bunn, *Butcher Boy Barrackers*, p. 6; Quinn, *Legends of League*, p.14. Tom (listed as treasurer) appears seated first left in front of the third row – to his left is the Crawford Cup, at the end of the seated row is the Mullally Shield. In Bryden & Bunn, *Butcher Boy Barrackers*, p. 95 Tom is listed as a 'Central Senior Official' in the 1920s. Tom's Premiership Badge is in the possession of John Farrell – it is inscribed: 'Premiership Badge NRFL 1928 Mullally Shield Competition 1st Grade Won by Central Newcastle R E Farrell'.

7. For details of Tom's move to New Lambton see Farrell, 'Tom Farrell Biography' For comments by later commentator see Power, *The Saga of The Western Men*, p.55. For statistics of Western Suburbs' performance in the 1929 season see Power, *Saga of The Western Men*, pp.55-56. For comments by 'The Forward', football correspondent, see *NMH*, 26 June 1929 and 31 August 1929.

8. For details of the Great Depression on Newcastle see S.Gray, *Newcastle in the Great Depression*, Council of the City of Newcastle, 1989. Newcastle experience an unemployment rate of thirty per cent as the construction industry, steelworks, dockyard and associated plants suffered a severe economic downturn. Shanty towns were set up at Nobbys Beach, Stockton, Carrington, Adamstown, Lambton, Waratah and Hexham. For those facing unemployment or hardship, rugby league provided a relatively inexpensive form of entertainment. Although the region's rugby league clubs also faced economic hardship, their supporter base remained solid. For details of First and Reserve Grades' season see Power, *Saga of The Western Men*, p.57. For details of the reserve Grade match on 26 June 1930 see 'The Forward', *NMH*, 28 June 1930. For details of the Reserve Grade semi-final see 'The Forward', *NMH,* 15 September 1930. For details of the Reserve Grade Final see 'The Forward', *NMH*, 29 September 1930.

9. For 1931statistics see Power, *Saga of The Western Men*, p.60. For details of games see *NMH*, 2 July 1930; 18 July 1931. For details of Reserve Grade semi-final see *NMH*, 14 September 1931. For details of Reserve Grade final see *NMH*, 21 September 1931. It appears Tom ended his playing career for Wests at the end of 1931. He is not listed among the Reserve or Senior Grade players for the 1932 season – see *NMH*, 7 May 1932; 14 May 1932; 21 May 1932; 28 May 1932; June 11 1932; 18 June 1932; 25 June 1932; 2 July 1932; 16 July 1932; 23 July 1932; 30 July 1932 and 6 August 1932. See also Power, *Saga of The Western Men*, pp.65-66. Wests Reserve Grade's fortunes were poor during 1932 season, finishing eighth out of ten teams with eight wins, one draw and nine losses – see 'League Table', *NMH*, 6 August 1932. For details of the physical injury that forced Tom out of the game see Farrell, 'Tom Farrell Biography', p.4; Hincks, 'Memories of My Father'. For details of Tom's football friends see Farrell, 'Tom Farrell Biography', p.8. For statistics regarding number of grade games see 'Farrell's Favourite Town', *Sporting Times*, 1993, TFPJF.

10. For details of the financial difficulties of the club see Power, *Saga of The Western Men*, p.60. For Tom's role in the rescue plan see Power, *Saga of The Western Men*, p.69. It is clear that Dr Alfred Harker, a local medical practitioner and medical officer for the club, played a key role in putting Wests on a stronger financial footing – see Manson, 'Memories of My Father'. For Otto to Prospective Members, 18 May 1934, see Power, *Saga of The Western Men*, pp.69-70; see also J. Mathews, 'Man of Many Interests Well Worth Knowing', *NMH*, 24 October 1979.

11. For comment by daughter see Manson, 'Memories of Dad'. For recollections of John Farrell see Farrell, 'Tom Farrell Biography', pp.8-9. The Sportsman's Arms Hotel in Hobart Street, New Lambton, was a

popular meeting place for officials and players after the Wests' games – see 'The Sportsman's Arms Hotel', *Lambton & New Lambton Advertiser*, 25 November 1986 in 'Paper Clippings of New Lambton', Newcastle Public Library Local Studies, LHD919.442/NEW Vol., 2. The hotel was demolished in 1987 to make way for the expansion of Western Suburbs League's Club. For details of Tom's Committee positions see Power, *Saga of The Western Men*, p.94, p.154 and p.157; 'Hall of Fame – Club Officials', accessed 3 January 2012, <http://www. westrosellas.com.au/page19132/Club-Officials.aspx>. Note the sources provide different dates for Tom's second term as President. See also Farrell to Trip, 3 August 1980, TFP A8289 (viii). For details of Tom's Life Member ship of Newcastle Rugby League see 'Life Members', accessed 2 January 2012, <http://www. sportingpulse.com /assoc_page.cgi? c=0-2137-0-0-0&sID=17597>. Note this source gives a different date (1992) for Tom's Life Membership of the Newcastle Rugby League to Power, *Saga of The Western Men*, p.132. For details on Tom's involvement with the Western Suburbs Associated Clubs see Farrell, 'Tom Farrell Biography', p.8; see also Mathews, 'Man of Many Interests'. For involvement with the Country Rugby League see Farrell, 'Tom Farrell Biography', p.8. For 1978 comments see D. Rowe, 'Interview with Mr R. E. Farrell', Archive Tape 10017, Newcastle University Archives. For Tom's comment regarding the Newcastle Rugby League Competition see Farrell, 'League Standard Defended', Farrell to Editor (*NMH*), 1980, TFPJF. For Tom's interest in international football matches see Farrell, 'Tom Farrell Biography', p.8 – it is clear from the TFPJF that Tom attended a number of international games – see 'Souvenir Program Australia vs British Isles', *The Rugby News*, 28 May 1966, 'Souvenir of Australia vs Great Britain', *The Rugby News*, 25 May 1968. For Tom's attempt to join the Sydney Cricket and Sports Ground Club see Wood (Secretary) to Booth (Minister for Sport, NSW), 12 May 1978, TFPJF – it appears that Tom had enlisted the assistance of Booth to enquire why the membership application (dated 3 September 1966) had not been successful. Tom finally achieved membership sometime before 1987 – see 'Sydney Cricket and Sports Ground Certificate of Gold Membership', Gold Member Number S/005968, 31 December 1987, TFPJF. For newspaper articles dealing with football issues in the 1950s and 1980s see TFP A8289 (vi); see also various football publications (*League News*, 1 May 1966, 5 September 1966, *The Rugby League News*, 18 September 1965, *Looking at League* , 23 and 25 April 1988, 21 and 22 May 1988, *Big League*, 15 September 1987) in TFPJF. For Tom's mistrust of Sydney Football Authorities see Farrell to Editor (*NMH*), 21 February 1978, 16 March 1978 and 9 April 1978; Editor (*NMH*) to Farrell, 31 March 1978 TFPJF – the Editor had decided not to publish Tom's original letter (dated 21 February 1978) because of the 'verbiage' he had used in opposing the Sydney Football Authorities' decision not to organise a Newcastle v Sydney competition. This led to a heated written exchange between Tom and John Allan, Editor (*NMH*). Tom did not give up on this issue – see Farrell to Editor, *NMH*, 17 June 1980. For poem commenting on Tom's role as delegate to the Newcastle Rugby League see Power, *Saga of The Western Men*, pp.122-123 – it is clear that Tom met such comment with good humour. Power comments that 'after reading this poem Tom came back with his usual quip now known as 'Tom's Retort'. For Tom's interest in other football codes see Farrell, 'Tom Farrell Biography', p.9. For comment by friend in 1968 see Still to Farrell, 31 October 1968, TFP A8289 (v). For testimonial for Life Membership of Wests see Farrell to The Secretary, Western Suburbs RLFC, 10 November 1975 TFPJF. For Life Membership of Newcastle Rugby League see 'Farrell's Favourite Town', *Sporting Times*, 1993, TFPJF. For testament comments see Power, *Saga of The Western Men*, p.132; see also B. Power, *Continuing Saga of The Western Men*, Western Suburbs Leagues Club, 1966-1967, TFPJF – the author has inscribed on Tom's copy, 'yours for RL, Bob Power'; see also B. Power,*The Rebels of Rugby The Bolshevicks v The Lilywhites 1907-1920* , Western Suburbs League Club, 1992 – the author has inscribed on Tom's copy (TFPJF) 'Tom Yours for the Old Times', 'Keep Punching'. For Mathew's comments see Mathews, 'Man of Many Interests'.

12. For details of CHLSSC see J.Ramsland, *Cook's Hill Life Saving & Surf Club The First Hundred Years*, Brolga Publishers, Melbourne, 2011. For the importance of the club to footballers see Ramsland, *Cook's Hill Club*, pp.127-132. For the dates of Tom's association with the club see Farrell to Trip, 3 August 1980, TFP A8289 (viii). For Tom and Charles' listing on patrol at Bar Beach see *NMH*, 29 November 1929. For the fitness level and skills involved in lifesaving see Ramsland, *Cook's Hill Club*, pp.92-98. For fatalities see Committee Meeting, 15 April 1928, 17 March 1931, Minutes Book of Cook's Hill Life Saving & Surf Club, 1927/28 to 1933/34, Cook's Hill Life Saving & Surf Club Archives; Ramsland, *Cook's Hill Club*, p.98. For details of death of John Welsh see Ramsland, *Cook's Hill Club*, pp.109-110. For the rate of successful rescues see Ramsland, *Cook's Hill Club*, pp.90-92 and p.95. For Warton's rescue see *NMH*, 14 February 1924.

13. Tom's Bronze Medallion is in the possession of John Farrell. For Farrell brothers' involvement in swimming competition see *NMH*, 12 January 1922, 2 February 1922, 11 January 1923, 13 January 1923, 22 January 1923, 25 January 1923, 29 January 1923, 10 January 1924, 24 January 1924, 14 February 1924, 12 February 1925, 16 February 1925, 15 December 1925, 22 December 1925, 5 January 1928, 12 January 1928, 26 January 1928, 23 February 1928, 1 March 1928, 29 March 1928, 3 January 1929, 10 January 1929, 14 January 1929, 16 January 1929, 31 January 1929. See also Stan E. Baker, Newspaper Clippings (Surfing), 1929-1932, Cook's Hill Life Saving & Surf Club Archives. For the comments of the Swimming Club's Secretary see Baker, Newspaper Clipping, no date, p.39. The 'Green Cup' 1926-1927 is in the possession of John Farrell – it is inscribed: 'Green Cup Presented by Green Brothers To the Cooks' Hill Amateur Swimming Club for the Point Score Competition Season 1926-1927 Won by R Farrell'.

14. See *NMH*, 12 February 1925, Minutes of 16th Annual Meeting, 23 September 1927, Minutes Book of Cook's Hill Life Saving & Surf Club, 1927/28 to 1933/34. Charles Farrell's nomination for Life Membership in 1929 was unsuccessful – see Minutes of 18th Annual Meeting, 18 September 1929, Minutes Book of Cook's Hill Life Saving & Surf Club, 1927/28 to 1933/34. In this year all six nominations were unsuccessful. It was an ambition few obtained – Tom and Charles Farrell are not listed among the seventy-one Life Members of the Club – see Ramsland, *Cook's Hill Club*, p.334. For details of Tom's friendship with Arthur Gow see Farrell, 'Tom Farrell Biography' – John Farrell recalls that Gow visited Tom and his family regularly each Christmas.

15. For details of the 'glory years' see Ramsland, *Cook's Hill Club*, pp.94-98. For quotation see Ramsland, *Cook's Hill Club*, p.92. For the swimming greats of the club see Ramsland, *Cook's Hill Club*, p.98. For

1928 photograph see Ramsland, *Cook's Hill Club*, p.91. Although the exact year is not indicated, it most likelihood the photograph should be dated to 1928, the year the CHLSSC held more trophies won in surf lifesaving competitions than any other club.

16. Tom indicated in his recruitment papers that he still enjoyed amateur swimming – see 'Farrell Air Force Recruitment Papers. For ongoing commitment to sport and physical recreation see Farrell, 'Tom Farrell Biography', pp.3-4, pp.6-7. For recollection of friend see Talty, 'Memories of My Father'; see also Hincks, "Memories of My Father".

CHAPTER THREE

1. Editorial, 'Tom Farrell', *NMH*, 27 July 1996.

2. For details concerning the history of the Newcastle Abattoir see Farrell to Editor, *NMH*, 19 April 1980, 13 September 1980, 26 June 1981, 8 July 1981, 10 August 1981 and 20 November 1981. The letters reveal the former General Manager's depth of knowledge in regards to the meat industry and his commitment to upholding the original charter. See also Newcastle Abattoir Feature, 'Hygiene Need Realised', *NMH*, 8 November 1966; see also M. Scanlan,'Brooking the Slaughter', *NMH*, 31 July 2010.

3. For educational qualifications see 'Application for Administrative Branch, Royal Australian Air Force', R E Farrell War Records – Tom had been successful at the Intermediate & Final examination of the Federal Institute of Accountants. See also Tripp, 'Profile on a Successful Man', p.1 – Tom had returned to night school at Newcastle Technical College to undertake his accounting training before finally being accepted into the Institute of Accountants. See also Waldron (National President of the Australian Society of CPAs) to Tom, 1 May 1951, TFPJF. He also held a Meat Inspectors Full Certificate having successfully passed Inspection of Meat & Animals Examination and Practical Sanitation Examination; see also The City of Newcastle, 'Resignation from the Service of the Council', 5 November 1968, TFP, A8289 (v); 'Letter of Application', Farrell to The Chairman, Metropolitan & Export Abattoirs Board, 19 August 1952, TFP A8290 (viii). For details of Tom's appointment as Senior Accountant see 'Minutes of Council Meeting', 3 July 1951, 17 July 1951; 'The Council of the City of Newcastle Lord Mayoral Minute', No 2, 2 July 1951, Newcastle City Council Archives (NCCA), File Number 2/97 1951. For details of Tom's appointment as Assistant General Manager see 'Report of Special Finance Committee Meeting', 13 November 1951; 'Report of Abattoir Sub-Committee ', 6 September 1951, NCCA File No 2/97 See also 'Our Managers in 50 Years', *NMH*, 8 November 1966. Comments by leading businessman see Donaldson (General Manager of the Shortland County Council) to Farrell, 1 April 1966, TFP A 8289 (v), on retirement see *NMH*, 6 November 1968; photograph entitled 'The Men of the Meat World', *Newcastle Sun*, 2 July 1980; for Alderman Bell's comments see *NMH*, 24 April 1968. Tom's membership of the Newcastle Club seems to have dated from 1967 – see A .A .Rankin, *Newcastle Club Centenary*, Reg C Pogonoski, Newcastle, 1985, p.65. For details of Tom's appointment as a director to Dark's Ice see Farrell, 'Tom Farrell's Biography', pp.6-7. For details on Dark's Ice Pty Ltd see 'Dark's Ice Works', Local Studies Newcastle Regional Library, 338.76215/DAR. Tom remained committed to the business until its redevelopment in the early 1980s. For Tom's role in the development of Dark's Ice Works see Farrell, 'Tom Farrell Biography' – against local opposition, Tom ensured the commercial success of the venture.

4. R.E.Farrell, 'Future Progress Outlined', *NMH*, 8 November 1966. See also from Newcastle Abattoir Feature, 'All but the Squeak', 'Big Export Boom', 'Medical', 'Training Ground', 'Family Network at Abattoir', 'Impressive Records', 'Glands for Medicine', 'Special Carcase Competition', 'Newcastle Abattoir Celebrates

Jubilee of Service', 'Message from the Mayor' 'Hides & Skins', 'Rapid Growth Sustained' and 'Greater Newcastle Council', *NMH*, 8 November 1966. See also 'Newcastle Abattoir NSW', *Daily Commercial News and Shipping* List, 31 December 1962. For comments by Meat & Allied Trades Federation of Australia see Brown to Farrell, 16 October 1968, TFP A 8289 (v). For comments by employee see Tripp to Farrell, 21 October 1968 & 10 May 1966, TFP A 8289 (v). See also 'Newcastle Abattoir File', Local Studies Newcastle Regional Library, LH 664.9029. For details of Tom's opposition to 'city hall bureaucracy' see Farrell, 'Tom Farrell Biography', p.13.

5. For details of William Farrell's association with pig producers on the North Coast, particularly in the Kempsey area, and his attempt to challenge a Sydney cartel see Farrell, 'Tom Farrell Biography', pp.2-3. For details of the Royal Commission see *Report of the Royal Commission of Enquiry (Captain W.J.Wade, MBE) into the Newcastle District Abattoir Board Administration*, 1930, pp.1-35 [p.4 and 16 quoted], TFP A8289 (iii); see also 'Rapid Growth Sustained', *NMH*, 8 November 1966; for detail on Bacon Division see 'Large Abattoir Bacon Section', *NHM* 8 November 1966. Given the sequence of events (change of government from Bavin Nationalist to Lang ALP) it appears that the establishment of the Commission and its subsequent review may have been (in part) due to political factors .

6. For details of the controversy surrounding the Town Clerk's advertising of the position of General Manager see *NMH*, 23 March 1966, 3 April 1966; see also President of the Abattoir Staff Officers' Union to McDougall, 23 March 1966, TFPJF. For 1968 controversy see 'Town Clerk Accused of Intrusion', *NMH*, 24 April 1968; 'Report of the Abattoir General Manager: Proposed Overseas Study of the Assistant General Manager & Accountant' Greater Newcastle Council Committee Papers May 1968,TFP A8289 (v); see also Farrell to Lord Mayor, 19 April 1968, TFPJF – in the letter Tom pointed out that 'I do not oppose the principle of sending officers overseas but I feel that I should be given the opportunity to organise the form the tour should take and the matters to be investigated and the countries visited'.

7. 'Message from Lord Mayor' & 'Greater Newcastle Council' *NMH*, 8 November 1966; 'Resignation from the Service of the Council', 5 November 1968; 'Lord Mayor's Memorandum to Mr R E Farrell', 1 October 1968 TFP A8289 (v); McMullin to Farrell, 21 November 1968 TFP A8289 (v); Rumbold to Farrell, 8 November 1968 TFP A8289 (v) – see also Still (General Manager, Ryland Brothers) to Farrell, 31 October 1968 TFP A8289 (v); see also 'Letter Regarding R E (Tom) Farrell Farewell Function', Newcastle Abattoir Department, 28 October 1968, TFPJF. For correspondence regarding Meat Industry and Newcastle Abattoir see Farrell to Editor, *NMH*, 19 April 1980, 13 September 1980, 26 April 1981, 10 August 1981, 14 November 1981 and 2 July 1982

8. For details on NHRSBS see 'Photographs & History of the Greater Newcastle & Hunter River Starr Bowkett Society', Rodd Papers, UNA A5400 (iv); 'Fifty Years of Service', *Interest: Magazine of The Greater Newcastle Permanent Building Society Ltd'*, No 3, November 1973, pp.12-16; see also P. Baker, 'Greater Building Society – Our History', no date, TFPJF. For information on Starr Bowketts including

definition see M.Darnell, 'The Alternative Building Society – Starr-Bowkett Societies: function, growth and operation', Paper presented at Asia Pacific Economic and Business History Conference, Sydney, 12-14 February 2007, <http:// ehsanz.econ.usyd.edu.au/papers/darnell> accessed 5 October 2011; see also M.Darnell, 'Ataining the Australian Dream: The Starr-Bowkett Way', *Labour History*, vol 91, November 2006, accessed 6 October 2011, <http://www. History cooperative.org /journals /lab /91/darnell.html>; E.Balnave, *Review of the Operation and Failure of Starr-Bowkett Type Building Societies*, Department of Co-operative Societies, 1981, ML NQ334.10994. For Tom's comments see Farrell to Bill,1986,'Greater Newcastle Co-operative Building Society Correspondence, Statistical Information', TFP A8288 (xxi). On the history of mortgage lending in Australia see M R Hill, *Housing Finance in Australia 1945-1956*, MUP, 1959, pp.10-14. For details of NHRSBS see 'Second Co-operative Registered Under Act', *NMH*, 6 November 1973. For Tom's membership of the NHRSBS see 'Receipt Book Register Number 77 The Newcastle Hunter River Public Service Starr-Bowkett Building Society Ltd', TFPJF. For details of the original location of the NHRSBS see Hincks, 'Memories of My Father' – before moving to premises on the corner of Beaumont and Tudor Streets, Hamilton, the NHRSBS operated out of a two storey building purchased at 77 Tudor Street.

9. Much of the archival material of The Greater Newcastle Building Society Ltd was lost as a result of the 1989 Newcastle earthquake. For details of the membership of the original committee see 'Fifty Years of Service', p.12. For 'List of Directors' see Baker, 'History of the Greater'. For cooperative entities which made up the Association see Baker, 'History of the Greater'. For Farrell comment see Farrell to Bill, 1986. For details on No 2 Starr Bowkett see 'Cooperative Societies Report of the Registrar for the Year Ended 30th June 1948', NSW Parliamentary Papers, ML NQ328.94401/8, p.316. This report gives some statistical information of the cooperative entities which made up the Association. See also P. Baker, 'Notes from the Deputy CEO & Corporate Secretary, Greater Newcastle Building Society', email 7 October 2011, in possession of author.

10. 'Newcastle Needs 6114 Homes', *NMH*, 30 January 1944. See also '£350 Cottages for Newcastle', *NMH*, 21 August 1942; 'Seek Better Housing Deal', *NMH*, 7 June 1945; Editorial, *NHM* 4 June 1945; 'Housing Authority Seek Subdivision', *NMH*, 14 July 1945; 'Provide Homes Not Finance', *NMH*, 20 July 1945; 'Plan to Expand Cooperative Housing Societies', *NMH*, 8 November 1945. It is clear that Tom remained concerned about the housing shortage in the 1950s – see various newspaper clippings held in TFP A8289 (vi): 'We must Double our Present Building Rate', *Sunday Telegraph*, 12 February 1950; 'Prefabs Could Check Our Housing Misery', *Daily Telegraph*, 19 February 1950; 'Mr McGirr's Housing Figures Don't Add Up', *Daily Telegraph*, 2 June 1950.

11. For Tom's comment see Farrell to Bill, 1986. For Mathieson comment see 'Boost Housing in Newcastle', *NMH*, 6 December 1945. For details of capital and lending rates of the various entities in the Association see 'Photographs & History of the Greater' (Rodd Papers). For median house price and basic wage statistics see (in part) J.Wilkinson, 'Affordable Housing in NSW Past to Present', NSW Parliamentary

Library Research Service, Briefing Paper No14/05, 2005, accessed 12 October 2011, <http://www. parliament.nsw.gov.au/prod/parlment/publications.nsf/0/c43281eba16c7f36ca2570c40003081c/$FILE/ Finalaffordable.pdf >. Partisan commentary provided by author of 'Photographs & History of the Greater' (Rodd Papers). For details of the methods of operation and sources of funding for various cooperative entities see Hill, *Housing Finance*, pp.14-41. See also *The Greater Newcastle Co-operative Permanent Building and Investment Society Limited Rule Book*, Newey & Son General Printers, Newcastle, no date, NLHRL LH332/Pam Box.

12. For comments by Registrar see Balnave, *Review of Starr-Bowkett Societies*, p.7. Starr-Bowkett Societies had been banned in England since 1894 when the practice of balloting for the right to advances was declared illegal – see Hill, *Housing Finance*, p.20. For comments by Tom see Farrell to Bill, 1986.

13. For Tom's position on Boards associated with the Greater Newcastle Building Society Ltd see Baker, 'Notes' - the earliest extant record of Tom holding a position is 1962 when he was Chairman of the Board; he was also Chairman of the Board in October 1975 and May 1976. He resigned from the Board in August 1976. Regarding the Greater Cooperative Association the earliest extant record of Tom as a director is November 1949; Chairman of the Board 1971, 1977, 1980 and 1986, resigned from the Board in April 1991. In regard to the Greater Credit Union the earliest extant record of Tom as a director is June 1967 when he was Chairman of the Board; again Chairman in 1967, 1974 and 1976; resigned from the Board in 1997. For comments by Tom see 'From the Chairman', *Interest*, No 3, November 1973, p.1, pp13-16.

14. For details of housing shortage in the Greater Newcastle and Hunter regions see 'Housing Chief for Newcastle', *NMH*,12 February 1953; 'Conference on Home Finance', *NMH*, 13 April 1955, 'Homes Finance Conference', *NMH*, 23 July 1955; 'Lord Mayor on Home Finance Problem', *NMH*, 5 August 1955; 'Council Moves on Home Loans', *NMH*, 28 September 1955; 'Appeal for More Money For Homes', *NMH*, 10 November 1955; 'Housing Delegation', *NMH*, 9 November 1955, 25 November 1955; 'Lord Mayor Claims Homes Lag Planned', *NMH*, 14 March 1957; 'Housing Talks on Monday', *NMH*, 23 July 1957; '6000 Homes Short', *NMH*, 23 July 1957; 'Finance for Housing Appeal by Leaders to Minister', *Newcastle Sun* 3 July 1961. For comments by Mr Mathieson and fellow directors see 'Hamilton Office Plan', *NMH*, 25 September 1964. For details of planned construction see *NMH*, 25 September 1964.

15. For examples of Tom's reading see 'Greater Newcastle Cooperative Building Society, Correspondence & statistical Information' TFP A8288 (xxi); 'Supplement to Euromoney', 'Abbey National Building Society' TFP A8288 (xxvii); 'Australian Overseas Investment Limited', TFP A8288 (xxviii); 'Taxation, Northumberland County Council, Housing', TFP A8289 (vii); 'North Rothbury Land Sale' TFP A8290 (v); 'Correspondence', TFP A290 (viii). For work with the Association of Cooperative Building Societies in regard to the 'rating issue' see R E Farrell, 'Local Government Rating', Paper Presented to the Conference of Association of Cooperative Building Societies, Sydney, 1954, TFPJF. For details of public meeting on 8 October 1954 and subsequent activity see 'Flyer-Cardiff Heights New Lambton Lookout

Progress Association Public Meeting', TFPJF; Farrell, 'Notes on Rating', no date, TFPJF. For attendance at International Conferences see 'International Union of Building Societies and Saving Associations 11th International Congress, Sydney, 1968', TFP A8291; Secretary of the Building Societies Association (London) to Farrell, 16 March 1961, TFPJF; 'Program Building Societies Association (London) Annual Conference', 1961, TFPJF. It is clear from the newspaper clippings (TFPJF) that Tom maintained an interest in the 'rating system' – see for example 'Saturation in Local Government Tax', *Daily Telegraph*, 4 November 1952; Richley to Editor, *NMH*, 18 October 1975; 'V-G Wants New Rating System', *NMH*, 16 February 1977; 'City Rates Rise less than 8%', *NMH*, 10 November 1984; 'UK Plans to Scrap Land Rates', *NMH*, 30 January 1986; 'Government to Hold Inquiry into Council Rates', *NMH*, 25 July 1988; 'Fairer Council Tax Needed', *NMH*, 3 April 1989. Tom also followed the issue overseas – see 'Paying for Local Government: The Common Charge', Greater London Council, 1990, TFPJF.

16. For details of the expansion of the Greater Newcastle Building Society see '¼m. Addition to building at Hamilton' *NMH*, 14 March 1972; 'Hamilton Grows Upward', *NMH*, 13 July 1972; 'Extensions Show Faith', *NMH*, 12 July 1973. For comments by journalist and computerisation in 1980s see 'Membership Rising', *NHM* 23 March 1983. For details of Board Meetings see 'Greater Newcastle Cooperative Building Society, Correspondence & statistical Information', TFP A8288 (xxi). The 'Minutes Monthly Meeting of the Board of Directors, Held Tuesday 8th July 1986 reveal that the following matters were discussed: reports, correspondence, staff, board fees, wage increases for staff, computer costs, superannuation, appointment of consultants, taxation (Fringe Benefits Tax), vehicle report, finance, strategic planning, senior management, competition with competitors, advertising. Tom had also been appointed to a sub-committee to investigate a fire at the Cabana Coffee Lounge – the subcommittee report is included. It appears from Baker, 'Notes' that Mr R E Farrell resigned from the Greater Cooperative Association in April 1991. He retired from the Board of the Greater Credit Union a year before in August 1990. For comments by retiring director see Hutchinson to Farrell, 14 June 1983, TFPJF.

17. For details of Tom's retirement and consultancy position see Prince to Farrell, 27 August 1990 (two letters), TFPJF. For latter recollections by a colleague see J. Arnold, 'Memories of R E (Tom) Farrell', 2011, TFPJF. For 'Minutes of Building Society', July 1996 see B. Prince, 'Tom Farrell', 2011, TFPJF.

CHAPTER FOUR

1. For Tom's views about the establishment of the university see R.E.Farrell, 'Notes concerning the Establishment of the University', TFP A5581 (vi). For attempts to establish the university prior to 1949 see D. Wright, *Looking Back A History of the University of Newcastle*, The Pot Still Press, Sydney, 1992, pp.1-4. Although a University Committee had been established in 1942 progress towards establishing university facilities had been slow – see Wright, *History of the University*, pp.5-13. For details of the educational establishments in Newcastle see Wright, *History of the University*, pp.4-5. For Tom's frustration with the Education Minister see Farrell, 'Notes on University'. For comments in November 1950 see 'New England' to Editor, *NMH*, 3 November 1950. As noted Tom regularly used a pseudonym when writing to the press – there is no doubt that 'New England' was Tom Farrell – see Farrell to Ellis, 11 November 1985, TFP A8289 (viii). For details on the opposition to Tom's stance on the university see Rowe, 'Interview'. Tom explained that 'people laughed at me pointing out that I was wasting my time but Armidale showed that you could conduct a university in a country setting'.

2. For details of Tom's involvement with the Liberal Party and the formation of the New Lambton Branch see Farrell, 'Notes on University'; R .E .Farrell, 'Newcastle University', TFP A8289 (viii); Farrell to Trip, 3 August 1980, TFP A8289 (viii); Farrell to Ellis, 11 November 1986; Ellis to Farrell, 7 August 1986, TFP A8289 (viii). For Mabel Whiley's involvement see Ellis to Farrell, 7 August 1986; Farrell to Ellis, 11 November 1986. For Tom's detailed proposal for the university (including the motion of the New Lambton Branch to the 1950 State Convention of the Liberal Party) see 'R.E Farrell, 'The Basis of a Scheme to Establish an Academic University College in Newcastle Commencing in 1951 and Developing to Ultimate Autonomy in Say 5 or 6 Years', TFP A5581 (iv). See also attached to this document 'A List of Suggested Part Time Lecturers Already in Newcastle Their Subjects & Their Academic Qualifications'. For details of the debate surrounding the resolution see Ellis to Farrell, 7 August 1986; Farrell, 'Newcastle University'. Interestingly, George Whiley was the only member of the New Lambton Branch who witnessed the demise of the original motion –the other members, including Tom, had to leave the debate late in the afternoon in order to catch the 'Flyer' back to Newcastle.

3. For details of the press controversy see *NMH*, 4, 5 and 11 August 1950; see also Ellis to Farrell, 7 August 1986. The *NMH* had incorrectly reported that the Liberal Party had opposed the establishment of a university college in Newcastle. Ellis on behalf of the New Lambton Branch approached the editor and asked for a retraction, this, however, was not forthcoming. With further pressure the paper published a factual account of the Liberal Party's position on the issue. For Tom's comments on the importance of the resolution see Rowe, 'Interview'. On the formation of the 'Centaur Group' see Ellis to Farrell, 7 August 1986; Farrell to Tripp, 3 August 1980; Farrell, 'Newcastle University'; Farrell, 'Notes on University'. See also Wright, *History of the University*, pp.12-13. For the role of Mabel Whiley in the group see Farrell to Tripp, 3 August 1980; Farrell, 'Newcastle University'; Farrell, 'Notes on University'. Wright, *History of the*

University, p.12 refers to Mabel as 'dynamic'. Tom commented that 'Mrs Whiley, a Science Mistress at Newcastle Girls' came out strongly for a university for this city' – see Farrell, 'Newcastle University'. For the role of George Whiley see Farrell, 'Notes on University'. For Tom's role see Farrell to Tripp, 3 August 1980. For Darby's support see Farrell to Darby, 18 February 1951and 24 October 1951 TFP A5881 (iv).; see also Farrell to Darby, 24 October 1950, TFPJF – Tom had been impressed with Darby's concern for the local area after hearing him speak at the Newcastle Business Men's Luncheon. For details of the plan's demise see *NMH*, 27 and 30 November 1950, 2 and 9 December 1950; Rowe, 'Interview'. For the opposition of the labour aldermen see Farrell, 'Notes on University'; Farrell, 'Newcastle University'. For Tom's comment see Farrell to Tripp, 3 August 1980.

4. For details of the formation of the NUEG see Wright, *History of the University*, pp.13-16. .For details of the strong community support see Ellis to Farrell, 7 August 1986. For details of the public meeting see Ellis to Farrell, 7 August 1986; Farrell to Tripp, 3 August 1986. For details of Mabel Whiley's involvement and the executive see Ellis to Farrell, 7 August 1986; Farrell to Tripp, 3 August 1986. For details on how Tom saw his role in the NUEG see Farrell, 'Notes on University'. For Tom's words see Farrell to Tripp, 3 August 1986. For details on Ellis and Eddy see Wright, *History of the University*, pp.14-15. For details of the Newcastle Technical College see A. Barcan, 'Three Pathways to Education Change in NSW', *Education & Perspectives*, Vol.36, No.2, 2009, pp.69-71, accessed 27 March 2013, <http://erpjournal.net/wp-content/uploads/2012/07 /ERPV36-2_Barcan-A.-2009.pdf >. For Tom's frustration with Eddy's view see Farrell to Eddy 26 January 1954 TFP A5581 (iv); 'Notes on University'. For Tom's advice to Ellis see 'Notes on University'.

5. For Tom's comment in regard to community support see Farrell, 'Newcastle University'. See also Wright, *History of the University*, p. 16.For details of Mabel's street drive see '8000 Sign Petition For University', *NMH*, 4 May 1951; see also 'Canvas For University' *NMH*, 3 May 1951, A photograph shows Miss Jabe Campbell, captain of Newcastle Girls' High getting a supporter's signature. For the meeting schedule of the NUEG see H. Eddy, 'Draft History of the Newcastle University Establishment Group', 1953, Bentley Papers 1914-1986, MLMSS 7763, Box 4, Mitchell Library, Sydney. For details of the NUEG's first action see Wright, *History of the University*, p. 16. For details of the families Tom & Kath Farrell visited see 'List of Students Allocated to Tom Farrell', TFP A5581 (iv). For details of the delegation on 7 and 13 May 1951 see Eddy, 'Draft History of the NUEG'. For Tom's views on subsequent delegations see Farrell to Tripp, 3 August 1980; Ellis to Farrell, 7 August 1986. For Tom's dealing with the Premier, Mr McGirr, see Rowe 'Interview'. For Tom's view on the means to maintain pressure on politicians see Farrell to Eddy, 26 January 1954, TFP A5581 (iv). For Heffron's response see *NMH*, 17 May 1951. For Tom's earlier criticism of Heffron in the *SMH* see Farrell to Tripp, 3 August 1980. For Tom's letters questioning the Minister's motives see 'Evening Student' to Editor, *NMH*, 16 May 1951 and 'Maitland' to Editor, *NMH*, 3 May 1951. For Ellis' reply see Ellis to Editor, *NMH*, 18 May 1951. For Ellis' position see *NMH*, 18 May 1951. For Editorial see *NMH*, 17 May 1951. For Tom's criticism of the press see Farrell to Eddy, 26 January 1954. For the Executive's criticism of Tom and his response see Farrell to Eddy, 26 January 1954.

6. Report of Minutes 7 June 1951 in Eddy, 'Draft History of the NUEG'. See Eddy, 'Draft History of the NUEG' for details of the onerous work load involved in completing the home visits. For details of the delegation to Minister on 10 June 1951 see Wright, *History of the University*, p.17. For names of intending students and details of petition see 'A Case for a Newcastle College of the University of Sydney', no date, Eddy Papers, USA ; 'Typed List of Students Available for Newcastle University College', SUA G3/13/18320.

7. For details of the delaying tactics employed by Roberts see Wright, *History of the University*, pp.18-20. For an interesting perspective on this issue see 'A Country Bloke's Impressions on a Visit to the City of Sydney via the Hawkesbury River – Subject the Newcastle University', TFP A 5581 (iv). For the position of the *SMH* see 'Hard Facts of Higher Education', *SMH*, 21 May 1951; 'Minister to Establish More Universities', *SMH*, 20 May 1951. For Ellis comment see *NMH*, 23 October 1951. For insight into continued support see comments by Professor Copland, Vice-Chancellor of the National University, Canberra in "Varsity College Advocated', *NMH*, 4 October 1951. See also Holt to Editor, *NMH*, 30 June 1951; H. Eddy, 'Courses of A University', *NMH*, 2 July 1951. For Eddy's proposal see Eddy to Roberts, 10 and 29 November 1951, Eddy Papers, SUA G3/13/18320. See also *NMH*, 9 November 1951.

8. For details of the establishment of the University College by the University of Technology see Wright, *History of the University*, pp.20-25. For the NUEG's dealings with the government in early 1952 see Wright, *History of the University*, pp.25-28. For critics of the University of Technology see *Newcastle Sun*, 12 December 1951; see also *Newcastle Sun*, 4 December 1951; *NMH*, 3, 4 and 12 December 1951. For Tom's opposition to McGirr see Rowe 'Interview'. For Tom's view on external studies see Farrell to Eddy, 26 January 1954. For details of the continued agitation by NUEG in 1953 see 'NUEG Annual Report 1953', TFP A5581 (iv). For Tom's reaction to Cahill's policy speech see 'Parent' to Editor, *Newcastle Sun*, 14 February 1953. Quotation taken from Farrell, 'Notes on University'. For Tom's letter to the Editor see Farrell to Editor, *NMH*, 20 August 1952.

9. For details of NUEG action during August 1952 see Wright, *History of the University*, pp.28-29. For commentary in press see *NMH*, 8 August 1952. For details of NUEG action in 1953 see 'NUEG Annual Report 1953'; see also Wright, *History of the University*, pp.30-32. For details of the NUEG Conference see 'NUEG Annual Report 1953'; 'Keen Interest in Varsity, Hunter Valley Conference' *NMH*, 30 April 1953.

10. For details of the Kahibah Bi-Election and Heffron's announcement see Wright, *History of the University*, pp.32-38. For Tom's comments regarding the pressure applied to the ALP during the bi-election see Farrell, 'Notes on University'. For Electoral pamphlet see *Kahibah News*, Vol.1, No.1, October 1953, TFP A8289 (vii). For details of the Shortland site see Wright, *History of the University*, pp.12-13. The site (much of it underwater) had been given to the government by BHP in 1949. In 1950 it had been set aside for possible use by tertiary education institutions. For details of Heffron's plan and the reaction to it see Wright, *History of the University*, pp.33-38. For Heffron's comments see *NMH*, 23 October 1953. For support for the plan in Newcastle see *NMH*, 23 October 1953; *SMH*, 1 December 1953. For Ellis' view see *NMH*, 23 October 1953; 24 October 1953 For Eddy's opposition and subsequent NUEG response see NUEG Annual Report, 1953, 'Minutes of NUEG Executive Meeting', 20 December 1953, Eddy Papers SUA 1953 Bundle. For Eddy's comments to the press see *NMH*, 23 October 1953. For Tom's views as President of the Newcastle Branch of the New England New State Movement see *NMH*, 23 October 1953. In the letter Tom urged 'in the interests of decentralisation' that a further college be established at Lismore or Grafton. For Griffith Duncan's support of the plan see *NMH*, 23 October 1953. For Tom's support of the proposal see Farrell to Tripp, 3 August 1980, Farrell, 'Notes on University'. For correspondence see Booth to Farrell, 10 November 1953; Farrell to Booth, 17 November 1953 TFP A5581 (vi); Farrell to Wright, 23 October 1953 and 10 November 1953; Wright to Farrell, 14 November 1953, TFP A5581 (iv). For references about Tom and Eddy's character see Farrell, 'Notes on University'. For results of Kahibah bi-election see Farrell, 'Notes on University'.

11. Eddy to Farrell, 23 December 1953 TFP A5581(iv). See Eddy to Farrell, 15 and 29 January 1954, 25 February 1954 TFP A5581 (iv). The letters dated 15 January and 25 February contain annotations made by Tom. See also Eddy to Farrell, 5 March 1954; Farrell to Eddy, 22 March 1954 TFP A5581 (iv). For Eddy's view of Baxter see H. Eddy, 'Notes for State Executive on Newcastle University College and Other Matters', no date, Eddy Papers, USA, Series 1 006-008, P196/06/08, point 48-59. For Eddy's view of Auchmuty see Ellis to Farrell, 20 March 1987. It appears while Eddy remained firm on his view of Baxter, he later develop a closer relationship with Auchmuty – see Eddy to Auchmuty, 5 February 1973 and 6 February 1973; Auchmuty to Eddy, 6 February 1973, Eddy Papers, USA, Series 1 006-008, P196/01; see also Auchmuty to Beryl Anderson, 26 April 1974, Eddy Papers, USA, Series 1 006-008, P196/01/021. For Bentley's views see *The Australian Highway Journal of the Workers' Educational Association*, August 1959, in 'Press Clippings', Bentley Papers, MLMSS 7763, Box 2. For Eddy's request for money for the WEA see Eddy to Farrell, 31 October 1953 TFP A5881 (iv).

12. Farrell to Eddy, 26 January 1954 see also Farrell to Eddy, 22 February 1954, TFP A5581 (iv). For details of NUEG meetings see 'Minutes of Regular Monthly Meeting of the NUEG held in the WEA Rooms 71 King Street Newcastle', 8 February 1954 and 8 March 1954, CF Bentley Papers 1914-1986, ML MSS 7763, Box 4. A copy of minutes also held in TFP A5581 (iv). See also 'Extracts from Draft of NUEG Minutes' attached to Eddy to Farrell, 17 March 1954 TFP A5581 (iv). For details of the deep divisions that were emerging in the NUEG see Farrell to Tripp, 3 August 1980; Farrell, 'Notes on University'; Rowe, 'Interview'; Ellis to Farrell, 20 January 1984; Farrell, 'Untitled Notes'; Farrell to Ellis, 11 November 1986; Ellis to Farrell, 7 August 1986; Ellis to Farrell, 20 March 1987. For Tom's view of Baxter and Auchmuty see Farrell to Tripp, 3 August 1980; Farrell to Editor, *NMH*, 21 November 1954.

13. Wright, *History of the University*, p.43. For Tom's isolation in the NUEG see Rowe, 'Interview'. For Kath's continual support see Ellis to Farrell, 11 November 1986. For views on Eddy see Ellis to Farrell, 11 November 1986; see also Ellis to Farrell, 7 August 1986. Even Auchmuty had to acknowledge the work of Eddy in establishing a university in Newcastle – see Auchmuty to Beryl Anderson, 26 April 1974; see also

Barcan to Eddy, 21 November 1973, Eddy Papers, USA, Series 1 006-008, P196/01/033. See also Eddy to Farrell, 25 March 1964 TFP A5881(iv) – Tom was kind enough to send Eddy a note when the University of Newcastle gained its autonomy. For Tom's view about the 'colossal blunder' see Ellis to Farrell, 11 November 1986. For Professor Anderson's support see 'Copy Letter to Professor John Anderson' attached to Eddy to Farrell, 29 March 1954 TFP A5581 (iv). For details of the State Conference see 'Report for NUEG on Preliminary Meeting on Conventions on Universities held at St James Hall, Sydney', 27 March 1954, Eddy Papers, USA, Series 1 006-008, P196/01/033. - Ellis, Eddy, Anderson, Morgan and Butcher attended from the NUEG; see also 'NUEG Annual Report 1954', TFP A5581 (iv), pp.7-9. Interestingly, Eddy asked Tom for his 'press-clippings to assist him to prepare a pamphlet for the conference – see Eddy to Farrell, 13 October 1953, TFP A5581 (iv). For details of the University Convention see 'NUEG Annual Report 1954', pp.5-9 – for details of 'charter' see p.6. For Batty's defence see Wright, *History of the University*, p.43. For Tom's reply see 'Parent' to Editor, NHM, 7 January 1954. The author of the letter was definitely Tom – see signed copy of letter in TFP A5881 (iv). For Eddy's article see *Opus*, volume 1, August 1954 in Bentley Papers, MLMSS 7763, Box 2.

14. For Tom's unsuccessful attempts concerning Eddy's position and an open membership see 'NUEG Annual Report 1954', pp.10-14. For developments of the NUC in the period 1954-56 see Wright, *History of the University*, pp.47-53. For details of the NUEG's opposition see Wright, *History of the University*, pp.52-59. For details of Tom's position see 'Parent' to Editor, *NMH*, 20 November 1954 – the author of this letter is definitely Tom, see annotation (R E Farrell) on copy of letter, TFP A5881 (iv). For dispute with 'WEA Clique' see Farrell to Editor, *NMH*, 15 January 1958; Bentley to Editor, *NMH*, 18 January 1958; Farrell to Editor, *NMH*, 24 January and 28 January 1958; Bentley to Editor, *NMH* 28 January 1958. For Tom's 'final word' comment see Farrell to Editor, *NMH*, 25 March 1958; see also a typed copy of this letter (no date) in TFP A8289 (viii). For details of the last meeting of the NUEG see 'Minutes of meeting 28 March 1958', Eddy Papers, NUEG minutes 1957. For Baxter's summation see Baxter to Harant, 5 February 1957, 'Private Correspondence', Bentley Papers, Box 2. For Ellis comment see Ellis to Farrell, 7 August 1986. For Tom's comment see 'Notes on Newcastle University'. See also Eddy to Auchmuty, 6 March 1973, Eddy Papers, USA, Series 1, P196/01/08. For commentator's view of Tom's role in NUEG see Wright, *History of the University*, p.61. For Tom's 'call to arms' over Baxter proposal see Farrell to Editor, *NMH*, 30 May 1958. For details of the Public Meeting see *NMH*, 30 May and 31 May 1958; see also Farrell to Tripp, 3 August 1980; Farrell, 'Notes on Newcastle University'; Rowe, 'Interview'. Interestingly, Tom's detail about the number who attended the meeting differs – somewhere between 300-400 (Rowe, 'Interview') to 500-600 ('Notes on University'). For details concerning Tom's decision not to join the committee see Farrell to Tripp, 3 August 1980. For the role of the committee see Wright, *History of the University*, p.63.

15. For details of the NUC movement towards autonomy see Wright, *History of the University*, pp.64-89. For Tom's comment see 'Notes on University'. For the environmental credentials of the Shortland campus (established in 1966) see A.Gamble, *Campus at Shortland*, Cambridge Press, Newcastle, 1987; Campus Book Committee, *Bushland Campus*, Canberra Press, 1994, pp.22-26. For details of the Honorary Master of Arts degree see 'Letter of Recommendation', Talty & Relf (Wardens of Convocation) to The Chairman Honorary Degrees Committee of Council, University of Newcastle, 16 April 1986 TFPJF; see also attachment: V.Tripp, 'History of the University with Archival Material'. See also George (Vice-Chancellor) to Farrell, 24 April 1986 TFPJF; Alexander (Secretary) to Farrell, 29 April 1986 TFPJF; The University of Newcastle, 'Conferring of Degrees Faculties of Arts and Medicine', 3 May 1986 TFPJF; *NMH*, 5 May 1986 (photograph); see also Wheeler to Farrell, 6 May 1986 TFPJF; B. Power, 'New Lambton Memo', 3 May 1986 TFPJF; Sargent (Secretary New Lambton Branch of the Liberal Party of Australia, New South Wales Division) to Farrell, 26 May 1986. For details regarding Tom's grandsons see 'Newsletter for the University of Newcastle', Vol 12, No 6, May 12 to 26 1986, p.8 TFPJF – photograph caption reads: 'the Farrell and Talty families were well represented at the UN graduations brothers John Talty and James Talty were awarded BCom degrees. They are pictured with their grandfather, Mr R.E. Farrell, who had an honorary MA degree conferred upon him the next day and their mother, Kay Talty'. For details of the academic success of Tom's grandchildren see Hincks, 'Memories of My Father' – Tom also supported his other grandchildren to achieve success at other tertiary institutions.

CHAPTER FIVE

1. For Tom's admiration for the work of John Muir see Hincks, 'Memories of My Father'. For an overview of Tom's community involvement after the war see Farrell to Tripp, 3 August 1980. For Tom's comments about Blackbutt Reserve see Farrell to Editor, *NMH*, 30 October 1987; Rowe, 'Interview'. For details of Tom's first exposure to the beauty of the Blackbutt area see Tripp, 'Profile on a Successful Man'; J.Ramsland, 'A History of Blackbutt Nature Reserve', Unpublished Manuscript, 1988, p.4.

2. For details of the disposal of land owned by the Scottish-Australian Company see Ramsland, 'History of Blackbutt Reserve', pp.2-7.; see also B.Gilligan, *The Blackbutt Book*, Association of Environmental Education (Hunter Region), 1982, p.6. For details of Tom's purchase see Tripp, 'Profile on a Successful Man', p.4; Farrell to Keith, 10 May 1988, TFP A8285 (x). For details of the Cardiff Height Progress Association see Ramsland, History of Blackbutt Reserve', pp.4-5. For details of the New Lambton Council's proposal see 'National Reserve Blackbutt Wanted', *NMH*, 25 July 1931. For details of the Municipal Conference see 'Blackbutt Area – National Park Plans', *NMH*, 5 January 1932. For Tom's comments see Farrell to Barnett, (President of the Blackbutt Reserve Committee), 10 July 1984 TFP A8285 (ix). For details of second conference see 'Blackbutt New Committee Formed', *NMH*, 4 June 1932.

3. See R.E.Farrell, 'Address to the Northern Parks & Playgrounds Movement', 30 November 1984, NPPM Minute Book, November 1983-December 1985, Newcastle University Archives, C831; 'Northern Parks and Playground Movement' 2001, in Wesley Mission, 'Green Conscience – The Ongoing Struggle for a Clean, Green Newcastle', 2011, accessed 14 April 2012 <http://radicalnewcastle. files.wordpress.com /2011/05/greenconscience.pdf >. For details of the goals of the Parks and Playgrounds Movement NSW see 'Park Lover' to Editor, *NMH*, 6 April 1936. As Tom later admitted he was the author of the letter (dated 31 March 1936) – see Farrell, 'Address to the NPPM'. For details of the Cardiff Heights Progress Association's support for the NPPM see Farrell & Marshall to Editor, *NMH*, 8 April 1936 TFP A2885 (ix). For Tom's involvement in establishing the NPPM see Tripp, 'Profile on a Successful Man', pp.4-5; Farrell to Barnett, 10 July 1984. See also Ramsland, 'History of Blackbutt Reserve', pp.7-9.

4. For details of the purchase of Lot 51 see Tripp, 'Profile on a Successful Man', p.5; Farrell to Burgess (Town Clerk), 10 May 1988 TFP A8285 (x); Farrell to Barnett, 10 July 1984; R. E .Farrell, 'Address to Mark the Dedication of the Joe Richley Blackbutt Reserve', November 1983, TFP A8286 (i); Farrell to Editor, *NMH*, 30 October 1985. See also Ramsland, History of Blackbutt Reserve', p.9. See also *NSW Government Gazette*, No 36, 4 March 1938, p.1014 TFP A8285 (ix). The local government area of Newcastle has undergone a number of name changes in its history – The Borough of Newcastle (1867-1938), The City of Greater Newcastle (1938-1949), The City of Newcastle (1949-1993) and The Newcastle City Council (1993-) – see NSW State Archives, 'Sesquicentenary of Local Government in Newcastle', accessed 1 April 2013, <http://archivesoutside.records. nsw.gov.au/sesquicentenary-of-local-government-in-newcastle>.

5. See Ramsland, 'History of Blackbutt Reserve', pp.10-12. See *NMH*, 10 December 1937; 28 March 1940; 26 October 1941. See also Farrell to Barnett, 10 July 1984; Farrell to Burgess, 10 May 1988; Farrell to Editor, *NMH*, 30 October 1987 TFP A8285 (ix); J. Richley & R.E. Farrell, 'Submission to the National Estate', 14 October 1973 TFP 8285 (v) and (viii). See also *NSW Government Gazette*, No 136, 11 October1940, p.1200 TFP A8285 (ix).

6. For 1943 plan see *NMH*, 11 December 1943. For 1949 plan see *NMH*, 4 May 1949; 11 May 1949. For the establishment of the Blackbutt Reserve Special Committee see *NMH*, 15 June 1949; 3 November 1949. For Tom's plans for a zoo at Blackbutt and the action of the Cardiff Heights Progress Association see *NMH*, 15 October 1949; 3 November 1949; 23 November 1949; 10 December 1949 and 11 February 1950. For McGirr's refusal of funds see *NMH*, 13 January 1950. For the Blackbutt Reserve Special Committee's plans for the area see *NMH*, 11 and 22 February 1950. For the plan to establish a trust see *NMH*, 15 March 1950; 1 August 1951; 5 September 1951. For the establishment of the trust see *NMH*, 8 August 1954. For details of the mine see *NMH*, 1 August 1951; 25 February 1954. See also Ramsland, 'History of Blackbutt Reserve', pp.12-17.

7. For details of the formation of the NPPM see Wesley Mission, 'Northern Parks and Playground Movement'; Farrell, 'Address to NPPM'; For details of the Northumberland County Council see NSW State Records Archives, 'The Cumberland County Council', accessed 19 April 2012, <http://investigator. records.nsw.gov.au/ Entity.aspx?Path =%5CAgency% 5C423> see also E.C. Wilmott, *Twenty Five Years of Planning in the Hunter Valley*, NCC Publication, Newcastle, 1983. For details of the Northumberland County Plan see 'County Plan On Display Soon', *NMH*, 21 August 1951; see also *NMH*, 31 October & 1 November 1951; V. Neech, Transcript of Interview with Doug Lithgow, 'Conservation and the History of the Northern Parks & Playgrounds Movement', Community Oral Histories, NUA A6968 (ii)(B), pp.14-15. For objectives of movement, notes from Second Annual Report, nature of membership see Wesley Mission, 'Northern Parks and Playgrounds Movement'. For Tom's simple view of the objectives see Farrell, 'Address to NPPM'. For Tom's view of Joe Richley see Farrell, 'Address to NPPM'. For comments by Hay see Wesley Mission, 'Northern Parks and Playgrounds Movement'.

8. For details of Richley's proposal see 'Plan For City Zoo', *NMH*, 13 August 1954; see also Ramsland, 'History of Blackbutt Reserve', pp.16-17. For details of the final plan see *NMH*, 14 June 1956; 18 July 1956. For further details see Ramsland, 'History of Blackbutt Reserve', pp.18-19.

9. For details of the plans to extend the reserve in 1954 see *NMH*, 1 September 1954; 13 October 1954. For Richley's comment at the Annual General Meeting of the NPPM see *NMH*, 28 September 1957. For details of community opposition to the plan see *NMH*, 14 December 1957. For Tom's comments in regard to the Council's policy in regard to subdivision of public land see Farrell, 'Address to NPPM'. For Tom's role in the NPPM's continued agitation see NPPM Minute Book, August 1958-July 1965, Newcastle University Archives, C830, 26 August 1958; 28 November 1958; 30 January 1959; 27 February 1959; 10

April 1959; 24 April 1959. For details of the 'Special Conference' see NPPM Minute Book, 10 December 1958. For details of the public meeting see *NMH*, 5 June 1959; see also 'Minutes of Public Meeting Held in the Mechanics' Institute Hall, New Lambton', 4 June 1959, NPPM Minute Book, 4 June 1959. For further details see Ramsland, 'History of Blackbutt Reserve', pp.17-21.

10. For details of Richley's compromise plan see *NMH*, 24 July 1959. For Dunkley's plan see *NMH*, 25 July 1959. For the Baddeley plan see *NMH*, 22 July 1959. For details of the Newcastle City Council Works Committee meeting on 21 July 1959 see *NMH*, 22 July 1959. For Tom's motion see NPPM Minute Book, 25 September 1959. For Tom's comments regarding pressure being brought to bear on council aldermen see Farrell, 'Address to NPPM'. For details of the NCC's decision see *NMH*, 18 November 1959; 20 November 1959. For attempt to involve the Lands Minister see 'Annual Report NPPM', 11 December 1959, in NPPM Minute Book. For the NCC's confirming of its decision see *NMH*, 2 December 1959. For Richley's remarks see 'Annual Report NPPM', 11 December 1959. For further details see Ramsland, 'History of Blackbutt Reserve', pp.21-23. For details of Richley's candidature in the Local Government Election see J. Richley, 'Newcastle Council Election', 5 December 1959, TFP 8289-7. See also 'Obituary', *NMH*, 15 July 1978.

11. For details of the Special Works Committee see *NMH*, 10 August 1960. For details of the plan for Blackbutt see *NMH*, 15 August 1960; 18 July 1962. For adoption of a more ambitious plan see *NMH*, 10 January 1963; 31 January 1963. For improvements to Blackbutt see *NMH*, 1 August 1962; 18 May 1963. For comments by Earp and Purdue see *NMH*, 10 January 1963. For further details see Ramsland, 'History of Blackbutt Reserve', pp.23-25. For details of Tom's activities see NPPM Minute Book, 24 June 1960; 27 January 1961; 24 February 1961; 24 November 1961.

12. For the proposal of the Department of Education see *NMH*, 22 May 1963; see also Tripp, 'Profile of a Successful Man', p.5. For details of the public meeting see *NMH*, 1 August 1963. For Tom's proposal regarding P & C Associations see NPPM Minute Book, 30 August 1963. For the Minister's decision and Richley's comment see *NMH*, 11 September 1963. For further details see Ramsland, 'History of Blackbutt Reserve', pp.25-27.

13. For Power's comments see B. Power (Guest Writer), 'Blackbutt Reserve', *Newcastle Sun*, 30 January 1964. For Tom's comment about Bob Power see Farrell to Editor, *NMH*, 27 December 1986. For details of progress at Blackbutt Reserve see J. Armstrong, 'Better than Lantana in Blackbutt', *NMH*, 6 November 1964. For Short's comments see P. Short, 'When One Man's Garden is Another Man's Thorn', *NMH*, 11 June 1973. For comment about Blackbutt see I. Macara, 'A Little Eden for Newcastle', *NMH*, 25 July 1966. For further details see Ramsland, 'History of Blackbutt Reserve', pp.27-28. For an example of the reports that NPPM members read see J.E. Mosley, 'Functional Classification – A Method of Improving National Parks & the Pioneering Zoning Plan for the Kosciusko State Park, January 1966, NPPM Minute Book C830. For details of the presentations made at NPPM meetings see NPPM Minute Book', 22 August

1958; 30 January 1959; 11 December 1959; 23 September 1960; 24 November 1961; 26 October 1962; 24 October 1964 and 4 December 1964. For details of NPPM activity in 1965-1966 see Short, 'One Man's Garden'; see also Blackbutt Preservation Society to Editor, *NMH*, 1 August 1966.

14. For details of Tom's suspicions about the DMR see NPPM Minute Book, 26 March 1965. For details of the DMR proposal see 'Betrayal on Blackbutt', *NMH*, 4 August 1966. For the Lord Mayor's support see 'Highway Plan Approved 'In City's Interest'', *NMH*, 5 August 1966. For details of the Northumberland County Scheme and Tom's views regarding County Road 23 see Farrell to Editor, *NMH*, 12 June 1979. For Tom's statement before the House of Representatives Standing Committee see Evidence of Mr Rolfe Everist Farrell, House of Representatives Standing Committee on Environment and Conservation, Sub-Committee, Impact of Proposed State Highway 23 on Blackbutt Reserve, Newcastle, 16 March 1974, TFP A8286 (ii). See also R .E. Farrell, 'Notes on the Value of Blackbutt Reserve', TFP A8285 (x). For details of the proclamation of the Northumberland County District Planning Scheme maps see Lithgow to Editor, *NMH*, 12 June 1979. For Bassan's comments see C.Alison, 'How Blackbutt Reserve was Saved', *Sydney Morning Herald*, 3 April 1974. For comments by Lithgow see *NMH*, 5 August 1966. For Richley's comments see 'All Energy to Oppose Road Plan', *NMH*, 18 August 1966. For Earp's comments see 'The Real Threat to Blackbutt', *NMH*, 21 September 1966. For details of the protest meeting see '500 Attend Blackbutt Protest', *NMH*, 22 September 1966. For further details see Ramsland, 'History of Blackbutt Reserve', pp.27-29. For details of Tom's motion at the September meeting see NPPM Minute Book, August 1965-July 1967, UNA, C831, 25 September 1966. For the hand written copy of Tom's unpublished letter to the *Sydney Morning Herald* see TFP A2885 (ix). For details of the Minister for Local Government and Highways' reaction see ''Blackbutt May Be Saved', *NHM*, 2 December 1966. For details of the Special Meeting see NPPM Minute Book, 18 March 1967. For details of the October visit by aldermen to Blackbutt Reserve see C.Watson, 'Balckbutt Saga On Again', *NMH*, 22 May 1979. For details of the action by various Progress Associations see Watson, 'Blackbutt Saga'. For further details see Ramsland, 'History of Blackbutt Reserve', pp.27-29.

15. For details of the BAC proposal see 'Committee Move New Route on Blackbutt', *NMH*, 12 May 1967. For Mr Hope's comments and details of the Marshall Street Route see 'Committee Move New Route on Blackbutt', *NMH*, 12 May 1967. For details of the Council meeting in March 1967 see Watson, 'Blackbutt Saga'. For details of the meeting in July see 'Alderman Vote 15-4 for DMR on Blackbutt', *NMH*, 5 July 1967; see also Alison, 'Hoe Blackbutt was Saved'. For Richley's comments see 'Sixteenth Annual Report NPPM', 23 August 1967, NPPM Minute Book, C832. For comment regarding the period 1968-1970 see Watson, 'Blackbutt Saga'. For further details see Ramsland, 'History of Blackbutt Reserve', pp.27-30.

16. For details of the BAC's canvassing of candidates see Woodgate to Farrell, 13 November 1968, TFP A8289 (vii). For details of Tom's candidature for the 1968 Local Government elections see 'R. E. Farrell Electioneering Paraphernalia', TFP A8289 (vii). For Tom's reason for running see R .E. Farrell, 'Points of Policy', TFP A8289 (vii). For details of the election result for Central Ward see 'Election of Three

Aldermen for Central Ward', 7 December 1968, TFP A8289 (vii) – Tom received the third highest number of votes (314) behind Henderson and Gosper but lost on preferences to Bailey. For the split in the protest movement see Farrell, 'Notes on Value of Blackbutt Reserve'; *NMH*, 15 April 1970. For comments by the Editor see *NMH*, 17 April 1970. For details of October Council meeting see Watson, 'Blackbutt Saga'. For Morton's announcement see Watson, 'Blackbutt Saga'. For the protest meeting of New Lambton Height's residents see *NMH*, 8 December 1970. For Tom's comments see Farrell to editor, *NMH*, 27 February 1971. For protest meeting in June 1971 see *NMH*, 25 June 1971; Watson, 'Blackbutt Saga'. For further details see Ramsland, 'History of Blackbutt Reserve', p.30. For the comments by NPPM see 'Twentieth Annual Report of the NPPM', 20 October 1971, NPPM Papers, UNA, C832.

17. For details of Tom's ability as a lobbyist see Farrell Evidence, Select Committee, pp.522-523. For Tom's role in the Blackbutt Reserve Committee see Farrell Evidence, Select Committee, p.523; p.531. For Tom's strongly worded letter see Farrell to Bill, 28 May 1972, TFP A8285 (viii). For Tom's later view about the aldermen see Farrell to Editor, *NMH*, 27 December 1986; see also Farrell, 'Address to NPPM' – it was Tom's view that 'Joy Cummings was the only one that was really solid. All the rest gave you promises but then did nothing about it'. For the Editor's view see *NMH*, 12 March 1973. For the comments of Mr Brown see Farrell, 'Notes on the Value of Blackbutt Reserve'. For Joe Richley's words see 'Twenty-First Annual Report NPPM', 13 October 1972, NPPM Papers, UNA C832. Richard Hincks (Tom's ten year old grandson) was present at the decisive Council vote on the 28 March 1972 – Tom had asked Peter Podmore to accompany his grandson to the Council chambers. As Hincks, 'Memories of My Father' points out Tom was very keen to ensure that all his grandchildren were educated on these matters. For Alderman Purdue's comments see Purdue to Editor, *NMH*, 8 May 1973. For Tom's reply see Farrell to Editor, *NMH*, 15 May 1973; see also handwritten copy of letter TFP A8285 (v). For details of the Council meetings on 28 March 1973 and 30 May 1973 see *NMH*, 29 March 1973; 31 May 1973; see also *NMH*, 2 June 1973; Farrell, 'Notes on the Value of Blackbutt Reserve'. For details of 'Save Blackbutt' pamphlet see TFP A285 (v). For Tom's response to rescission motion see Farrell to Editor, *NMH*, 23 May 1973. For Tom and Joe Richley's meeting with the Lord Mayor see "Blackbutt Study Welcome Says McDougall', *NMH*, 2 June 1973. For details of Joe Richley's retirement see NPPM Minutes, 13 September 1972. For Short's comments see P. Short, 'It's Been A Rough Ride Into the Expressway Era', *NMH*, 12 March 1973. For the Lord Mayor's announcement regarding the response by the Federal Government see *NMH*, 2 June 1973.

18. J. Richley & R.E. Farrell 'Submission on Behalf of the Blackbutt Reserve Committee to the House of Representatives Standing Committee on Environment and Conservation', Report of the Select Committee, pp.513-515, TFP A8286 (ii). R. S. Woodgate (For and on behalf of the Blackbutt Action Committee), *Save Blackbutt: The Case Against State Highway 23 Violating Blackbutt Reserve*, Phelps & Samuels, Newcastle, no date, pp.1-29. Farrell Evidence, Report of the Select Committee, pp.516-534; see also R. E .Farrell, 'Notes Federal Parliamentary Sub Committee Route 23', 16 March 1974, TFP A8285 (vii). For details of Blackbutt's educative role see "Blackbutt: An Open-Air Classroom', *NMH*, 21 November 1970. Tom's plea in his own hand writing appears on Report of the Select Committee, p.516.

19. For details regarding the NPPM's canvassing of candidates see 'Questionnaire for Candidates', 28 June 1974, NPPM Minute Book, UNA, C833. For Ramsland's comment see Ramsland, 'History of Blackbutt Reserve', p.31. For details of the Findings of the Select Committee see 'Canberra Snag for Motorway', *NMH*, 3 December 1974; see also Watson, 'Blackbutt Saga'. For position of Fife in regards to the motorway see Farrell, 'Notes on Value of Blackbutt Reserve'. It was Tom's view that Sir Charles Cutler, Fife's predecessor, 'had been in favour of the motorway going through the reserve'. For the Council decision on 22 October 1974 see *NMH*, 23 October 1974; see also Farrell, 'Notes on Value of Blackbutt Reserve'. For decision of the Federal Transport Minister see Farrell, 'Notes on Value of Blackbutt Reserve'; see also Tripp,' Profile of a Successful Man', p.6. For Tom's comments regarding the outcome see Farrell to Editor, *NMH*, 9 December 1974. For Morris' later role see Farrell, 'Notes on Value of Blackbutt Reserve'. For details of Morris' maiden speech see Wesley Mission, 'Birdwood Park' in 'Green Conscience'.

20. For Tom's comments see Farrell to Editor, *NMH*, 23 November 1976; see also a copy of the letter in TFP A8285 (iv). See also Farrell Motion (seconded by Richley), NPPM Minute Book, 26 November 1976 – the motion reads 'that we write to the Lord Mayor congratulating him for his public stand advocating that State Highway 23 should be built in accordance with the County Plan in the vicinity of Blackbutt Reserve'. See also Woodgate to Editor, *NMH*, no date, TFP A8285 (iv). In regard to Tom's interest in the National Highway being built west of Lake Macquarie see Shields' Motion (seconded by Farrell), NPPM Minute Book, 25 July 1975, UNA, C833 – the motion requested 'that a submission be made to MSJ Keys Young Planners Pty Ltd on the Investigation for a National Highway through the Hunter Valley and further we propose that all road development on the eastern side of Lake Macquarie be in accordance with the County Plan'. For Tom's comments on the DMR's decision regarding Highway 23 see Farrell to Editor, *NHM* 12 June 1979. See also Alison, 'How Blackbutt was Saved'; Watson, 'Blackbutt Saga'. For Tom's motion see NPPM Minute Book, 25 May 1979.

21. For details of the history of mining in the Blackbutt area see Farrell, 'Notes on Value of Blackbutt Reserve'. For Tom's motion see NPPM Minute Book, 31 July 1970. For details of the NPPM's delegation to Mr Fife and comments by Mr Woodgate see "Blackbutt Protest", *NMH* Press Clipping, TFP A8286 (i). For Joe Richley's comment see 'Twentieth Annual Report NPPM", 20 October 1971, NPPM Minute Book, UNA, C832. For Lumsdon cartoon see *NMH*, 12 May 1971. For details of NPPM's canvassing of candidates see Barnett to Candidates, 28 June 1974, NPPM Minute Book. For Council's decision not to extend the lease and the response of the Company see 'Blackbutt Pit Phasing Out', *NMH*, 12 August 1976. For Lithgow's comments see *NMH*, 12 August 1976. For Barnett's motion see NPPM Minute Book, 25 August 1978. For comments about Joe Richley and Tom see 'Twenty-Sixth Annual Report NPPM', 10 November 1978, NPPM Minute Book. For Tom's appointment as a 'Life Patron' see 'Minutes of the Annual General Meeting', 10 November 1978, NPPM Minute Book. For details of 'Life Membership' see NPPM Minute Book, 10 December 1987. For details of the mine's closure see 'Blackbutt Mine Closed', *NMH*, 27 March 1973; see also 'Notes on Value of Blackbutt Reserve'. For the opening of the Joe Richley Reserve see 'New Blackbutt Area to Open', *NMH*, 11 November 1983; Farrell, 'Address at Dedication of Joe Richley

Blackbutt Reserve'. For Lithgow's reflections see 'Annual Report NPPM Year 1982-1983', 25 November 1983, NPPM Minute Book. For Tom's comments about Doug Lithgow see Farrell, 'Address to NPPM'.

22. For Lithgow's comment see Neech, 'Lithgow -Transcript History of the NPPM', p.5. For comments on the Blackbutt Management Plan see 'Annual Report NPPM', 22 October 1976, NPPM Minute Book. For Tom's opposition to sectional use of public parks see Farrell motion, NPPM Minute Book, 29 May 1987. For Town Clerk's reply see NPPM Minute Book, 27 August 1987. For Tom's reiteration of his view see NPPM Minute Book, 27 May 1988. For comments about funding see 'Annual Report NPPM', 23 September 1977, NPPM Minute Book. For comments by President in 1979 see 'Annual Report NPPM', 26 September 1979, NPPM Minute Book. For comments by President in 1980 see 'Annual Report NPPM', 31 October 1980, NPPM Minute Book. For Tom's interest in the issue see *Northern Parks & Playgrounds Movement Quarterly Review*, June 1982, NPPM Minute Book. For details of the Blackbutt Reserve Management Plan see B. Mackenzie & Associates and P. Parker, *Blackbutt Reserve Plan of Management*, NCC, 1989. The fact that the Draft Management Plan was not ratified by the NCC for some time because of ongoing concerns about the wildlife and aviary exhibits caused some consternation in the NPPM see '1989-1990 Annual Report NPPM', 29 November 1990, NPPM Minute Book, UNA, C837; '1992-1993 Annual Report NPPM',26 November 1993, NPPM Minute Book, UNA, C837. 'The Blackbutt Reserve Management Plan' was ratified in 1993.

23. For Bob Power's comment see hand written note alongside letter Farrell to Editor, *NMH*, 27 December 1986, TFP A8285 (iii). For Lithgow's comments see '1991-1992 Annual Report NPPM', 7 December 1992. For Tom's comments see Farrell, 'Address to NPPPM'. For details of the Australia Day award see Lithgow to Farrell, 18 February 1988, NPPM Minute Book.

CHAPTER SIX

1. For details of the Northumberland County Council see State Records Archives, 'The Cumberland County Council' accessed 20 May 2012, <http://investigator.records.nsw.gov.au/Entity.aspx?Path =%5C Agency% 5C423>; see also E. C. Wilmott, 'Twenty Five Years of Planning in the Hunter Valley', 1974, NRLLSA, Q711/ PAM Box1; see also 'County Plan On Display Soon', *NMH*, 21 August 1951; *NMH*, 31 October & 1 November 1951; Neech, Interview with Doug Lithgow, pp.14-15. For Joe Richley's comments see J. Richley, 'Public Parks and Recreation Facilities of the Future', Hunter Valley Local Government Association Seminar, 1967, NPPM Minute Book, C831. For Tom's view of the objectives see Farrell, 'Address to NPPM'.

2. For Tom's involvement with the Pit Paddock rezoning issue see R.E. Farrell, 'Rezoning of Pit Paddock', Cardiff Heights-New Lambton Lookout Progress Association, no date, TFPJF. Tom submitted the following papers for the Minister's consideration A.S. Oakes, 'Glass Works Pit Paddock, New Lambton'; Town Clerk to Butler, November 1945; County Clerk to Barnett, 19 June 1951; County Clerk to Town Clerk, 19 June 1951, TFPJF. For the NPPM's advice to the City Council regarding parks in the New Lambton Area see J. Richley, 'Report of Meeting with Newcastle Businessmen's Club Regarding Parks', NPPM Minute Book, 26 March 1965. For Tom's motions regarding Armstrong Park see NPPM Minute Book, 22 March 1968; 22 May 1970. For Tom's defence of Tauranga Park see Farrell, 'Address to NPPM'; see also Tom's motion (seconded by Munro) that a letter be sent to Minister 'protesting the proposal to establish a library on park land at New Lambton', NPPM Minute Book, 22 May 1964.

3. For Tom's plan to establish a Land Usage Sub-committee see 'Special Conference at the Residence of Mr J. Richley', NPPM Minute Book, 10 December 1958. For Richley's comments see 'NPPM Annual Report 1960-1961', NPPM Minute Book, 14 November 1961; 'NPPM Annual Report 1964-1965', NPPM Minute Book , 10 November 1965; 'NPPM Annual Report 1966', NPPM Minute Book, 24 August 1966. For details of the formation of the Park Alienation Committee see 'NPPM Annual Report 1964-1965'. For details about Nesca Park see Tom's report NPPM Minute Book, 30 January 1959; 'NPPM Annual Report 1964-1965'. For details regarding Campbell Park and Toronto Park see 'NPPM Annual Report 1960-1961'. For the 1963 motion see NPPM Minute Book, 30 August 1963. For the 1967 motion see NPPM Minute Book, 27 October 1967. For the action regarding Harker Oval and Adamstown Park see NPPM Minute Book, 22 March 1968; 'NPPM Annual Report 1967-1968', NPPM Minute Book, 27 September 1968. For motion regarding Mitchell Park, Flaggy Creek Reserve, Jefferson Park and Charlestown Oval see NPPM Minute Book, 28 February 1969; 22 May 1970; 31 July 1970; 'NPPM Annual Report 1970', NPPM Minute Book, 25 September 1970. For political lobbying in 1970-1971 see Farrell motion (seconded by Shields), NPPM Minute Book, 27 November 1970; Farrell motion (seconded by Shields), NPPM Minute Book, 21 January 1971. For the action regarding Throsby Creek and Merewether Beach front see Farrell motion (seconded by Lithgow), NPPM Minute Book, 24 September 1971; Farrell motion (seconded by Shields), NPPM Minute Book, 24 September 1971. For details of the court's decision see 'NPPM Annual Report 1972', NPPM Minute Book, 13 October 1972. For details of Tom's opposition to the fencing of parkland see Farrell motion (seconded by Shields), NPPM Minute Book, 23 March 1971. For details about Tom's activity in Tarro and Sandgate see NPPM Minute Book, 21 January 1968. For Alder Park motion see NPPM Minute Book, 23 March 1973. For Tom's motion (seconded by Doug Harris) regarding the prosecution of those driving motor vehicles in park areas see NPPM Minute Book, 22 March 1974. For letter to council regarding suitable play areas for children see NPPM Minute Book, 25 July 1975. For Croudace Bay matter see 'NPPM Annual Report 1976', NPPM Minute Book, 22 October 1976. For motion regarding Rathmines see Farrell motion (seconded by Shields), NPPM Minute Book 25 March 1977. For motions regarding Valentine Bowling Club and Hunter District Water Board see NPPM Minute Book, 24 February 1978.

4. For Richey's comments about the state of affairs in 1978 see 'NPPM Annual Report 1978', NPPM Minute Book,10 November 1978. For achievements a year later see 'NPPM Annual Report 1979', NPPM Minute Book, 9 November 1979. For Tom's motion regarding payment in lieu of parkland see NPPM Minute Book, 24 November 1978. For Lithgow's motion see NPPM Minute Book, 25 May 1979. For Richley's views on the lack of town planning see 'NPPM Annual Report 1966'; 'NPPM Annual Report 1967'; 'NPPM Annual Report 1968'.

5. For an overview of the difficulties faced by the NPPM as it fought to preserve open space see D. Lithgow, 'Address to a Seminar of the Royal Australian Planning Institute, Newcastle Branch, on the Retirement of Bob James, City Planner', Newcastle, NPPM Minute Book, 30 June 1963. For details of the attempt by the NPPM to fight against the haphazard nature of town planning see 'NPPM Annual Report 1966', 'NPPM Annual Report 1967', 'NPPM Annual Report 1968', 'NPPM Annual Report 1981', NPPM Minute Book, 24 November 1981; 'NPPM Annual Report 1982', D. Lithgow, 'Outdoor Recreation Seminar in Conjunction with the Newcastle and Lake Macquarie City Councils', NPPM Minute Book, 1 December 1985. For details of the attempt by the NPPM to fight against inadequate public funding see D. Lithgow, 'Report on The Northumberland Development Fund and The Cumberland Development Fund', NPPM Minute Book, 19 May 1982; 'NPPM Annual Report 1981'; 'NPPM Annual Report 1982'. For details of the attempt by the NPPM to win greater support from State Government see 'NPPM Annual Report 1977', NPPM Minute Book , 23 September 1977; 'NPPM Annual Report 1981'; 'NPPM Annual Report 1982'. For comments by Lithgow see 'Address to a Seminar of the Royal Australian Planning Institute'; Lithgow, 'Outdoor Recreation Seminar'. For details of the work undertaken by Lithgow, 'our hardworking and efficient secretary' see 'NPPM Annual Report 1967', NPPM Minute Book, 23 August 1967.

6. For details regarding Tom's efforts to improve town planning see motion (seconded by Shields) NPPM Minute Book, 28 June 1974. In regards Federal and State funding see Tom's motions - NPPM Minute Book, 22 March 1968 (seconded by Barnett) 24 May 1968 (seconded by Lithgow); 27 November 1970 (seconded by Shields); 29 June 1985 (seconded by Dews); 30 August 1985 (seconded by Wright). For

motion (seconded by Wright) regarding audit of parks in Greater Newcastle region see NPPM Minute Book, 24 February 1984. For subsequent motions (seconded by Adamthwaite) see NPPM Minute Book, 30 August 1985; 30 May 1986. For details of meetings where Tom moved or seconded the majority of motions see (for example) NPPM Minute Book, 25 September 1966; 24 May 1968; 26 November 1976; 28 July 1984; 1 May 1987.

7. For criticism of the NPPM see 'Annual Report of the NPPM 1976', NPPM Minute Book, 22 November 1976. For details of the leadership role played by NPPM see 'Annual Report of the NPPM 1986 ', NPPM Minute Book, 24 November 1986. It is clear that the NPPM did not always have a good working relationship with the media – the following motion was passed at the October 1967 meeting 'that we ask the Editor of the *Newcastle Morning Herald* to receive a deputation to discuss the work of the movement and ask why the press has withheld public statements and information about the Movement' – see NPPM Minute Book, 27 October 1967. For comments regarding the improved working relationship with the media see 'Annual Report of the NPPM 1964-1965'; 'Annual Report of the NPPM 1980', NPPM Minute Book, 31 October 1980. In the 'Annual Report of the NPPM 1985', NPPM Minute Book, 6 December 1985 the President paid 'special thanks to the local media, the *Newcastle Herald* in particular for providing a platform for the discussion of environmental issues; Channel 3 and the *Star* should also be thanked'. For Lithgow's comment regarding the achievements of the NPPM see 'Annual Report of the NPPM', Minute Book 1992, NPPM Minute Book, 7 December 1992. For details regarding Tom's motions in regard to Nobby's Beach see NPPM Minute Book, 23 July 1981; King Edward Park see NPPM Minute Book 23 May 1983; 29 July 1983, 25 May 1984, 28 July 1984; 1 February 1985; 21 January 1986; Belmont see NPPM Minute Book 1 May 1987; 21 January 1989; Speers Point see NPPM Minute Book 1 May 1987; Charlestown see 'Annual Report of the NPPM 1992'. For details regarding insolvent clubs see Molesworth motion (seconded by Farrell), NPPM Minute Book, 30 May 1986.

8. For details regarding Reid Park see 'Annual Report of the NPPM', NPPM Minute Book, 24 November 1981. For details regarding King Edward Park and Empire Park see NPPM Minute Book, 27 August 1987. For opposition regarding off-road vehicles and roads see NPPM Minute Book, 23 May 1983; 31 July 1987.

9. For details of motions regarding West Park and No 1 Sports Ground see NPPM Minute Book, 30 May 1986. For motions opposing further development at Bar Beach see NPPM Minute Book, 31 July 1987; 27 May 1988; 29 July 1988; for opposition to Redhead Pumping Station see NPPM Minute Book, 29 April 1988. For details regarding BHP see James motion (seconded by Farrell), NPPM Minute Book, 1 February 1985; Farrell motion (seconded by Gaudry), NPPM Minute Book , 29 July 1985. For motions regarding landscaping at Wangi Point, Warners Bay and Eleebana see 'Annual Report of the NPPM', NPPM Minute Book , 24 November 1981. For details of Tom's motions regarding tree planting programs at Westend Park see NPPM Minute Book, 28 May 1982; 31 July 1987; at Speers Point see NPPM Minute Book, 30 October 1987; for 'arboreal screen from the overhead bridge at Hamilton to Hannell Street' see NPPM Minute Book, 28 May 1982.

10. For details of Tom's motions regarding Adamstown Park see NPPM Minute Book , 30 May 1986; 27 May 1988; regarding the old rifle range site see NPPM Minute Book, 25 June 1980; 27 May 1983; 22 February 1985; 26 April 1987; 31 January 1988. For motions regarding Shortland Wetlands see NPPM Minute Book, 25 May 1984; 29 May 1987; 26 September 1987; see also 'Annual Report of the NPPM', NPPM Minute Book , 6 December 1985.

11. For Tom's motions regarding the Abattoir site see NPPM Minute Book, 25 May 1972; 21 January 1986; see also 'Annual Report of the NPPM', NPPM Minute Book, 25 November 1983. For Tom's motions regarding Dixon Park see NPPM Minute Book , 22 May 1958; 24 March 1961; 26 March 1965; see also 'Flyer Save Dixon Park Beach Front', NPPM Minute Book, 4 December 1964; Wesley Mission, 'Northern Parks and Playground Movement'. For comments by President see 'Annual Report of the NPPM, NPPM Minute Book, 1 September 1965.

12. For details of Tom's motions regarding Braye Park see NPPM Minute Book, 30 January 1959; 28 May 1971; 24 February 1978; see also 'Annual Report of the NPPM', NPPM Minute Book, 1 September 1965; 'Annual Report of the NPPM', NPPM Minute Book, 13 October 1972; 'Annual Report of the NPPM', NPPM Minute Book , 22 October 1976; 'Annual Report of the NPPM', NPPM Minute Book, 23 September 1977. For the work of Tom and the NPPM in the Stockton, Fern Bay area see NPPM Minute Book , 26 February 1960; 27 January 1971; 23 June 1962; 25 January 1963; 27 October 1967; see also 'Annual Report of the NPPM', NPPM Minute Book, 1 September 1965. For activity in Port Stephen's Shire see NPPM Minute Book, 23 February 1962; 23 March 1962; 27 April 1962; 25 May 1962; 26 March 1965; 30 August 1985; see also 'Annual Report of the NPPM', NPPM Minute Book, 1 September 1965; 'Annual Report of the NPPM', NPPM Minute Book, 23 September 1977; 'Annual Report of the NPPM', NPPM Minute Book, 31 October 1980; 'Annual Report of the NPPM', NPPM Minute Book , 31 October 1980. For Tom's comments regarding reserves in Port Stephens see NPPM Minute Book, 30 August 1985. For Lithgow's comments regarding Tomaree National Park see 'Annual Report of the NPPM', NPPM Minute Book, 25 November 1984.

13. For Tom's role in protecting District Park see NPPM Minute Book , 22 August 1958; 22 January 1960; 25 March 1960; 22 April 1960; 23 February 1962; 23 March 1962; 27 April 1962; 26 June 1962; 28 September 1962; 26 October 1962; comment taken from NPPM Minute Book , 24 May 1963. For Tom's motion regarding District Park see NPPM Minute Book, 29 June 1985. For details regarding National Park see D. Lithgow, 'National Park and Parkland in the Hamilton South and Cooks Hill Area', 22 March 1984, NPPM Minute Book C835; see also 'Annual Report of the NPPM', NPPM Minute Book , 28 November 1984. For 1986 Gaudry motion (seconded by Hartley) see NPPM Minute Book, 30 May 1986; see also NPPM Minute Book, 30 May 1986 for Farrell motion.

14. For details of Lithgow's proposal for the Civic precinct see D. Lithgow, 'Report on Civic Park and Its Environs', 29 March 1968, NPPM Minute Book C833. For Tom's motion see NPPM Minute Book, 24 May

1968. For the slow progress of the Council's consideration see '1967-1968 Annual Report of the NPPM', NPPM Minute Book, 22 November 1968 – the report comments 'it would appear from our enquiries that the proposal has been pigeon-holed somewhere'. For comments in 1976 see 'Annual Report of the NPPM', NPPM Minute Book, 22 October 1976. For President's comments in 1977 see 'Annual Report of the NPPM', NPPM Minute Book, 23 September 1977. For Tom's motion see NPPM Minute Book, 27 January 1989. For President's comments in 1982 see 'Annual Report of the NPPM', NPPM Minute Book, 29 November 1982. For details of some of the unreal projects suggested for the precinct see C. Hunter, *Newcastle Civic and Cultural Precinct History,* January 2003, pp.28-33, accessed 4 June 2012, <http://www.newcastle.nsw.gov.au / __data /assets/ pdf_file/0020/8804/civichistory_post1920.pdf>.

15. For Tom's comment regarding lost park land in the inner-city see Farrell, 'Address to NPPM'. For details of planning proposal and its impact on Birdwood Park see Wesley Mission, 'Northern Parks and Playground Movement'; see also Wesley Mission, 'Birdwood Park' in *Green Conscience The Ongoing Struggle for a Clean, Green Newcastle A History,* accessed 5 June 2012, <http://radicalnewcastle.files.wordpress.com /2011/05/ greenconscience.pdf >. For comment by contemporary commentator (John Turner) see Wesley Mission, 'Northern Parks and Playground Movement'. For Tom's motion see NPPM Minute Book, 25 September 1966; see also 25 November 1966. For the report entitled 'Criticisms of the Present Plan and Suggestions for Alternate Measures' see Wesley Mission, 'Northern Parks and Playground Movement'. For details of the protest meeting see Wesley Mission, 'Birdwood Park'. For Richley's comments and Council's response see 'Annual Report of NPPM 1971'. For the position of the Lord Mayor, the Council and the Works Committee see Wesley Mission, 'Birdwood Park'. For Richley's comment see 'Annual Report of the NPPM 1972'. For details of the action of SAPS see Wesley Mission, 'Birdwood Park'; see also *NMH,* 24 & 25 February 1973. For a report of the Council meeting see *NMH,* 26 February 1973. For details of the destruction of trees in Birdwood Park and Lithgow's comments see *NMH,* 27 February 1973; see also Wesley Mission, 'Birdwood Park'. For subsequent action by Council and the aftermath see Wesley Mission, 'Birdwood Park'. For Tom's motion see NPPM Minute Book, 23 March 1973. For Tom's criticism of the Council and DMR see Farrell evidence, Report of the Select Committee, p.516. For Tom's subsequent motions see NPPM Minute Book, 28 June 1974; 23 July 1981. For details of letter to candidates see NPPM Minute Book, 28 June 1974. For the election result see Wesley Mission, 'Birdwood Park'. For Tom's view of Joy Cummings see Farrell, 'Address to NPPM'. For Lithgow's view of Joy Cummings see 'Annual Report of the NPPM 1983-1984'. For the new Lord Mayor's more enlightened approach see Wesley Mission, 'Birdwood Park'.

16. For details of problem of pollution emanating from Kooragang see Neech, 'Interview with Doug Lithgow'; E. J .Coffey, *Report and Findings of the Commission of Inquiry into Pollution on Kooragand Island,* NSW State Pollution Control Commission, 1973; W. J. Streever, 'Kooragang Wetland Rehabilitation Project: Opportunities and Constraints in an Urban Wetland Rehabilitation Project', *Urban EcoSystens,* Vol.2, 1998, p.208 accessed 7 June 2012, <http://carmelacanzonieri. com/library/6123/Streever-Koorangang WetlandRehab-Urban.pdf >. For details of the *Hunter 2000 Report* see 'NPPM Annual Report 1972'

– Joe Richley regarded this report of the National Trust (requested by the State Planning Authority) as 'the most significant document for conservation since the gazettal of the Northumberland County Plan because it gives us aims in our battle to ensure the adequate provision of open space for the citizens of this area'. For quotation from report see Coffey, *Report Kooragang*, p.14. For Tom's motions see NPPM Minute Book, 22 March 1974; 25 July 1974. For Lithgow's motion see NPPM Minute Book, 25 June 1976. For Barnett's comments see 'Annual Report of the NPPM 1978'; 'Annual Report of the NPPM 1979', NPPM Minute Book, November 1979. For details of the various studies see NSW National Parks and Wildlife Service, *Kooragang Nature Reserve and Hexham Swamp Nature Reserve Plan of Management*, August 1998, accessed 8 June 2012, <http://www.environment.nsw.gov.au/resources/parks/pomfinalhexhamkoorangang.pdf>. For Lithgow's comments see 'Annual Report of the NPPM 1980'. For details of the establishment of the SEPP see NSW National Parks and Wildlife Service, *Kooragang Nature Reserve*. For Tom's motions see NPPM Minute Book, 29 June 1985; 30 October 1987. For the importance of Kooragang see NSW National Parks and Wildlife Service, *Kooragang Nature Reserve*.

17. For Richley's optimistic comments see 'NPPM Annual Report 1970', NPPM Minute Book, 25 September 1970. For details of sand mining in the Myall Lakes area and the recommendations of the Sim Committee see Office of Environment & Heritage, NSW National Parks & Wildlife Service, 'History of the Myall Lakes', accessed 9 June 2012, <http://www.environment.nsw.gov.au/NationalParks/parkHistory.aspx?id=N0026>. For details of the work of Richley and Earp see Farrell, 'Address to NPPM''; Rowe, 'Interview'. For details of the establishment of the Myall Lakes National Park and the banning of all sand mining in the area see NSW National Parks & Wildlife Service, 'History of Myall Lakes'. For the report of the President see 'NPPM Annual Report 1977'. For Tom's description of Joe Richley see Rowe, 'Interview'. For Tom's comment about the role of the NPPM see Farrell, 'Address to NPPM''.

18. For the role of the NPPM and the Hunter Manning National Parks Association in the establishment of the Barrington Tops National Park see Wesley Mission, 'Northern Parks and Playground Movement'; Neech, 'Interview with Doug Lithgow'. For details of the history of the area see Office of Environment & Heritage, NSW National Parks & Wildlife Service, 'History of Barrington Tops National Park', accessed 9 June 2012, <http://www.environment.nsw.gov.au/ NationalParks/park Heritage. aspx?id=N0002>. For Lithgow's comments see 'NPPM Annual Report 1992-1993', NPPM Minute Book, 26 November 1993. For comments by Editor see *NMH*, 7 July 1996.

19. For details of the NPPM's development of the plan for Mt Sugarloaf Park see Wesley Mission, 'Northern Parks and Playground Movement'; 'Annual Report of the NPPM 1964-1965'. For Dewes' motion and Richley's comment see NPPM Minute Book, 23 June 1961. For the Morris Plan see 'Proposed Mount Sugarloaf Park', June 1965, attached to 'NPPM Annual Report 1964-1965'. For Morris' role in developing the proposal see 'NPPM Annual Report 1971'. For details of the support of Lewis and Booth see 'NPPM Annual Report 1966'. Richley was particular grateful for the support of Lewis, a man he described as 'a citizen who had long been associated with park organisations' According to Richley, one of the first

directions Lewis gave to officers of his Department was to classify parks. For LMSC's failure to take up the Lewis' proposal see 'NPPM Annual Report 1967'. For details of Lewis' address to the NPPM and the company's response see Wesley Mission, 'Northern Parks and Playground Movement'. For events in 1969 see Wesley Mission, 'Northern Parks and Playground Movement'. For Tom's comment see Farrell, 'Address to NPPM'. For comments by President see 'NPPM Annual Report 1970', NPPM Minute Book, 25 September 1970. For comment by Joe Richley see 'NPPM Annual Report 1971'. For Tom's part in the tree planting activity see NPPM Minute Book, 25 May 1979. For details of the Sugarloaf State Conservation Area see Office of Environment & Heritage, NSW National Parks & Wildlife Service, 'The Vertebrate Fauna of Sugarloaf State Conservation Area', accessed 10 June 2012, <http://www. environment.nsw.gov. au/resources/nature/surveys/SugarloafSCAvertebratefauna.pdf>.

20. For details of the area see Office of Environment & Heritage, NSW National Parks & Wildlife Service, 'The Glenrock State Recreation Area', accessed 11 June 2012, <http://www.environment.nsw.gov.au/ NationalParks /parkHeritage.aspx?id=N0616 >; see also J. F. Grothen, *The History In and About Glenrock*, Newcastle, 1982. For the history of the Flaggy Creek Reserve see Wesley Mission, 'Glenrock', *Green Conscience The Ongoing Struggle for a Clean, Green Newcastle A History*; see also Neech, 'Interview with Doug Lithgow'. For Tom's recollection see Farrell, 'Address to NPPM'. For details of the coal operation in the area see Newcastle Industrial heritage Association, 'Industries of Glenrock Reserve', accessed on 11 June 2012, <http://www.niha.org.au/staticpages/index.php /20110830001925853>. For Tom's attempt to organise a meeting with Mr Wilkinson see Farrell motion (seconded by Sladen), NPPM Minute Book, 26 March 1965. For Tom's motions see NPPM Minute Book, 23 October 1970, 22 January 1971. For President's comments see 'NPPM Annual Report 1971'. For details of Lithgow's work see Newcastle Flora and Fauna Protection Society, *Glenrock Natural History A Proposal for the Establishment of a Coastal State Recreation Reserve Between the Newcastle Suburbs of Merewether and Dudley*, 1983. For details of the Newcastle-Lake Macquarie Coastal Study, February 1980, see Wesley Mission, 'Glenrock'; Neech, 'Interview with Doug Lithgow'. For Tom's motion see NPPM Minute Book, 24 November 1978. For details of the problem regarding leaking sewerage mains see 'NPPM Annual Report 1980'. For details of Annual Reports 1980, 1981 and 1983 see 'NPPM Annual Report 1980'; 'NPPM Annual Report 1981'; 'NPPM Annual Report 1983'. For Tom's motion see NPPM Minute Book, 29 July 1983. For Lithgow's comment see Neech, 'Interview with Doug Lithgow'; see also Lithgow motion (seconded by Farrell), NPPM Minute Book, 24 February 1984 – 'that we congratulate Richard Face in his inspiring address and that we offer him help in his deputation if required'. For details of free-hold land purchases by State Government and LMSC see 'NPPM Annual Report 1982-1983'. For details of the submission to the Bicentennial Authority see 'NPPM Annual Report 1983-1984'. For Tom's motion opposing land exchanges see NPPM Minute Book, 20 October 1984. For Carr's announcement and details of agreement between the State Government and BHP see Wesley Mission, 'Glenrock'. For Lithgow's comments see 'NPPM Annual Report 1984-1985', NPPM Minute Book, 6 December 1985. For the Jackson motion (seconded by Farrell) see NPPM Minute Book, 21 January 1986. For details of the Glenrock Community Advisory Committee see Wesley Mission, 'Glenrock'. For Tom's motions opposing mining at Burwood

Beach and the NCC's quarry activity see NPPM Minute Book, 30 May 1986; 1 May 1987. For Lithgow's comments regarding the ongoing challenges see 'NPPM Annual Report 1986'. For Tom's motion calling for the cessation of all quarry activities see NPPM Minute Book, 29 May 1987. For details of the Protest Meeting see NPPM Minute Book, 29 May 1987. For President's report on quarry see 'NPPM Annual Report 1987', NPPM Minute Book, 10 December 1987. For details of the NPPM's activities in the 1990s see "NPPM Annual Report 1990', NPPM Minute Book, 29 November 1990; 'NPPM Annual Report 1991-1992', NPPM Minute Book , 7 December 1992. For the difficulties faced by the NPPM in the early 1990s see 'NPPM Annual Report 1993-1994', NPPM Minute Book, 23 November 1994; 'NPPM Annual Report 1994-1995', NPPM Minute Book, 23 November 1995. For details about the purchase of 'the Bailey land' see Wesley Mission, 'Glenrock'. For Lithgow's comments regarding closure of quarry and wastewater plant see Neech, 'Interview with Doug Lithgow'. For details of the expansion of the reserve see Wesley Mission, 'Glenrock'. For information regarding the Glenrock State Conservation Area see NSW Government Environment, Climate Change & Water, National Parks & Wildlife Service 'The Glenrock State Conservation Area Plan of Management', September 2010, accessed on 13 June 2012 <http://www. environment.nsw.gov.au/resources/planmanagement/final/20100835 Glenrock SCA.pdf>. For Lithgow's comments see Neech, 'Interview with Doug Lithgow'.

21. For Tom's motion see NPPM Minute Book, 28 November 1958. For Barnett's comments see 'NPPM Annual Report 1977'. For Tom's motion in June 1980 see NPPPM Minute Book, 25 June 1980. For Lithgow's comments regarding capital expenditure on Sydney's Botanic Garden see 'NPPM Annual Report 1980'. For details of the Botanic Gardens Committee see 'NPPM Annual Report 1981'; 'NPPM Annual Report 1982; 'NPPM Annual Report. For Lithgow's comments in 1985 see 'NPPM Annual Report 1984-1985'. For details of the Hunter Region Botanic Gardens see 'Hunter Region Botanic Gardens', accessed 12 June 2012, <http://www. huntergardens.org.au/>. For Barnett's address see 'Minutes of Annual General Meeting 1986', NPPM Minute Book, 28 November 1986. For Tom's continued support of the Botanic Gardens see Farrell motion (seconded by Wright), NPPM Minute Book, 29 February 1988. The motion read 'that we write to Peter Morris MHR thanking him for his continued interest in the Botanic Gardens'.

22. For an overview of the aims of the NPPM in regard to the East End see Wesley Mission, 'Northern Parks and Playground Movement'. For Tom's motions regarding open space for the inner city see NPPM Minute Book, 27 October 1967; railway lands associated with Zaara Street Power Station (seconded by Jones) see NPPM Minute Book, 28 January 1966; the area of Fort Scratchley becoming parkland (seconded by Lithgow) see NPPM Minute Book, 28 February 1969; Pacific Park (seconded by Woodgate), NPPM Minute Book, 31 July 1970. For Lithgow's motion (seconded by Farrell) see NPPM Minute Book, 27 June 1969. For Lithgow's presentation see NPPM Minute Book, 31 May 1969; see also *SMH*, 5 September 1947. For Tom's motion regarding the parking area at Nobby's see NPPM Minute Book, 28 February 1969. For details of the groups that successfully opposed the parking area proposal see Wesley Mission, 'Northern Parks and Playground Movement'. For Lithgow's proposal regarding historic sites see 'NPPM

Annual Report 1970'. For details of the Newcastle East Residents Group proposal see Wesley Mission, 'Northern Parks and Playground Movement'. For Tom's motions regarding Pacific Park see NPPM Minute Book, 25 July 1975; 25 June 1976. For Lithgow's motion regarding Pacific Park see NPPM Minute Book, 25 June 1976. For details of Lithgow's involvement with the Newcastle East Development Committee see 'NPPM Annual Report 1977'; see also NPPPM Minute Book, 25 June 1976. For details of the Interim Development Plan see 'NPPM Annual Report 1979'. For Tom and Lithgow's motions see NPPM Minute Book, 25 June 1976. For Tom's motions regarding Pacific Park see NPPM Minute Book, 25 July 1975; 25 June 1976. For President's report see 'NPPM Annual Report 1976'; 'NPPM Annual Report 1977'; 'NPPM Annual Report 1978'; 'NPPM Annual Report 1979'.

23. For the President's comments regarding the gazetting of the Interim Development Order and the progress made regarding Pacific Park, Harbour Foreshore and Fort Scratchley see 'NPPM Annual Report 1980'. For details of the winning entry of the Harbour Foreshore Competition see 'NPPM Annual Report 1981', For Tom's motion regarding Dark's Ice Works see NPPM Minute Book, 23 July 1981. For details regarding the budget for restoration work at Fort Scratchley, the development of Pacific Park and the East End Task Force see 'NPPM Annual Report 1981'. For the announcements by Federal and State Governments in 1983 see 'NPPM Annual Report 1982-1983'. For Tom's motion regarding: working party for the East End historic site see NPPM Minute Book, 27 May 1983; discussion paper and open space at the site of the Old Teachers College see NPPM Minute Book, 27 October 1983. For details regarding Pacific Park and the *Herald's* fountain see 'NPPM Annual Report 1982-1983'.

24. For details of the Newcastle East Historic Site Working Party see 'NPPM Annual Report 1983-1984'. For President's comments see 'NPPM Annual Report 1983-1984'. For details of the changes to the winning landscape scheme see 'NPPM Annual Report 1984-1985'. For Tom's motion see NPPM Minute Book, 26 July 1985. For Wright's motion (seconded by Tom) see NPPM Minute Book, 21 January 1986. For Tom's motion regarding Carr's reply see NPPM Minute Book, 28 February 1986. For Tom's activism in 1986 see NPPM Minute Book, 30 May 1986; 25 July 1986. For President's comments see 'NPPM Annual Report 1986'. For Tom's attempt to rally support see NPPM Minute Book, 26 June 1987; 31 July 1987; 26 September 1987; 30 October 1987. Concerning Bob Brown's visit see NPPM Minute Book, 30 October 1987. For recognition of Cummings and Lithgow see NPPM Minute Book, 30 October 1987. There is no doubt that Joy Cummings was an important figure in the environmental and conservation movement in Newcastle – in his speech to the Legislative Assembly on her death in 2003, Bryce Gaudry, the Member for Newcastle, made the following remarks: 'Joy Cummings left our city with a tremendous legacy – Blackbutt Reserve and its extension into Richley Reserve, the saving of Civic Park, the Newcastle East Plan and, in particular, the Harbour Foreshore Park, which is a special tribute to her' – see B. Gaudry, 'Death of Mrs Joy Cummings', 3 July 2003, 'Private Members Statements', Hansard, NSW Legislative Assembly, accessed 17 June 2012, <http://www.parliament.nsw.gov.au/prod/parlment/hansart.nsf/V3Key/LA20030703034>.

25. For details of activism in 1987 see 'NPPM Annual Report 1987'. For Wright motion (seconded by Tom) see NPPM Minute Book, 24 February 1989. For Tom's motion regarding public land and historic sites in Newcastle East see NPPM Minute Book, 31 March 1989. For details of the NPPM's proposals after the Newcastle Earthquake see 'NPPM Annual Report 1990'. For details of the ongoing struggle to secure the NPPM's vision for the East End and Harbour Foreshore Park see 'NPPM Annual Report 1991-1992', pp.7-8; 'NPPM Annual Report 1992-1993'; p.4; 'NPPM Annual Report 1993-1994', p.8; 'NPPM Annual Report 1994-1995', pp.14-15; "NPPM Annual Report 1998', pp.4-5.

26. For Tom's motion regarding the setting aside of 500 acres as park land between Valentine and Belmont see NPPM Minute Book, 25 September 1959. For the NPPM's position regarding the establishment of a national park in Lake Macquarie see NPPM Annual Report 1984-1985, pp.2-3. For Tom's reflections twenty-five years later see Farrell, 'Address to NPPM'. For Tom's motions regarding Lake Macquarie and the Northumberland County Plan see NPPM Minute Book, 23 June 1967. For details of the proposed levy on rate-payers see Wesley Mission, 'Northern Parks and Playground Movement'. For details of Tom's motions regarding Lake Macquarie see NPPM Minute Book, 25 June 1976 See also Tom's motion (seconded by Shields) and Shields' motion (seconded by Farrell), NBPM Minute Book, 24 November 1978 and 25 May 1979; see also NPPM Minute Book, 29 June 1985; 26 July 1985 (regarding Speer's Point). For President's comments about the activity of the NPPM in 1985 see 'NPPM Annual Report 1985', p.6. For details of the NPPM's attempt to stop pollution in Lake Macquarie see Wesley Mission, 'Northern Parks and Playground Movement'; 'NPPM Annual Report 1971, p.3; 'NPPM Annual Report 1972, p.2. For Tom's motion see NPPM Minute Book, 22 January 1971. For details of the establishment of the committee in October 1972 see Wesley Mission, 'Northern Parks and Playground Movement'; 'NPPM Annual Report 1971, p.2; see also Open Foundation, 'Summary of Transcript Interview with Doug Lithgow', p.18. For details regarding the Committee's ongoing work see 'NPPM Annual Report 1977, p.1. See also D. Lithgow, 'Lake Macquarie – A Lake Under Threat', NPPP Minute Book, 17 September 1983; 'Pollution – Lake Macquarie like Sydney Harbour', NPPM Annual Report 1982-1983, p.3. For the establishment of URGE see 'NPPM Annual Report 1987', p.6. For Lithgow's comments regarding URGE in 1989 see Neech, 'Interview with Doug Lithgow', p.18. See also 'NPPM Annual Report 1990', p.2. For Molesworth's motion (seconded by Farrell) see NPPM Minute Book, 30 October 1987. For press clippings see 'Tom Farrell Press Clippings' (two folders) in possession of Bev Hincks – see for example: 'Lake Erosion Hazard', *The Star*, 28 June 1989; 'Warning Sounded on Lake's Future', *The Post*, 31 May 1989; 'A Duck Shaving Danger to Lake', *NMH*, 15 January 1987; 'Tackling Lake Pollution', *NMH*, 24 March 1986.

27. For Tom's motions regarding Rathmines see NPPM Minute Book, 22 May 1970; 31 July 1970; 26 June 1971. For President's comments see 'NPPM Annual Report 1970', p.1; 'NPPM Annual Report 1971', p.2. For Tom's opposition to the caravan park see NPPM Minute Book, 26 May 1972. For President's comments at the end of 1972 see 'NPPM Annual Report 1972, p.3. For Tom's motion in July 1975 see NPPM Minute Book, 25 July 1975. For details of the campaign's success see 'NPPM Annual Report 1976, p.2. For Tom's role in the following years see NPPM Minute Book, 25 March 1977 and 29 October 1982. See also 'NPPM Annual Report 1977, p.2.

28. For Tom's early attempt to preserve Green Point see Farrell, 'Address to the NPPM'; Wesley Mission, 'Green Point', in 'Green Conscience'; Lake Macquarie Shire Council, 'A Case Study of Green Point Foreshore Reserve', accessed 27 August 2012, <http:www.lakemacquarielandcare.org/Files/Uploads/File/Resources/Green%20Point%20foreshore%20Reserve%20Case%20Study.pdf>. For the optimism within the NPPM see 'NPPM Annual Report 1964-1965', p.2. For President's comments see 'NPPM Annual Report 1966', p.2. For Tom's motions see NPPP Minute Book, 25 September 1966; 23 June 1967; 26 January 1969 and 28 February 1969. For Tom's part in the delegation see NPPM Minute Book, 23 June 1967.

29. For details of development proposal see Wesley Mission, 'Green Point'; see also S. Croxton, 'Marina, Motel, Shops, Part of Lake Plan', *NMH*, 3 November 1984

30. For Tom's response to the threat to Green Point see Farrell motion (seconded by Dews), NPPM Minute Book, 23 May 1983; Farrell motion (seconded by Wright), NPPM Minute Book, 23 May 1983.

31. For delegation to Booth see NPPM Minute Book, 24 February 1984; see also NPPM Minute Book, 25 May 1984.

32. For Lithgow's comments see 'NPPM Annual Report 1983-1984', p.6.

33. For Tom's motions see NPPM Minute Book, 1 February 1985.

34. For details of the Green Point Action Committee see Wesley Mission, 'Green Point'; see also 'NPPM Annual Report 1984-1985', p.3; Neech, 'Interview with Doug Lithgow', p.18.

35. For the ongoing campaign to establish a national park see 'NPPM Annual Report 1984-1985', p.1, p.3 and p.5.

36. For Tom's motions in support of the Lake Macquarie National Park see NPPM Minute Book, 28 August 1987.

37. For details of the NPPM's plans for a Bicentennial Lakeside Park and the landscaping and urban design competition see 'NPPM Annual Report 1987', p.7. For the NPPM's reaction to LMSC's allocation of Bicentennial funding see 'NPPM Annual Report 1987', p.8.

38. For Tom's motions regarding the Bicentennial Park see NPPM Minute Book, 30 October 1987.

39. For Tom's motions re contacting State and Federal Members see NPPM Minute Book, 31 January 1988

and 29 February 1988. For the NPPM's request that Tom write a history of Green Point see NPPM Minute Book, 29 February 1988. For Tom's effort to enlist the support of the Newcastle Trades Hall Council see Farrell motion (seconded by Wright), NPPM Minute Book, 29 February 1988.

40. For details of the revised development proposal in 1988 and the NPPM and Green Point Action Committee's response see Wesley Mission, 'Green Point'.

41. For the Lord Mayor's *volte-face* see *NHM*, 25 February 1988. For NPPM Press Release see NPPM Minute Book, 26 February 1988.

42. For details of Tom's motions regrading representations to the new Greiner Government see NPPM Minute Book, 29 April 1988.

43. For details of Tom's motions regarding Mr Clarke and Mr Jones see NPPM Minute Book, 27 May 1988.

44. For Tom's motions regarding Sydney Development Fund see NPPM Minute Book, 29 July 1988.

45. For motions regarding representations to Carr, Jones and Keegan see NPPM Minute Book, 29 July 1988.

46. NPPM Minute Book, 29 July 1988.

47. For Lithgow's motion see NPPM Minute Book, 29 July 1988.

48. For details of Tom's letter see Farrell to Editor, *NMH*, 31 December 1988. For details of the letters written by Tom's children see B. Hincks to Editor, *NMH*, 11 November 1987; J. Manson to Editor, *NMH*, 10 February 1987 & 24 June 1989; J. Farrell to Editor, *NMH*, 12 October 1988. It is clear that other members of the family contributed letters – see S. Farrell to Editor, *NMH*, 4 December 1987.

49. For details of meeting at Green Point in December 1988 see NPPM Minute Book, 25 November 1988.

50. For *Herald's* opinion piece see *NMH*, 15 December 1988.

51. For details of the pressure applied by the *NMH* in regard to the Green Point issue see the following editorials: 'Fight for Green Point to Go On', *NMH*, 9 May 1989; 'Green Point is Above Politics', *NMH*, 15 June 1989; 'Alderman Welsh and Green Point', *NMH*, 20 July 1989; 'Sharing the Bill for Green Point', *NMH*, 15 February 1990; 'Council Puts Freeze on Green Point Funds', *NMH*, 6 March 1990.

52. For details of Tom's motions at the January and February 1989 meetings of the NPPM see NPPM Minute Book, 27 January 1989 and 24 February 1989.

53. For Tom's letter to the paper see Farrell to Editor, *NMH*, 26 August 1989.

54. For the opinion of the concerned resident see J. McIvor to Editor, *NMH*, 28 March 1989. Clearly Tom had won the respect of his neighbours – Mr McIvor was a resident of Russell Road, New Lambton.

55. Wesley Mission, 'Green Point'. In regards to the mixed-support of the LMSC see 'NPPM Annual Report 1992-1993', p.7.

56. See NPPM Annual Report 1993-1994, p.9.

57. See Wesley Mission, 'Green Point'.

58. See A. Watson, 'New Twist for Green Point', *The Post*, 22 December 1992. See also Wesley Mission, 'Green Point'; NPPM Annual Report 1993-1994, p.9.

59. See N. Jameson, 'Think Big', *SMH*, 'Good Weekender', 28 February 2009, pp.8-9; NPPM Annual Report 1993-1994, p.9; 'NPPM Annual Report 1994-1995', pp.17-18. See also Lake Macquarie Shire Council, 'A Case Study of Green Point', pp.3-4.

60. Wesley Mission, 'Green Point'; Lake Macquarie Shire Council, 'A Case Study of Green Point', p.4.

CHAPTER SEVEN

1. For Tom's remark in 1965 see Farrell to Ellis, 5 November 1965, TFPJF. For Tom's campaign to improve public transport in his local area see 'Cardiff Asks for Bus Load Investigation', *NMH*, 13 February 1950; 'Electric Railway Agitation', *NMH*, 13 February 1950; Farrell to Darby, 10 September 1950, TFPJF. For Tom's views on trains and the passenger service into Newcastle see Rowe, 'Interview'. Among the Farrell Papers (TFPJF) are a number of newspaper clippings which clearly show Tom's interest in public transport in 1950: 'Short Sections', *NMH*, 2 September 1950; 'Editorial', *Maitland Mercury*, 27 July 1950; 'Mr Winsor Talks on Problems of Transport', *SMH*, 30 July 1950; 'Interview Sought To Speed Rail Link', *Newcastle Sun*, 2 August 1950; 'May Increase Railway Fares, Freight', *Newcastle Sun*, 23 August 1950 and 'Minister Accused of 'Cheap Jibe' at Newcastle Council', *Newcastle Sun*, 27 August 1950.

2. For Tom's involvement with the Liberal Party and the New Lambton Branch see Farrell, 'Notes on University' TFP A5581 (iv); R.E.Farrell, 'Newcastle University', TFP A8289 (viii); Farrell to Trip, 3 August 1980, TFP A8289 (viii); Farrell to Ellis, 11 November 1986; Ellis to Farrell, 7 August 1986, TFP A8289 (viii). For details of the Richardson Commission see K. Jones, 'Parliamentarians' Staff and the Professionalisation of Australian Politicians', Paper Presented to the Australasian Political Studies Association Conference, University of Adelaide, 29 September-1 October 2004, p.4, accessed 1 October 2012,<http://www.adelaide.edu.au/apsa /docspapers/Aust%20Pol/Jones%20K.pdf>. For details of Richley's attempt to secure the State Seat of Kahibah in 1956 see J. Richley, 'Seat of Kahibah State Election', 26 February 1956, TFP 8289 (vii). For the result of the election see A. Green, 'New South Wales Election Results 1856-2007', 5 July 2007, accessed 10 October 2012, <http://www.parliament.nsw.gov.au/ resources/nswelectionsanalysis/DistrictIndexes/Kahibah.htm>. See also electioneering paraphernalia for Richley's campaign including a sticker which reads 'Liberal Save Blackbutt! Vote Richley 1', TFP A 8289 (vii). For details of the public reaction to the Richardson Recommendations see Jones, 'Professionalisation of Australian Politicians'. For the reaction of the New Lambton Branch (including Tom's reaction) see T. Farrell, 'Notes on the Disbanding of the New Lambton Branch of the Liberal Party', TFP A82897. For Tom's comment regarding Reg Ellis see Farrell, 'Notes on Disbanding of the New Lambton Branch'. For details of the letters sent by Federal Liberal Parliamentarians to the disbanded New Lambton Branch see Pearce to Ellis, 17 June 1959; Holmes to Ellis, 19 June 1959; Bland to Ellis, 17 June 1959, TFP A82897. For the attempt by the State Executive to overturn the decision to disband the New Lambton Branch see Farrell, 'Notes on Disbanding of the New Lambton Branch'. For coverage in the press see *NMH*, 12 July 1959. For Tom's comments regarding those behind the State Executive's move and the 'Sydney Steam Roller' see Farrell, 'Notes on Disbanding of the New Lambton Branch'.

3. For details of the New State Movement see J. Farrell, 'Amending 'the lion in the path': the hurdles, thrusts and ploys of the New State Movement in northern NSW 1920-1930', *Journal of the Royal Australian History Society*, Vol.97, Part I, 2011, pp.44-64; J. Belshaw, 'Ulrich Ellis: journalist, political agitator and theorist, public servant and historian', *Canberra Historical Journal*, September 1982, pp.16-22; J. Belshaw, 'History of the New England New State Movement', accessed 4 October 2012, <http://newenglandhistory.blogspot.com.au /2010/02/ history-of-new-england-new-state 04.html>. For the role of Page see C. Bridge, 'Sir Earl Christmas Grafton Page (1880-1961)', *ADB*, accessed 4 October 2012, <http:// adb.anu.edu.au/biography/page-sir-earle-christmas-grafton-7941>. For the role of Drummond see J. Benshaw, 'David Henry Drummond (1890-1965)', *ADB*, accessed 4 October 2012, <http://adb.anu.edu.au/biography/drummond-david-henry-6019>. For details of the notes Tom prepared for Darby see Farrell to Darby, 23 November 1950, TFPJF. For details of the New Lambton Branch's successful motion at the 1951 NSW State Liberal Conference T. Farrell to U. R. Ellis, 10 June 1952, TFPJF. It is clear that Tom identified with the position Drummond adopted on the establishment of new states – see Rowe, 'Interview'.

4. For the reasons for Tom's interest in the New State Movement see 'New Stater' to Editor, *Maitland Mercury*, 5 May 1952; 'New England' to Editor, *NMH*, May 1952, TFPJF. See also notes (no author) entitled 'The Fallacy of Bigness', TFPJF. The author of the notes is certainly not Tom – the notes were found in an envelope (post-marked Five Dock, Sydney, 27 August 1953) addressed to Mr R. E. Farrell. Although Ellis may be the author, it is difficult to determine. See also Farrell to Darby, 23 November 1950; 'Notes on the New State Movement', TFPJF. In all probability these typed notes were compiled by Tom – the annotations are written in his hand writing.

5. For details on Ellis see A. Moore, 'Ulrich Ruegg Ellis (1904-1981)',*ADB*, accessed 7 October 2012, <http:// adb.anu. edu.au/biography/ellis-ulrich-ruegg-12459>; see also J. Belshaw, 'A Meander with Special Focus on Ulrich', accessed 5 October 2012, <http://belshaw.blogspot.com.au /2010/ 11/ meander-with-special-focus-on-ulrich.html>. For Ellis' correspondence with Tom see Schofield to Farrell, 4 June 1952; Farrell to Ellis, 10 June 1952, TFPJF. See also Tom's comments about Ellis – Rowe, 'Interview'. For details of the objectives of 'Operation Seventh State' see Tom's copy of U. Ellis, *For Australia A Seventh State*, New England State Movement, Armidale, 1968, p. 4,TFPJF. For details of the educational material distributed by NBNENSM see 'A New State Means Development for Newcastle', Apollo Transfer, Sydney; 'Self Government For New England', Express Print, Armidale; T. Noffs, 'New States', reprinted by New England New State Movement from *Australian Country Magazine*, October 1957, TFPJF. For Tom's membership of the Seventh State Executive see Ellis, *Seventh State*, p.67 – Tom joined Mr W.J. Hutchinson as the representatives from Newcastle on the ninety-nine member executive. For Tom's part in senior delegations see Scholfield to Farrell, 4 June 1952, TFPJF; Rowe, 'Interview'. For details of the 'Action Programme' see Ellis, *A Seventh State*, pp.65-66. For details of the petitions see Ellis, *A Seventh State*, p.22. For details of the NBNENSM's flyer see Newcastle Branch, 'New England New State Movement', March 1958, TFPJF. For details of Ellis' speech at the Twelfth Convention of the New England New State Movement in Newcastle see U. Ellis, 'A New Vision of Australian Development Through the Creation of New States', Examiner Print, Grafton, March 1958, TFPJF. For comments by Wright see Wright to Farrell, 7 July 1968, TFPJF. For Ellis' comment see Ellis, *Seventh State*, p.54. For details of the Indian Government's policy regarding the disposal of British imperial paraphernalia see *SMH*, 23 August 1957. For Tom's correspondence with the Indian Government see Farrell to

Nehru, 23 May 1957; Ram to Farrell, 29 May 1957; Farrell to Ram, 23 July 1957, TFPJF. For details of the Constitution of New England New State see Ellis, *Seventh State*, pp.22-24.

6. For details regarding the 1967 referendum see Belshaw, 'Ellis: journalist, agitator and theorist', p.22. For Tom's role in the campaign see U. Ellis, 'New England New State Campaign', 27 October 1966, TFPJF. For details concerning local Labor opposition to the New State Movement see 'Newcastle 'Joke' Over New State', *NMH*, 7 June 1950. It is clear that Breen's comment regarding the lack of support for a New State Committee in Newcastle was an exaggeration – as Tom (see Rowe, 'Interview') later pointed out 'our branch at New Lambton was one hundred per cent behind the New State Movement.' In the same interview Tom pointed out that fifty per cent of the NUEG were 'new staters'. Given this, it is highly likely that Tom would have been able to attract more than one other person to show interest in forming a New State Committee. The NBNENSM Committee that did form included R. R. Farrell (President), L. Saddington MLC (Vice President), A. McWilliams (Vice President), W. Hutchinson (Hon. Secretary) and J. Richley (Hon. Treasurer) – see NBNENSM, 'New England New State Movement'. For opposition within the coalition and the Dairy Industry see Belshaw, 'Ellis: journalist, agitator and theorist', p.22; Farrell, 'Lion in the Path', p.62. For details about the result of the referendum see Belshaw, 'Ellis: journalist, agitator and theorist', p.22; Farrell, 'Lion in the Path', p.62. For Tom's comments regarding the referendum's poor showing in Newcastle see Rowe, 'Interview'.

7. For details of the lack of success of the New State candidates in the 1968 State election see Belshaw, 'Ellis: journalist, agitator and theorist', p.22. For comment by daughter see Talty, 'Memories of My Father'. For Tom's correspondence with the President of the New England New State Movement see Wright to Farrell, 7 July 1968. For Tom's views in 1978 see Rowe, 'Interview'. For Tom's view in 1988 see Farrell to Editor, *NMH*, 8 March 1988.

8. For details of Tom's attempt to run for Council in 1965 see Farrell to Burgess (Town Clerk), 27 October 1965, TFP A 8289 vii; Farrell to Ellis, 5 November 1965, TFP 8289 vii; Hughes to Ellis, 17 November 1965, TFP 8289 (vii).

9. For details of the Citizens Group platform see K. Moon, Campaign Director, 'The Citizens Group Candidates of Ability and Integrity', Newey & Beath Printers, Newcastle, December 1968, TFP 8289 (vii).

10. For details of Tom's candidature see K. Moon, Campaign Director, 'R. E. (Tom) Farrell A Member of the Independent Citizens Group Team', Newey & Beath Printers, Newcastle, December 1968, TFP 8289 (vii).

11. For details of Tom's policy see K. Moon, Campaign Director, 'R. E. Farrell Points of Policy', Davies & Cannington, Newcastle, December 1968, TFP 8289 (vii). See also Woodgate to Farrell, 13 November 1968, TFP A8289 (vii) – like all other candidates Tom received a letter from the Blackbutt Action Committee 'to inquire where you, as a candidate for the Council elections, stand in respect to saving Blackbutt'. The BAC did not need to waste the cost of a stamp to know Tom's views on this matter.

12. For election result in Central Ward see Returning Officer, 'Election of Three Aldermen – Central Ward', 7 December 1968, TFP A 8289 (vii). For Tom's reaction to his loss see Farrell to Supporter, 17 December 1968, TFP A 8289 (vii). Tom was informed formally of the result by the Town Clerk see Burgess to Farrell, 10 December 1968, TFP A8289 (vii).

Select Bibliography

Unpublished Primary Sources:

Farrell Papers:
The Tom Farrell Papers, UNA, A8286 (i-xiv); A8287 (i-viii); A8288 (i-xxx); A8289 (i-viii); A8290 (i-viii); A8291.

The Tom Farrell Papers (in possession of John Farrell).

Farrell Children's Recollections:
Farrell, John, 'Tom Farrell Biography: As Experienced By His Son', 17 February 2010, TFPTFI.

Hincks, Beverley, 'Memories of My Father', 28 April 2012, TFPTFI.

Manson, Joan, 'Memories, Perspectives and Recollections of My Father', 6 January 2012, TFPTFI.

Nelmes, Claire, 'Recollections of My Father', 28 February 2012, TFPTFI.

Talty, Kay, 'Memories of My Father', 13 April 2012, TFPTFI.

Family & Friends Recollections:
Arnold, J., 'Memories of R E (Tom) Farrell', 2011, TFPJF.

Boutillier, N., 'Memories of Tom Farrell', 24 April 2012, TFPTFI.

Harris, M.J., 'Personal Memory of Mr Tom Farrell', 28 March 2012, TFPTFI.

Maher, K, 'Details of Uncle Tom's Life', 3 April 2012, TFPTFI.

Prince, B., 'Tom Farrell', 2011, TFPJF.

Unpublished Manuscripts:
'A Case for a Newcastle College of the University of Sydney', no date, Eddy Papers, USA; G3/13/18320 .

'A Typed List of Students Available for Newcastle University College', USA G3/13/18320.

Baker, S.E., Newspaper Clippings (Surfing), 1929-1932, Cook's Hill Life Saving & Surf Club Archives.

'Cooperative Societies Report of the Registrar for the Year Ended 30th June 1948', NSW Parliamentary Papers, ML, NQ328.94401/8.

Eddy, H, 'Draft History of the Newcastle University Establishment Group', 1953, Bentley Papers 1914-1986, ML, MLMSS 7763, Box 4.

Eddy, H, 'Notes for State Executive on Newcastle University College and Other Matters', no date, Eddy Papers, USA, Series 1 006-008, P196/06/08.

Farrell, R. E., 'The Basis of a Scheme to Establish an Academic University College in Newcastle Commencing in 1951 and Developing to Ultimate Autonomy in Say 5 or 6 Years', NUA, A5581 iv.

'Letter of Recommendation' (Wardens of Convention) to The Chairman Honorary Degrees Committee of Council, University of Newcastle, 16 April 1986, TFPJF.

Minutes Book of Cook's Hill Life Saving & Surf Club, 1927/28 to 1933/34, Cook's Hill Life Saving & Surf Club Archives.

'Minutes of NUEG Executive Meeting', 20 December 1953, Eddy Papers, USA, 1953 Bundle.

'Minutes of Regular Monthly Meeting of the NUEG held in the WEA Rooms 71 King Street Newcastle', 8 February 1954 and 8 March 1954, Bentley Papers 1914-1986, ML, Library MSS 7763, Box 4.

Neech, V., 'Transcript of Interview with Doug Lithgow, Conservation and the History of the Northern Parks & Playgrounds Movement', Community Oral Histories, UNA, A6968 (ii) (B).

Northern Parks & Playgrounds Movement, Minute Books, UNA, C830 (22/8/1958 – 23/7/1965); C831 (27/8/1965 – 28/7/1967); C832 (23/8/1967 – 24/11/1972); C833 (23/3/1973 – 24/9/1980); C834 (31/10/1980 – 25/11/83); C835 (25/11/1983 – 6/12/1985); C836 (1/1/1986 – 30/9/1988); C837 (17/11/1988 –28/11/1994); C838 (30/1/1995 – 29/2/2003).

Northern Parks & Playgrounds Movement, 'Proposal – Newcastle East 'Historic Site', 28 May 1969, NUA, C839.

Papers related to Cooks Hill Superior Public School, NSW State Archives (Kingswood) NRS 19083/1/1 (Cooks Hill Roll Book 1911-1920); NRS 5/15485 A & B (Cooks Hill School Administrative File 1905-1913).

'Photographs & History of the Greater Newcastle & Hunter River Starr Bowkett Society', Rodd Papers, UNA, A5400 (iv).

'Press Clippings', Bentley Papers, ML, MLMSS 7763, Box 2.

Ramsland, J., 'A History of Blackbutt Nature Reserve', 1988, UNA, RB Q719.320 99442 RAMS.

'Record of War Service, R.E. Farrell', Australian National Archives, Canberra, Series 9300/5243117.

'Report for NUEG on Preliminary Meeting on Conventions on Universities held at St James Hall, Sydney', 27 March 1954, Eddy Papers, USA, Series 1 006-008, P196/01/033.

Rowe, D., 'Interview of Mr R.E. Tom Farrell of 137 Russell Road, New Lambton Heights', NUA, Archive Tape, 10017.

Tripp, V., 'Open Foundation History Project Profile on a Successful Man Mr R. E. (Tom) Farrell', 1987, TFPJF.

Wesley Mission, 'Green Conscience – The Ongoing Struggle for a Clean, Green Newcastle', 2011, <http://radicalnewcastle.files.wordpress.com./2011/05greenconscience.pdf>.

Unpublished Papers:
'Farell, R. E., Citizen Air Force Recruitment Papers', Air Force Personnel, National Archives of Australia, A9300/5243117.

Bentley Papers 1914-1986, Mitchell Library, Sydney, ML, MLMSS 7763, Box 2; Box 4.

Eddy Papers, USA; G3/13/18320; 1953 Bundle; Series 1 006-008, P196/06/08.

Northern Parks and Playground Papers, UNA, Minute Books, C830-C838.

Papers related to Cooks Hill Superior Public School, NSW State Archives (Kingswood) NRS 19083/1/1; NRS 5/15485 A&B.

Rodd Papers, UNA, A5400 (iv).

Published Primary Sources:

Report of The House of Representatives' Standing Committee on Environment and Conservation, Sub-Committee, Impact of Proposed State Highway 23 on Blackbutt Reserve, Newcastle, 16 March 1974, Commonwealth Government Printer, 1974.

Report of the Royal Commission of Enquiry (Captain W.J. Wade, MBE) into the Newcastle District Abattoir Board Administration, Government Printer, Sydney, 1930.

The University of Newcastle, *Conferring of Degrees Faculties of Arts and Medicine*, The University of Newcastle, 3 May 1986.

Published Secondary Sources:

Books:

Bryden, T. & Bunn, T., *Butcher Boy Barrackers: A Brief History of Central Charlestown Rugby League Football Club 1910-2001*, Central Newcastle Rugby League Football Club, Charlestown, 2001.

McKey, N., *Pioneering Family: A History of the Warlters Family*, Howe Government Printer, Sydney, 1976.

Power, B., *The Saga of the Western Men: Story of Western Suburbs (Newcastle) RLFC,* Western Suburbs Leagues Club, 1966.

Ramsland, J., *Cook's Hill Life Saving & Surf Club The First Hundred Years,* Brolga Publishing, Melbourne, 2011.

Wright, D., *Looking Back A History of the University of Newcastle,* The Pot Still Press, Sydney, 1992.

Newspapers:

Daily Telegraph

Maitland Mercury

Newcastle Morning Herald & Miners' Advocate

Newcastle Sun

Sunday Telegraph

Sydney Morning Herald

The Post Newcastle & Lake Macquarie

Websites:

Australian Dictionary of Biography, National Centre of Biography, Australian National University, <http://adb.anu.edu.au/>

Index

A POWERHOUSE OF A MAN
Tom Farrell

CHRISTOPHER MOONEY

		Qty
ISBN 9781922175793		
RRP	AU$29.99	.....
Postage within Australia	AU$5.00	.....
	TOTAL* $_____	
	* All prices include GST	

Name:..

Address: ....

....

Phone:..

Email: ....

Payment: ❑ Money Order ❑ Cheque ❑ MasterCard ❑ Visa

Cardholders Name:..

Credit Card Number: ....

Signature:...

Expiry Date: ....

Allow 7 days for delivery.

Payment to: Marzocco Consultancy (ABN 14 067 257 390)
PO Box 12544
A'Beckett Street, Melbourne, 8006
Victoria, Australia
admin@brolgapublishing.com.au

BE PUBLISHED

Publish through a successful publisher.
Brolga Publishing is represented through:
• **National** book trade distribution, including sales,
marketing & distribution through **Macmillan Australia.**
• **International** book trade distribution to
  • The United Kingdom
  • North America
  • Sales representation in South East Asia
• Worldwide e-Book distribution

For details and inquiries, contact:
Brolga Publishing Pty Ltd
PO Box 12544
A'Beckett St VIC 8006

Phone: 0414 608 494
markzocchi@brolgapublishing.com.au
ABN: 46 063 962 443
(Email for a catalogue request)

www.ingramcontent.com/pod-product-compliance
Lightning Source LLC
Chambersburg PA
CBHW062357090426
42740CB00010B/1309